THE SUBALTERN SPEAK

THE SUBALTERN SPEAK

CURRICULUM, POWER, AND
EDUCATIONAL STRUGGLES

MICHAEL W. APPLE

AND

KRISTEN L. BURAS

EDITORS

Routledge
Taylor & Francis Group
New York   London

First published in 2006 by
Routledge
Taylor & Francis Group
711 Third Avenue
New York, NY 10017

Published in Great Britain by
Routledge
Taylor & Francis Group
2 Park Square, Milton Park
Abingdon, Oxon OX14 4RN

This edition published 2012 by Routledge

Routledge	Routledge
Taylor & Francis Group	Taylor & Francis Group
711 Third Avenue	2 Park Square, Milton Park
New York, NY 10017	Abingdon, Oxon OX14 4RN

International Standard Book Number-10: 0-415-95081-3 (Hardcover) 0-415-95082-1 (Softcover)
International Standard Book Number-13: 978-0-415-95081-7 (Hardcover) 978-0-415-95082-4 (Softcover)
Library of Congress Card Number 2005013542

Library of Congress Cataloging-in-Publication Data

Apple, Michael W.
  The subaltern speak : curriculum, power, and educational struggles / Michael W. Apple and Kristen L. Buras.
        p. cm.
  Includes bibliographical references and index.
  ISBN 0-415-95081-3 (hb : alk. paper) -- ISBN 0-415-95082-1 (pb : alk. paper)
  1. Educational sociology--United States. 2. Discrimination in education--United States. 3. Critical pedagogy--United States. 4. Education--United States--Curricula. 5. Education and state--United States. I. Buras, Kristen L. II. Title.

LC191.4.A665 2005
370.11'5--dc22   2005013542

Taylor & Francis Group
is the Academic Division of Informa plc.

Visit the Taylor & Francis Web site at
http://www.taylorandfrancis.com

and the Routledge Web site at
http://www.routledge-ny.com

Contents

Acknowledgments

Michael would like to thank the Friday Seminar at the University of Wisconsin–Madison for helping to keep alive and vibrant an insistence on connecting critical analyses and critical action in education. He also wants to express thanks to Rima D. Apple for her careful comments on a number of the issues raised in this book.

Kristen would like to especially acknowledge Michael Apple, Keffrelyn Brown, Mary Ann Doyle, Carl Grant, Diana Hess, Gloria Ladson-Billings, Paulino Motter, Bekisizwe Ndimande, Thomas Pedroni, Júlio Diniz Pereira, Bill Reese, Simone Schweber, and the members of the Friday Seminar—past and present. She would also like to thank her husband, Joe Aguilar, who surely deserves an honorary Ph.D. in light of the many lifetimes he has spent discussing educational issues. As for her parents, Christine and Michael Buras, a simple word of thanks could never convey how indebted she is to them for their support. Finally, Kristen wishes to express her appreciation to Minnie and Joe Aguilar.

It is also essential to extend a word to Catherine Bernard at Routledge and her assistant, Brook Cosby, for their assistance and commitment. Appreciation is also due to Eva Lewarne, who kindly granted us permission to place her compelling art on the cover of this book.

Introduction

The Subaltern Speak
Curriculum, Power, and Educational Struggles

KRISTEN L. BURAS AND MICHAEL W. APPLE

Whose Knowledge Is of Most Worth?

Sagoyewatha was a Seneca chief, an orator, and a pivotal figure in the Six Nations of the Iroquois. His name means "he keeps them awake." Befittingly, Sagoyewatha is well known for a speech he gave in 1805 in response to Missionary Cram of the Boston Missionary Society. Missionary Cram sought Indigenous converts and proclaimed to the Senecas:

> I had a great desire to see you, and inquire into your state and welfare. ... You will recollect [the Boston Missionary Society] formerly sent missionaries among you, to instruct you in religion and labor for your good.... Brothers, I have not come to get your lands or your money, but to enlighten your minds. (Velie, 1991, p. 136)

Speaking in defense of Native land and spirituality, Sagoyewatha replied in part:

> Brother, our seats were once large and yours were small. You have now become a great people, and we have scarcely a place left to spread our blankets. You have got our country, but are not satisfied; you want to force your religion upon us. (pp. 137–138)

On another occasion, he called into question the religious and educational practices of Christian missionaries who viewed Seneca culture as backward, asserting:

> You have taken a number of our young men to your schools. You have educated them and taught them your religion. They have returned to their kindred and color neither white men nor Indians. The arts they have learned are incompatible with the chase, and ill adapted to our customs. They have been taught that which is useless to us.... We believe it is wrong for you to attempt further to promote your religion among us or to introduce your arts, manners, habits, and feelings.

1

...Perhaps you think we are ignorant and uninformed. Go, then and teach the whites.... Improve their morals and refine their habits—make them less disposed to cheat Indians. (pp. 141–143)

Sagoyewatha's words—uttered at least two centuries ago—remind us of the long history of the struggles of oppressed groups (in this specific case, nations) against domination, particularly though not only around issues of deep cultural and educational significance.

His voice also reminds us that encounters among unequally empowered groups and contests over knowledge have never unfolded along simple lines, as evidenced by the young men who returned "neither white men nor Indians." In the context of colonialism, Indigenous communities in North America, including the Senecas, were often divided between traditional and Christian factions, among neutralists, francophiles, and anglophiles, and later, between militants calling for pan-Indian unity against whites and those advocating varying levels of accommodation to "American" power (Calloway, 1997; Dowd, 1992; Richter, 1992). Yet even accommodation was not a straightforward matter, as Indigenous peoples often found ways to speak through particular European forms in trade goods, architecture, clothing, and religion, and to redefine them along Amerindian lines—though not without conflict, contradiction, and consequence (Calloway, 1997).

This history of struggle has echoes in the present. As one Diné student attending an urban high school in the southwest recently protested (see Martinez, chapter 4, pp. 134–135):

In my [United States] history classes they always turn things around, the opposite way.... They always try to make the White people or the Spaniards better than the Native Americans.... It got me mad and I was about to go up in front of the class and about to show them [alternative] information.... [But] I thought they might just kick me out.

That such voices have often been placed at the margins in cultural theory and educational work caused Cameron McCarthy (1998) to remind us that in too much of our analyses:

Absent are the voices, cultural practices, and meaning of style of concrete, historical postcolonial and indigenous minority subjects. Even more disturbing is the... tendency to abrogate the whole field of accommodations, negotiations, and trestles of association and affiliation that link dominant and dominated political and cultural entities both locally and globally. (pp. 5–6)

It is precisely these absences and these kinds of historic and contemporary struggles to be heard, and the complexities surrounding them, which also compelled Gayatri Chakravorty Spivak (1988, 1999) to pose the well-known question, "Can the subaltern speak?" She raised a number of compelling issues surrounding the politics of who can speak and in what ways, and about the politics of how such voices are and are not heard. We will return later in this chapter to the work of Spivak and its relationship to understanding educational struggles, but it is important to realize that the issues involved are complicated. When they are brought into the field of education, their complexity increases because educators ultimately need to act on this complexity in the real world.

In essence, critical work in the field of education stands on the shoulders of Sagoyewatha and others who have fought for recognition and survival. One early educational statement that is part of this tradition is *Ideology and Curriculum* (Apple, 1979/2004), in which one of us posed the question: "Whose knowledge is of most worth?" That book raised the issue of whose perspective, experience, and history are privileged in the curriculum as well as in educational institutions more generally. In light of the unequal distribution of political, economic, and cultural power that characterizes the United States and other nations, this issue is as relevant today as it was when *Ideology and Curriculum* was first written, perhaps even more so. Educational struggles over knowledge and voice thus comprise the focus of the present volume— one in which critical educators respond with new insights on changing circumstances and conditions.

To appreciate the ongoing necessity of such a focus, one needs only to consider recent interventions in Texas to "restore" traditional definitions of marriage to high school health textbooks. State Board of Education member Terri Leo and others associated with the Christian Right called for textbook publishers to uphold the state's Defense of Marriage Act by making clear in textbooks that marriage is a union between a man and a woman. This definition, they believed, was undermined by the use of words, such as "couple," which might be read by students as endorsements of same-sex couples rather than as references to a man and a woman (Ledbetter, 2004). While gay and lesbian activists criticized the mandate, organizations such as the conservative Family Research Council hailed the effort, indicating, "The truth is that such activists are themselves attempting to overturn the time-honored definition of marriage that has been honored by societies and cultures for millennia" (Perkins, 2004). Such battles, we must understand, are constitutive; they create insiders and outsiders and reveal the often tense relationship between "popular" and "official" understandings (e.g., see Buras, 2005a).

There are many histories of educational struggle, some of which contributors to this book will attempt to trace. Together, we hope to illustrate the complexities of the contests among differentially empowered groups to influence the construction of knowledge and appropriation of resources in the arena of education. We especially aim to highlight the possibilities for and limitations of subaltern agency. But before saying more about this, it is important to first say something about the history of the "subaltern." The concept has played a key role in our understanding of and struggles against relations of domination and subordination. It is in the works of Antonio Gramsci—someone who appreciated the power of cultural struggles, the significance of popular sensibilities, and the importance of building oppositional movements and whose work has had a profound influence on critical educational research and action—where we can locate the genesis of some of the concept's most profound cultural and political insights.

Gramsci and the Subaltern

Like all words, "subaltern" has a history. In late-medieval English, the word referred to vassals and peasants, and by 1700 had come to signify those in the lower ranks of the military. Writers embracing a "subaltern perspective" thus authored narrative accounts of military campaigns throughout the 1800s and early 1900s (Ludden, 2002). Antonio Gramsci, a political activist jailed in Fascist Italy during the late 1920s, used the word in his *Prison Notebooks*—a collection of writings that centered on the dynamics of ideology and power and the struggles of subordinated classes to transform oppressive state and economic formations (Hoare & Nowell Smith, 1971). In these writings, "subaltern" functioned as a code word for oppressed groups, such as industrial laborers and peasants, while it simultaneously sheltered Gramsci from prison censors. Ultimately, the circulation of the *Notebooks* in the 1960s and 1970s ensured Gramsci's conceptualization of the subaltern a future in cultural studies, postcolonial studies, new histories from below, and quite importantly, critical educational theory and research.

Speaking of the subaltern allowed Gramsci to underscore the position of an array of groups within unequal relations of power. While he held that subaltern classes were oppressed by ruling groups, he also believed that power was less often exercised through force than consent. By this, Gramsci meant that the prevailing matrix of power was sustained ideologically as elites built on existing forms of common sense—"spontaneous," often unexamined worldviews held by collectivities—and compromised with subordinate groups to secure their assent. Gramsci emphasized:

> Hegemony presupposes that account be taken of the interests and the tendencies of the groups over which hegemony is to be exercised, and that a certain compromise equilibrium should be formed—in other words, that the leading group should make sacrifices. (Hoare & Nowell Smith, 1971, p. 161)

While material compromises secured partial victories, it was equally important to recognize that consciousness, or subjectivity, likewise constituted a battleground on which the powerful maneuvered to defend their position within the existing order.

If this was the case, it followed that consciousness might also be a space where an emancipatory politics could be forged. Indeed, Gramsci contended that:

> All men [and women] are intellectuals.... There is no human activity from which every form of intellectual participation can be excluded.... Each man, finally, outside his professional activity, carries on some form of intellectual activity, that is, he is a "philosopher," an artist, a man of taste, he participates in a particular conception of the world, has a conscious line of moral conduct, and therefore contributes to sustain a conception of the world or to modify it, that is, to bring into being new modes of thought. (Hoare & Nowell Smith, 1971, p. 9)

Though conceptions of the world were sustained by subaltern groups and even embedded in their daily lives, these conceptions required explicit examination and ultimately some degree of renovation. It was necessary, in other words, to distinguish the "various strata" embedded in everyday sensibilities and to separate the "conservative and reactionary" elements while building on those "which consist of a series of innovations, often creative and progressive ... and which are in contradiction to or simply different from the morality of the governing [elites]" (Forgacs & Nowell Smith, 1985, p. 190). In short, elements of both good and bad sense were understood to be in tension in the day-to-day consciousness of people (Apple, 1996, 2006).

For Gramsci, it was the role of the "organic intellectual" to maintain subaltern roots and "make coherent the principles and problems raised by the masses in their practical activity" (Hoare & Nowell Smith, 1971, p. 330). It was this critical refinement and elaboration that transformed a fragmentary and spontaneous common sense into a "creative philosophy," an intellectual order rooted in criticism, grounded in historical knowledge of popular and elite thought, and productive in guiding the active interventions of the subaltern in history. In the end, fighting a "war of position"—the ideological struggle to create a new and more just set of understandings (in essence, a "new hegemony") conducive to the accession of state power by the oppressed—required subaltern subjects who mobilized on the basis of collective forms of critical consciousness. An emancipatory cultural politics, Gramsci argued, could change the course of history and engender the conditions necessary for a more equitable existence.

Before his own imprisonment Gramsci wrote for a number of socialist journals, including *L'Ordine Nuovo*—a paper he cofounded and produced in Turin. As its name implies, Gramsci aimed to facilitate the birth of a new order by reworking prevailing forms of common sense. He attended to a host of cultural forms, writing reviews of books and theater. He organized and participated in study circles, which he also viewed as central to the project of political education. He was also active in Turin's Factory Council Movement, a working-class effort that sought to establish proletarian institutions. In April 1920, a general strike was announced in Turin as workers fought for control of production through the factory councils. Defeated some ten days later, the uprising demonstrated the potential for subaltern mobilizations as well as the difficulties of building and sustaining a mass movement (Fiori, 1970).

While in prison, Gramsci proposed in his *Notebooks* the development of a history of the subaltern classes and actually began to author such a history with regard to the Italian Risorgimento—the period of unification between 1815 and 1871 during which the Italian national state was forged. This history, Gramsci believed, would render more visible the possibilities for constructing critical consciousness and practice. It might be said that the book you are reading was conceived as part of such a project, as it represents an attempt to trace encounters between elite and subaltern groups in the field of education with the intent of making more visible possibilities for transformative action.

History and Educational Struggles

The essays in this volume focus on the struggles of dominant and subaltern groups to define what counts as knowledge and to appropriate political, economic, cultural, and social resources in a range of educational contexts, both national and international in scope. Whether in boardrooms or class-rooms, home schools or school communities, universities or foundations, each arena is characterized by the dynamics of differential power and the complexities and contradictions of identity and agency. In the areas of curriculum, educational policy, and reform, struggles of all kinds ensue along circuits of production, distribution, and reception. Some of these conflicts are organized, with particular factions pursuing rather defined agendas. Free market experiments with school choice, funded by powerful right-wing foundations, would be one example where dominant groups attempt to connect to elements of people's good sense, and hence to bring people under their leadership. Other struggles entail more subtle actions that emerge in the context of everyday life, as when students resist teacher or textbook constructions of knowledge in, say, geography, history, or literature (see Dance, 2002; Dolby, Dimitriadas, & Willis, 2004).

Most of these conflicts take shape under, or are generated out of, the conditions of *conservative modernization*. Conservative modernization refers to the growing power of a new "hegemonic bloc"—a new alliance of rightist forces that is currently exerting leadership in society. It is bent on pushing education and all things social, cultural, and economic in strikingly conservative directions. But this bloc is not simple. Indeed, it is quite complex. As one of us has argued (Apple, 1996, 2000, 2006), neoliberals have worked to redefine democracy in free market terms, with "consumers" choosing educational "products" in self-interested ways rather than citizens collectively mobilizing over education as a public good. Neoconservatives, religious fundamentalists, and

Christian evangelicals have meanwhile struggled over the cultural and moral underpinnings of the nation, fearing a loss of national cohesion if not a loss of souls. Moreover, the managerial middle class has sought to honor the neoliberal code of efficiency in schools, while also determining, through endless forms of measurement, the degree to which (generally) neoconservative standards have been met. With these specific economic and cultural groups working to maintain their dominance, the agenda of the right is both advanced and undermined in educational contests—small and big—as the efforts of less powerful groups complicate the process of exercising power.

So far we have been rather historical and general in our treatment of subaltern politics and the politics of education. Perhaps a concrete example of educational struggle that is simultaneously local and global and that illustrates some of the dynamics of identity and power that we have been discussing would be useful here. As we will see, this story relates to and raises questions about the complex issues involved in the act of subaltern "speaking," in what actually counts as "speech," and about how dominant groups may respond.

The Alliance for Democracy, an organization of student activists at the University of Wisconsin-Madison, directed a campaign in the late 1990s that focused on pressuring the board of regents—the body appointed by the governor to oversee the policies of the university—to engage in socially responsible investment. Socially responsible investment would require the university to divest of shares in companies known for abusing human rights and the environment and instead invest in those committed to a living wage, labor rights, and more humane, sustainable practices. This effort by the alliance was connected to earlier work by the Free Burma Coalition (ZarNi & Apple, 2000). That coalition was successful in getting the board of regents to relinquish over $200,000 of Texaco stock due to human rights violations in Burma (Evers, 1998). This victory required immense labor as students challenged university elites to acknowledge how their investment practices contributed to the oppression of people beyond the borders of Wisconsin and the United States.

Later organizing with the Alliance for Democracy, student activists assembled at a meeting of the regents. The action was intended to push the regents even further on the issue of socially responsible investment. Initially, activists constituted a silent presence at the meeting. With protest signs held in hands, the group awaited their moment on the agenda. When the time came, activists, one by one, read aloud cards with the names of people exploited or killed by corporations in the university's portfolio. One of the people memorialized was Ken Saro-Wiwa, a Nigerian environmental activist whose "speaking" against a major oil corporation and the prevailing military regime cost him his life. Each card was placed in front of a member of the board. Sitting quietly in positions of power, most regents seemed unmoved by the symbolic protest and less than willing to consider associated demands for alternative investment. As activists left the meeting and passed a small alcove where coffee was brewing for the regents, voices echoed: "There's blood in their coffee, too!"

The instances of activism detailed above raise a host of complex questions about who "speaks" and how they speak, who remains silent or is silenced, and who speaks for whom. Most centrally, these examples illustrate how groups with unequal power struggle to speak and act around complicated and often divergent sets of interests. They reveal how power can be exercised in silence, but also how silencing does not necessarily foreclose possibilities for expression and resistance (see Kelley, 1993; Scott, 1990). They are likewise about how those who speak can simultaneously be unspoken. These are precisely the kinds of issues that we wanted this book to address, particularly in the realm of education.

We might ask what made these activists think they had the power to speak, or to at least attempt to interrupt the existing regime of power. Part of the answer, we would like to argue, has to do with identity. This was made especially clear when the Alliance for Democracy planned another effort—a Democracy Teach-In—part of which centered on the Theater of the Oppressed (Boal, 1985). At the most fundamental level, this kind of theater is about the process of identity formation; as you will see, it is an educational experiment that aims to foster in the oppressed a sense of consciousness and agency. In this way, the Theater of the Oppressed also helps us to further introduce some of the issues most closely related to the title and content of this volume: *The Subaltern Speak.*

The Theater of the Oppressed was developed by Augusto Boal, a Brazilian theater activist who, in 1971, was imprisoned and tortured by the military regime for his revolutionary activities with workers and peasants (Boal, 1985; Schutzman & Cohen-Cruz, 1994). Consisting of an entire arsenal of dramatic games and exercises developed over several decades, the Theater of the Oppressed is premised on the assumption that "the aesthetic space possesses … properties which stimulate knowledge and discovery." "Theatre," Boal contends, "is a form of knowledge" (1995, p. 20). But whose knowledge, more precisely?

Developing an exercise called Forum Theater, Boal (1985, 1992) sought to directly involve "spectators" in the dramatic action. Based on an experience of oppression familiar to members of the community, a skit is improvised up to the point of conflict between the antagonist (oppressor) and protagonist (oppressed). After the initial exhibition of the skit, those present are invited to become "spect-actors," enter the role of the protagonist, and attempt to confront the antagonist. In short, the forum continues as various community members enter the skit and explore alternatives for challenging the oppression.

Boal (1985) described the educational significance of the theatrical confrontation in this way:

In order to understand this *poetics of the oppressed*, one must keep in mind its main objective: to change the people—"spectators," passive beings in the theatrical phenomenon—into subjects, into actors, trans-formers of the dramatic action.... He himself assumes the protagonist role, changes the dramatic action, tries out solutions, discusses plans for change—in short, trains himself for real action. In this case, perhaps theatre is not revolutionary in itself, but it is surely a rehearsal for the revolution. (p. 122)

Boal reminds us of the unequal relations of power that define personal and social experience and underscores the intimate transactions that occur when "oppressor" and "oppressed" endeavor to secure their related, though gener-ally oppositional, interests. It is this give-and-take between dominant and subaltern actors that contributors to this volume seek to better understand. We find, in fact, that there is much theater on the ground as multiple groups engage in "real action" aimed at shaping and reshaping the educational land-scape. We also find that clashes may have both microlevel and macrolevel implications, that strategies and outcomes may embody both progressive and retrogressive tendencies, and that actions may be taken both by specific groups and by broader networks of groups whose affiliations are often tense and rooted in ongoing compromises.

Perhaps most relevant to the present volume, however, is Boal's under-standing that many "masks" may be assumed and many "rituals" undertaken by each of us. In other words, our identities and actions are multiple and complicated; we are positioned in different ways along various axes of power and within a nexus of shifting relations and contexts. The line between oppressor and oppressed is not always a clear one, something Boal (1995) recognized when he developed his Cop in the Head/Rainbow of Desire tech-niques. In part, these theatrical forms were invented to make visible the conflicts of identity, spectrum of interests, and range of contexts that inform the behavior of actors. In education, we likewise want to show how dominance and subalternity mix and mingle, forming a tangled web of interrelations based on class, race, gender, sexual orientation, "ability," religion, language, and local, national, and global affiliations.

In light of this book's focus on the efforts of subaltern actors to speak and associated questions about what counts as speaking, the theatrical work at the Democracy Teach-In has something else to teach us—the world is not solely discursive in the usual sense of that word. This is something centrally addressed by Image Theater, another theatrical form included in the Theater of the Oppressed. Unlike Forum Theater, Image Theater (Boal, 1985, 1992) does not rely on spoken language. Rather, members of the community use their own bodies or "sculpt" the bodies of others to produce a visual representation of oppression. The embodied image, then, is a site of interpretive struggle and transformation as the actors "speak," or convey their perspectives and critiques, without words. After multiple images have been shared, the images may then be "dynamised," or put in motion. "Real" images represent the way things are (or are understood to be) in the present and "ideal" images represent how things might be made in the future. Moving between real and ideal images requires incrementally reshaping the initial images, ultimately revealing various possibilities for reshaping reality through action. In this case, Boal's theater underscores the myriad ways that actors may "speak" and demonstrates that interventions do not rely on language alone. Acting (or refusing to act) also matters, as a number of chapters in this book will show.

Yet none of this means that Boal or contributors to this collection are overly romantic about possibilities for resistance. In one game called the Machine of Rhythms (Boal, 1992), for example, each participant enacts a repetitive motion and corresponding sound or sound bite that captures the way in which the daily rigors of life often regiment the oppressed—the factory worker becomes an extension of the pounding machine (Boom! Boom!), the secretary an extension of the ever-ringing phone ("How may I help you? How may I help you?"), teachers and students extensions of the test (A, B, or C? A, B, or C?). Oppressive conditions do not necessarily inspire constructive rebellion, but may instead blunt critical consciousness and lead the oppressed to act in ways that reinforce existing structures of power, as will be evident later. In a similar way, Boal's (1985) Invisible Theater—a sort of theater enacted under circumstances where open political activity is unwelcome or even dangerous—forces us to recognize that "speaking" cannot be done directly or openly at all times, but must often be disguised or done under structural arrangements not always of one's own making (Kelley, 1993; Scott, 1990). Rather than assuming that subaltern actors are enlightened and resistant in all circumstances, contributors to this book explore the limitations of particular interventions as well as the constraints that limit agency.

The Theater of the Oppressed resonates with the historical, theoretical, and empirical investigations in this book. Much like the theatrical work that occurred during the Teach-In, the chapters in this volume pull back the curtain and allow readers to consider the stage on which educational actors compete for influence over the production, distribution, and reception of curriculum, policy, and reform. Who speaks and acts, the spaces for speaking and acting, and the effects and implications are illuminated in diverse ways by each of the contributors. Collectively, the chapters constitute a reflection on how dominant and subaltern groups "speak" in the theater of education.

It is important to understand that attempts to speak and be heard generate dynamics of reaction as well. This "theater" has many actors, some of whom are from dominant groups. And members of dominant groups may, in turn, *reappropriate* the language and actions of dominated groups in the intense conflicts that organize and disorganize power relations inside and outside of education. Indeed, as we shall see later in this book, it is not unusual for some members of powerful groups to claim subaltern status in their attempts to interrupt and take back the gains made by members of less powerful groups (Apple, 2006).

A case in point occurred during this same period of activism at the University of Wisconsin-Madison. Scott Southworth and several other conservative activist students claimed that they were in essence the "new oppressed" and filed a lawsuit to prevent the university from mandating the payment of student fees used to support campus organizations they opposed. Funded by the Alliance Defense Fund, an outside organization affiliated with the Christian Right, the lawsuit was intended to "defund" leftist activism and thereby compromise the ability of many progressive and traditionally oppressed groups to speak on issues of central importance to them (Evers, 1998). *Board of Regents of the University of Wisconsin System v. Southworth et al.* went all the way to the U.S. Supreme Court. In 2000, the Supreme Court reversed the decisions of lower federal courts, which determined that the payment of such fees violated the right of students to refuse funding forms of expression offensive to them (*Board of Regents of the University of Wisconsin System v. Southworth et al.,* 2000). This dispute provides powerful evidence of the energies invested by specific groups to control the circulation of particular forms of knowledge in educational contexts.

Had Southworth and his outside ultraconservative ideological and financial backers been successful in their attempt to take on the mantle of being oppressed, it would have made it that much harder for progressive student activists and their community allies to actually interrupt such things as the university's economic policies, which supported profits over people. Instead, student activists persuaded the university to adopt a policy on socially responsible investment, one that at least symbolically undermined the increasingly corporate culture of the university as well as the neoliberal regime supported by particular kinds of investments. However, the Alliance for Democracy and other organizations still found it necessary to subsequently occupy Bascom Hall, where the offices of the university chancellor are located, for nearly 100 hours in order to make additional progress on the anti-sweatshop front (Manski, 1999).

This kind of collective voice proved essential. Such collective mobilizations and the *constant* labor to make such voices heard are crucial and can ultimately change the ideological and cultural terrain in significant ways.

Take the case of Augusto Boal once more. Silenced by the military regime in Brazil, Boal was ultimately forced into exile in Argentina, and was later forced to flee to Peru. Yet his work continued throughout Latin America, Europe, Africa, and North America where the Theater of the Oppressed came to be used and reinterpreted in an array of educational and political sites, and where his "techniques" provided the tools for the silenced to have a real voice (Boal, 1992;

Schutzman & Cohen-Cruz, 1994). Boal eventually returned to Brazil where he continued his theatrical/educational work, became active in the Workers' Party (one of the first political parties in Brazil centered on the interests of subaltern classes) and was elected city counselor in Rio de Janeiro (Boal, 1995).

In the end, then, these histories reveal that educational struggles over values—moral, cultural, and economic—are not simple or straightforward conflicts, but are instead contests that continue amid gains and losses. Struggles are engaged by the right and the left, invested in by dominant and subaltern actors and movements, and pursued through avenues that are highly personal and broadly political. This was the case in Brazil in the 1970s and at the University of Wisconsin-Madison in the late 1990s, and it continues to be the case for schools locally, nationally, and globally.

Education as Political Theater

The struggles over higher education noted in the previous section and the constant dialectical interactions between hegemonic and counterhegemonic actions that involve being heard are ongoing—and they are not limited to higher education. Educational struggles are closely connected to conflicts in larger economic, political, and cultural arenas. Thus, the steadily growing influence of rightist positions in each of these arenas is pronounced and has had major effects in education on the politics of identity and culture, struggles over the production, distribution, and reception of curriculum, and the connections between national and international mobilizations. Together, these domains form the "stage" on which the political theater of education is currently unfolding.

Understanding the Context of Conservative Modernization

As we noted earlier, over the past two decades the politics of what has been called *conservative modernization* has advanced. Nations such as the United States, Britain, Sweden, Norway, New Zealand, and many others have experienced a disintegration of the social democratic accord in education and in almost every social arena. At the same time, globalization has become the new colonial form, sustaining and even worsening the historic inequalities suffered by the so-called third world (Apple et al., 2003; Apple, Kenway, & Singh, 2005; Chomsky, 1999). Indeed, on national and global scales, neoliberals have promoted and instituted policies to commercialize, managerialize, and marketize schools and to transform the inherently collective endeavor of education into an "individual market choice." Neoconservatives have likewise contributed to the rightward turn, advocating a "return" to traditional knowledge, often through the mechanisms of standardized curriculum and assessment. As neoconservatives work to stem the tide against the "multicultural threat," authoritarian populists—religious fundamentalists and conservative evangelicals—seek to manage the secular threat by calling for a return to (their) God in all of our institutions. And finally, a fraction of the managerial and professional middle class stands ready to assist the process of conservative modernization by offering various forms of technical and organizational expertise; they will measure student and teacher performance, manage schools more efficiently, and hold the faltering public school system accountable (Apple, 1996, 2006; Buras, 1999).

The alterations of social democratic policies, the rise of new left and post-colonial positions, and the concomitant advance of restorational cultural movements and global economic policies have produced a conservative and frequently contradictory terrain. This terrain is dominated by a set of tense alliances between fractions of dominant groups, such as neoliberals and neoconservatives, and among dominant and dominated fractions, such as hegemonic neoconservatives and traditionally oppressed groups (Apple, 1996, 2006). In fact, the forces of conservative modernization, particularly those most invested in the maintenance of dominant cultural configurations, have only intensified in the wake of September 11th (Buras, 2005b).

These alliances are built through the exchange of material benefits, but are also sutured ideologically through the appropriation, reconfiguration, and welding of an assemblage of cultural and historical conceptions. Take, for instance, the notion of "choice" in relation to President George W. Bush's educational initiative—No Child Left Behind (NCLB). Much of this initiative is intended to push forward a free market agenda in education by mandating that schools "in need of improvement" provide very specific remediation and exit routes for students—routes that promise profits to private educational entities providing tutorial services or (potentially) seats in alternative classrooms when students seek transfers (Karp, 2003). Yet NCLB has not been framed in neoliberal terms only.

Instead, Keita Takayama (2005) reveals that a number of "historically constituted 'choice' discourses are creatively mobilized and stitched together ... to bring groups of a wide range of political interests under the Bush administration's hegemonic leadership" (p. 2).

"Choice" first emerged in the United States after the *Brown* decision in 1954 and was used by southern segregationists who claimed that the continuing pattern of school segregation reflected the fact that whites and blacks simply preferred to remain among their own. When public schools were desegregated, racist whites then argued that they had the right to choose private schools for their children, a "choice" facilitated by state tuition grants. With the rise of the civil rights movement in the 1960s, James Coleman proposed controlled "choice" and "redefined [it] as a means to allow poor minorities to escape inner city 'ghetto' schools, thus disarticulating it from its racist and segregationist legacy" (p. 6). Choice for this sector of students, in other words, would function to equalize opportunity. Under the emerging neoliberal regime in the 1980s, choice was imbued with new meaning as it circulated less as an equity-oriented discourse than one focused on the value of uncontrolled market choice—something Milton Friedman had actually begun advocating in the 1950s.

An analysis of texts by former secretary of education Rod Paige demonstrates how these various discourses "are utilized to make NCLB and other contemporary choice programs speak to multiple publics" (Takayama, 2005, p. 13). In an article titled "A Child's Hope," Paige weaves together equity-oriented and market-oriented discourses:

> We want schools to improve. School improvement requires change. Positive change requires creativity and innovation. Market forces power creativity and innovation. School choice will drive this process. There's also the matter of social justice. A child should not have his educational circumstances limited by his parent's income, the color of his skin, or the dialect of his speech.... Disadvantaged parents should have the same right to make choices for their children as other parents have. (quoted in Takayama, 2005, pp. 15–16)

This is how consent is generated, in part, as policies are made to "speak" to a variety of constituencies. Yet the process of building alliances between dominant and subaltern groups requires more than the manufacturing of layered arguments. As Thomas Pedroni (2003) has documented and as will be discussed in his chapter later on, conservative organizations such as the Bradley Foundation have financed groups such as the Black Alliance for Educational Options as part of a wider effort to promote educational choice schemes, including tuition tax credits and school vouchers (see also Apple & Pedroni, in press). These sorts of affiliations and their associated tensions and implications will be further explored in upcoming chapters.

Associations have likewise been forged between other factions under conservative modernization. One of us (Apple 1996, 2006) has shown how the Christian Right has exercised exceptional power through activism, populist rhetoric, and a large financial base. Recasting liberalism around their own concerns, religious conservatives have presented themselves as an embattled minority suffering discrimination under a secular educational system that disrespects their beliefs, traditions, and even their right to free speech. Tapping also into particular national sentiments, they portray the United States as a Christian nation in which prosperity and liberty will continue to reign only if the (alleged) moral crisis is abated. Speaking these "truths" in churches and through well-financed television and radio programs, and through organizations such as the Christian Coalition and Focus on the Family, the case is made that public schools might be saved if instruction is purified of ungodly influences—permissive forms of sex education, antiracist, feminist, and anti-homophobic brands of multiculturalism, values clarification, antinationalist histories and global education, evolution science, and more. Yet if the existing public school system cannot be pushed to respect their traditions, then charter schools and vouchers are advocated, much to the pleasure of market advocates.

Meanwhile, neoconservative concerns about cultural disintegration, national cohesion, and the decline of Western traditions (Bennett, 1992; Leming, Ellington, & Porter, 2003) have partly resonated with the Christian Right. As Kristen Buras's research has unveiled, Core Knowledge—the back-to-basics curriculum inspired by the work of E. D. Hirsch (1987) and promoted by his Core Knowledge Foundation (1999)—has earned the allegiance of many home schoolers who use Core materials. It does not hurt that Core also pays special attention to Bible knowledge, and that the curriculum is parent-friendly with sequenced content and aligned resources. Core Knowledge, moreover, has attracted the interest of not only cultural and religious conservatives, but many traditionally oppressed groups, including low-income African American, Latino/a, and Native American communities. Hirsch (1996) has, in fact, articulated a vision of schooling that skillfully (and problematically) blends criticisms of cultural illiteracy with promises of civil rights and social mobility, a vision that has encouraged an array of communities to join the nationwide Core Knowledge movement, as Buras will discuss in Chapter 1 (see also Buras, 1999; Apple, 2005a; Hirsch, 2005).

The maintenance of social, cultural, and economic advantages—not only their acquisition—is a central preoccupation in the present political context that we have been charting. One group that occupies a contradictory location (Wright, 1997) within this nexus of relations is the middle class, including professional and technical experts who simultaneously serve the interests of more elite factions bent on cultural and economic control (Apple, 1995, 2006). This type of location implies that one's interests are *simultaneously* aligned with and antagonistic to those of more powerful elites. The middle-class subject is manager and worker, exploiter and exploited.

This contradictory location results in what Stephen Ball (2003) has characterized as a sense of "risk," "uncertainty," and "fear." In short, middle-class groups are anxiously engaged in a variety of class strategies aimed at securing both present and future educational benefits for their children. Through the mobilization of forms of social, cultural, and economic capital, parents of middling status negotiate their way through state and private educational institutions; obtain remedial resources and preparatory guidance for their children; rely on networks to access relevant information, developmental activities and career-related placements, and advice on applications and interviews; and ultimately seek the admission of their children to respected schools and universities. Participating in what is not only classed but gendered work—it is generally women who manage educational decision making in Britain, France, and the United States (see Andre-Bechely, 2005; Griffith & Smith, 2005)—one mother reports an exchange with her daughter:

I said to her—you've got … eight weeks before your modules, can't we get you a tutor? No, no, no, no, no! She was insistent. So the best we could do was to go to W. H. Smith and buy her a revision book which she found very useful…. Then when her module results came and she'd done so badly for her needs for university, then she really got a fright. And she said—OK, she would have a tutor…. She actually [also] agreed to go and have … [a] revision course. (Ball, 2003, p. 93)

Middle-class students likewise described the following sorts of opportunities:

When I did work experience, I spoke to a lot of doctors. And one of the doctors … I've kept in contact with, and he's helped me through my interviews and advised me. (p. 86)

There have been teachers like Miss Plummer who went to Cambridge herself and have … been really helpful and been right behind me and helped me with my personal statement and my application and helping me for the interview and stuff, so, I mean, that sort of stuff makes a difference really. (p. 87)

While the politics and policies of conservative modernization do create particular opportunity structures, it is important to remember that the middle classes (and other groups) must act within those spaces in order to secure and maximize advantage. In other words, class position is not given, but is instead reproduced and maintained through the purposeful application of available resources and through the making of a series of careful, sometimes tortured, and not-always-"rational" decisions (see Ball, 2003).

From what we have said here, it is clear that conservative modernization provides much of the ideological context for educational policy and practice in the United States and elsewhere. It has established the conditions under which so many of us operate, but it should also be clear that it is not a simple phenomenon—one group, one set of interests. Rather, it is an ideologically complex and often contradictory assemblage of forces, but one in which its general tendencies move us in rightist directions. Because of this, our analyses of who does speak and who does not speak, of how such speech is made public, of who is heard and who is not heard, of who claims subaltern status, and similar pressing concerns need to be subtle and nuanced. But at the same time, such subtlety must not lose sight of the winners and losers of the intense battles over recognition and redistribution in this society (Fraser, 1997). We need to be careful not to sacrifice our commitment to social and educational transformation on the altar of "complexity."

This requires a kind of balancing act. What we said about being cautious in the last paragraph should not cause us to ignore the gains that have been made in understanding the depth of the problems we face and the difficulties involved in more fully understanding them. The effects of conservative modernization on school knowledge and educational advantage do require more extensive investigation, particularly if more democratic alternatives are to be envisioned and potentially built. In this volume, several authors will empirically document and theorize the politics behind a number of largely conservative movements targeting school curriculum and access in the United States. In highlighting educational movements driven by the tendencies of conservative modernization, attention will also be given to the fragile relationship of rightist agendas to the interests of subaltern communities.

The Politics of Identity and Culture: Can the Subaltern Really Speak?

While these conservative movements have gained more power, less powerful groups have not been passive. This has led to significant theoretical and empirical developments with respect to issues of identity and culture. The 1960s and early 1970s were an unsettling time; a spectrum of social movements sought to challenge deeply rooted relations of unequal power. In the United States—from our homes, schools, buses, streets, and fields, to the courts, corporations, and the military-industrial complex—all were shaken by a chorus of overlapping and sometimes conflicting voices. These voices demanded the transformation of classist, racist, patriarchal, heterosexist, ablebodied, globally destructive structural arrangements.

This was accompanied by crucial intellectual developments as these same movements challenged the epistemological basis of many disciplines and even motivated the development of new fields, such as African American, Native American, and women's studies. The "new history," a rewriting of the past from the perspective of the oppressed, became increasingly accepted. Historian Eric Foner (1997) reflects:

> In the course of the past twenty years, American history has been remade.... The rise of "new histories," the emphasis on the experience of ordinary Americans, the impact of quantification and cultural analysis, the eclipse of conventional political and intellectual history—these trends are now so widely known (and the subject of such controversy) that they need little reiteration. (p. ix)

Accompanying this advance, more orthodox Marxist positions, which assumed a relatively unproblematic reproduction of class relations, were complicated by neo-Marxist work emphasizing the relative autonomy of superstructural institutions, contradiction, the agentic potential of subaltern groups, and the overall importance of struggles throughout civil society (Apple & Weis, 1986; Borg, Buttigieg, & Mayo, 2002). Beyond this blossomed the field of cultural studies, including the subaltern and postcolonial (Chaturvedi, 2000; Dimitriadis & McCarthy, 2001). Complicating the terrain even more, various traditions of postmodernism emerged, with their emphasis on the local, particular, fragmented, and hybridized nature of identity and culture. Some of the more radically deconstructive forms question the very notion of identity, reject any understanding of culture as a coherent construction, and instead focus on the impossibility of knowledge itself (Ellsworth, 1997). In turn, criticisms developed that questioned the legitimacy of understanding identity as inevitably fragmented and were accompanied by alternative accounts that emphasized efforts to generate coherence across multiple axes of identity (Carlson & Apple, 1998).

These theoretical gains and debates are important, not the least because when we ask *whose* knowledge is most valued, we invoke a form of identity politics. That is, this invocation requires us to closely consider the aforementioned advances in identity work and the debates this scholarship has generated. The significance of these debates for more fully grappling with the issues surrounding the subaltern can be seen in another example, one that returns us to Spivak's question—"Can the subaltern speak?"—which lies at the heart of this book. Let us consider the work of the South Asian Subaltern Studies Collective. This group was formed in the late 1970s to write a history of India from below, a project conceived in the spirit of subaltern history first envisioned by Gramsci. The first of many volumes of subaltern studies was published under the editorship of Ranajit Guha in 1982 (see Guha, 1988b, p. 35). Guha (1988a) argued that the historiography of India had long been dominated by "colonial elitism and bourgeois-nationalist elitism" (p. 37). Colonial histories, in other words, applauded British rulers, culture, and institutions for the advancement of India, while nationalist histories credited Indian elites, ideas, and efforts. "What is clearly left out of this unhistorical historiography," contended Guha, "is the *politics of the people*" (p. 37). "Elitist historiography," he elaborated, "should be resolutely fought by developing an alternative discourse based ... on the recognition of the co-existence and interaction of the elite and subaltern domains of politics" (p. 43).

Aside from Guha's own research (1983), other members of the collective likewise challenged dominant narratives (Guha & Spivak, 1988). For example, Gyan Pandey (1988) traced the peasant movement in Awadh from 1919 to 1922. The British had extended privileges to *taluqdars*, a native landowning class, in exchange for maintaining order in the countryside, while the majority of the native population remained landless laborers. As a result, *Kisan Sabhas*, or peasant associations, were organized locally and independent of the involvement of urban leaders in the Indian National Congress, the major nationalist party in colonial India. Pandey explains:

> The peasant associations now raised the cry for ... resistance to demands for anything more than the recorded rent. They called at the same time for non-cooperation with the colonial regime. Before long, colonial observers were complaining that ... the Criminal Procedure Code had "no provision for a whole countryside arrayed against law and order."

Yet the Congress leadership spared little time for the protagonists ... and this new phase of the movement was suppressed by a large force of armed police and military men. (p. 239)

Pandey shows how nationalist leaders such as Gandhi attempted to downplay the significance of the conflicts between landlords and peasants in the interest of promoting a wider unity against the British—an approach that was likely read by peasants as "a statement in favour of the *status quo* and against any radical change in the social set-up when the British finally handed over the reins of power" (p. 277). Perhaps more than urban nationalist leaders, Pandey suggests, the peasants of Awadh understood the alliance that supported colonial power and what would be required to undermine it.

As subaltern studies advanced, however, the complexities inherent in the project inspired heated debate—complexities and debates that are evident in the chapters that follow our introduction. Debates centered on a number of substantial issues, including the degree of subaltern autonomy from elite groups, the nature of resistance, and the danger of essentializing subaltern subjectivity while overlooking the heterogeneity and margins within subaltern communities (see Chaturvedi, 2000; Spivak, 1996a). Perhaps most crucially, issues were raised regarding the *possibility* of the historical subaltern speaking. Each of these debates is relevant to work on subalternity in critical educational studies. We have opted here to discuss the two latter debates because it is clear that this volume is partly situated in relation to this earlier work and even appears by title to challenge Gayatri Spivak's (1988) well-known declaration: "The subaltern cannot speak."

Joining subaltern studies in 1985, Spivak (1996a) reflected on the historiographic work of the group up to that point, especially in relation to the issue of essentialism. She conceded that the work of the group had often implied a single and unitary underlying consciousness that constituted the basis of subaltern solidarity and resistance. At the same time, she argued that the group's work was concurrently deconstructive in that it questioned the "sovereign subject," particularly the voice of authority embodied in the imperial archive. As such, Spivak claimed that the work of subaltern studies should be read "as a *strategic* use of positivist essentialism in a scrupulously visible political interest" (p. 214). Put another way, constructing the subaltern *as* coherent collective consciousness was a method for restoring the subaltern as an agent and force in history—even if the method concurrently required the historian to recognize the partiality of his or her construction and the impossibility of knowing the subjects of the past in all their complexity.

The most fundamental question engaged by these debates was articulated by Spivak in her classic essay, "Can the Subaltern Speak?" When Spivak first published the essay in 1988, she answered in the negative. The "recovery" of the (sexually) subaltern subject in Indian history, she contended, was complicated by the position of the investigating historian, the imperialism of British colonial records, and the patriarchy of indigenous elites—all of which seemed to leave "no space from which the subaltern subject can speak" (p. 307). These are exactly the issues faced by critical educators when they claim to speak for the silenced, and are among the most powerful issues faced by marginalized students when they confront the official curriculum, attempt to construct alternative understandings and knowledge, and press for a space where such knowledge is recognized as legitimate.

Spivak believes that the nature of her claim has been misunderstood by critics who argued, in opposition, that the subaltern *could* speak. In an interview in 1993, Spivak (1996b) clarified: "Subaltern insurgency... *is* an effort to involve oneself in representation, *not* according to the lines laid down by the official institutional structures of representation. Most often it does not catch. That is the moment that I am calling 'not speaking'" (p. 306). Further clarifying her argument, Spivak explained, "By speaking I was obviously talking about a transaction between the speaker and the listener," including attempts to speak through "actions" that ultimately address observers who must hear, or read the meaning of, such actions (p. 289). In short, subaltern attempts at representation and the reception of those representations within existing circuits of power are two very different things.

Considering the significance of the debate, Spivak rewrote her essay in 1999 and more clearly elaborated on the context of her statement "the subaltern cannot speak." She explains that this assertion reflected the frustration she felt as she attempted to reconstruct the histories of two Indian women. In the first case, Spivak confronted a scant historical record in which the Rani of Simur, a woman who declared her intention to self-immolate (a rite sometimes undertaken by Hindu widows which the British called *sati*) only appeared in documentation when her actions were of concern to either indigenous patriarchs or colonial authorities. In the second case, Spivak sought to investigate the suicide of Bhubaneswari Bhaduri, a young woman involved in armed struggle for Indian independence, who hanged herself rather than undermine the trust of her comrades who were depending on her to commit a political assassination—a plan she could not bring herself to execute. Spivak suggests that by waiting until the onset of menstruation to take her life, Bhubaneswari may have avoided commission of the assassination while simultaneously "rewriting the social text of *sati*-suicide" by both displacing and denying "in the physiological inscription of her body" the "interdict against a menstruating widow's right to immolate herself" (p. 307).

In 1926, the suicide was considered a puzzle by authorities, who did not grasp Bhubaneswari's symbolic speech. Perhaps even more disconcerting were the responses of a Bengali woman who questioned why Spivak would want to research this woman, and Bhubaneswari's nieces who contended that the suicide resulted from an illicit relationship—an interpretation invalidated by the onset of Bhubaneswari's menstruation. In light of these reactions, Spivak (1999) professed: "Her Speech Act was refused. She was made to unspeak herself, posthumously, by other women.... I had [earlier] summarized this historical indifference and its results as: the subaltern cannot speak" (p. 273). In this way, the silences and distortions of the archival record and the indifference of later generations motivated Spivak to conclude as she did. Rather than signifying a definitive statement about the im/possibilities of subaltern resistance and representation, however, Spivak hoped the pronouncement would underscore the genuine difficulties manifest in such historical work as well as the mediating effects of power on how the subaltern voice is heard.

Yet Spivak (1999) also underlined the political necessity of this challenging project, declaring that "the alternative of *not* attending to the subaltern past with all of its difficulties would be not to attend to it at all" (p. 307). Recognizing the difficulties—even the masquerade—involved in the processes of defining and representing "true" subaltern consciousness and experience, Spivak concluded even in the first version of her piece (1988): "Reporting on, or better still, participating in, [anti-oppressive] work ... is undeniably on the agenda. We should ... welcome all the information retrieval in these silenced areas that is taking place in anthropology, political science, history, and sociology." At the same time, she stressed that "the assumption and construction of a consciousness or subject sustains such work and will ... [thus] mingle epistemic violence with the advancement of learning and civilization" (p. 295).

We have detailed the history of Spivak's intervention in debates over the subaltern because we wish to take her points seriously. The complexities of subaltern "speech" and the politics of how it is heard and advanced lie at the very center of this book.

Putting the Subaltern on the School Bus

In dealing with the issues and cautions raised by Spivak about the "genuineness" of subaltern speech and about the complex identities that are performed, we are guided by a position taken by Stuart Hall, one of the cultural analysts to think creatively about the relationships among identity, voice, and power. Hall (1996) argues for "not an abandonment of 'the [subaltern] subject' but a reconceptualization—thinking it in its new, displaced or decentered position" (p. 2). Embracing a reconceptualized understanding of the subaltern subject, the many contributors to this book incisively renovate and carefully redeploy the concepts of identity and culture to illuminate pivotal debates, both past and present, over what counts as knowledge in schools. In short, we aim to put Spivak on a school bus. That bus will travel across the educational landscape, navigating its way through the curriculum, urban classrooms, home schools, the academy, educational policy and reform, and social movements. Along the way, we need to ask: To what degree and to what effect have subaltern groups been able to resist or rearticulate conservative practices, policies, and movements?

By the time the bus returns, we hope to have a more nuanced understanding of the limits of and possibilities for subaltern communities speaking and acting within education. This can only be accomplished by situating the complex dynamics of subaltern agency in the process of how differential power currently works within education. Thus, we combine an analysis of the ways in which various forms of dominance now operate, with a specific focus on the spaces that are created in which subaltern groups can act to reassert their own perceived identities, cultures, and histories. In so doing, we aim to participate in a larger project—one focused on imagining the kind of work that will be necessary to challenge conservative hegemony and to build schools that support the affiliations and sensibilities conducive to a radically democratic "new order."

All of this is especially important in light of current cultural clashes. Indeed, the assertions of subaltern groups have ignited what some have come to call the "culture wars" (Gates, 1992). Against waves of multiculturalism, and in opposition to the above political and intellectual developments, neoconservatives have waged a battle against the "balkanization" of society, decomposition of national unity, and the crisis of "common" culture and the Western tradition (Bennett, 1992; Hirsch, 1996). These battles continue to be quite intense, especially within education, where the idea of a "return" to "real knowledge" and a "common culture" are now generating increasing power.

Let us consider briefly an example that takes seriously the dual task mentioned above and highlights the stakes of present-day battles. In his book *Holler If You Hear Me*, Gregory Michie (1999) reflects on his struggle as a teacher to develop pedagogy relevant to the Chicano/a students he taught in Chicago. Dismayed by how English-speaking Chicano/a students in the school "kept their distance from those who only spoke Spanish," he discusses how the school itself contributed to this:

> The kids' rejection of their ethnic identity seemed to stem, at least in part, from a clash of cultures that they experienced between life at home and life in school. At home, most kids spoke Spanish; at school, there was a teacher who fined them—literally, made them *pay money*—for every word of Spanish they uttered in class. (p. 73)

One project that Michie developed with several Chicana students was the production of an audio book of Sandra Cisneros's *The House on Mango Street*, a series of vignettes about a Mexican American, working-class girl growing up in Chicago—much like his own students. As the project got underway, it revealed how a curriculum that relates to students' lives can begin, in ways big and small, to open up spaces for learning that recognize as valuable the cultures of subaltern groups. For example, while reading one vignette entitled "Chanclas [Flip Flops]," Michie's students began to giggle. When he inquired why they were laughing over a word that referred to shoes, one student explained: "It's like a nickname or something. I've just never seen that word printed in a book before. It's not that it's funny, it's just—it's like an inside word, you know? Like a word nobody outside knows. You get me?" (p. 58) In a compelling way, this moment speaks to the power of dominant cultural forms to create insiders and outsiders in educational institutions, but it also provides a glimpse into the spirit ignited when alternative forms of knowledge infuse schools and the "outside" makes its way "in" (see also Buras, 2005a).

This example speaks to a larger issue. Dolores Delgado Bernal (1999, 2002) has argued for the epistemological relevance of the subjectivity and cultural intuitions of students of color in schools. She has demonstrated how divergent interpretations of student culture and knowledge follow from Eurocentric and Chicana feminist perspectives. Based on white privilege, the privileging of English, capitalism, and "scientific" theories of intelligence, she contends that for generations a Eurocentric epistemological orientation has positioned Chicano/as "as 'culturally deficient' and characterized them as ignorant, backward, unclean, unambitious, and abnormal" (2002, p. 112; see also Valenzuela, 2005). By comparison, a Chicana feminist perspective brings into focus the fact that valuable "community and family knowledge is taught to youth through legends, *corridos*, and storytelling," a kind of knowledge generally invisible within a Eurocentric epistemology (p. 113). Delgado Bernal stresses that "learning to listen to [these] counterstories within the educational system can be an important pedagogical practice for teachers and students," one that exposes a "nonmajoritarian perspective," which more advantaged students are generally unaccustomed to hearing (p. 116). If we think here of Spivak's contention that while the subaltern *may* speak, the powerful often refuse to hear the stories told, then we are reminded of the real difficulties that arise when members of dominant and subaltern groups confront one another.

Yet even subaltern cultural forms may contain dominant elements and engender their own "constitutive outside" (Butler, 1993). It is important, then, to distinguish those dimensions of culture and history that are to be defended from those that deserve critique (Apple, 2005b)—an undertaking of the sort recommended by Gramsci who called for examining the "various strata," conservative and progressive, within consciousness. This ultimately requires us to both appreciate the elements of insight in the positions assumed by subaltern groups, but also to acknowledge those aspects that may have less democratic implications. All of this must be done in an unromantic way. Reality is complex and contradictory, as are the politics coming out of it. "Speaking back" may have contradictory results; and as we shall see, it may even involve groups with whom progressives may disagree. Subalternity does *not* always mean political and educational progressivism. This point is a crucial realization and will be taken up in a number of chapters, especially in section one.

In this regard, the work of Kevin Kumashiro has been insightful (2002). "It is a problem," he writes, "to speak of identities always and only in their separate(d) incarnations, which not only denies ways in which identities are already intersected, but more importantly, masks ways in which certain identities are already privileged" (p. 56). Rather than valorizing subaltern culture and emphasizing a singular collective identity rooted in oppression, Kumashiro shows how particular dimensions of subaltern culture and consciousness are worthy of preservation while other aspects may warrant critique (see also McCarthy, 1998).

More precisely, Kumashiro (2002) reveals how subaltern cultures sometimes "cite" and "supplement" dominant ideologies, meaning they incorporate forms of dominant ideology while simultaneously adding something new. In one illustration, he points out that queer Asian American boys experience both racism and heterosexism within mainstream society. In the same moment, they also experience different forms of heterosexism and racism from within Asian American and queer communities. Thus, Asian American communities often "normalize heterosexuality and denigrate queer sexualities [cite], but they also assign racial markers to different sexual orientations [supplement]." While heterosexuality is frequently racialized as "a requirement of Asianness," queer sexuality is often racialized as white so that Asian Americans who are queer "are not 'really' Asian, are more White than Asian, [and] have the 'White disease'" (p. 83). Meanwhile, queer Asian men may be embraced within queer communities, but the terms are racialized as they are viewed as "exotic" and thus "hyperdesirable" (p. 84). Much like Spivak, Kumashiro emphasizes that both dominant and subaltern constructions of identity create their own margins. Such are the contradictions engendered when the subaltern speak.

Circuits of Curricular Production, Distribution, and Reception

While we pointed to questions of identity in the previous section, identity does not exhaust the issues with which we must deal. Other issues are also intimately connected to the question we mentioned earlier—"Whose knowledge is of most worth?" The politics surrounding the production, distribution, and reception of curricular knowledge are intense and complex. Struggles over the curriculum—over whose experience would be represented as valid or whose language or history would be taught—are unquestionably long-standing (Apple, 2000; Kaestle, 1983; Zimmerman, 2002). These conflicts have continued into the present as multiculturalists of all stripes call for greater diversity in the curriculum (Grant & Sleeter, 2003). Neoconservatives, by comparison, strive to maintain the dominance of particular (e.g. "Eurocentric") traditions, while authoritarian populists urge a return to school prayer and even a return to the home for schooling when the evil of secular humanism appears unconquerable (Apple, 2006; Buras, 1999). The textbook—perhaps the most concrete embodiment of that which counts as knowledge in schools—has engendered content-related campaigns from both the left and right (Delfattore, 1992)—campaigns that have led to all kinds of maneuvering by textbook publishers to capture the market in state textbook adoptions (Apple, 1988; Apple & Christian-Smith, 1991). On top of this, the push for national and state standards as well as standardized assessment (McNeil, 2002; Ravitch, 1995) has only heightened the stakes.

Many of the aforementioned struggles have focused on the production and distribution of curricular knowledge. At the same time, however, there has been an increasing focus on how schools themselves function as sites for the recontextualization of the formal corpus of school knowledge (Bernstein, 2000). The emphasis here rests on the fact that knowledge is never unproblematically transmitted from the state curriculum to the teacher, the textbook to the student, or even the teacher to the student (Epstein, 1998; Grant, 2001; Willis, 1977). In short, the official curriculum is always reconstructed at the level of reception as teachers and students engage in the unending process of sense-making, resistance, and day-to-day teaching and learning. Of course, none of the conflict associated with the politics of curricular production, distribution, and reception occurs on even ground. Not all parties have access to equivalent resources, channels of communication, or power—a fundamental point that is interrogated throughout this book.

These inequalities are made strikingly visible in recent work on how such channels have been controlled by conservative policy makers. Mary Lee Smith and her colleagues (2004) endorse a "theory of political spectacle" when it comes to explaining the formation of educational policy and the distribution of values associated with policy. They explain:

> This theory holds that contemporary politics resemble theater, with directors, stages, casts of actors, narrative plots, and (most importantly) a curtain that separates the action onstage—what the audience has access to—from the backstage, where the real "allocation of values" takes places. (p. 11)

This is definitely *not* the type of theater advanced by Boal, whose aim, as we saw, is to undermine dominance rather than to perpetuate it. In the theater of political spectacle, by contrast, the audience gets—for the most part—only symbolic benefit from the reassuring language and appeals of policy makers; elites acquire concrete benefits behind the curtain. "Rational" explanations of policy making assume that stakeholders negotiate their interests together, with an eye toward the common good. What is too often overlooked, however, are the politics that shape the development of policy.

Tracking educational assessment programs in Arizona during the 1990s provides a glimpse into the theater of policy making. Embracing rhetoric focused on a need to raise standards and make schools accountable, state officials killed the deficient testing program of the previous administration and quickly replaced it with another similarly flawed system. Although both programs were doing more harm than good to students, the revision of standards and development and implementation of a new testing regime promised to remedy the achievement crisis, and simultaneously boosted confidence in the latter administration. While state and district budgets were drained throughout this process, politicians and their allies in the testing industry accrued great profits and public applause. Meanwhile, the waste of educational resources and instructional time, as well as poor test reliability and validity, have undermined academic advancement, particularly for poor students and students of color. At the level of reception, high stakes tests have actually spurred resistance in a number of states, as not all groups have been equally entertained by policy makers' performances (Smith et al., 2004; see also Valenzuela, 2005).

Such resistance reminds us that the circuits of policy and curriculum production, distribution, and reception consist of a dense and dynamic network of relations (Johnson, 1983). Actors at one level may find their mandates challenged by actors elsewhere in the circuit. The use of curricula at the school level may be quite different from the curricula originally produced and distributed, may serve ends unforeseen by producers, and may even inspire unanticipated lessons or resistance. In the end, the curricular script must be enacted or brought to life, but the broader platform on which the reproduction occurs poses challenges to the integrity of the official vision (e.g., see Schweber, 2004).

The complexities of this circuit are apparent when we look closely not only in the United States, but internationally as well. In Singapore in the late 1980s, for example, the government tightly controlled the development of a religious knowledge curriculum intended (at least onstage) to protect Singapore against the perceived "moral decline" occurring in the West. Although it claimed neutrality and invited parents to choose from several course options, the Confucian Ethics option was given disproportionate political and media attention—an intervention shaped by the government's backstage desire to bolster its own rule. On the ground, however, parents more often opted for Buddhist studies, which they believed was easier for students to pass, and thereby prioritized "which option promised 'easier returns' in the competitive educational system" (Tan, 2000, p. 89). Although unanticipated, Buddhist and Christian Evangelical revivalism was actually strengthened by the religious knowledge curriculum. This mediation reveals that despite the government's "rigid control" over curriculum, implementation was "fraught with numerous contradictions and tensions which in turn sowed the seeds for the eventual review of the programme" (p. 96). Clearly, curriculum development cannot be understood apart from contexts of adoption and implementation (see also Wong, 2002).

In another international setting, Nadine Dolby (2000) has shown how two different "sites of memory" about apartheid exercised disparate influence on the historical understandings of white students in an elite South African high school. The first site, the government-sponsored Truth and Reconciliation Commission initiated in 1995, focused on the narratives of black victims and white perpetrators of human rights violations, and emphasized truth-telling, forgiveness, healing, and national unification. The second site was the history classroom of Mrs. West. By comparison, she asked students to consider the agency of black South Africans who collectively sought to change apartheid. Dolby explains that students tended to "refuse" their teacher's interpretations. "Many of them overlaid her historical presentation with the predominant themes emerging from the Truth and Reconciliation hearings, thus replacing her concentration on agency and struggle with an emphasis on morality, pity, and confession" (p. 183). Considering students' uneven receptivity, she concludes that "Mrs. West's history lessons, designed to convey to students the vibrancy and power of collective change, *cannot speak* to the students' understandings of history, which are framed through the national discourse of reconciliation" (italics added, p. 190). In this case, subversive histories were elided for more conciliatory narratives of the past, revealing how the efforts of teachers are mediated by students' own class and racial backgrounds and the broader political context in which schools are situated.

Clearly, it is imperative that scholars be specific in tracing these circuits. We agree with Catherine Cornbleth (2000) when she emphasizes, "Saying that education in general or curriculum in particular is political isn't saying much unless one describes what political means, how the politics operate, and why politics matters.... Relatively few contemporary observers or analysts have explicated education politics beyond abstractions" (p. 2). How, we ask, have dominant and subaltern groups—poor and working classes, people of color, queer students, progressive scholars in the corporate academy, increasingly powerful groups such as conservative evangelicals, and even various nationalist groups and social movements—intervened in the circuits of curricular production, distribution, and reception? In what ways have the opportunity structures created by specific educational policies been taken up by different groups? Both dominant and subaltern collectivities seek to influence the production and circulation of knowledge and to reinterpret the representations that permeate everyday school life. Contributors to this volume address the contests, compromises, and reconstructions associated with the circuits of curriculum and educational policy. By analyzing a range of contexts, the power dynamics, stakes, and democratic possibilities, we hope, can be more clearly grasped.

National and International Contexts

Our use of examples from Singapore and South Africa points to our final set of arguments. The worldwide nature of conservative modernization and the globalization of economic and cultural relations have necessitated a deeper analysis of the connections between national and international contexts. Indeed, advances in subaltern and postcolonial studies have revealed the utter importance of understanding the interconnected and often shifting relations between "periphery" and "center," particularly in terms of struggles over knowledge (Mignolo, 2000; Hardt & Negri, 2000).

In following up on these insights, scholars have explored the relevance of neoliberal educational policy and its effects in nations as different as Chile, China, South Africa, and England, and have demonstrated the relevance of these nations' experiences to debates over school choice, equality, and curricular innovation in the United States. The weight of evidence from these diverse contexts reveals that market-based educational plans have only heightened advantages for those already relatively privileged and worsened existing disparities (Plank & Sykes, 2003; see also Whitty, Power, & Halpin, 1998; Apple, 2006). What is equally disturbing is that despite such evidence, conservative modernizers in nations such as the United States, where market forms in education are less advanced, still persist in making promises about the redemptive quality of educational markets. This refusal to learn from other nations, we submit, is a dangerous practice rooted in both a will to ignore and hierarchical assumptions about whose experience is most useful in guiding educational reforms (see Buras & Apple, 2005).

A fuller perspective on issues of identity, curricular knowledge, and resistance can be gleaned from work that takes seriously the insights made possible by connecting the local, national, and global—a project that has been hampered by Western nationalism and exceptionalism. The extent of resistance to this project is exemplified in neoconservative denunciations of not only leftist multiculturalism, but global education within the United States. In the mid-1980s, Phyllis Schafly charged that global education promoted "the falsehood that other nations, governments, legal systems, cultures, and economic systems are essentially equivalent to us and entitled to equal respect" (cited in Lamy, 1990, p. 52). This kind of condemnation of even the most basic forms of transnational education has only escalated (Burack, 2003). We reject this insular view and the retrogressive nationalism on which it is based. In fact, several scholars in this book assert the value of border thinking or "the recognition and transformation of the hegemonic imaginary from the perspective of people in subaltern positions" (Mignolo, 2000, p. 736). In what ways, we ask, may disputes over school knowledge in specific contexts inform educational and cultural workers both within and across national borders? What are the possible implications of and barriers to constructing a curriculum that is subaltern, critically multicultural, and transnational in its emphasis?

These are pivotal questions. Globalization in all its guises has contributed to an increasingly cosmopolitical world, albeit one in which exchanges are highly uneven. Dominated by the interests of elites in Western nations, international financial entities, such as the International Monetary Fund [IMF] and the World Bank, have imposed neocolonial forms of debt slavery on less powerful nations, and have proceeded with little regard for basic democratic practices. Joseph Stiglitz (2002) makes this point:

> Underlying the problems of the IMF and other international economic institutions is the problem of governance: who decides what they do.... The institutions are dominated not just by the wealthiest industrial countries but by commercial and financial interests in those countries, and the policies of the institutions naturally reflect this. (pp. 18–19)

Here again, the issue arises of elite and subaltern voices and their corresponding ability to be heard and to influence crucial decision-making processes. Using our theater imagery once more, we might say that onstage the IMF proclaims that it does not dictate loan agreements—it negotiates them. Backstage, however, it is quite dictatorial and "effectively stifles any discussions within a client government—let alone more broadly within the country— about alternative economic policies" (p. 43). Poor nations, in turn, have demanded the right to participate more significantly in the formation of development policies. These demands prompted the IMF and World Bank to acquiesce and begin conducting "participatory" poverty assessments in which client governments assist in evaluating the extent of existing problems, at least as an initial step. Illustrating the spectacle at play, the IMF, *prior* to its consultative visit to a particular country, demanded that the World Bank send it a draft of the country's poverty assessment "asap [as soon as possible]" (p. 50). Clearly, there is a world of difference between the real and the ideal, with moves such as this powerfully demonstrating the length to which dominant groups will go to control who speaks, and the conditions under which the "dialogue" will occur.

Artifice thus substitutes for democracy and the struggles continue. In recognition of this fact, some scholarship has actually centered on the complicated ways in which neoliberal and neoconservative discourses and policies have been partially interrupted by historic social democratic arrangements or rearticulated by subaltern groups across a range of international contexts (Apple et al., 2003). It is paramount that we not forget that globalization can be remade as subaltern groups resist the role of spectator and instead act to challenge current economic structures that undermine access to health care, education, and other fundamental social entitlements—something powerfully illustrated by Luís Armando Gandin in Chapter 9.

But we need to be careful. These global economic forces are too often viewed as the only thing structuring international relations. Cultural flows and exchanges facilitated by new technologies, postcolonial migration, international education, and displacement have had a profound impact on everyday life, political practice, and imagination (Apple, Kenway, & Singh, 2005;

Burbules & Torres, 2000; Cheah & Robbins, 1998). Transnational advocacy networks have developed, have facilitated international mobilizations, and have even reinforced national ones (Keck & Sikkink, 1998). These processes, much like the economic ones we just discussed, have been similarly uneven as cultural exchanges within nations and among them unfold in the midst of gross inequities. Earlier we alluded to the "culture wars" within the United States. It may be argued that the present "war on terrorism" (since September 2001) is *the* culture war par excellence—although it is undeniably clear that naked economic interests are also driving this most brutal campaign. Since that fateful moment, cultural exchanges have come to be viewed by many elites as even *more* polluting and dangerous than before. Specific racial and religious groups, immigrants and "aliens," "unpatriotic" protesters, civilians in "terrorist" states, and other "suspicious" classes are profiled, interrogated, detained, deported, and tortured. It is therefore the case that we cannot overlook the "terms" of cultural contact and mixing, as all cultural forms do not merit positive recognition within this context (see Apple, 2002; Buras, 2005b; Pieterse, 2004). The globalization of culture combined with oppressive streams of nationalism and national identity, neocolonial forms and practices, and mobile police states mean that circulations of knowledge from below are all the more difficult *and* all the more essential.

With all the talk about a new global and *post*colonial world order, there is much that is not so "new." Colonial forms manifest as reconfigured but familiar imperialisms that fuel ongoing struggles and new social movements. For example, since the "end" of apartheid in South Africa, a number of neocolonial, or (re)colonizing tendencies, have emerged. Although IsiZulu is both an official national language and one that is more widely spoken than English, language policy in the realm of education facilitates the continuing hegemony of English (Ndimande, 2004; see also Singh, Kell, & Pandian, 2002). In many public schools, despite attempts to democratize and desegregate them, English is the only official medium of communication all the way to sixth grade. Textbooks used in the schools exhibit comparable tendencies. The structure of one such text and its content followed a comfortable pattern: Histories of Europe and the United States were given priority, with the history of Africa covered last. Colonialism in Africa was virtually absent, with disproportionate attention given to the period of decolonization. The coverage of South African history was no better, with the period between 1976 and 1994—a time of worldwide contestation against apartheid—treated as an add-on not even worthy, according to the history syllabus, of examination. "Textbooks that are [racially] biased," concludes Ndimande (2004), "reflect one of the tendencies of neocolonial[ism]," namely the tendency to "erase the collective memory of oppressed peoples" (p. 208). These (re)colonizing tendencies, as well as oppositional movements that seek to rewrite national geographies and pasts from the view and in the language of subalterns, involve struggles over "center" and "margins" and will be emphasized in forthcoming chapters.

Paulo Freire (1993) early understood the liberating potential of viewing the world from the vantage point of those living on the margins, as do many activists involved in more recent counterhegemonic movements in education. With regard to this philosophy, Michael Apple recalls, "During one of the times I was working in Brazil with Paulo Freire, I remember him repeatedly saying to me that education must begin in critical dialogue" (Apple, 2001, p. 218). The importance of such a dialogue extends not only to individuals and groups within nations, but also implies "the efficacy of turning to the experiences of other nations to learn about what the effects of neoliberal and neoconservative policies actually are," as well as how marginalized groups in such nations "are helping to build support for more progressive and democratic policies" (p. 219). In this tradition of dialogue, the present book incorporates scholarship on both national and international educational contexts to encourage a critical reflexivity that crosses borders.

Dominance and Subalternity—Right and Left

It should be clear, then, that the purpose of this volume is to articulate powerful historical, theoretical, and empirical responses to the many questions generated when one considers voice, identity, and "whose knowledge is most valued" under present-day political, economic, and cultural conditions. The authors who contributed to this volume rigorously evaluate the effects of conservative modernization on school knowledge; carefully and unromantically examine the struggles of subaltern groups for cultural recognition and economic redistribution within various educational contexts; explore the ways in which dominant and subaltern actors and formations intervene in the circuits of curricular production and distribution and recontextualize knowledge at the school and classroom level; and critically analyze the politics of knowledge in national and international contexts, with an emphasis on both the locally specific and transnational significance of particular controversies and projects. Considered collectively, the chapters in this collection clarify many of the major contests over knowledge, which characterize the contemporary moment and provide a lens for considering how dominant and often antidemocratic efforts to construct and reconstruct school curriculum and policy might be interrupted by progressive and sometimes contradictory subaltern mobilizations.

We want to challenge some of the predominant ways of understanding the subaltern. Our ordinary assumptions about who are the subaltern and the voices in which they speak nearly automatically assume that oppressed groups speak in progressive voices. Further, we too often neglect the fact that subaltern status has increasingly been claimed by a larger number of groups, some of which may occupy both dominant and subaltern positions. We need to take seriously Fraser's (1997) argument that, at times, struggles over recognition may interrupt dominance and even powerfully influence struggles over redistribution, but we also wish to go further than Fraser by highlighting the fact that struggles over recognition can and do go on equally among dominant groups.

The Subaltern Speak is divided into three sections. The first section is "The Subaltern Speak: In Whose Voices?" In light of the issues raised previously, the chapters in this section trace and analyze curriculum initiatives and educational movements under the primary direction of dominant factions of the conservative alliance in the United States, including neoconservatives, religious conservatives, and neoliberals. Authors focus on the efforts made by these groups to influence curriculum production, distribution, and reception, educational reform, and the relationship of these efforts to various subaltern groups. A primary focus will be on the contradictory voices, efforts, and movements of those who rightly or wrongly claim subaltern status, or who claim to speak for the subaltern. We put this section first because we want to complicate and trouble the notion of subalternity at the outset of the book.

In Chapter 1, Kristen Buras argues that we are entering an era in which progressive forms of multiculturalism are being redefined by powerful groups along conservative lines and embraced as part of a decisive compromise— one intended to win the consent of subaltern communities for particular educational reforms. She critically assesses the assumptions underlying E. D. Hirsch's neoconservative vision of schooling, which has helped to usher in what she calls "rightist multiculturalism." In turn, Buras traces the diverse interests and peculiar alliances that have contributed to the nationwide Core Knowledge Movement and that have strengthened and challenged it over the past two decades. Equally significant, she details how Hirsch's Core curriculum constructs a "*new* old history" in classroom textbooks, which potentially appeals to groups below and above. Concentrating on a different vein of conservative modernization in Chapter 2, Michael Apple assesses the ways in which traditional gender roles for women, access to new technologies such as the Internet, the growth of Christian publishing houses, and even the development of charter school legislation have facilitated a blossoming of home schools headed by religious fundamentalist and conservative evangelical women. He illuminates the contradictions in conservative movements that simultaneously position women as subservient and yet provide these same women with identities as powerful actors. In the process, he raises complex and troubling questions about the way in which this faction has assumed the language and identity of a subaltern community. In Chapter 3, Thomas Pedroni examines the identity formation and agency of low-income, African American parents involved in the Milwaukee private school voucher program. More specifically, he analyzes the conditional alliance formed with dominant groups—particularly neoliberals—around vouchers, and suggests that subaltern groups do not necessarily become right (politically) when they support market-based school reform. In fact, he reveals various tensions that characterize this alliance, but suggests that even tactical support for vouchers by subaltern groups may nonetheless bolster conservative power and undermine the interests of the dispossessed.

In short, the chapters in the first section highlight understudied educational movements driven by the tendencies of conservative modernization as well as the fragile and often contradictory relationship of rightist agendas to the interests of oppressed communities.

Because one of our purposes in section one is to make more complicated our understanding of the politics of subalternity in relation to the aggressive forces of conservative modernization, there is a danger in forgetting the justifiable struggles of those groups who are clearly among the most oppressed culturally, economically, and politically in this nation and so many others. Thus, we wish to also pay particular attention to the voices and struggles of those groups that continue to suffer the often murderous consequences of racism, patriarchy, homophobia, and capitalism. In the process, we aim to give a clearer sense of the agency and crucial struggles of these groups within the sphere of education.

As such, the second section, "The Subaltern Speak: National Contexts," concentrates on the positionality and participation of various subaltern groups in the United States, including Native American students, Chicana feminist educational activists, queer students and students of color, and progressive scholars, in a range of educational struggles. More specifically, the authors examine the efforts of subaltern groups to challenge the effects of conservative modernization on schooling, intervene in circuits of curricular production, distribution, and reception, and exercise agency in response to issues of recognition and redistribution.

In Chapter 4, Glenabah Martinez concentrates on the reception of "regular" and Native American Studies curricula by Indigenous students in an urban high school, and reveals how domination, compromise, and resistance unfold at the classroom level. Moreover, she explores the complicated relationship between students' understandings of what counts as educationally useful and notions of "white" required knowledge and "red" elective knowledge. In Chapter 5, Dolores Delgado Bernal focuses on a historic protest by Chicano/a students against racist curricula and unequal resources in the public schools of East Los Angeles. Attempting to first be heard through official channels—only to be ignored by school authorities—student activists organized and sustained a massive strike. Yet ironically, Chicanas involved in the mobilization were not perceived as leaders. Through oral histories, Delgado Bernal shows how particular constructions of agency masked women's contributions and thereby expands what counts as "speaking" at the grassroots level. This again shows that subaltern agency is often complex and contradictory. In Chapter 6, Kevin

Kumashiro reflects on the racial and sexual dynamics of the post–9/11 context and interrogates how such dynamics relate to forms of "difference" in schools. Within society and within education, he argues, racial and sexual differences have engendered fear and assimilation-oriented reforms that encourage conversion, passing, and covering—all of which burden the identities of subaltern students while leaving the power of dominant forms unquestioned. Anti-oppressive educational efforts, he asserts, are too often willing to go "only so far" in addressing issues of recognition. Stanley Aronowitz shows in Chapter 7 how military and corporate interests have infected the production, distribution, and reception of knowledge in postsecondary institutions of education and diminished possibilities for more enlightened forms of teaching and research. Scholars in the academy dedicated to producing knowledge for the public rather than the private good will be rendered subaltern, he contends, as intellectual work is increasingly commodified and compromised by the dictates of economic elites and conservative state forces. Aronowitz's challenge is this: Public intellectuals, even those with relative privilege, must act in solidarity against global capital.

Mapping the educational conditions and mobilizations of a broad range of subaltern groups, the authors in the second section thus reveal the possibilities and contradictions involved in how such groups have resisted or organized (or potentially could) on the basis of particular identifications and within the spaces made available by both progressive and conservative forces.

The third section, "The Subaltern Speak: International Contexts," charts the significance of subalternity to the production, distribution, and reconstruction of school knowledge in contexts beyond the United States. It takes seriously one of the major tasks of this book—to help us understand the specifics of how contests unfold in a range of contexts. The realities of globalization compel us to think across borders and to recognize that our histories and struggles are connected to those of so many other nations throughout the world. In essence, we want to remember that much of the history of those nations that arrogate the center to themselves occurs outside their borders (see also Hardt & Negri, 2000).

Hence, in Chapter 8, Jyh-Jia Chen documents the conflicts in Taiwan surrounding the recognition of indigenous history, language, and culture in school curricula. She examines the treatment of a historically significant massacre under Chinese domination and of the geographic representation of territory in relation to issues of sovereignty, and discusses how activists sought to counter official representations. Chen then turns to an examination of the dominant language policies that reinforced the value of standard Mandarin over native languages. Her analysis sheds important light on the power of oppositional movements to reconstruct curriculum and identity and to mediate state action. Extending our critical international focus, in Chapter 9, Luís Armando Gandin traces subaltern efforts in Porto Alegre, Brazil, a site that has generated worldwide attention because of its progressive educational policies. He underscores how oppressed communities have rearticulated neoliberal discourses on international competition and devolution in an effort to support greater educational investment, participatory school governance, and grassroots curriculum within the Citizen School project. At the same time, he considers some of the challenges of democratizing knowledge and decision making within a context shaped by unequal power as well as competing conceptions of what constitutes "conservative" versus "revolutionary" educational change. In Chapter 10, Kristen Buras and Paulino Motter examine how traditions of Western multiculturalism—left and right—are embedded in a framework that stresses affiliation and difference *within* the nation. To expand the emancipatory potential of more critical traditions, they advocate and detail the complexities involved in building a "subaltern cosmopolitan multiculturalism" that places epistemological subalternity and a more complex and far-reaching sense of identification at the curriculum's center. This is not a choice, they contend, between critical localized multiculturalism and counter-hegemonic cosmopolitanism, but rather a challenge to imagine and develop a curriculum that nurtures a range of solidarities, advances the interests of subaltern communities locally, nationally, and globally, and enables students to think and act within and across borders.

By examining the campaigns waged by activists in Taiwan to challenge the legacy of colonialism in the representation of knowledge, highlighting the efforts of poor communities in Brazil to democratize education and counter the effects of global policies, and constructing a curricular vision that crosses borders and redefines the relationship between insurgent forms of multicultural and global education, the authors in the third section provide starting points for transnational reflection, dialogue, and action.

The book concludes with a final chapter, "Speaking Back to Official Knowledge," which poses a number of crucial questions about what it might mean to develop more complicated theories of cultural recognition and how they might help us better understand the complexities, contradictions, limits, dangers, and possibilities of the educational struggles presently unfolding.

References

Andre-Bechely, L. (2005). *Could it have been different?* New York: Routledge.

Apple, M. W. (1979/2004). *Ideology and curriculum.* New York: Routledge.

Apple, M. W. (1988). *Teachers and texts: A political economy of class and gender relations in education.* New York: Routledge.

Apple, M. W. (1995). *Education and power* (2nd ed.). New York: Routledge.

Apple, M. W. (1996). *Cultural politics and education.* New York: Teachers College Press.

Apple, M. W. (2000). *Official knowledge: Democratic education in a conservative age* (2nd ed.). New York: Routledge.

Apple, M. W. (2001). *Educating the "right" way: Markets, standards, god, and inequality.* New York: RoutledgeFalmer.

Apple, M. W. (2002). Patriotism, pedagogy, and freedom: On the educational meanings of September 11 [Electronic version]. *Teachers College Record, 104* (8).

Apple, M. W. (2005a). Comment on E. D. Hirsch. In D. Ravitch (Ed.), *Brookings papers on education policy 2005* (pp. 186–197). Washington, DC: Brookings Institution.

Apple, M. W. (2005b). Education, markets, and an audit culture. *Critical Quarterly, 47* (1–2), 11–29.

Apple, M. W. (2006). *Educating the "right" way: Markets, standards, god, and inequality* (2nd ed.). New York: Routledge.

Apple, M. W., et al. (2003). *The state and the politics of knowledge.* New York: RoutledgeFalmer.

Apple, M. W., & Christian-Smith, L. K. (Eds.). (1991). *The politics of the textbook.* New York: Routledge.

Apple, M. W., Kenway, J., & Singh, M. (Eds.). (2005). *Globalizing education: Policies, pedagogies, and politics.* New York: Peter Lang.

Apple, M. W., & Pedroni, T. C. (in press). Conservative alliance building and African American support for voucher reforms: The end of *Brown's* promise or a new beginning? *Teachers College Record.*

Apple, M. W., & Weis, L. (1986). Seeing education relationally: The stratification of culture and people in the sociology of school knowledge. *Journal of Education, 168* (1), 7–33.

Ball, S. J. (2003). *Class strategies and the education market: The middle classes and social advantage.* New York: RoutledgeFalmer.

Bennett, W. J. (1992). *The de-valuing of America: The fight for our culture and our children.* New York: Simon & Schuster.

Bernstein, B. (2000). *Pedagogy, symbolic control and identity.* New York: Rowman & Littlefield.

Boal, A. (1985). *Theatre of the oppressed.* New York: Theatre Communications Group.

Boal, A. (1992). *Games for actors and non-actors.* New York: Routledge.

Boal, A. (1995). *The rainbow of desire.* New York: Routledge.

Board of Regents of the University of Wisconsin System v. Southworth et al. (2000). Available: http://laws.findlaw.com/us/000/98-1189.html

Borg, C., Buttigieg, J., & Mayo, P. (2002). *Gramsci and education.* New York: Rowman & Littlefield.

Burack, J. (2003). The student, the world, and the global education ideology. In J. Leming, L. Ellington, & K. Porter (Eds.), *Where did social studies go wrong?* (pp. 40–69). Washington, DC: Thomas B. Fordham Foundation.

Buras, K. L. (1999). Questioning core assumptions: A critical reading of and response to E. D. Hirsch's *The Schools We Need and Why We Don't Have Them. Harvard Educational Review, 69* (1), 67–93.

Buras, K. L. (2005a, January). Review of Parker, W. C. Teaching democracy: Unity and diversity in public life. *Education Review.* Available: http://edrev.asu.edu/reviews/rev341.htm

Buras, K. L. (2005b). The (un)patriotic teacher: Schooling, dissent, and the "war on terrorism." Unpublished manuscript, University of Wisconsin-Madison.

Buras, K. L., & Apple, M. W. (2005). School choice, neoliberal promises, and unpromising evidence. *Educational Policy, 19* (3), 550–564.

Burbules, N. C., & Torres, C. A. (2000). *Globalization and education: Critical perspectives.* New York: Falmer Press.

Butler, J. (1993). *Bodies that matter: On the discursive limits of "sex."* New York: Routledge.

Calloway, C. G. (1997). *New worlds for all: Indians, Europeans, and the remaking of early America.* Baltimore, MD: Johns Hopkins University Press

Carlson, D. & Apple, M. W. (Eds.). (1998). *Power-knowledge-pedagogy: The meaning of democratic education in unsettling times.* New York: Westview Press.

Chaturvedi, V. (Ed.). (2000). *Mapping the subaltern and the postcolonial.* New York: Verso.

Cheah, P., & Robbins, B. (Eds.). (1998). *Cosmopolitics: Thinking and feeling beyond the state.* Minneapolis: University of Minnesota Press.

Chomsky, N. (1999). *Profit over people: Neoliberalism and global order.* New York: Seven Stories Press.

Core Knowledge Foundation (1999). *Core knowledge sequence: Content guidelines for grades K–8.* Charlottesville, VA: Author.

Cornbleth, C. (Ed.). (2000). *Curriculum politics, policy, and practice: Cases in comparative context.* Albany: State University of New York Press.

Dance, L. J. (2002). *Tough fronts: The impact of street culture on schooling.* New York: RoutledgeFalmer.

Delfattore, J. (1992). *What Johnny shouldn't read: Textbook censorship in America.* New Haven, CT: Yale University Press.

Delgado Bernal, D. (1999). Using a Chicana feminist epistemology in educational research. *Harvard Educational Review, 68* (4), 555–582.

Delgado Bernal, D. (2002). Critical race theory, Latino critical theory, and critical raced-gendered epistemologies: Recognizing students of color as holders and creators of knowledge. *Qualitative Inquiry, 8* (1), 105–126.

Dimitriadis, G., & McCarthy, C. (2001). *Reading and teaching the postcolonial: From Baldwin to Basquiat and beyond.* New York: Teachers College Press.

Dolby, N. (2000). Curriculum as a site of memory: The struggle for history in South Africa. In Catherine Cornbleth (Ed.), *Curriculum politics, policy, and practice: Cases in comparative context* (pp. 175–194). Albany: State University of New York Press.

Dolby, N., Dimitriadis, G., with Willis, P. (Eds.). (2004). *Learning to labor in new times.* New York: RoutledgeFalmer.

Dowd, G. E. (1992). *A spirited resistance: The North American Indian struggle for unity, 1745–1815.* Baltimore, MD: Johns Hopkins University Press.

Ellsworth, E. (1997). *Teaching positions: Difference, pedagogy, and the power of address.* New York: Teachers College Press.

Epstein, T. (1998). Deconstructing differences in African-American and European-American adolescents' perspectives on U.S. history. *Curriculum Inquiry, 28* (4), 397–423.

Evers, T. (1998, November 19). The state of student activism 1998 [Electronic]. *Shepherd Express, 19* (47).

Fiori, G. (1970). *Antonio Gramsci: Life of a revolutionary.* London: NLB.

Foner, E. (1997). *The new American history.* Philadelphia, PA: Temple University Press.

Forgacs, D., & Nowell Smith, G. (Eds.). (1985). *Antonio Gramsci: Selections from cultural writings.* Cambridge, MA: Harvard University Press.

Fraser, N. (1997). *Justice interruptus.* New York: Routledge.

Freire, P. (1993). *Pedagogy of the oppressed.* New York: Continuum.

Gates, H. L., Jr. (1992). *Loose canons: Notes on the culture wars.* New York: Oxford University Press.

Grant, C. A., & Sleeter, C. E. (2003). *Turning on learning: Five approaches for multicultural teaching plans for race, class, gender, and disability.* New York: John Wiley & Sons.

Grant, S. G. (2001). An uncertain lever: Exploring the influence of state-level testing in New York State on teaching social studies. *Teachers College Record, 103* (3), 398–426.

Griffith, A., & Smith, D. (2005). *Mothering for schooling.* New York: RoutledgeFalmer.

Guha, R. (1983). *Elementary aspects of peasant insurgency in colonial India.* Delhi: Oxford.

Guha, R. (1988a). On some aspects of the historiography of colonial India. In R. Guha & G. C. Spivak (Eds.), *Selected subaltern studies* (pp. 37–43). New York: Oxford University Press.

Guha, R. (1988b). Preface. In R. Guha & G. C. Spivak (Eds.), *Selected subaltern studies* (pp. 35–36). New York: Oxford University Press.

Guha, R., & Spivak, G. C. (1988). *Selected subaltern studies.* New York: Oxford University Press.

Hall, S. (1996). Introduction: Who needs "identity?" In S. Hall & P. du Gay (Eds.), *Questions of cultural identity* (pp. 2–17). Thousand Oaks, CA: Sage Publications.

Hardt, M., & Negri, A. (2000). *Empire.* Cambridge, MA: Harvard University Press.

Hirsch, E. D., Jr. (1987). *Cultural literacy: What every American needs to know.* New York: Vintage Books.

Hirsch, E. D., Jr. (1996). *The schools we need and why we don't have them.* New York: Doubleday.

Hirsch, E. D., Jr. (2005). Education reform and content: The long view. In D. Ravitch (Ed.), *Brookings papers on education policy 2005* (pp. 175–186). Washington, DC: Brookings Institution.

Hoare, Q., & Nowell Smith, G. (Eds.). (1971). *Selections from the prison notebooks of Antonio Gramsci.* New York: International Publishers.

Johnson, R. (1983). What is cultural studies anyway? Unpublished manuscript, University of Birmingham Centre for Contemporary Cultural Studies.

Kaestle, C. F. (1983). *Pillars of the republic: Common schools and American society, 1780–1860.* New York: Hill & Wang.

Karp, S. (2003, November 7). The no child left behind hoax [Address to Portland Area Rethinking Schools] at www.rethinkingschools.org/special_reports/bushplan/hoax.shtml

Keck, M. E., & Sikkink, K. (1998). *Activists beyond borders: Advocacy networks in international politics.* Ithaca, NY: Cornell University Press.

Kelley, R. D. G. (1993). "We are not what we seem": Rethinking black working-class opposition in the Jim Crow south. *Journal of American History, 80* (1), 75–112.

Kumashiro, K. (2002). *Troubling education: Queer activism and antioppressive education.* New York: RoutledgeFalmer.

Lamy, S. L. (1990). Global education: A conflict of images. In K. A. Tye (Ed.), *Global education: From thought to action* (pp. 49–63). Alexandria, VA: Association for Supervision and Curriculum Development.

Ledbetter, T. R. (2004, November 9). Traditional definition of marriage restored to Texas textbooks. Retrieved March 8, 2005, at www.bpnews.net/bpnews.asp?Id=19504.

Leming, J., Ellington, L., & Porter, K. (Eds). (2003). *Where did social studies go wrong?* Washington, DC: Thomas B. Fordham Foundation.

Ludden, D. (Ed.). (2002). *Reading subaltern studies: Critical history, contested meaning, and the globalization of South Asia.* London: Anthem Press.

Manski, B. (1999, May). 97 hours of struggle. *Z Magazine.*

McCarthy, C. (1998). *The uses of culture.* New York: Routledge.

McNeil, L. M. (2002). *Contradictions of reform: Educational costs of standardized testing.* New York: Routledge.

Michie, G. (1999). *Holler if you hear me: The education of a teacher and his students.* New York: Teachers College Press.

Mignolo, W. D. (2000). *Local histories/global designs: Coloniality, subaltern knowledges, and border thinking.* Princeton, NJ: Princeton University Press.

Ndimande, B. S. (2004). (Re)Anglicizing the kids: Contradictions of classroom discourse in Post-Apartheid South Africa. In N. K. Matua & B. B. Swadener (Eds.), *Decolonizing research in cross-cultural contexts: Critical personal narratives* (pp. 197–214). Albany: State University of New York Press.

Pandey, G. (1988). Peasant revolt and Indian nationalism: The peasant movement in Awadh, 1919–1922. In R. Guha & G. C. Spivak (Eds.), *Selected subaltern studies* (pp. 233–287). New York: Oxford University Press.

Pedroni, T. C. (2003). *Strange bedfellows in the Milwaukee "parental choice" debate: Participation among the dispossessed in conservative educational reform.* Unpublished doctoral dissertation, University of Wisconsin, Madison.

Perkins, T. (2004, November 9). Washington update: Texas textbooks will teach truth about marriage. Retrieved March 8, 2005, at www.frc.org/get.cfm?i=WU04K08&v=Print.

Pieterse, J. N. (2004). *Globalization and culture: Global mélange.* New York: Rowman & Littlefield Publishers.

Plank, D. N., & Sykes, G. (Eds.). (2003). *Choosing choice: School choice in international perspective.* New York: Teachers College Press.

Ravitch, D. (1995). *National standards in American education: A citizen's guide.* Washington, DC: Brookings Institution Press.

Richter, D. K. (1992). *The ordeal of the Long-House: The Peoples of the Iroquois League in the era of European colonization.* Chapel Hill, NC: University of North Carolina Press.

Schutzman, M., & Cohen-Cruz, J. (1994). *Playing Boal: Theatre, therapy, and activism.* New York: Routledge.

Schweber, S. A. (2004). *Making sense of the Holocaust: Lessons from classroom practice.* New York: Teachers College Press.

Scott, J. (1990). *Domination and the arts of resistance.* New Haven, CT: Yale University Press.

Singh, M., Kell, P., & Pandian, A. (2002). *Appropriating English: Innovation in the global business of English language teaching.* New York: Peter Lang.

Smith, M. L., Miller-Kahn, L., Heinecke, W., & Jarvis, P. F. (2004). *Political spectacle and the fate of American schools.* New York: RoutledgeFalmer.

Spivak, G. C. (1988). Can the subaltern speak? In C. Nelson & L. Grossberg (Eds.), *Marxism and the interpretation of culture* (pp. 271–313). Urbana: University of Illinois Press.

Spivak, G. C. (1996a). Subaltern studies: Deconstructing historiography (1985). In D. Landry & G. Maclean (Eds.), *The Spivak reader: Selected works of Gayatri Chakravorty Spivak* (pp. 203–235). New York: Routledge.

Spivak, G. C. (1996b). Subaltern talk: Interview with the editors (1993–94). In D. Landry & G. Maclean (Eds.), *The Spivak reader: Selected works of Gayatri Chakravorty Spivak* (pp. 287–308). New York: Routledge.

Spivak, G. C. (1999). *A critique of postcolonial reason: Toward a history of the vanishing present.* Cambridge, MA: Harvard University Press.

Stiglitz, J. E. (2002). *Globalization and its discontents.* New York: W. W. Norton & Company.

Takayama, K. (2005, March). "Choice" as a hegemonic policy keyword: Mobilization of multiple "choice" discourses in NCLB. Paper presented at the annual meeting of the International Comparative Education Society, Stanford, California.

Tan, J. (2000). The politics of religious knowledge in Singapore. In C. Cornbleth (Ed.), *Curriculum politics, policy, and practice: Cases in comparative context* (pp. 77–102). Albany: State University of New York Press.

Valenzuela, A. (Ed.). (2005). *Leaving children behind: How "Texas-style" accountability fails Latino youth.* Albany: State University of New York Press.

Velie, A. R. (Ed.). (1991). *American Indian literature: An anthology.* London: University of Oklahoma Press.

Whitty, G., Power, S., & Halpin, D. (1998). *Devolution and choice in education: The school, the state and the market.* Philadelphia, PA: Open University Press.

Willis, P. (1977). *Learning to labor: How working class kids get working class jobs.* New York: Columbia University Press.

Wong, T. H. (2002). *Hegemonies compared.* New York: RoutledgeFalmer.

Wright, E. O. (1997). *Class counts: Comparative studies in class analysis.* Cambridge: Cambridge University Press.

ZarNi, & Apple, M. W. (2000). Conquering Goliath: The free Burma coalition takes down Pepsico. In G. White (Ed.), *Campus incorporated: Corporate powering the ivory tower* (pp. 280–290). Amherst, NY: Prometheus Books.

Zimmerman, J. (2002). *Whose America? Culture wars in the public schools.* Cambridge, MA: Harvard University Press.

I
The Subaltern Speak
In Whose Voices?

1

Tracing the Core Knowledge Movement
History Lessons from Above and Below

KRISTEN L. BURAS

Nearly two decades ago, E. D. Hirsch (1987) authored *Cultural Literacy: What Every American Needs to Know*. This bestseller generated a wave of debate as it declared not only the importance of common culture to national unity, but defined the relevant content of that culture and blamed multicultural education for undermining it. Deemed Eurocentric by critics (Aronowitz & Giroux, 1991), *Cultural Literacy* nonetheless metamorphosed into Core Knowledge—a pre-kindergarten through eighth grade curriculum that includes specific content guidelines in history, language arts, math, science, and the musical and visual arts (Core Knowledge Foundation [CKF], 1998), and resources such as literary collections and history textbooks aligned with those guidelines (Hirsch, 2002). The first school to implement the curriculum opened in 1990. Since that time, Hirsch's vision has shaped a nationwide movement focused on reforming education through Core Knowledge, which has been adopted by nearly 1000 schools in a diverse array of communities (CKF, 2003e, 2004b). Why is it, we might wonder, that an educational initiative developed to mediate against the "threat" of multiculturalism has garnered support from a range of communities—some constituted by traditionally oppressed groups?

I plan to consider that question by critically examining Hirsch's vision of education and the ways in which his guiding assumptions appeal to unequally empowered groups. Moreover, I trace the growth of the movement, analyze the allegiance of dominant and subaltern groups to Core Knowledge, and underscore the tensions generated by diverse actors and interests within the movement.[1] In turn, I assess the representation of various groups in the narratives of Core history textbooks and the relationship of those narratives to history from above and below. What might be learned from these analyses, I ultimately argue, is that we are entering an era in which more progressive forms of multiculturalism focused on subaltern experience, elite power, and emancipatory struggle (Freire, 1993; Giroux, 1995), are being redefined by dominant groups along distinctly conservative lines and embraced as part of a decisive compromise. Through such compromise, select reforms partly speak to the concerns of marginalized communities and often win their consent while they simultaneously sustain relationships of cultural domination.

In the late 1990s, Nathan Glazer (1997) declared "we are all multicultural-ists now." By this he meant that the multiculturalism advocated by oppressed groups had gained enough strength that "simple denunciation ... would no longer do" (p. 33). "Multiculturalism of some kind there is, and there will be," he conceded. "The fight is over how much, what kind, for whom, at what ages, under what standards" (p. 19). When considering what kind of multicultural-ism Glazer envisioned, it helps to recall his clarification that the declaration "we are all multiculturalists now" mirrors past resignations "pronounced wryly by persons who recognized that something unpleasant was nevertheless unavoidable; it [does not] indicate a whole-hearted embrace" (p. 160).

Glazer's pronouncement points toward the first history lesson of this chap-ter and offers a way to begin thinking about the advance of Core Knowledge. The 1960s and 1970s were indeed decades of spirited social activism during which many subaltern groups—African Americans and women to name just two—struggled for a more equitable distribution of resources as well as cultural respect and recognition. Issues related to the production and legiti-mization of knowledge were central to these groups as they demanded that their perspectives and histories contribute to reconstructing the nation. The demands expressed by movement activists inspired the rise of refashioned rightist politics in the 1980s, including neoconservative reform efforts aimed at curtailing the influence of progressive multiculturalism in schools and soci-ety (Apple, 1996). In short, this kind of multiculturalism—focused on oppressed identities and ignored histories—was understood as divisive and threatening to cultural cohesion, shared national identity, and the supremacy of Western civilization (Bennett, 1992; Kramer & Kimball, 1997).

Cultural conservatives, it is true, began working to "restore" the traditions under siege, but this is where the story gets more complicated than generally recognized. To say that "we are all multiculturalists now," even if some are reluctant multiculturalists, actually masks the diverse strategies employed by various neoconservative factions. It complicates any attempt to critically assess these different strategies for their relative success or failure in helping neocon-servatives build alliances with subaltern groups, and in either reinforcing or undermining hegemony. If the power of the right only betrays more radically democratic conceptions of existence, and those dedicated to such conceptions hope to wage a "war of position" (Hoare & Nowell Smith, 1971), then we need to understand the processes through which the right forwards its agenda and bolsters its influence. Close study of the Core Knowledge movement provides a good deal of insight, particularly when compared with kindred initiatives.

Allow me to briefly illustrate what I mean by "diverse strategies of neocon-servative factions." First consider the Free Congress Foundation (2004b), which announces its purpose in this way: "Our main focus is on the Culture War. Will America return to the culture that made it great, our traditional, Judeo-Christian, Western culture? Or will we continue that long slide into the cultural and moral decay of political correctness?" In its proposed "Declaration of Cultural Independence," the foundation's (2004a) Center for Cultural Conservatism suggests the following:

> Until recently, the objective of cultural conservatives ... was to retake existing cultural institutions—the public schools, the universities, the media, the entertainment industry, and the arts—from those hostile to our culture and make them once again forces for goodness, truth, and beauty.... Unfortunately, we must acknowledge that this strategy has not been successful.... We [therefore] seek nothing less than the creation of a complete, alternate structure of parallel cultural institutions.

Unwillingness to compromise with the assumed-to-be-dominant multicultural tradition represents one strategy that has been pursued. However, other neoconservative factions have aimed to foster alliances with grassroots, even traditionally marginalized, communities. In an effort to win the consent of Latino parents, for example, Hirsch's Core Knowledge Foundation has begun translating its encyclopedic *What Your K–6 Grader Needs to Know Series* into Spanish and distributing the volumes free of charge. These translated readers are intended "to provide supplements to the original books for concerned Spanish-speaking parents, to enable them to help their children read and learn from the corresponding English-language volume" (Hirsch in Hirsch & Holdren, 2001, About Supplement). Unlike the Free Congress Foundation, which advocates an intolerant and separatist doctrine as a means for rebuilding power, the Core Knowledge Foundation has instead engaged in the complex task of fostering alliances on the battlefield of culture.[2] In fact, its effort to defend dominant cultural forms—in this case, to utilize Spanish as a bridge to both the inculcation of English and Core content—has been far more successful than the Free Congress Foundation would suggest.

The propensity toward particular forms of compromise—those capable of appealing to the cultural sensibilities of marginalized groups while at the same time steering those sensibilities in dominant cultural directions—reveals the emergence of a new and potentially more "successful" hegemonic strategy; this strategy might be called *rightist multiculturalism*. In calling this a new strategy, I mean to underscore that it is more sophisticated and encompassing than additive multiculturalism (McCarthy, 1998) or curricular "mentioning" of "limited and isolated elements of the history and culture of less powerful groups" (Apple, 1993, p. 56) that have often characterized conservative cultural work. This point will be further elaborated when I analyze Core history textbooks. For now, let us move to an examination of Hirsch's educational vision and its appeal to the often disparate concerns of dominant and subaltern groups.

E. D. Hirsch's Educational Vision

Long before Hirsch presented his views on culture and curriculum, a neoconservative vision was being constructed. The assumed hegemony of the left in major social institutions, the threat posed by countercultures to American and Western civilization, and the fragility of national unity in light of identity politics were frames that had given shape to neoconservative work in a variety of areas, including domestic and foreign policy, the arts, religion, and ultimately education (Gerson, 1997; Steinfels, 1979). The marks of this history are apparent in Hirsch's educational vision, which he has presented in published works and speeches. *The Schools We Need and Why We Don't Have Them* (Hirsch, 1996) is his most comprehensive treatment of education, and may actually be read as a manifesto for the Core Knowledge movement. As such, I focus most heavily on that text, offer a critical reading of its guiding assumptions, and suggest how those assumptions may resonate with groups above and below (see also Buras, 1999).

To begin, Hirsch contends that progressivism reigns supreme in schools. "Critics have long complained," he writes, "that public education in the United States is an institutional and intellectual monopoly" (1996, p. 63). He describes this monopoly as a corpus of guiding educational beliefs and practices that values student-centered, naturalistic, hands-on, process-driven, and thinking-skills-oriented schooling. Opening his manifesto with the foreboding words, "Failed Theories, Famished Minds," Hirsch laments "our national slowness … to cast aside [the] faulty theories that have led to the total absence of a coherent, knowledge-based curriculum" (p. 2). After quoting Romantic poets who wrote about the inherent goodness of the child and citing academic passages on child-centered schooling authored by early progressive curriculum scholars, Hirsch infers:

> Education schools … converted to progressivism in the 1920s and '30s. From these cells, the doctrine emerged victorious in the public schools in the 1950s…. Thereafter, it took a full generation of progressive students, extending from preschool to high school, before the full effects of Romantic progressivism manifested themselves in the graduating seniors of the 1960s. (pp. 78–79)

According to him, progressivism in schools has supplanted verbal instruction focused on the transmission of a solid body of knowledge reinforced by repetitive practice.

In contrast to Hirsch's chronicle stands work by Herbert Kliebard (1995) on four ideologies active in the struggle to define the American curriculum between 1893 and 1958. The perspectives of humanists and developmentalists are most relevant here, with the first focused on the study of Western civilization and the second centered on the nature of the child and a corresponding curriculum. Unlike Hirsch, Kliebard addresses how social context shaped the relative impact of these ideologies on curriculum. Meanwhile, Hirsch characterizes the field of education as one mired in progressive doctrine only, and ignores the schism between theory and practice. Scholars have documented that overall, schools remain traditional institutions that offer teacher-centered, whole-class, textbook-focused instruction (Cuban, 1993; Goodlad, 1984). That demands by marginalized groups for cultural recognition have been at least partially accommodated in schools may account, however, for Hirsch's unfounded and more generalized fear that traditional authority has been undermined.

A second assertion made by Hirsch is that the existing curriculum is incoherent. "The idea that there exists a coherent plan for teaching content," he writes, "is a gravely misleading myth" (1996, p. 26). According to Hirsch, the progressive monopoly has cultivated schools that lack an agreed upon scheme for the transmission of specific content to students. He rails against what he calls formalism (the emphasis on acquiring the formal intellectual tools needed for lifelong learning), and denounces that under the current regime, "The particular content used to develop those tools need not be specified" (p. 21). He also faults naturalism, or the belief that education is a natural process that should be connected to real goals and settings, for curriculum incoherence. He stresses that although natural pedagogy "assumes that the proper way of learning involves lifelike, holistic projects," it nonetheless "turns out to be a very insecure way of learning" (p. 86). Such teaching methodologies, broadly applied and prescriptively weak, are thus responsible for the curriculum's indistinct state. Finally, Hirsch believes that localism, the tradition of determining locally what children should learn, has only displaced valued content.

Yet Hirsch overlooks the way in which various mechanisms indirectly lend coherence to the curriculum, including textbook adoptions, patterns of textual representation, standards, and standardized tests. State textbook adoptions, for example, have tremendous influence on the regulation of school knowledge, with just a handful of states controlling enough of the market to determine which texts will be sold nationally (Apple & Christian-Smith, 1991). Since the late 1970s, conservative groups have organized campaigns to influence textbook content and their influence has been notable (Cornbleth & Waugh, 1999; Delfattore, 1992). In fact, studies examining textbooks across grade levels and subject areas have noted relatively coherent patterns of representation of class, race, gender, and disability (Banks, 1969; Sleeter & Grant, 1991; Cobble & Kessler-Harris, 1993). In the end, though Hirsch is partially insightful in recognizing the absence of an explicit curricular logic, he fails to recognize those mechanisms that indirectly combine to lend coherence. For Hirsch, such mechanisms do not adequately serve the goal of cultural restoration. Moreover, the possibility that conflict over what constitutes legitimate knowledge might provide students with an opportunity to discover "what is at stake in one way of knowing against another" (Graff, 1992, p. 186) is not on Hirsch's register.

Hirsch's failure to consider what is at stake relates to his third assumption —education is a cognitive-technical process through which factual content is transmitted. He complains that a major barrier to improving education has been "the politicization of educational issues that are at bottom technical rather than political" (1996, p. 66). Appropriating both cognitive psychology and neurophysiology to support his vision of schooling, Hirsch argues that educational excellence depends on an appreciation of short- and long-term memory, repetition, and automation, the development of mental schemas consisting of vocabulary and specific facts, and the continuous chunking, assimilation, and stocking of new information in an accurate fashion. Learning, for Hirsch, is the consumption of what he calls core content, relevant background knowledge, intellectual capital, traditional subject matter, shared national culture, and solid facts.

Such referents shelter Hirsch from having to discuss the political nature of knowledge and schooling. In fact, he consciously chooses not to explore the role of power in determining what and whose knowledge is considered relevant, reasoning: "Once you start down that road, where will you stop?" (1996, p. 31) Instead of exploring this political slippery slope, Hirsch emphasizes the need to reach an agreement on a common sequence in the curriculum, "at least in those areas like math and science and the basic facts of history and geography, which, unlike sex education, are not and should not be subjects of controversy" (p. 37). That the construction of knowledge is a political process and that the privileging and obliteration of culture have been central to the educational history of this nation are issues that Hirsch evades. In challenging the cognitive-technical view of education that Hirsch embraces, it is crucial to ask: Is education about depositing information into the minds of people, or is it about engaging in a critical process of reflection and action, naming the world in order to transform it (Freire, 1993)?

A fourth and related assumption made by Hirsch is that schools must compensate for the knowledge deficits of children from culturally impoverished backgrounds. He reasons that "students from good-home schools will always have an educational advantage over students from less-good home schools" (1996, p. 43). Drawing startling parallels between knowing and unknowing students, Hirsch praises the benefits of traditional knowledge and pedagogy for "the palace-tutored prince as well as the neglected pauper" (p. 226). He does not address why the cultural traditions, linguistic practices, or social mores of one home are considered good, while others are viewed as symptomatic of illiteracy, ignorance, and cultural deficit. Instead, he expresses guarded optimism:

> Young children who arrive at school with a very small vocabulary and a correspondingly limited knowledge base, *can* fortunately be brought to an age-adequate vocabulary by intelligent, focused help ... [but] when this

language and knowledge deficit is not compensated for early, it is nearly impossible ... in later grades. (p. 146)

Though articulated with benevolence and even declared part of the "new civil rights frontier," Hirsch's position is founded on a sort of cultural supremacy that fails to recognize itself as such.

His perspective prevents him from recognizing that children—whether working class, of color, or Spanish-speaking—bring to the classroom lived experiences, cultural traditions, and languages that are diverse and rich sources of knowledge. Based on her ethnographic research in schools, Gloria Ladson-Billings (1994) suggests that successful teaching occurs not when students are required to abandon their cultural identities in order to learn, but when educators view student culture as an asset rather than an impediment. She discovered that successful teachers of African American students saw "teaching as 'digging knowledge out' of students" and had "an overriding belief that students come to school with knowledge and that that knowledge must be explored and utilized" (p. 52). These findings and others (Apple & Beane, 1995; Delgado Bernal, 2002; Michie, 1999) imply a view of schooling —a promise—that Hirsch denies.

Finally, Hirsch assumes that a common culture is shared by all members of society and should be promoted through a national curriculum in support of democracy. Providing a questionable reading of history, for example, he claims that the founding of the common school was based on "the goal of giving all children the shared intellectual and social capital" necessary for participation in "the economy and policy of the nation" (1996, p. 233). Such a rendering of history allows Hirsch to forget that the intellectual capital transmitted by the common school was not shared. As Carl Kaestle (1983) has shown, common schools were built on a native, Anglo-American, Protestant, republican, capitalist ideology that left many groups alienated. Further, the underlying purpose of the common school was to promote moral, social, and cultural stability rather than genuine educational and political development. Such evidence is not considered by Hirsch, who rejects the idea that "common culture" has long represented a selective tradition.

Hirsch's educational vision is instead built on the notion that an inclusive and shared culture—a mythic one that has never existed—is being undermined by a "retrogressive kind" of multiculturalism he calls "ethnic loyalism." Rather than allowing this "particularistic" tradition, which emphasizes allegiance to one's local or ethnic culture, to promote social divisions, Hirsch advocates a "universalistic" tradition he calls "cosmopolitanism," which stresses being "a member of humanity as a whole" (Hirsch, 1992b, p. 3). He also argues that the United States should adopt a national curriculum to defend shared culture, and promises that such a curriculum will remedy the deficiencies of culturally impoverished students. Although he acknowledges that the formation of such a curriculum may initially involve some conflict, he indicates that it should be possible to reach a consensus on some core of knowledge. This belief is bolstered by the fact that he views knowledge as relatively static and uncontested, asserting, "For most problems that require critical thought by the ordinary person ... the most needed knowledge is usually rather basic, long-lived, and slow to change" (1996, p. 155). In the end, Hirsch's cosmopolitanism relies on a mythical consensus that overshadows the reality of cultural and economic inequality. His quest to settle on common curricular content also overshadows the fact that what should be shared in a democracy is an ongoing process of negotiation over what counts as knowledge, rather than adherence to some unchanging canon (see Apple, 1996).

Hirsch's neoconservative imaginary rests on a host of problematic assumptions. Still, the discourses adopted by him have resonated with the experiences, anxieties, and hopes of differently situated groups—something that partly explains why the Core Knowledge movement has attracted wide support. His call for a return to tradition—in the guise of reinstating curricular coherence —appeals to prevalent fears about race, gender, and sexuality. In the midst of demands for the recognition of diverse cultural perspectives, cultural and religious conservatives tired of Latinos, gays and lesbians, women, and others politicizing everything conceivably find themselves attracted to the position that the school curriculum need not generate political struggles, but should rather be recognized as an avenue for transmitting "factual" content. Those who feel anxious about losing privileges afforded by traditional social arrangements believe that Core Knowledge can partly mediate the threat.

In another vein, Hirsch's claim that the acquisition of intellectual capital through Core Knowledge will secure upward mobility addresses the concerns of marginalized groups. He asserts, "Wherever public schools have offered the choice of truly effective mainstream academic training ... minority families have signed up in disproportionate numbers.... These parents clearly recognize the direct connection between economic advancement for their children and the mastery of ... mainstream culture" (1996, p. 208). While Hirsch fails to note the predicament in which many minorities find themselves (they must submit to cultural dominance or risk economic hardship) and also ignores market realities, his assertion nonetheless manages to associate Core with greater access to material resources. It is not hard to appreciate why poor or even anxious middle-class parents would mobilize around a curriculum that provides children with the background knowledge needed to "succeed economically."

It is equally significant that Hirsch frames his initiative in terms of civil rights and compensation. Building on this argumentation, Hirsch (1999) has inveighed, "In the wake of the *Brown* decision, at the very moment of our highest hopes for social justice, the victory of progressivism over academic content had already foreclosed the chance that school integration would equalize achievement and enhance social justice" (para. 2). Forging an even closer relationship between Core Knowledge and racial equality, he highlights: "The late James Farmer, the great civil rights activist, once honored our annual Core Knowledge conference by giving a keynote address in the tradition of Du Bois which said, in effect, that strong common content in the early grades is the new frontier of the civil rights movement" (para. 9). Interestingly, this is not what Farmer said—as I will later show—yet such a bold statement powerfully connects Core to histories of struggle from below and to civil rights, a long-standing concern for communities of color and for many other subaltern groups, too.

On multiple levels, Hirsch's educational vision synthesizes and redirects a plethora of feelings and convictions, evidenced by the growth of the Core Knowledge movement. However, it took more than a vision to build the movement. It also took a curriculum. Let us look at its history.

From Cultural Literacy to Core Knowledge

In the late 1970s, Hirsch, a professor at the University of Virginia, began formulating his ideas on cultural literacy and circulating them at professional meetings. In 1983 he published an essay titled "Cultural Literacy" in the *American Scholar*. He declared English and history "central to culture making," then charged:

> In English courses, diversity and pluralism now reign without challenge. … If we want to achieve a more literate culture than we now have, we shall need to restore the balance between [the] two equally American traditions of unity and diversity. We shall need to restore certain common contents to the humanistic side of the school curriculum. (pp. 160–61)

Professing his emergent philosophy, Hirsch captured the attention of the Exxon Education Foundation, which supported his production of a tentative list of cultural literacy items (Hirsch, 1987). Meanwhile, he established the Cultural Literacy Foundation. In a maneuver to depict his educational initiative as detached from politics, Hirsch (1996) explained the decision to change the organization's name to the Core Knowledge Foundation as follows: "The term 'Cultural' raised too many extraneous questions, whereas the term 'Core Knowledge' better described the chief aim … to introduce solid knowledge in a coherent way into the elementary curriculum" (p. 13). Since 1986, the foundation has provided a good part of the organizational structure and resources needed to transform his vision into a national reform effort. With the publication of Hirsch's *Cultural Literacy* in 1987 and *The Dictionary of Cultural Literacy* the next year (Hirsch, Kett, & Trefil, 1988), the *Core Knowledge Sequence*—content guidelines for the various subject areas—soon followed (CKF, 1998).

According to the Core Knowledge Foundation, the content guidelines were "the result of a long process of research and consensus-building." Reports issued by state departments of education and professional associations were examined for recommended educational outcomes. Additionally, the organization "tabulated the knowledge and skills specified in the successful educational systems of several other countries, including France, Japan, Sweden, and West Germany." An advisory board on multiculturalism was invited to suggest "diverse cultural traditions that American children should all share." "Three independent groups of teachers, scholars, and scientists around the country" were provided with the materials and asked to generate master lists. Those lists were used to create a "draft master plan," which was finalized by "some 100 educators and specialists" who formed "twenty-four working groups" at a gathering in March 1990. The *Sequence* was then piloted and refined during its first year of implementation at Three Oaks Elementary School, the first Core Knowledge school, in Florida. The foundation clarifies, however, that there has been "more stability than change in the Sequence," particularly considering the "inherent stability of the content of literate culture" (CKF, 1998, pp. 1–2).

The foundation's description may appear to render transparent the process by which Core was produced, but the issues associated with its production are more complex than acknowledged. The politics that shaped the standards advocated in state reports, for example, were not considered. These standards, along with those assumed to guide successful educational systems in other nations, were apparently embraced without criticism. The process is described in highly technical terms—content recommendations were tabulated and a list was developed. The commissioning of an advisory board on multiculturalism raises a host of issues that remain unarticulated, including the issue of how its members and participants at the 1990 meeting were chosen. Reflecting several years later on the convocation that met in 1990, Hirsch explained, "I mean, we didn't have Lithuanians, but we did have 24 working groups" (Goldberg, 1997, p. 84). Such a statement hardly addresses the most fundamental questions. Who determined what should count as Core Knowledge? Did particular conflicts emerge during the process? If so, how were they resolved? If the politics of knowledge were not explicitly engaged, as suggested by the foundation's technical approach, then what implicit interests might have determined the content? Questions about *whose* knowledge is valued in schools are worthy of continuous and collective reflection, and the answers reveal a good deal about the quality of democratic life within the nation. Yet the politics surrounding the production of Core Knowledge have been rendered to a significant degree invisible and beyond the pale of inquiry.

That the process for determining state standards and texts is often comparably opaque does not exempt Core from such critiques. The scope of the foundation's agenda and the ever-increasing popularity of Core warrant the posing of scrutinizing questions. Hirsch advocates a national curriculum; an effort is even underway to align Core with educational standards in all fifty states, meaning that a plan for schools would exist in each state that charts how to blend Core with state-specific content requirements (CKF, 2003e). Unlike state standards and testing, Core Knowledge has been pursued with missionary zeal and has evidenced a grassroots appeal not associated with state educational mandates. Core has indeed generated an educational movement—one that has, in part, been facilitated by the foundation.

The Role of the Core Knowledge Foundation

The development of local, regional, and national networks around Core Knowledge has been assisted by the Core Knowledge Foundation. The foundation's work has progressed from piloting Core in a single school in 1990, to working with some 300 schools by mid-1996 (CKF, 1996b), to coordinating a network of nearly 1,000 Core Knowledge schools in forty-four states by 2004 (CKF, 2003e, 2004b). Although Core initially covered grades K–6, the curriculum for pre-kindergarten and grades 7–8 was subsequently developed (Marshall, 1997d, 1997e). Approximately half of Core Knowledge schools are public, another quarter are charter schools, and the remaining fraction are private or religious schools. In urban, suburban, and rural areas, Core has likewise captured attention; a quarter of the schools are rural, with the remaining percentage divided almost evenly between urban and suburban areas (CKF, 2004b, 2004c).

With such an array of communities on board, the foundation has mandated that schools comply with increasingly rigorous implementation and reporting standards in order to gain recognition. A school can qualify as either a "friend of Core Knowledge," an "official Core Knowledge school," or a "visitation site" deemed "model." Depending on its status, the school may need to complete an annual profile, but may also be required to participate in professional development offered by the foundation, fully implement the curriculum, host site visits by foundation representatives, and accommodate a strong push to utilize Core resources, such as Core Knowledge history textbooks, and provide achievement data through standardized Core Knowledge–referenced tests (CKF, 2003b, 2003c, 2003d, 2004b). This heightened monitoring, I will later argue, may be driven by a desire to discipline the very diversity that has enabled the movement's growth. But we should first consider the role the foundation has played in facilitating this growth and why differently situated communities have embraced Core.

The foundation has organized a National Core Knowledge Conference annually since 1992. The 1st national conference was attended by 50 people (Goldberg, 1997). In comparison, the 13th gathering in Atlanta in 2004 was attended by 2,100 administrators, teachers, and parents (Hassett, 2004). At the conference, participants attend formal addresses by invited speakers, receive awards for their school's progress in implementing Core, and even tour local Core Knowledge schools. An entire day is dedicated to teachers presenting lesson plans based on the *Sequence*. Actually, it is difficult to overstate the role such activities have played in mobilizing teachers around Core. Under conditions where teachers are generally blamed for the failures of the educational system, Core Knowledge teachers are viewed as professionals whose curricular ideas contribute to enhancing the quality of education in Core schools. At the 2004 National Conference, Hirsch called teachers "the heart and soul of the movement." He continued:

> Our potential is being realized because of you great people in this room. I feel that every time I come to one of these conferences.... Even though it's hard work to do Core Knowledge and it's hard to get up and teach the knowledge that's in the *Sequence* and it's hard to convey it well to students, it's work that dedicated teachers are engaging in because they realize that it is best for children.... And it's also very rewarding for teachers. Many of you have told me that. (Buras, 2004)

The populist tenor of the movement is apparent in Hirsch's words and throughout the conference, where names are put to faces and hugs are exchanged between foundation staff and their grassroots allies. Foundation staff carefully listens to teachers, as revealed in one session during which draft teacher handbooks for Core were shared with teachers for their feedback (Buras, 2004). Though the balance between teachers' professional autonomy and the foundation's production of resources has generated tensions, the national conference is clearly a time for building community among a national network of Core Knowledge advocates.

The foundation also distributes a newsletter called *Common Knowledge*. Browsing its pages reveals a great deal about the philosophy of the foundation, and partly illuminates the character of the movement. Skimming *Common Knowledge*, the reader will often find essays by Hirsch that elaborate the guiding vision behind Core, such as "Why General Knowledge Should Be a Goal of Education in a Democracy" (1998b). Typically, feature articles such as "The Bad News about Discovery Learning" (Marshall, 1998b) or "What Do Scientists Know About How We Learn?" (Willingham, 1999) convey the foundation's endorsement of direct instruction techniques. Other pieces announce important developments and communicate a sense of progress. One headline reads "Coast to Coast, Trainers Spread Core Knowledge with Enthusiasm" (Siler, 1999), while another declares "Core Knowledge Offers Blueprint for Content-Rich Teacher Education" (Davis, 2002). It is also not uncommon to discover an odd convergence of "traditional" and "multicultural" elements on the page, albeit with no regard for how those elements might be critically connected. Newsletter highlights of one national conference illustrate this point:

From the school visits ... to the closing comments by Foundation President E. D. Hirsch ... the theme of "Content Counts" was underscored by speakers, presenters, and teachers. They talked of math and land bridges, of women's rights and classical music. Teachers shared slides of Antarctica and Japanese snacks.

One picture from the meeting shows two older, white, female teachers with huge eyeglasses performing "a ceremonial dance of the Aztecs" with an olive-complexioned, longhaired man dressed in Native American garb. Another reveals elementary students wearing bonnets and performing "songs from the Civil War" for conference attendees. Other photos portray students at a local Core Knowledge school marching "a Chinese dragon through the halls" and a charter school board member reading *Cultural Literacy* during the conference (Siler, 1998, pp. 10–11).

While the conference and newsletter attempt to define the movement's vision and foster a collective sense of mission, other foundation resources provide more tangible home and classroom support. The *What Your K–6 Grader Needs to Know Series* (e.g., Hirsch, 1998a) is a wildly popular, encyclopedic set of volumes sequenced in accordance with the Core curriculum. By title, these books summon parents based on myriad anxieties about the knowledge required for upward mobility. The literary *Core Classics* (Marshall & Hirsch, 1997) are child-friendly versions of works covered by Core, including *Robinson Crusoe, Treasure Island, Pollyanna,* and *Don Quixote.* The historical *Rats, Bulls, and Flying Machines: A History of the Renaissance and Reformation* is a text meant to introduce students to early European history (Prum, 1999). Such resources exist alongside the recently published *Pearson Learning–Core Knowledge History and Geography Textbooks* on U.S. and world history (Hirsch, 2002). To pull it all together, *Teacher Handbooks* detail "what teachers need to know" to teach the curriculum (CKF, 2004d).

Curriculum resources have multiplied in recent years, but support services have also been enhanced. The foundation sponsors Core adoption seminars and professional development workshops (CKF, 1997, 2003a). It offers guidance to low-income schools that want to adopt Core, but need help applying for funds under the federal Comprehensive School Reform Program (Shields, 2003b). The foundation likewise maintains a website (CKF, 2004e) that serves as an avenue of communication, and continuously produces informational literature and books that help sustain the organization financially, assist teachers and parents pedagogically, and support the movement ideologically (e.g., CKF, 1996a, 2004f; Hirsch, 1992a, 1996).

The Making of a Movement

The foundation's work has been pivotal in advancing Core Knowledge as a reform, but it is important to look more broadly at the movement. Core has flourished due to the motivations and efforts of a variety of actors, communities, and foundations. It is essential to provide just a few highlights.

In several areas, Core has been adopted districtwide in the public school system. In the small district of Hobbs, New Mexico, Core is taught in every K–8 school (Rounds, 2004). Larger districts have likewise implemented Core, including Polk County, Florida, and Nashville, Tennessee (Jones, 1997a). In Polk County, sixty-three elementary schools with 37,000 children adopted Core, and middle schools joined later. Recalling his election campaign, District Superintendent Glenn Reynolds explained the decision to adopt the program districtwide: "I kept hearing that the public schools were not competitive.... Our public schools were losing credibility and trust. The public was ready for major change" (in Marshall, 1997c, p. 1).

Though not part of a districtwide effort, there are notable concentrations of Core Knowledge schools elsewhere. Baltimore, where approximately fifteen Core Knowledge schools have developed, is home to the Baltimore Curriculum Project. Funded by the Abell Foundation, which aimed to support a "promising education reform model," the project is dedicated to generating lesson plans that correspond with Core content guidelines. Several Baltimore schools are directly affiliated with the project and have piloted the lessons (Marshall, 1997a; Baltimore Curriculum Project, 2004; Buras, 2004). Another effort in Baltimore has revolved around the implementation of Core in three elementary schools in the Sandtown-Winchester neighborhood. In this low-income, predominantly African American community, educator Sylvia Peters collaborated with the Enterprise Foundation to facilitate the initiative—one supported by an annual budget of more than $500,000 (Scherer, 1996; Enterprise Foundation, 2000). Attending the National Core Knowledge Conference, Peters addressed teachers and called them the "most important links in recivilizing our society" (in Siler, 1997, p. 1). "Core Knowledge is about the soul of our country," she declared (p. 8). Words used by Peters like "recivilizing" and "soul" capture the missionary spirit of the Core Knowledge movement, which partly seeks to effectuate the cultural conversion of poor communities, particularly those of color.

In Atlanta, there are nine Core schools, though the state of Georgia has about twenty-five (CKF, 2004b). The city of Atlanta was the site for the 2004 annual meeting, where attendees watched students from a local Core Knowledge school perform songs from the curriculum. With Hirsch sitting in the front row of a packed ballroom, a student choir from Morningside Elementary put on a well-polished show. The rapid-fire performance of a selection of songs that included the patriotic "America," country western "The Yellow Rose of Texas" (which in popular myth refers to an indentured mulatto woman), and African American spiritual "Swing Low, Sweet Chariot" revealed the awkward and uncritical relationship between the traditions of knowledge embodied in Core. Nonetheless, this parade of songs assured that there was something for everyone, which is one of the reasons for Core's popular appeal (Buras, 2004).

In Colorado there are over sixty Core Knowledge schools (CKF, 2004b). William Moloney, the former school superintendent of Calvert County, Maryland (the first system to adopt Core districtwide) was appointed commissioner of education in Colorado in 1997 (Siler, 1997; Jones, 1997b). He became a member of the Core Knowledge Foundation's board of trustees that same year, and gave a keynote address at the national conference in Atlanta the next year. Moloney's (1998) speech resounded with concerns about the stability of tradition and nationhood:

> The odyssey of Core Knowledge is a remarkable story of the American journey in search of better schools.... I would first take us back to 1983 and the landmark report, "A Nation at Risk," which served as a springboard for the current school reform movement in general and for the Core Knowledge movement in particular.... Americans wanted answers to questions and concerns that had been building for many years.... Why did every survey of public opinion reveal our people's concern that the schools were failing to uphold the values, the discipline, and the work ethic that have been the foundations of our national heritage?

The reason for this decline, Moloney pronounced, was that "serious mission confusion began when schools were declared the ideal forum to resolve explosive issues of class, language, race, religion, and sexuality." Dismissing multiculturalism as mission confusion, he next invoked a racially coded discourse to explain the erosion of national order, emphasizing, "In more stable settings, it would be possible to paper over the cracks in the edifice, but in less stable settings, notably our large urban systems, it was impossible to mask the descent into educational chaos" (p. 5). For Moloney, the descent into educational chaos called for ongoing advocacy of Core, and he was not alone in this crusade. Holly Hensey, originally a Core Knowledge teacher in Texas where some fifty Core schools exist (CKF 2003e; Hitchcock, 2002), was recruited by the Core Knowledge Foundation to organize in the Colorado region. She has raised nearly $900,000 in grant money and has instituted many initiatives in the state, including a website, an annual Summer Writing Institute for Core teachers to develop lesson plans, an annual Colorado Core Knowledge Conference, and a project that aligned Core with educational standards in Colorado (Colorado Schools, 2003; National Core Knowledge Coordinator of Colorado, 2004).

A seminar intended to introduce interested groups in the state to Core Knowledge was arranged by the Minnesota Humanities Commission in 1997 (Jones, 1997b, 1997c). Mae Schunk, a gifted and talented teacher at a Core Knowledge school in St. Paul, assisted in aligning Core with Minnesota standards and became Minnesota's Lieutenant Governor in 1999. In this position,

Schunk introduced Core to parents and school officials across the state, explaining that "Core is just common sense" (in Marshall, 1999, p. 3). St. Paul is home to the Midwest Core Knowledge Center sponsored by the Minnesota Humanities Commission. The state presently has twenty-one Core Knowledge schools, and another twenty-two exist in nearby Michigan (CKF, 2004b).

In California, few Core Knowledge schools existed in the late 1990s. Perhaps most significant to increasing interest in the state was Hirsch's invitation to address the California State Board of Education. "If I were a member of your Board," Hirsch admonished, "I would begin to shift rather large resources into academically effective, very-early education" (1997, p. 7). Concluding, he stressed, "If reliable research does become your guide ... it may come to be said that this was the Board that put an end to the era of educational fad and failure" (p. 8). The exhortation to adopt an educational reform based on "reliable research," a reference that often invokes rather narrow conceptions of scientific method, evidence, and educational performance, is an approach frequently taken by Hirsch and the foundation—and it has some allure. There are presently twenty-nine Core Knowledge schools in California (CKF, 2004b).

With the diffusion of Core in regions across the United States, it is not surprising that media attention has followed. Widely circulated publications such as the *Wall Street Journal* (Putka, 1991), *Life* (Meyer, 1991), *Newsweek* (Kantrowitz, Chideya, & Wingert, 1992), *Reader's Digest* (Perry, 1994), and *Forbes* (Summers, 1999) have positively highlighted the movement.

The growth of the Core Knowledge movement and the limelight it has enjoyed are indicative of the appeal this reform has secured in diverse kinds of communities. Having an even closer look at specific schools and particular associates of Core may illuminate further why certain groups are drawn to the reform, how those groups are differently positioned, and what interests are at play when alliances are formed.

Peculiar Alliances

At the predominantly European American, middle-class Washington (now Traut) Core Knowledge School in suburban Fort Collins, Colorado, parents' descriptions of the curriculum in non-Core public schools are "often filled with images of erosion. Many describe how the curriculum they knew as children, the one rooted in the granite truths of Western civilization, has disappeared from most schools." Concerned about cultural disintegration and loss of tradition, these parents petitioned the school district for the solution—a Core Knowledge school that would "emphasize a content-rich curriculum that would leave nothing to chance ... [and] be teacher-directed from beginning to end" (Ruenzel, 1996–97, p. 8). In this community, it appears that Core made possible a return to "better" days before the multicultural assault on truth and the dominant order.

In contrast, Nathaniel Hawthorne Elementary School is a mostly Latino/a, low-income, urban Core Knowledge school in San Antonio, Texas. Two teachers (Mentzer & Shaughnessy, 1996) at Hawthorne reflect on the school before its adoption of Core:

> We, as teachers, were frustrated. Things were not working well. We did not know what to do.... We were all scared about what was going to happen to our children if we couldn't find an intervention.... We could see that if we did not do something to stop the cycle of failure our children would end up on the streets or dead. (pp. 14–16)

After a careful look at Core by teachers and parents, the teachers report, "We found our missing piece.... What we had not had was a common content." For this school, Core was understood as contributing to renewal by providing a unifying educational vision and plan conducive to the advancement of struggling children. Though the specificity of content was deemed important, teachers underscored their partial renovation of the curriculum, stating, "We then added items we thought were important for our students to learn such as Hispanic culture and traditions" (p. 20).

In the rural town of Crooksville, Ohio, the adoption of Core by Crooksville Elementary—a largely low-income, European American school—has meant that "students will get to see and understand the world beyond the mountains." For example, students will "learn the stories of Zeus and Hades and Persephone, ... attend Renaissance Fairs, read *Don Quixote*, listen to Shakespearean actors, research and re-enact Civil War events," and "eat with chopsticks, and pantomime treaty agreements with Native Americans" (Vail, 1997, p. 14). Timm Mackley, the Superintendent of Crooksville, emphasizes, "We are dealing with kids who are narrowly confined to their small world. We are trying to share the wealth of human knowledge with them" (in Vail, p. 15; see also Mackley, 1999). This particular rural school thus views Core Knowledge as connecting isolated students to a wider multicultural world.

That schools in such different contexts could embrace Core reveals the complex alliances that have been forming in the movement. Hirsch is quite aware of this situation, stating, "To be liked by the Bushies [Bush allies] and by the AFT [American Federation of Teachers]—there's something peculiar going on" (in Lindsay, 2001, p. W24). The reality is that Hirsch and the foundation have worked to build such affiliations. Hirsch's relationship with former AFT president Albert Shanker goes back to the mid-1980s. It was then that Shanker began praising Hirsch's newly articulated theory of cultural literacy as the means to greater educational equity, with the union later arguing that Core was a more promising reform for school improvement than vouchers (AFT, 2003; Lindsay, 2001). The AFT granted Hirsch the QuEST (quality educational standards) Award in 1997, and Sandra Feldman, president of the AFT, accepted a seat on the Core Knowledge Foundation's board of trustees in 1998 (Marshall, 1997b, 1998a).

Moreover, scholars and members of historically marginalized groups were courted by the foundation, particularly after *Cultural Literacy* had been attacked for its Eurocentric content. For instance, Henry Louis Gates, professor of humanities and Afro-American studies at Harvard, was invited to be on the Core Knowledge multicultural advisory committee (Hirsch, 1992b). Yet the formation of such alliances has not been without rifts. James Farmer, the well-known founder (and civil rights activist) of a different CORE—the Congress of Racial Equality—was invited to speak at the 1996 national conference. He underscored in his speech the idea that "we are bound together," then prompted Core Knowledge teachers and the foundation:

> What I'm asking for is something that maybe you have as a part of your curriculum. And that is a pluralistic culture. It's not difficult for a people in a society like ours to love themselves and at the same time join with others in loving their history and traditions. I … *urge you* to come together with me and us in *celebrating ourselves* as well as *you celebrate yourselves*. It's not difficult at all if people are taught that way. *Perhaps the teaching of that should also be part of the core curriculum* [italics added]. (Farmer, 1996, p. 2)

While Farmer's presence at the conference might be read as an endorsement of Core Knowledge—as suggested by Hirsch—it may also be read as a challenge to more significantly incorporate the knowledge, culture, and history of oppressed groups into the curriculum rather than teaching children about the culture of more powerful groups only.

Equally telling, Richard Rodriguez, a noted Chicano author and lecturer, was welcomed to the conference the following year. In comparison to Farmer's talk, his speech emphasized that "assimilation happens." He declared to Core Knowledge advocates:

> This is not the voice I talked with in the first grade. It is not the way I sounded. This is *your* voice. This is the voice *you* shoved down my throat. … There was a time in my life I would describe myself as a minority and because of you I am not a minority in the cultural sense. (1997, p. 12)

Relegating his own language and culture to the private sphere, Rodriguez stressed the necessity of minority children embracing public culture, meaning dominant ways of speaking, acting, and knowing. He went on:

> There are lots of teachers in this bilingual, ebonics age that simply do not get the point that the point is not mere self-expression. The point is trying to get children to be able to speak in a way that other people can understand them. That is what we mean by "public school." (p. 13)

To a much more significant degree than Farmer, Rodriguez supported accommodating dominant culture rather than demanding cross-cultural literacy. The fact that both have given addresses at the conference highlights the varying ideological commitments that inform the movement and the tensions that characterize existing alliances. The foundation's desire to build such relationships is even more interesting when one recalls the aforementioned effort to translate the *Grader Series* into Spanish for use alongside the English version. Clearly, the force behind this intervention is more aligned with the views of Rodriguez than Farmer, though both have been welcomed under the canopy of Core Knowledge.

As Hirsch has noted, the canopy stretches far and wide. Efforts have been made by Hirsch and his supporters to invite not only parents and children into the Core coalition, but even those at the highest levels of government. In 1996, a cadre of individuals associated with Mathematically Correct issued a letter to President Clinton, asserting, "There is every reason to believe that standards based on content and academics will be subverted before they ever reach the classrooms of America" (para. 2). Opposed to *whole math*, a method that emphasizes conceptual understanding and exploratory problem solving, this organization has called for ongoing drill and memorization of formulas—approaches they believe have disappeared from schools. With such educational conditions in mind, the group implored Clinton:

> All we ask is that you, personally, read *The Schools We Need & Why We Don't Have Them*.... It is our belief that in reading this book you will gain important insight into the gravity of the problem.... We even believe that you will come to feel, as we do, that it is imperative that you bring E. D. Hirsch into your service to advise you directly. (para. 3–4)

A year later, Wayne Bishop (one of those who signed the letter and a math professor) analyzed, at the Core Knowledge Foundation's request, various math textbooks for their usefulness in teaching Core; those emphasizing heavy review and scripted teacher guides came out on top (Marshall, 1997f). These approaches are the same as those advocated by the "Bushies," who have been supporters of the educational forms endorsed by Hirsch and Mathematically Correct (Hoff, 2002).

Not surprisingly, Hirsch has spent some time building alliances in Washington, D.C., where in April 2003 he addressed the White House Forum on Civic Literacy and was honored at a dinner by the vice president and his wife, Lynne Cheney. A few months later Hirsch returned for a celebration sponsored by the Center for Education Reform, which was attended by Secretary of Education Rod Paige, Florida Governor Jeb Bush, and John Walton of the Walton Foundation, a financial backer of Core Knowledge. Regarding these networking efforts, the Core Knowledge Foundation observes, "Hirsch continues to be our roving ambassador, promoting educational reform and seeking like-minded allies" (CKF, 2003e, p. 20).

Yet Hirsch himself has acknowledged that not all his allies are exactly like-minded. How is it, then, that privileged suburbanites and low-income urban and rural communities, assimilationists and cultural pluralists, subaltern parents and state officials, the American Federation of Teachers and conservative foundations are brought together around Core Knowledge? Why is it, to use the words of Minnesota's lieutenant governor, that Core is "just common sense?" As we have seen, Core Knowledge is officially framed in terms of social mobility and civil rights—concerns central to subaltern groups. Beyond this, its curricular coherence offers a promising horizon for urban schools facing various challenges. The association of well-known people of color with Core—some of whom have quite moderate positions on culture and schooling—also gives the reform an air of respectability in marginalized communities. Moreover, poor communities and communities of color that have adopted Core are strategically highlighted by the foundation. The message is that Core has the interests of these groups at its center. All of this serves to shield the reform from criticisms of elitism and Eurocentrism and helps to further the foundation's agenda on this front.

Additionally, cultural restorationists in the government, with right-wing foundations or on the ground in suburban school districts may also securely advocate Core—a reform partly premised on a defense of tradition and order. Those who believe the national heritage is "at risk," and even those who forward a rightist cultural agenda under the banner of "reliable research" and science find Core Knowledge a comfortable home. In these cases, however, the foundation generally eschews directly propounding the classed and raced demands of such groups and uses instead democratically appealing language about common culture and national unity that masks the more coercive aspects of the reform.

Autonomy, Discipline, and the Remaking of a Movement

The disparate social positioning of Core Knowledge advocates and the various interests being folded into the movement are indeed "peculiar," as Hirsch points out. The tensions generated by this balance of forces within the movement should not be overlooked. After all, these diverse investments have led the foundation to redefine its relationship with Core Knowledge schools.

With the movement nearly a decade in the making, Hirsch (1998b) assured teachers that they were its vanguard rather than the foundation: "Core Knowledge has been from the start a *bottom-up not a top-down movement.* . . . *You've done it without coercion* and with dedication, and with ever-increasing numbers" (italics added; pp. 1, 14). Guided by Core content guidelines, teachers across the nation have spent countless hours searching for relevant materials and developing original lesson plans (CKF, 2004e, 2004g). In the beginning, this work was essential because the content guidelines were virtually all that existed. After the first Core school opened in 1990, its principal Connie Jones (1991) reported:

> Our teachers were pleased with the *amount of independence and autonomy* that the Core Knowledge Sequence afforded them.... Selection and use of resources and materials were *completely at the discretion of the teachers....* Our faculty *would not look favorably on publication of a strict Core Knowledge textbook with teacher's guides.* (italics added; p. 10)

This relative autonomy, in diverse hands, has led to interpretations of Core that fall outside the ambit of the official vision. Researchers (Datnow et al., 2000) solicited by the foundation to study Core's implementation across various sites interviewed students and reported:

> All Core Knowledge schools are to teach fifth graders about Thomas Jefferson.... At a school serving a majority African-American population, the students recalled that Jefferson fathered children with one of his slaves. However, students at a majority white school in a suburban area told us that Jefferson was a hero. (p. 183)

Aside from this, researchers also found disparate implementation levels and teaching methods. It is well known that teachers mediate educational initiatives within their classrooms (Grant, 2001; Schweber, 2004), and the lesson plans independently developed by Core Knowledge teachers indicate that a degree of diversity has historically prevailed when Core content is taught. At the same time, this kind of curricular deviance has only been encouraged by a lack of standardized resources to accompany Core content guidelines. There was indeed something to Hirsch's acknowledgement, "You've done it without coercion," but it was becoming increasingly apparent that some schools were not doing it fully or appropriately. In recent years, various disciplinary mechanisms—Core Knowledge history textbooks and teacher guides, *Teacher Handbooks*, refined foundation requirements for Core schools, Core curriculum-referenced tests (CKF, 2004a, n.d.), achievement data collection (Telling, 2003), and a nascent elementary teacher education reform initiative (CKF, 2002)—have begun to take shape.[3]

Core Knowledge history textbooks (Hirsch, 2002), which I will discuss shortly, must be understood in this context. The major issue, of course, is the degree to which these materials will exercise a disciplinary influence. The aforementioned study on Core is relevant here. While Core Knowledge teachers valued the autonomy afforded by relatively scarce Core resources, autonomy had an underside—most notably the intense demands of such work (Datnow et al., 2000). The labor associated with implementing the curriculum independent of Core resources, combined with an overall lack of alternative elementary-level resources pertaining to Core history content, will likely engender greater dependence on Core history textbooks. As such, it is important to assess whose knowledge informs the histories officially endorsed by the foundation. It is equally important to think about how those histories might concurrently and strategically appeal to diverse groups within the movement, support teachers in Core classrooms, and potentially discipline more radically inclusive mediations of Core content guidelines.

Core Knowledge and the *New* Old History

History in schools has generally been taught in narrative form, a speech genre embodied in textbooks used by teachers and read by students. Regarding speech genres, Mikhail Bakhtin emphasized:

> Utterances are not indifferent to one another, and are not self-sufficient; they are aware of and mutually reflect one another.... Each utterance is filled with echoes and reverberations of other utterances to which it is related.... Every utterance must be regarded as primarily a *response* to preceding utterances of the given sphere.... Each utterance refutes, affirms, supplements, and relies on the others, presupposes them to be known, and somehow takes them into account. (in Morris, 1994, p. 85)

If each utterance contains "echoes and reverberations" of past utterances in related social fields and takes these into account, then we must carefully consider the broader conversations, debates, and contexts (see also Gee, 1999) relevant to the writing of Core Knowledge history. The trajectory of struggle between old and new histories—meaning history from above and from below—is most pertinent. Much of the neoconservative reaction, after all, has been driven by a desire to sustain a particular epistemological orientation to studying the past—one that centers on founding fathers and more powerful groups, and what they did to build the nation. Defending the tradition of old history against the onslaught of the new is what compelled Arthur Schlesinger (1992) to warn of "the disuniting of America." "The militants of ethnicity," he wrote, "now contend that a main objective of public education should be the protection, strengthening, celebration, and perpetuation of ethnic origins and identities." Sounding the alarm, he continued, "Separatism, however, nourishes prejudice, magnifies differences and stirs antagonisms.... The result can only be the fragmentation, resegregation, and tribalization of American life" (pp. 17–18). New histories focused on subaltern groups, and conflict rather than consensus, were to blame. In turn, historians of long-ignored pasts—those of African Americans, women, Asian Americans, immigrants, the working class, and so forth—defended such work as legitimate and long overdue (Foner, 1997; Stearns, 1993; Wiener, 1989).

This is the conversation and context in which Core history texts are embedded and to which they respond. Unlike additive multiculturalism, in which "one half of a page here and one half of a page there" discusses subaltern groups

(McCarthy, 1998, p. 115), Core Knowledge history, I argue, represents a strategic innovation that moves beyond additive multiculturalism to something that I have termed the "*new* old history."[4] By this I mean that Core texts reflect to a *greater degree* the tendencies of *both* the old and the new histories, and that the relationship between these traditions within Core is more complex than the additive approach that has characterized so many school texts over past decades (e.g., see Zimmerman, 2002). I will only be able to provide select illustrations here, but it is important to say that the illustrations provided reflect the broader patterns that I found in the many Core history texts that I analyzed.[5] Offering these illustrations, I aim to show how Core texts, as *new* old history, are themselves contributors to the "disuniting of America's history."

More to the point, the pattern that I document (see also Buras, 2005) is one in which both elite and subaltern groups are recognized within Core history texts, but their recognition is premised on two main conditions. First, reflecting the old and the new, the pasts of groups above and below are narrativized, but *not in relation* to one another; elites are powerful but they do not exercise power over any group, subalterns are oppressed but they do not live amid oppressors. Second, the pasts of groups above and below are narrativized *in relation* to one another through a frame that stresses *consensus* (the bulwark of old history) and overshadows or ignores conflict and power (pivotal to new history). Moreover, it is the major storyline that reflects the old history, while the minor storyline "takes into account" and "echoes" the new history. Similarly, images in the texts generally respect those conditions. Core narratives do not represent what has been called *integrative* (Said, 1988) or *synthetic* history (Bender, 1989); this does not mean a total history, but rather any number of partial histories in which "groups interact to make national politics and culture" and do so in "a continuing contest ... to define both themselves and the nation as a whole" (Bender, pp. 198–199). Rather, the *new* old history constructed through Core texts constitutes a strategy of rightist multiculturalism at the epistemological level.

Significantly, Hirsch (2001) has asserted that "people who have called this [reform] ... 'Eurocentric' and 'elitist' have not bothered to find out just what is in Core Knowledge" (p. 4). Let us begin to find out, while keeping in mind that "every written history is a selection and arrangement of facts.... And the selection and arrangement of facts ... is always an act of choice, conviction, and interpretation" (Beard, 1934, p. 220). The point, then, is to assess what kind of selection and arrangement of "facts" characterizes Core Knowledge school history—facts, we should recall, that Hirsch believes "are not and should not be subjects of controversy."

Immigrants

Before even turning a page, one cannot help but notice that Core school history, despite Hirsch's criticism of "ethnic loyalism," is framed in terms of identity politics. Upper-grade textbook covers, for example, do not feature a unifying image such as the American flag. Rather a collage that includes not only a president and a general, but a Native American and an immigrant adorns the covers. A flip through the series further suggests that the national past is a story of diverse groups, from Mount Rushmore presidents and civil rights leaders to industrial giants and workers. Yet the deep structure of the narratives and the connections and disconnections they foster raise serious questions about the legitimacy of this appeal.

As an example, let us consider a sixth grade text on immigrants (Hirsch, 2002). This text, it is worth noting, is twenty-one pages long and seems at first to be an extensive exploration of immigrant experience during the mid-nineteenth and early twentieth centuries. The major storyline is one in which immigrants are *pushed* to emigrate due to terrible conditions in the homeland and are *pulled* toward America, the land of opportunity. The old country was a place, one Irish immigrant says, "where there will be nothing for us but to lie down and die" (p. 244). In contrast, the United States is generally presented in a positive light. When the subaltern speak in this text, it is usually to hail America's greatness. This is illustrated by the inclusion of seven long excerpts from the letters of European immigrants, one right after the other. "Listen to the voices of these earlier immigrants," the text reads, "and you will have no trouble understanding why a struggling European farmer or town worker would consider giving up everything and moving." From the pens of immigrants, it is submitted to students: "One sees no poor here.... One cannot discern any differences between the cobbler's wife and the wife of a prominent gentleman" (p. 245). There is, however, a minor storyline too. In this storyline, success in America is not absolute. Students read that "living conditions for most immigrants in American cities were simply dreadful" (p. 249). Notably, far fewer immigrants in the text speak about this.

This is history from below in that the voices and experiences of immigrants are centered, but the narrative is actually more complicated. It is only European immigrants who speak—Asian immigrants are virtually absent—and when they do, they are only "allowed" to speak in ways that support the major storyline. The minor narrative on hardship and inequality in America is consistently undermined by its relationship to the broader narrative. This occurs through a process that includes *acknowledgement, qualification, comparison,* and *affirmation*. First there is an acknowledgement of immigrant struggle: "Making a living in the city was not easy.... Usually [immigrants] wound up with the hardest jobs, the longest hours, and the lowest pay" (p. 254). Then after a paragraph or two on pay and working conditions for immigrants, and a quote from "someone" who wrote that "the streets [of America] were not paved with gold" and that it was immigrants who "were expected to pave them," the text indicates:

Hard as life may have been for them, however [qualification], these new Americans knew they were far better off than they had been in their native lands [comparison].

In time, many learned new skills and improved their earnings. They were able to afford better housing.... Within one generation, or sometimes two, many of [their] children were entering the fields of medicine, education, business, [and] law [affirmation]. (p. 255)

In this way, the minor storyline, and the history of immigrant struggle that it represents, is consumed by an affirmative narrative of success and consensus in the United States.

One of the most telling instances in which experience from below is reframed from above relates to persecution in the old country and the opportunity to become American in the new. Early on, students read that many immigrants:

had been persecuted in their native lands simply because they spoke a different language, had different customs, or followed a [different] religion.... They weren't allowed to have newspapers or books in their own language, or to get very far in school or in work unless they gave up their language. (p. 253)

Yet later these same tendencies are described as desirable in the United States and are actually a core part of becoming American. With regard to first-generation immigrants, the question is posed, "Did living in their own neighborhoods, and reading newspapers in their own language slow down the process of becoming American?" It was the third generation, the text lauds, that felt "fully, comfortably American," something facilitated by the fact that "foreign language newspapers no longer existed" and few in this generation still felt "torn between the ways of the old and the ways of the new" (p. 262). In short, immigrants flee persecution for a similar experience called "becoming American," only this experience is portrayed as positive.

Significantly, the major storyline is sustained through a nonrelational history. Rather than confronting immigration officials, the captains of industry, or native-born citizens, immigrants mainly encounter geographic locations (e.g., New York City), the American nation (e.g., new world), disembodied forces (e.g., mood of the country, American ways, demands that the government limit who entered), symbols (e.g., Statue of Liberty), institutions (e.g., Americanization programs), and unidentified presences (e.g., those who would take down the welcome sign). Only 20 of 170 references to dominant individuals or groups correspond to actors embodied with specific attributes of class, race, religion, language, or national origin; among these few are an official on Ellis Island, skilled workers born in America, a Congressman, and Protestants. On the whole, this is not a narrative in which subaltern and dominant groups relate—each as identified, embodied groups. Even when the narrative turns to nativism, students are told that some "Americans" favored immigration, while others were troubled by those unlike "themselves" (p. 258). The "mood of the country" and "nativist sentiment" are far more present than "Protestants" who "called for laws" to stop immigration. One drawing does depict violence against the Chinese, but the caption says that "riots ... resulted in the beating of Chinese immigrants." The text later explains that "those responsible" were rarely punished (p. 259).

Civil Rights Leaders

In second grade, students read a Core history text dedicated to Civil Rights Leaders, particularly African Americans (Hirsch, 2002). Old and new, above and below, are also conditionally incorporated into this narrative. The major storyline is that all Americans worked to ensure equal rights. In tension with this is a minor storyline that some groups did not have equal rights. More specifically, this story unfolds as utterances on black experience alternate with ones on white benevolence. Thus, the text indicates that Mary McLeod Bethune, whose parents "had been slaves," believed that "every black child should get an education." She "started a school" for African American girls with whom she is pictured. In this narrative frame, Bethune's experience is raced; she seeks to equalize educational conditions for *black* children (p. 4). Next appears Eleanor Roosevelt who "wanted to help others" (p. 5). Bethune and Roosevelt, finally, are shown together in a photo as they relate to one another with smiles. Students read that they "worked together to help all American children get a good education" (p. 6). In this frame, Bethune's racial struggle is transformed into a cooperative effort with Roosevelt to help all *American* children.

This pattern persists as the narrative continues: "White people played in the major leagues and black people played in the Negro leagues," but Branch Rickey, the white manager of the Brooklyn Dodgers, "still wanted Jackie Robinson" to play on his team (pp. 7–8). Martin Luther King "wanted integration," but at the Lincoln Memorial, he spoke to thousands who "wanted a better life for all Americans." Students are told that King knew Gandhi had freed his country "without violence" (pp. 12–13). These alternating discourses—one focused on unequal conditions and the other on cooperative relations and an "all American" effort to ensure equality—are only reinforced by the textual images. Jackie Robinson and Branch Rickey are pictured together shaking hands and smiling. Martin Luther King is pictured at the Lincoln Memorial with the statue elevated behind him—itself an image of nonviolent relations as Lincoln "watches over" King.

Notably, this narrative is simultaneously non-relational and relational. Unequal conditions prevail in the minor storyline, but Africans Americans never encounter whites exercising power in direct or explicit ways. Violent southern segregationists did not work to help "all" Americans. And the struggle for integration saw much violence—namely that perpetrated by whites against blacks. Yet all of this is absent within a nonrelational frame that manages to convey a story from below of the black civil rights struggle, but without malevolent whites. At yet another point the text explains: "Black people had to sit at the back of the bus. Rosa Parks broke the law in Alabama. She would not move to the back of the bus to give a white man her seat" (p. 10). Accompanying these words, however, is a photo that shows Parks sitting *in front* of a white man who is calmly seated and does not recognize her presence. It thus seems that Parks was able to address unequal treatment without tension, much less arrest. The "Read Aloud" in the Teacher Guide—meant to be read by the teacher to the class—does, on occasion, allude to conflictual relations, for example, announcing that "Rosa Parks got arrested on the bus" and said she "was tired of being pushed around" (p. 14). But these representations are not reflected in the written or visual text that students directly engage. Instead, subaltern and dominant racial groups only meet within a consensual frame. The minor storyline on inequality, as lived from below, is subverted by a story in which blacks have cooperative relations with benevolent whites.

Lessons from Above and Below

Calling for a return to the old history, Glazer (1997) said, "would no longer do" (p. 33), though moving beyond additive history could certainly do Core Knowledge one better. This strategy might actually have the power to mobilize both dominant and subaltern groups around Core without either group feeling that its interests or history are being undercut. At the 5th National Core Knowledge Conference, Diane Ravitch (1996), a current member of the foundation's board of trustees, declared: "You, as teachers and leaders of Core Knowledge schools, must foment a revolution.... America needs *more* Core Knowledge schools" (p. 11). I have suggested that those of us dedicated to more progressive conceptions of democracy need to think about how precisely the revolution is being fomented. Groups from below may seek to redefine Core, but they are also surrounded by a network of very powerful conservative forces from above that will try, at every turn, to make and remake the movement and to write and rewrite the pages of history in ways that support dominant interests. The degree to which rightist multiculturalism will succeed in serving those interests is the question of the day. For now, let's just say the Free Congress Foundation might learn a lesson from the Core Knowledge Foundation. Strange as it may sound coming from someone in the field of education, I hope the lesson goes unlearned.

Endnotes

1. Those interested in how tensions have unfolded around other educational reforms involving alliances between differently situated groups should see Apple (1996), Pedroni (2003), and Apple & Pedroni (in press).
2. On one hand, it is important to think about what might be learned by the left from such an effort. Apple (2001), for example, has discussed the progressive potential of building coalitions among politically, economically, and culturally disparate groups. On the other

hand, I wish to follow his lead in underlining the dangers of learning from the right's success. There are lessons, in other words, that the left may wish to reject—as when the strategies employed rely on reappropriating subaltern voices and redefining subaltern concerns in ways that actually serve to undermine rather than advance the process of democratic transformation.

3. Some Core initiatives have been funded by conservative groups such as the Walton Foundation and John M. Olin Foundation.

4. Gertrude Himmelfarb (2004) has used the terms *new* new history and *old* new history, and has written about Lawrence Stone's proposal for a new old history, but none of these usages correspond with my invocation of the term *new* old history.

5. I can only provide select illustrations here, but interested readers should consult a forthcoming manuscript (Buras, 2005) in which I lay out more extensively the critical discourse analysis that I completed on purposefully sampled selections from the *Pearson Learning-Core Knowledge History and Geography Textbooks* (Hirsch, 2002). Readers should also see that text for a discussion of my methodology (Gee, 1999). The illustrations provided in this chapter reflect the patterns that I found more broadly in the many Core history texts that I analyzed, including all or significant portions of the following: civil rights leaders (Grade 2) and American reformers (4); exploring the west (1), the earliest Americans (3), and Native Americans: cultures and conflicts (5); immigration and citizenship (2) and immigration (6); industrialization and urbanization in America (6); Mount Rushmore presidents (K) and early presidents (4). I also closely read and did a cursory analysis of the Teacher Guides associated with any texts that I discursively analyzed from grades K–2, and closely read all of the U.S. history texts for grades K–6. Images in all discursively analyzed texts were also examined.

References

American Federation of Teachers (2003, March). American Federation of Teachers on Core Knowledge [Bound compilation of articles]. Washington, DC: Author.

Apple, M. W. (1993). *Official knowledge: Democratic education in a conservative age.* New York: Routledge.

Apple, M. W. (1996). *Cultural politics and education.* New York: Teachers College Press.

Apple, M. W. (2001). *Educating the "right" way: Markets, standards, god, and inequality.* New York: RoutledgeFalmer.

Apple, M. W., & Beane, J. (Eds.). (1995). *Democratic schools.* Alexandria, VA: Association for Supervision and Curriculum Development.

Apple, M. W., & Christian-Smith, L. K. (1991). *The politics of the textbook.* New York: Routledge.

Apple, M. W., & Pedroni, T. C. (in press). Conservative alliance building and African American support for voucher reforms. *Teachers College Record.*

Aronowitz, S., & Giroux, H. (1991). Textual authority, culture, and the politics of literacy. In M. W. Apple & L. K. Christian-Smith, *The politics of the textbook* (pp. 213–241). New York: Routledge.

Baltimore Curriculum Project (2004). Baltimore curriculum project: Draft month-by-month content lesson plans based on the Core Knowledge sequence. Available: http://www.cstone.net/~bcp/

Banks, J. A. (1969). A content analysis of the black American in textbooks. *Social Education, 33,* 954–957, 963.

Beard, C. (1934). Written history as an act of faith. *American Historical Review, XXXIX* (2), 219–229.

Bender, T. (1989). Public culture: Inclusion and synthesis in American history. In P. Gagnon and The Bradley Commission on History in Schools (Eds.), *Historical literacy: The case for history in American education* (pp. 188–202). New York: Macmillan.

Bennett, W. J. (1992). *The de-valuing of America: The fight for our culture and our children.* New York: Simon & Schuster.

Buras, K. L. (1999). Questioning Core assumptions: A critical reading of and response to E. D. Hirsch's *The Schools We Need & Why We Don't Have Them. Harvard Educational Review, 69* (1), 67–93.

Buras, K. L. (2004). [Notes from national Core Knowledge conference]. Unpublished data.

Buras, K. L. (2005). The disuniting of America's history: Core Knowledge and the new old history. Manuscript in progress. University of Wisconsin, Madison.

Cobble, D. S., & Kessler-Harris, A. (1993). The new labor history in American history textbooks. *Journal of American History, 79*, 1534–1545.

Colorado Schools (2003). Colorado schools grow through Holly Hensey's support [Electronic version]. *Common Knowledge, 16* (3).

Core Knowledge Foundation. (1996a). Common misconceptions about Core Knowledge. Available: www.coreknowledge.org

Core Knowledge Foundation. (1996b). Core Knowledge in the schools as of fall 1996 [Brochure]. Charlottesville, VA: Author.

Core Knowledge Foundation. (1997). Core Knowledge professional development workshops [Brochure]. Charlottesville, VA: Author.

Core Knowledge Foundation. (1998). *The Core Knowledge sequence: Content guidelines for grades K–6.* Charlottesville, VA: Author.

Core Knowledge Foundation. (2002). *What elementary teachers need to know: College course outlines for teacher preparation.* Charlottesville, VA: Author.

Core Knowledge Foundation. (2003a, March 1). Professional development workshops. Retrieved October 22, 2003, from http://www.coreknowledge.org

Core Knowledge Foundation. (2003b, September 15). Official Core Knowledge schools. Retrieved October 14, 2003, from http://www.coreknowledge.org/CKproto2/schools/schllst_O.htm

Core Knowledge Foundation. (2003c, August 25). Official Core Knowledge school application: Information for school year 2003–2004. Retrieved October 14, 2003, from http://www.coreknowledge.org/CKproto2/schools/schllst_O_app.htm

Core Knowledge Foundation. (2003d, December 1). Core Knowledge schools: How to get started. Retrieved July 20, 2004, from http://www.coreknowledge.org/CKproto2/schools/start.htm

Core Knowledge Foundation. (2003e). *Annual report of the Core Knowledge Foundation.* Charlottesville, VA: Author.

Core Knowledge Foundation. (2004a, March 10). Core Knowledge-TASA curriculum–referenced tests. Retrieved July 29, 2004, from http://www.coreknowledge.org/CKproto 2/schools/testing.htm

Core Knowledge Foundation. (2004b, May 25). Core Knowledge K–8 schools list. Retrieved June 15, 2004, from http://www.coreknowledge.org

Core Knowledge Foundation. (2004c, July 16). Becoming a Core Knowledge K–8 school [Breakdown of schools]. Retrieved July 20, 2004, from http://www.coreknowledge.org

Core Knowledge Foundation. (2004d). *Core Knowledge teacher handbook, grade 1.* Charlottesville, VA: Author.

Core Knowledge Foundation. (2004e). Home page. Available: www.coreknowledge.org

Core Knowledge Foundation. (2004f). Parent brochure. Retrieved March 31, 2005, from http://www.coreknowledge.org/CKproto2/schools/schools_parentbrochure.htm

Core Knowledge Foundation. (2004g). Share the knowledge: Core Knowledge national conference units and handouts. Charlottesville, VA: Author.

Core Knowledge Foundation. (n.d.). Q&A: Core Knowledge testing program [Brochure]. Charlottesville, VA: Author.

Cornbleth, C., & Waugh, D. (1999). *The great speckled bird: Multicultural politics and education policymaking.* Mahwah, NJ: Lawrence Erlbaum Associates.

Cuban, L. (1993). *How teachers taught: Constancy and change in American classrooms.* New York: Teachers College Press.

Datnow, A., Borman, G., & Stringfield, S. (2000). School reform through a highly specified curriculum: Implementation and effects of the Core Knowledge sequence. *Elementary School Journal, 101* (2), 167–191.

Davis, M. (2002). Core Knowledge offers blueprint for content-rich teacher education. *Common Knowledge, 15* (3), 4.

Delfattore, J. (1992). *What Johnny shouldn't read: Textbook censorship in America.* New Haven, CT: Yale University Press.

Delgado Bernal, D. (2002). Critical race theory, Latino critical theory, and critical raced-gendered epistemologies: Recognizing students of color as holders and creators of knowledge. *Qualitative Inquiry, 8* (1), 105–126.

Enterprise Foundation. (2000). Community Building in Partnership, Baltimore, Maryland: A case study from on the ground with comprehensive community initiatives. Available: http://www.enterprisefoundation.org/resources/ERD/browse.asp?c=35

Farmer, J. (1996). We are bound together. *Common Knowledge, 9* (1/2), 2.

Foner, E. (Ed.). (1997). *The new American history.* Philadelphia, PA: Temple University Press.

Free Congress Foundation. (2004a). Declaration of cultural independence. Retrieved June 22, 2004, from http://www.freecongress.org/centers/cc/culturalindependence.asp

Free Congress Foundation. (2004b). Home page. Retrieved June 22, 2004, from http://www.free-congress.org/about/index.asp

Freire, P. (1993). *Pedagogy of the oppressed.* New York: Continuum.

Gee, J. P. (1999). *An introduction to discourse analysis.* New York: Routledge.

Gerson, M. (1997). *The neoconservative vision: From the cold war to the culture wars.* New York: Madison Books.

Giroux, H. A. (1995). Insurgent multiculturalism and the promise of pedagogy. In D. T. Goldberg (Ed.), *Multiculturalism: A critical reader* (pp. 325–343). Oxford: Blackwell.

Glazer, N. (1997). *We are all multiculturalists now.* Cambridge, MA: Harvard University Press.

Goldberg, M. F. (1997). An interview with E. D. Hirsch, Jr.: Doing what works. *Phi Delta Kappan, 79* (1), 83–85.

Goodlad, J. I. (1984). *A place called school.* New York: McGraw-Hill.

Graff, G. (1992). *Beyond the culture wars: How teaching the conflicts can revitalize American education.* New York: W. W. Norton.

Grant, S. G. (2001). An uncertain lever: Exploring the influence of state-level testing in New York State on teaching social studies. *Teachers College Record, 103* (3), 398–426.

Hassett, M. K. (2004). A conference to remember [Electronic version]. *Common Knowledge, 17* (2).

Himmelfarb, G. (2004). *The new history and the old.* Cambridge, MA: Harvard University Press.

Hirsch, E. D., Jr. (1983). Cultural literacy. *American Scholar, 52,* 159–169.

Hirsch, E. D., Jr. (1987). *Cultural literacy: What every American needs to know.* New York: Vintage Books.

Hirsch, E. D., Jr. (1992a). Fairness and core knowledge. Charlottesville, VA: Core Knowledge Foundation.

Hirsch, E. D., Jr. (1992b). Toward a centrist curriculum: Two kinds of multiculturalism in elementary school. Charlottesville, VA: Core Knowledge Foundation.

Hirsch, E. D., Jr. (1996). *The schools we need & why we don't have them.* New York: Doubleday.

Hirsch, E. D., Jr. (1997). An address to the California State Board of Education. *Common Knowledge, 10* (1/2), 4–8.

Hirsch, E. D., Jr. (Ed.). (1998a). *What your second grader needs to know: Fundamentals of a good second-grade education* (Rev. ed.). New York: Doubleday.

Hirsch, E. D., Jr. (1998b). Why general knowledge should be a goal of education in a democracy. *Common Knowledge, 11* (1/2), 1, 14–16.

Hirsch, E. D., Jr. (1999). Why core knowledge promotes social justice [electronic version]. *Common Knowledge, 12* (4).

Hirsch, E. D., Jr. (2001). Breadth versus depth: A premature polarity. *Common Knowledge, 14* (4), 3–4.

Hirsch, E. D., Jr. (Ed.). (2002). *Pearson Learning—Core Knowledge history and geography textbooks, grades K–6.* Parsippany, NJ: Pearson Learning Group.

Hirsch, E. D., Jr., & Holdren, J. (Eds.). (2001). *Lo que su alumno de kindergarten necesita saber* [Field copy]. Charlottesville, VA: Core Knowledge Foundation.

Hirsch, E. D., Jr., Kett, J. F., & Trefil, J. (1988). *The dictionary of cultural literacy: What every American needs to know.* New York: Houghton Mifflin Company.

Hitchcock, S. T. (2002). Teaching the teachers: New education school programs promise to help Core Knowledge teachers. *Common Knowledge, 15* (1), 4–6.

Hoare, Q., & Nowell Smith, G. (Eds.). (1971). *Selections from the prison notebooks of Antonio Gramsci.* New York: International Publishers.

Hoff, D. J. (2002). Bush to push for math and science upgrade. *Education Week, 22* (12), 19, 24.

Jones, C. (1991). *A school's guide to Core Knowledge: Ideas for implementation.* Charlottesville, VA: Core Knowledge Foundation.

Jones, C. (1997a). School clips. *Common Knowledge, 10* (1/2), 10, 16.

Jones, C. (1997b). School clips. *Common Knowledge, 10* (3), 6, 12.

Jones, C. (1997c). School clips. *Common Knowledge, 10* (4), 6, 12.

Kaestle, C. F. (1983). *Pillars of the republic: Common schools and American society, 1780–1860.* New York: Hill & Wang.

Kantrowitz, B., Chideya, F., & Wingert P. (1992, November 2). What kids need to know: Putting cultural literacy into elementary school. *Newsweek*, 80.

Kliebard, H. M. (1995). *The struggle for the American curriculum, 1893–1958.* New York: Routledge.

Kramer, H., & Kimball, R. (Eds.). (1997). *The future of the European past.* Chicago, IL: Ivan R. Dee.

Ladson-Billings, G. (1994). *The dreamkeepers: Successful teachers of African American students.* San Francisco, CA: Jossey-Bass.

Lindsay, D. (2001, November 11). Against the establishment: How a U-VA professor, denounced as elitist and ethnocentric, became a prophet of the school standards movement. *Washington Post*, W24.

Mackley, T. A. (1999). *Uncommon sense: Core knowledge in the classroom.* Alexandria, VA: Association for Supervision and Curriculum Development.

Marshall, M. (Ed.). (1997a). Baltimore lessons are on the net. *Common Knowledge, 10* (3), 2.

Marshall, M. (Ed.). (1997b). Hirsch receives AFT's Quest Award. *Common Knowledge, 10* (3), 1.

Marshall, M. (1997c). In Polk County, Florida: Going for Core in a big way. *Common Knowledge, 10* (3), 1, 7, 11.

Marshall, M. (Ed.). (1997d). Preschool sequence now available. *Common Knowledge, 10* (3), 3.

Marshall, M. (Ed.). (1997e). Sequence for 7th and 8th finalized. *Common Knowledge, 10* (3), 4.

Marshall, M. (1997f). What math book to use? *Common Knowledge, 10* (3), 1, 8, 11.

Marshall, M. (1998a). Feldman joins Core Knowledge Foundation board of trustees. *Common Knowledge, 11* (3), 2.

Marshall, M. (1998b). The bad news about discovery learning: A nugget from the annals of research. *Common Knowledge, 11* (3), 6–7.

Marshall, M. (Ed.). (1999). Minnesota's Lt. Governor is a core knowledge teacher. *Common Knowledge, 12* (1/2), 3.

Marshall, M., & Hirsch, E. D., Jr. (Eds.). (1997). *Core classics series.* Charlottesville, VA: Core Knowledge Foundation.

Mathematically Correct (1996, November 20). A letter to the president. Retrieved July 14, 2004, from http://www.mathematicallycorrect.com/clinton.htm

McCarthy, C. (1998). *The uses of culture.* New York: Routledge.

Mentzer, D., & Shaughnessy, T. (1996). Hawthorne Elementary School: The teachers' perspective. *Journal of Education for Students Placed at Risk, 1* (1), 13–23.

Meyer, P. (1991, September). Getting to the core. *Life, 14* (11), 36–39.

Michie, G. (1999). *Holler if you hear me: The education of a teacher and his students.* New York: Teachers College Press.

Moloney, W. (1998). The place of Core Knowledge in American school reform. *Common Knowledge, 11* (1/2), 5–6, 12–13.

Morris, P. (Ed.). (1994). *The Bakhtin reader.* New York: Edward Arnold.

National Core Knowledge Coordinator of Colorado (2004). Home page. Available: http://www.ckcolorado.org

Pedroni, T. C. (2003). Strange bedfellows in the Milwaukee "parental choice" debate: Participation among the dispossessed in conservative education reform. Unpublished doctoral dissertation, University of Wisconsin, Madison.

Perry, C. (1994, October). Maverick principal. *Reader's Digest*, 134–138.

Prum, D. M. (1999). *Rats, bulls, and flying machines.* Charlottesville, VA: Core Knowledge Foundation.

Putka, G. (1991, September 5). Florida schools to put cultural literacy to test. *Wall Street Journal*, B1.

Ravitch, D. (1996). Why we need a literate core curriculum. *Common Knowledge, 9* (1/2), 1, 6–11.

Rodriguez, R. (1997). Assimilation happens. *Common Knowledge, 10* (1/2), 12–13.

Rounds, S. (2004, February). *Hobbs Municipal Schools: Comprehensive K–12 reform programs—the Core Knowledge sequence.* Hobbs, NM: Hobbs Municipal Schools.

Ruenzel, D. (1996–97). Washington Core Knowledge school: Fort Collins, Colorado. *American Educator, 20* (4), 8, 24–26, 28–29.

Said, E. (1988). Foreword. In R. Guha & G. C. Spivak (Eds.), *Selected subaltern studies* (pp. v–x). New York: Oxford University Press.

Scherer, M. (1996). On better alternatives for urban students: A conversation with Sylvia Peters. *Educational Leadership, 54* (2), 47–52.

Schlesinger, A. M, Jr. (1992). *The disuniting of America: Reflections on a multicultural society.* New York: W. W. Norton.

Schweber, S. A. (2004). *Making sense of the Holocaust: Lessons from classroom practice.* New York: Teachers College Press.

Shields, C. J. (2003b). Interview with CSR coordinator Yolanda Van Ness [Electronic version]. *Common Knowledge, 16* (4).

Siler, J. N. (1997). Report on the sixth national core knowledge conference: Bigger is still better. *Common Knowledge, 10* (1/2), 1, 8–9.

Siler, J. N. (1998). Atlanta '98: Core content with southern hospitality. *Common Knowledge, 11* (1/2), 10–11.

Siler, J. N. (1999). Coast to coast, trainers spread Core Knowledge with enthusiasm. *Common Knowledge, 12* (4), 5, 9.

Sleeter, C. E., & Grant, C. A. (1991). Race, class, gender, and disability in current textbooks. In M. W. Apple & L. K. Christian-Smith (Eds.), *The politics of the textbook* (pp. 78–110). New York: Routledge.

Stearns, P. N. (1993). The old social history and the new. In M. K. Cayton, E. Gorn, & P. W. Williams (Eds.), *Encyclopedia of American social history* (pp. 237–250). New York: Macmillan.

Steinfels, P. (1979). *The neoconservatives: The men who are changing America's politics.* New York: Simon & Schuster.

Summers, M. (1999, July 26). Defining literacy upward. *Forbes,* 70, 72.

Telling. (2003). Telling your story with test data [Electronic version]. *Common Knowledge, 16* (3).

Vail, K. (1997). Core comes to Crooksville. *The American School Board Journal, 184* (3), 14–18.

Wiener, J. M. (1989). Radical historians and the crisis in American history, 1959–1980. *The Journal of American History, 76,* 399–434.

Willingham, D. B. (1999). What do scientists know about how we learn? A brief summary of the most important principles of learning and memory. *Common Knowledge, 12* (1/2), 6–7.

Zimmerman, J. (2002). *Whose America: Culture wars in the public schools.* Cambridge, MA: Harvard University Press.

2

"We Are the New Oppressed"
Gender, Culture, and the Work of Home Schooling

MICHAEL W. APPLE

Introduction[1]

In *Educating the "Right" Way* (Apple, 2001; see also Apple et al., 2003), I spend a good deal of time detailing the world as seen through the eyes of *authoritarian populists*. These are conservative groups of religious fundamentalists and evangelicals whose voices in the debates over social and educational policies are now increasingly powerful. I critically analyzed the ways in which they construct themselves as the *new oppressed,* as people whose identities and cultures are ignored by or attacked in schools and the media. They have taken on subaltern identities and have (very selectively) reappropriated the discourses and practices of figures such as Dr. Martin Luther King to lay claim to the fact that they are the last truly dispossessed groups.

In this chapter, I examine the ways in which the claim to subaltern status has led to a partial withdrawal from state-run institutions, and to a practice of schooling that is meant to equip the children of authoritarian populist parents both with an armor to defend what these groups believe is their threatened culture and with a set of skills and values that will change the world so that it reflects the conservative religious commitments that are so central to their lives. I shall focus on the ways in which new technologies, such as the Internet, have become essential resources in what authoritarian populists see as a counter-hegemonic struggle against secular humanism and a world that no longer "listens to God's word" (Apple, 2001). Much of my discussion will center around the place of gender in these movements, because conservative women have multiple identities within them, as they are simultaneously able to claim subaltern status based on the history of dominant gender regimes and have dominant status given their positioning in relationship to other oppressed groups.

Technology and Social Movement Resources

There has been an explosion of analyses of the Internet in education, cultural studies, sociology, the social studies of technology and science, and elsewhere. Much of this material has been of considerable interest and has led to a good deal of discussion of the use, benefits, history, and status of such technologies (see, e.g., Bromley & Apple, 1998; Cuban, 2001; Godwin, 2003; Hakken, 1999; Jordan, 1999). However, much of this debate is carried on with limited reference to the contexts in which the Internet is actually used, or the context is mentioned as an issue but remains relatively unexamined. As one of the more perceptive writers on the social uses and benefits of the Internet has said, "We can only understand the impact of the Internet on modern culture if we see that symbolic content and online interaction are embedded in social and historical contexts of various kinds" (Slevin, 2000, p. ix). As Manuel Castells reminds us, rather than having a unitary meaning and use, the new communications networks that are being created "are made of many cultures, many values, many projects, that cross through the minds and inform the strategies of the various participants" (1996, p. 199).

New technologies have both been stimulated by and have themselves stimulated three overlapping dynamics: (1) the intensification of globalization, (2) the detraditionalizing of society, and (3) the intensification of social reflexivity (Slevin, 2000, p. 5). In the process, technologies such as the Web and the Internet have provided the basis for new forms of solidarity as groups of people seek to deal with the transformations brought about by these dynamics. Yet the search for such forms of solidarity that would restore or defend tradition and authority can itself lead to the production of new forms of social *disintegration* at one and the same time (pp. 5–6).

In this chapter, I examine a growing instance of this paradoxical process of solidarity and disintegration. By focusing on the social uses of the Internet by a new but increasingly powerful group of educational activists—conservative Christian evangelical home schoolers—I want to contribute both to our understanding of how populist conservative movements grow and support themselves ideologically, and to the complex ways in which technological resources can serve a multitude of social agendas. I argue that only by placing these technologies back into the social and ideological context of their use by *specific* communities (and by specific people within these communities) can we understand the meaning and function of new technologies in society and in education. In order to accomplish this, I also focus on the labor of home schooling, on how it is organized, on new definitions of legitimate knowledge, and on how all this has been partly transformed by the ways in which technological markets are being created.

Technology and the Growth of Home Schooling

The connections between conservative evangelical forms and technologies are not new by any means. Elsewhere, others and I have written about the creative use of electronic ministries both nationally and internationally by the authoritarian populist religious right (see, e.g., Apple, 2001). Technological resources such as television and radio have been employed to expand the influence of conservative religious impulses, and to make "the word of God" available to believers and "those who are yet to believe" alike.[2] While understanding that the increasing range and impact of such efforts is crucial, here I am less interested in such things. I want to point to more mundane but growing uses of technologies such as the Internet in supporting evangelical efforts that are closer to home. And I do mean *home* literally.

Home schooling is growing rapidly. But it is not simply the result of additive forces. It is not simply an atomistic phenomenon in which, one by one, isolated parents decide to reject organized public schools and teach their children at home. Home schooling is a *social movement*. It is a collective project, one with a history and a set of organizational and material supports (Stevens, 2001, p. 4).

While many educators devote a good deal of their attention to reforms such as charter schools, and such schools have received a good deal of positive press, there are many fewer children in charter schools than there are being home schooled. In 1996, home school advocates estimated that there were approximately 1.3 million children being home schooled in the United States. More recent estimates put the figure even higher. Given the almost reverential and rather romantic coverage in national and local media of home schooling (with the *New York Times* and *Time* magazine providing a large amount of very positive coverage, for example), the numbers may in fact be much higher than this, and the growth curve is undoubtedly increasing.

The home schooling movement is not homogeneous. It includes people of a wide spectrum of political/ideological, religious, and educational beliefs. It cuts across racial and class lines. As Stevens notes, there are in essence two general groupings within the home school movement, *Christian* and *inclusive*. There are some things that are shared across these fault lines, however: (1) a sense that the standardized education offered by mainstream schooling interferes with their children's potential, (2) that there is a serious danger when the state intrudes into the life of the family, and (3) that experts and bureaucracies are apt to impose their beliefs and are unable to meet the needs of families and children (Stevens, 2001, pp. 4–7). These worries tap currents that are widespread within American culture and they too cut across particular social and cultural divides.

Yet it would be wrong to interpret the mistrust of experts by many home schoolers as simply a continuation of the current of *anti-intellectualism* that seems to run deep in parts of the history of the United States. The mistrust of science, government experts, and rationality became much more general as a result of the Vietnam War, when the attacks on scientists for their inhumanity, on government for lying, and on particular forms of instrumental rationality for their loss of values and ethics spread into the common sense of society. This was often coupled with a mistrust of authority in general (Moore, 1999, p. 109). Home schoolers are not only not immune to such tendencies, but combine them in creative ways with other elements of popular consciousness concerning the importance of education in times of rapid change and economic, cultural, and moral threat.

Demographic information on home schoolers is limited, but in general home schoolers seem to be somewhat better educated, slightly more affluent, and considerably more likely to be white than the population in the state in which they reside (Stevens, 2001, p. 11). While it is important to recognize the diversity of the movement, it is just as crucial to understand that the largest group of people who home school have conservative religious commitments and are what I have called elsewhere "authoritarian populists" (Apple, 2001). Given the dominance of conservative Christians in the home schooling movement, this picture matches the overall demographic patterns of evangelical Christians in general (Smith, 1998).

Based on a belief that schooling itself is a very troubled institution (but often with widely divergent interpretations of what has caused these troubles), home schoolers have created mechanisms where "horror stories" about schools are shared, as are stories of successful home schooling practices. The metaphors that describe what goes on in public schools and the dangers associated with them, especially those used by many conservative evangelical home schoolers, are telling. Stevens puts it in the following way:

> Invoking the rhetoric of illness ("cancer," "contagion") to describe the dangers of uncontrolled peer interaction, believers frame the child-world of school as a kind of jungle where parents send their kids only at risk of infection. The solution: keep them at home, away from that environment altogether. (2001, p. 53)

Given these perceived dangers, through groups that have been formed at both regional and national levels, home schooling advocates press departments of education and legislatures to guarantee their rights to home school their children. They have established communicative networks—newsletters, magazines, and increasingly the Internet—to build and maintain a community of fellow believers, a community that is often supported by ministries that reinforce the "wisdom" (and very often godliness) of their choice. And as we shall see, the business community has increasingly begun to realize that this can be a lucrative market (Stevens, 2001, p. 4). Religious publishers, for profit publishing houses large and small, conservative colleges and universities, Internet entrepreneurs, and others have understood that a market in cultural goods—classroom materials, lesson plans, textbooks, religious material, CDs, and so forth—has been created. They have rushed to respond to the expressed needs and to stimulate needs that are not yet recognized as needs themselves. But the market would not be there unless what created the opportunity for such a market—the successful identity work of the evangelical movement itself—had not provided the space in which such a market could operate.

Understanding Social Movements

Conservative Christian home schoolers are part of a larger evangelical movement that has been increasingly influential in education, politics, and in cultural institutions such as the media (Apple, 2001; Binder, 2002). Nationally, white evangelicals constitute approximately 25% of the adult population in the United States (Green, 2000, p. 2). The evangelical population is growing steadily (Smith, 1998) as it actively provides subject positions and new identities for people who feel unmoored in a world where, for them, "all that is sacred is profaned" and where the tensions and structures of feeling of advanced capitalism do not provide either a satisfying emotional or spiritual life. The search for a "return"—in the face of major threats to what they see as accepted relations of gender/sex, of authority and tradition, of nation and family—is the guiding impulse behind the growth of this increasingly powerful social movement (Apple, 2001).

Social movements often have multiple goals that may or may not be reached. Yet it is also important to understand that they can produce consequences that are much broader than their avowed goals and that are not always foreseen. Thus, social movements that aim at structural transformations in state policies may produce profound changes in the realms of culture, everyday life, and identity. The mobilizations around specific goals as well can strengthen internal solidarities, cement individual and collective identity shifts in place, create a new common sense, and ultimately lead to perceptible shifts in public attitudes about a given issue (Giugni, 1999, pp. xxi–xxiii). They also create "innovative action repertoires" and have an influence on the practices and culture of mainstream organizations (Amenta & Young, 1999, p. 34). As we shall see, this is exactly what is happening both in the lives of home schoolers, and in the ways in which organized public school systems have responded to the perceived threat to their financial well-being by a growing home school population.

A key to all this is something I mentioned above—the importance of identity politics. For social movements to prosper, they must provide identities that constantly revivify the reasons for participating in them. They must, hence, have an emotional economy in which the costs of being "different" are balanced by the intense meanings and satisfactions of acting in opposition to dominant social norms and values. This doesn't happen all at once. People are changed by participating in oppositional movements such as home schooling. As social movement theorists have widely recognized, there are crucial biographical impacts of participating in movements. People become transformed in the process (see, e.g., McAdam, 1999). This point is clearly made by Meyer:

> By engaging in the social life of a challenging movement, an individual's experience of the world is mediated by a shared vision of the way the world works and, importantly, the individual's position in it. By engaging in activism, an individual creates himself or herself as a subject, rather than simply an object, in history and ... is unlikely to retreat to passive acceptance of the world as it is. (1999, p. 186)

Technology and Doing Home Schooling

A large portion of social movement activity targets the state (Amenta & Young, 1999, p. 30), and this is especially the case with the home schooling movement. While there is often a fundamental mistrust of the state among many religiously conservative home schoolers, there are a considerable number of such people who are willing to compromise with the state. They employ state programs and funds to their own tactical advantage. One of the clearest examples of this is the growing home schooling charter school movement in states such as California. Even though many of the parents involved in such programs believe that they do not want their children to be "brainwashed by a group of educators" and do not want to "leave [their] children off somewhere like a classroom and have them influenced and taught by someone that I am not familiar with" (Huerta, 2000, p. 177), a growing number of Christian conservative parents have become quite adept at taking advantage of government resources. By taking advantage of home school charter programs that connect independent families through the use of the Internet and the Web, they are able to use public funding to support schooling that they had previously had to pay for privately (pp. 179–180).

But it is not only the conservative evangelical parents who are using the home schooling charter possibilities for their own benefit. School districts themselves are actively strategizing, employing such technological connections to enhance their revenue flow by maintaining existing enrollments or by actively recruiting home school parents to join a home school charter.

For example, by creating a home school charter, one financially pressed small California school district was able to solve a good deal of its economic problems. Over the first two years of its operation, the charter school grew from 80 students to 750 (Huerta, 2000, p. 180). The results were striking.

> Along with the many new students came a surge of state revenue to the small district, increasing the district's budget by more than 300 percent. [The home schooling charter] garnered home school families by providing

them with a wealth of materials and instructional support. In exchange for resources, families would mail monthly student learning records to the school. Learning records are the lifeline of the school and serve a dual purpose—outlining the academic content completed by students and serving also as an attendance roster from which [the charter school staff] can calculate average daily attendance.... Thus, parents' self-reported enrollment data permit [the school district] to receive full capitation grants from the state. (Huerta, 2000, p. 180)

In this way, by complying with the minimal reporting requirements, conservative Christian parents are able to act on their desire to keep government and secular influences at a distance; and at the very same time, school districts are able to maintain that the children of these families are enrolled in public schooling and meeting the requirements of secular schooling.

We should be cautious of using the word *secular* here. It is clear from the learning records submitted by the parents that there is widespread use of religious materials in all of the content. Bible readings, devotional lessons, moral teachings directly from online vendors, and so on were widely integrated by the parents within the secular resources provided by the school. "Write and read Luke 1:37, memorize Luke 1:37, prayer journal" are among the many very nonsecular parts of the sample learning records submitted by the parents (Huerta, 2000, p. 188).

Such content, and the lack of accountability over it, raises serious questions about the use of public funding for overtly conservative religious purposes. It documents the power of Huerta's claim that "In an attempt to recast its authority in an era of fewer bureaucratic controls over schools, the state largely drops its pursuit of the common good as public authority is devolved to local families" (2000, p. 192). In the process, technologically linked homes are reconstituted as a "public" school, but a school in which the very meaning of *public* has been radically transformed so that it mirrors the needs of conservative religious form and content.

Home Schooling as Gendered Labor

Even with the strategic use of state resources to assist their efforts, home schooling takes hard work. But to go further we need to ask an important question: *Who* does the labor? Much of this labor is hidden from view. Finding and organizing materials, teaching, charting progress, establishing and maintaining a "proper" environment, the emotional labor of caring for as well as instructing children—and the list goes on—all of this requires considerable effort. Most of this effort is done by *women* (Stevens, 2001, p. 15).

Because home schooling is largely women's work, it combines an extraordinary amount of physical, cultural, and emotional labor. It constitutes an intensification of women's work in the home because it is added on to the already extensive responsibilities that women have within the home, and especially within conservative religious homes with their division of labor in which men may be active, but are seen as "helpers" of their wives who carry the primary responsibility within the domestic sphere. The demands of such intensified labor have consistently led women to engage in quite creative ways of dealing with their lives. New technologies, as labor saving devices, have played key roles in such creative responses (see Schwartz Cowan, 1983; Strasser, 1982).[3]

This labor and the meanings attached to it by women themselves need to be situated into a much longer history and a much larger context. A number of people have argued that many women see rightist religious and social positions and the groups that support them as providing a nonthreatening, familiar framework of discourse and practice that centers directly upon what they perceive to be issues of vital and personal concern: immorality, social disorder, crime, the family, and schools. Yet the feelings of personal connection are not sufficient. Rightist action in both the *public* and the *private* spheres (see Fraser, 1989, regarding how these concepts themselves are fully implicated in the history of gendered realities, differential power, and struggles) empowers them as women. Depending on the context, they are positioned as "respectable, selfless agents of change deemed necessary, or as independent rebels" (Bacchetta & Power, 2002, p. 6).

Historically, right-wing women have consistently exalted the family. It is seen as a privileged site of women's self-realization and power, but one that is threatened by a host of internal and external *others*. It is *the* family that is the pillar of society, the foundation of a society's security, order, and naturalized hierarchy that is given by God (Bacchetta & Power, 2002, p. 8).

Usually, fundamentalist and evangelical women are depicted as essentially dedicated to acting on and furthering the goals of religiously conservative men (Brasher, 1998, p. 3). This is much too simplistic. The message is more complex and compelling—and connected to a very clear understanding of the realities of many women's lives. Women should have not a passive but a very active engagement in their family life and the world that impinges on it. They can and must "shape their husband's actions and alter disruptive family behaviors." The latter tasks are becoming especially important because this is a time when all too many men are abdicating their family responsibilities, often impoverishing women and their dependent children (p. 3). Further, only a strong woman could mediate the pressures and the often intensely competitive norms and values that men brought home with them from the world of work. Capitalism may be "God's economy" (see Apple, 2001), but allowing its norms to dominate the home could be truly destructive. Women, in concert with "responsible" men, could provide the alternative but complementary assemblage of values so necessary to keep the world at bay and to use the family as the foundation for both protecting core religious values and sending forth children armed against the dangers of a secular and profane world.

To conservative religious women, what from the outside may look like a restrictive life guided by patriarchal norms, feels very different on the inside. It provides an identity that is embraced precisely because it improves their ability to direct the course of their lives and empowers them in their relationships with others. Thus, intense religiosity is a source of considerable power for many women (Brasher, 1998, pp. 4–5).

Based on her extensive research on conservative Christian women, Brasher is very clear on this. As she puts it,

> [Although such women] insistently claimed that the proper relationship between a woman and her husband is one of submission, they consistently declared that this submission is done out of obedience to God not men and is supposed to be mutual, a relational norm observed by both spouses rather than a capitulation of one to the other.... Submission increases rather than decreases a woman's power within the marital relationship. (1998, p. 6)

Divine creation has ordained that women and men are different types of beings. While they complement each other, each has distinctly different tasks to perform. Such sacred gender walls are experienced not as barriers, but as providing and legitimating a space for women's action and power. Interfering with such action and power in this sphere is also interfering in God's plan (pp. 12–13).

Echoes of this can be found in other times and in other nations. Thus, an activist within the British Union of Fascists—an anti-Semitic and proto-Nazi group before World War II—looked back on her activity and said that her active membership demonstrated that she had always been "an independent, free thinking individual" (Gottlieb, 2002, p. 40). This vision of independence of what might be called *counterhegemonic thinking* is crucial not just then but now as well. It connects with today's belief among conservative religiously motivated home schoolers that the world and the school have become too PC (politically correct). Bringing conservative evangelical religion back to the core of schooling positions secular schooling as hegemonic. It enables rightist women to interpret their own actions as independent and free thinking—but always in the service of God.

Solving Contradictions

One of the elements that keeps the Christian Right such a vital and growing social movement is the distinctive internal structure of evangelical Protestantism. Evangelicalism combines orthodox Christian beliefs with an intense individualism (Green, 2000, p. 2).

This is a key to understanding the ways in which what looks like never-ending and intensified domestic labor from the outside is interpreted in very different ways from the point of view of conservative religious women who willingly take on the labor of home schooling and add it to their already considerable responsibilities in the domestic sphere. Such conservative ideological forms do see women as subservient to men and as having the primary responsibility of building and defending a vibrant godly "fortress-home" as part of "God's plan" (Apple, 2001). But it would be wrong to see women in rightist religious or ideological movements as only being called upon to submit to authority per se. Such obedience is also grounded in a call to act on their duty as women (Enders, 2002, p. 89). This is what might best be seen as *activist selflessness*, in which the supposedly submerged self reemerges in the activist role of defender of one's home, family, children, and God's plan. Lives are made meaningful and satisfying—and identities supported—in the now reconstituted private and public sphere in this way.

There is an extremely long history in the United States and other nations of connecting religious activism and domesticity.[4] This has consistently led to mobilizations that cut across political lines that bridge the public and private spheres. In Koven and Michel's words:

> Essential to this mobilization was the rise of domestic ideologies stressing women's differences from men, humanitarian concerns for the conditions of child life and labor, and the emergence of activist interpretations of the gospel ... [including] evangelicalism, Christian socialism, social Catholicism, and the social gospel. Women's moral vision, compassion, and capacity to nurture came increasingly to be linked to motherliness. (1993, p. 10)

Often guided by a sense of moral superiority, when coupled with a strong element of political commitment, this became a powerful force. Maternalism could be both progressive and retrogressive, often at the same time. While it is the conservative elements of this ideological construction that have come to the fore today, forms of maternalism also had a major impact on many of the progressive programs and legislation that currently exist (see, e.g., Kessler-Harris, 2001; Koven & Michel, 1993; Ladd-Taylor, 1994).

The restorative powers of domesticity and "female spirituality" could be combined with a strong commitment both to democratic principles and education and opportunities for women (Koven & Michel, 1993, p. 17). The key was and is how democracy—a sliding signifier—is *defined*.

Protecting and educating one's children, caring for the intimate and increasingly fragile bonds of community and family life, worries about personal safety, and all of this in an exploitative and often disrespectful society—these themes are not only the province of the right and should not be only the province of women. But we have to ask how identifiable people are mobilized around and by these themes, and by whom.

The use of a kind of maternalist discourse and a focus on women's role as mother and as someone whose primary responsibility is in the home and the domestic sphere does not necessarily prevent women from exercising power in the public sphere. In fact, it can serve as a powerful justification for such action and actually *reconstitutes* the public sphere. Educating one's children at home so that they are given armor to equip them to transform their and others' lives outside the home, establishes the home as a perfect model for religiously motivated ethical conduct for all sets of social institutions (see Apple, 2001). This tradition, what has been called *social housekeeping*, can then claim responsibility for non-familial social spaces and can extend the idealized mothering role of women well beyond the home. In Marijke du Toit's words, it was and can still be used to forge "a new, more inclusive definition of the political" (2002, p. 67).

Such maternalism historically enabled women to argue for a measure of direct power in the redefined public arena. One could extol the virtues of domesticity and expand what counts as a home at the same time. Thus, the state and many institutions in the public sphere were "a household where women should exercise their ... superior skills to create [both] order [and a better society]" (du Toit, 2002, p. 67).[5]

All of this helps us make sense of why many of the most visible home school advocates devote a good deal of their attention to "making sense of the social category of motherhood." As a key part of "a larger script of idealized family relations, motherhood is a lead role in God's plan" for authoritarian populist religious conservatives (Stevens, 2001, p. 76). Again in Stevens's words, "One of the things that home schooling offers, then, is a renovated domesticity—a full-time motherhood made richer by the tasks of teaching, and [by] some of the status that goes along with those tasks" (p. 83).

Yet it is not only the work internal to the home that is important here. Home schooling is outward looking as well in terms of women's tasks. In many instances, home schooling is a collective project. It requires organizational skills to coordinate connections and cooperative activities (support groups, field trips, play groups, time off from the responsibilities that mothers have, etc.) and to keep the movement itself vibrant at local and regional levels. Here too, women do the largest amount of the work. This has led to other opportunities for women as advocates and entrepreneurs. Thus, the development and marketing of some of the most popular curriculum packages, management guides, self-help and devotional materials, and so on has been done by women. Indeed, the materials reflect the fact that home schooling is women's work, with a considerable number of the pictures in the texts and promotional material showing mothers and children together

(Stevens, 2001, pp. 83–96). A considerable number of the national advocates for evangelically based home schooling are activist women as well.

Marketing God

Advocacy is one thing—being able to put the advocated policy into practice is quite another. In order to actually *do* home schooling a large array of plans, materials, advice, and even solace must be made available. "Godly schooling" creates a market. Even with the burgeoning market for all kinds of home schooling, it is clear that conservative evangelicals and fundamentalists have the most to choose from in terms of educational and religious (the separation is often fictional) curricula, lessons, books, and inspirational material (Stevens, 2001, p. 54). Such materials not only augment the lessons that home schooling parents develop, but increasingly they become *the* lessons in mathematics, literacy, science, social studies, and all of the other subjects that are taught. This kind of material also usually includes homework assignments and tests as well as all of the actual instructional material. Thus, a complete package can be assembled or purchased whole in a way that enables committed parents to create an entire universe of educational experiences that is both rigorously sequenced and tightly controlled—and prevents unwanted "pollution" from the outside world.

The A Beka Book program provides a clear example. An offshoot of Pensacola Christian College, it markets material for nursery school up to the end of secondary school. It offers the home schooler a curriculum in which Christian teachings are woven into every aspect of knowledge. Little is left to chance. Preschool children learn through the use of Bible story flannelgraphs. At the age of five, they begin a complete Bible curriculum and as they move up in age their texts include *Bible Doctrines for Today* and *Managing Your Life Under God.* The elementary level science textbooks, *God's World,* are based on an inerrantist approach to the Bible and a literalist reading of Genesis and creation—one in which evolution is dismissed. The difference between right and wrong is seen as answerable only through reference to biblical teachings (Stevens, 2001, p. 55).

Easily ordered on the Web, similar kinds of material are made available by other religiously based publishers—Bob Jones University Press, Christian Liberty Academy, Alpha Omega Publications, KONOS, the Weaver Curriculum Series, and a number of others. While there are pedagogic differences among these sets of materials, all of them are deeply committed to integrating biblical messages, values, and training throughout the entire curriculum. Most not only reproduce the particular biblically based worldviews of the parents, but also create an educational environment that relies on a particular vision of "appropriate" schooling, one that is organized around highly sequenced formal lessons that have an expressly moral aim. Technological resources such as videos are marketed that both provide the home schooler with a model of how education should be done and the resources for actually carrying it out (Stevens, 2001, p. 56).

The *organizational form* that is produced here is very important. As I have argued elsewhere (Apple, 2001), because much of the religiously conservative home schooling movement has a sense of purity and danger in which all elements of the world have a set place, such an organization of both knowledge and pedagogy embodies the ideological structure underlying the evangelical universe. As Bernstein (1977) reminds us, it is often in the form of the curriculum that the social cement that organizes our consciousness at its most basic level is reproduced.

While the form of the curriculum is clearly a collection code in key ways (Bernstein, 1977), the content is partly integrated. Project methods are also used in many conservative home schoolers' practices. For example, at the same time as parents may use the detailed sequential curriculum purchased from the Weaver Curriculum Series because it enables lessons to be related as well to a sequential reading of the Bible, these same parents also approve of the ways in which such curricular material includes creative ideas for student projects. Thus, one parent had her children engage in brick-making as part of the study of the Tower of Babel. She also used the genealogies of the Old Testament to stimulate her children's study of their family tree (Stevens, 2001, p. 58).

This kind of integration is found in nearly all of the widely used material. Stevens clearly describes a common situation.

> By creative elaboration, curriculum authors spin out a wide range of lessons from biblical passages. Every word and phrase can be a metaphor for a revered character trait, a starting point for a science lesson. In this instance the first line of the first verse of the Sermon on the Mount, "Seeing the crowds, he went up the mountain," commences lessons on sight, light, and the biological structure of the eye, as well as character studies on the virtues of alertness. [The parent] noted that her children's "entire curriculum will be Matthew 5, 6, and 7. Through high school." Detailed lesson plans provide project descriptions and learning guides for children of various ages, so that the whole family can do the same lesson at once. "Our part in this," [the parent] explained, "is to read through the booklet." (2001, pp. 58–59)

This sense of the importance of structured educational experiences that are infused with strong moral messages is not surprising given the view of a secular world filled with possible sins, temptations, and dangers. The emphasis then on equipping children with an armor of strong belief supports a pedagogical belief that *training* is a crucial pedagogic act. While children's interests have to be considered, these are less important than preparing children for living in a world where God's word rules. This commitment to giving an armor of "right beliefs" "nourishes demands for school material" (Stevens, 2001, p. 60). A market for curriculum materials, workbooks, lesson plans, rewards for doing fine work such as merit badges, videotapes and CDs, and so many other things that make home schooling seem more doable is created not only out of a strategy of aggressive marketing and of using the Internet as a major mechanism for such marketing; but it is also created and stimulated because of the ideological and emotional elements that underpin the structures of feeling that help organize the conservative evangelical home schooler's world (see Apple, 2001).

Technology and the Realities of Daily Life

Of course, parents are not puppets. While the parent may purchase or download material that is highly structured and inflexible, by the very nature of home schooling, parents are constantly faced with the realities of their children's lives, their boredom, their changing interests. Here, chat rooms and Internet resources become even more important. Advice manuals, prayers, suggestions for how one should deal with recalcitrant children, and biblically motivated inspirational messages about how important the hard work of parenting is and how one can develop the patience to keep doing it—all of this provides ways of dealing with the immense amount of educational and especially *emotional* labor that home schooling requires.

The technology enables women who may be rather isolated in the home due to the intense responsibilities of home schooling to have virtual but still intimate emotional connections. It also requires skill—something that ratifies the vision of self that often accompanies home schooling parents. We don't need "experts"; with hard work and creative searching we can engage in a serious and disciplined education by ourselves. Thus, the technology provides for solace, acknowledging and praying for each other's psychic wounds and tensions—and at the same time enhances one's identity as someone who is intellectually worthy, who can wisely choose appropriate knowledge and values. What, hence, may seem like a form of anti-intellectualism is in many ways exactly the opposite. Its rejection of the secular expertise of the school and the state is instead based on a vision of knowledgeable parents—especially mothers who have a kind of knowledge taken from the ultimate source, God.

Thus, one of the most popular of the evangelically oriented websites that markets products for home schoolers sells such things as "The Go-to-the-Ant Chart." The wall chart contains pictures of common situations and biblical passages that speak to them. A list of the topics that the chart covers speaks to the realities that home schooling parents often face—serving God, gratefulness, honesty, perseverance, obedience, thoroughness, responsibility, initiative, consideration, and redeeming time. In language that not only home schooling parents will understand, it says:

This chart arms parents with Scripture for working with the easily distracted or "less than diligent" child. The chart covers every area of laziness we could think of, plus a Bible verse for each problem for easy reference when they are driving you crazy! Take your child to the chart, identify his slothful action or attitude, read what God says about it, and pray for his strength to obey. (http://doorposts.net/g_to_and.htm)

It is important to note that the Internet is not only an effective tool for marketing and for movement building, and as I have just noted, for dealing with the emotional and intellectual labor home schooling requires. Just as importantly, it has become an extremely powerful tool for advocacy work and lobbying. Thus, the Home School Legal Defense Association has been at the forefront of not only home schooling, but in active and aggressive efforts to coordinate lobbyists inside and outside the Washington Beltway. The HSLDA's Congressional Action Program has proven how powerful and responsive a tool such as the Internet can be in mobilizing for and against congressional and state laws and in defending the interests of its conservative positions (Stevens, 2001, pp. 178–179).[6] However, once again, such mobilizing about home schooling needs to be situated within its larger context if we are not to miss some crucial connections between conservative-oriented home schooling and the more extensive authoritarian movement of which it is a key part. In this regard, it is worthwhile remembering what I noted earlier—that one of the most visible leaders of the home school movement nationally is Michael Farris. Farris plays a crucial leadership role in the HSLDA (Green, Rozell, & Wilcox, 2000) and is the president of Patrick Henry College. Patrick Henry is a college largely for religiously conservative home schooled students and it has one academic major—*government*. The principles that animate its educational activities are quite clear in the following description:

> The Vision of Patrick Henry College is to aid in the transformation of American society by training Christian students to serve God and mankind with a passion for righteousness, justice and mercy, through careers of public service and cultural influence.

> The Distinctives of Patrick Henry College include practical apprenticeship methodology; a deliberate outreach to home schooled students; financial independence; a general education core based on the classical liberal arts; a dedication to mentoring and disciplining Christian students; and a community life that promotes virtue, leadership, and strong, lifelong commitments to God, family and society.

> The Mission of the Department of Government is to promote practical application of biblical principles and the original intent of the founding documents of the American republic, while preparing students for lives

of public service, advocacy and citizen leadership. (http://www.phc.edu/about/FundamentalStatements.asp)

These aims are both laudable and worrisome. Create an environment where students learn to play active roles in reconstructing both their own lives and the larger society, but make certain that the society they wish to build is based wholly on principles that are not open to social criticism by nonbelievers. Only those anointed by their particular version of God and only a society built upon the vision held by the anointed are legitimate. All else is sinful.

Thus, for all its creative uses of technology, its understanding of "market needs" and how to fill them, its personal sacrifices, the immense labor of the (mostly) women who are engaged in the work of actually doing it, and its rapid growth fostered by good press and creative mobilizing strategies, a good deal of home schooling speaks the language of authoritarian populism. There's an inside and an outside, and for many authoritarian populists, the only way to protect the inside is to change the outside so that it mirrors the religious impulses and commitments of the inside. Doing this is hard political, educational, and emotional work, and new technologies clearly are playing a growing role in such personal and social labor.

Conclusion

In this chapter, I have examined a number of the complexities involved in the cultural and political efforts within a rapidly growing movement that has claimed subaltern status. This has involved critically analyzing a set of technological resources—the Internet—and situating it within the social context of its use within a specific community and by specific people within that community. In so doing, I have suggested that in order to understand the social meaning and uses of these technologies, we need to examine the social movement that provides the context for their use and the identities that are being constructed within that social movement. I have also argued that we need to critically analyze the kind of labor that is required in home schooling, *who* is engaged in such labor, and how such labor is interpreted by the actors who perform it. Only in this way can we understand the lived problems such technologies actually solve. I have pointed to how the space for production of such "solutions" is increasingly occupied by ideological and/or commercial interests that have responded to and enlarged a market to fill the needs of religiously conservative home schoolers.

A good deal of my focus has been on the work of mothers—of "Godly women"—who have actively created new identities for themselves (and their children and husbands)[7] and have found in new technologies solutions to a huge array of difficult personal and political problems in their daily lives. Such Godly women are not that much different from any of us, but they are "dedicated to securing for themselves and their families a thoroughly religious and conservative life" (Brasher, 1998, p. 29). And they do this with uncommon sacrifice and creativity.

The picture I have presented is complicated; but then so too is reality. One of the dynamics we are seeing is social disintegration, that is, the loss of legitimacy of a dominant institution that supposedly bound us together—the common school. Yet, and very importantly, what we are also witnessing is the use of the Internet not to detraditionalize society, but in the cases I have examined here, to *retraditionalize* parts of it. However, to call this phenomenon simply retraditionalization is to miss the ways in which such technologies are also embedded not only in traditional values and structures of feeling. They are also participating in a more "modern" project, one in which self-actualized individualism intersects with the history of social maternalism, which itself intersects with the reconstitution of masculinities as well.

Such maternalism needs to be seen as both positive and negative, and not only in its partial revivification of elements of patriarchal relations —although obviously this set of issues must not be ignored in any way. We need to respect the labor and the significant sacrifices of home schooling mothers and the fathers as well (the question of altered masculinities in home schooling families is an important topic that needs to be focused upon in a way that complements what I have done here). This sensitivity to the complexities and contradictions that are so deeply involved in what these religiously motivated parents are attempting is perhaps best seen in the words of Jean Hardisty when she reflects on populist rightist movements in general.

> I continue to believe that, within that movement, there are people who are decent and capable of great caring, who are creating community and finding coping strategies that are enabling them to lead functional lives in a cruel and uncaring late capitalist environment. (1999, pp. 2–3)

However, recognizing such caring, labor, and sacrifice—and the creative uses of technologies that accompany them—should not make us lose sight of what this labor and these sacrifices also produce. Godly technologies, godly schooling, and godly identities can be personally satisfying and make life personally meaningful in a world in which traditions are either destroyed or commodified, but at what cost to those who don't share the ideological vision that seems so certain in the minds of those who produce it?

Endnotes

1. I would like to thank Harry Brighouse, Kurt Squire, and the members of the Friday Seminar for their comments on this chapter. An earlier draft was presented at the Wisconsin/London/Melbourne Joint Seminar on New Technologies, Madison, Wisconsin, October 6, 2003.
2. The right has been in the forefront of the use of the Internet for creating linkages among existing members on key issues of concern. In understanding that youth are among the heaviest users of the Internet, conservative organizations have creatively employed such

technology to build sophisticated websites whose form and content appeal to youth (Hardisty, 1999, p. 46).

3. Actually, many of these technologies in fact were *not* labor saving ultimately. See Schwarz Cowan (1983) and Strasser (1982).

4. Much of this literature, however, draws upon the experiences of *white* women. The meaning of domesticity and the discourses of motherhood among black women cannot be understood from the standpoint of dominant groups. For more on this crucial point, see Boris (1993). Since the vast majority of right-wing home schoolers are indeed white, I have drawn upon a literature that is based on their experiences.

5. I would like to thank Rima D. Apple for her helpful comments on this section.

6. One of the most powerful figures in HSLDA is Michael Farris. He acts as both a public spokesperson for conservative home schoolers and as a legal advocate in court cases around the country. Farris has a long history of rightist activism. He ran for lieutenant governor of Virginia in 1993 on a strikingly conservative platform. Interestingly enough, he did not receive the endorsement of a number of other conservative Christian groups and national figures who believed that his public positions might alienate swing voters and actually harm the rightist cause. See Rozell and Wilcox (1996).

7. I am not assuming the normative heterosexual family here. There is no literature on gay and lesbian home schoolers. Given the ideological position that the vast majority of conservative evangelicals take on the question of sexuality, I am simply reflecting their own assumptions.

References

Apple, M. W. (2001). *Educating the "right" way*. New York: Routledge.

Apple, M. W., et al. (2003). *The state and the politics of knowledge*. New York: Routledge.

Amenta, E., & Young, M. P. (1999). Making an impact: Conceptual and methodological implications of the collective goods criterion. In M. Guigni, D. McAdam, and C. Tilly (Eds.), *How social movements matter* (pp. 22–41). Minneapolis: University of Minnesota Press.

Bacchetta, P., & Power, M. (2002). Introduction. In P. Baccetta & M. Power (Eds.), *Right-wing women* (pp. 1–15). New York: Routledge.

Bernstein, B. (1977). *Class, codes, and control* (Vol. 3, 2nd Ed.). London: Routledge & Kegan Paul.

Binder, A. (2002). *Contentious curricula*. Princeton: Princeton University Press.

Boris, E. (1993). The power of motherhood: Black and white activist women redefine the "political." In S. Koven & S. Michel (Eds.), *Mothers of a new world* (pp. 213–245). New York: Routledge.

Brasher, B. (1998). *Godly women*. New Brunswick, NJ: Rutgers University Press.

Bromley, H., & Apple, M. W. (Eds.). (1998). *Education/technology/power*. Albany: State University of New York Press.

Castells, M. (1996). *The rise of network society* (Vol. 1). New York: Oxford University Press.

Connell, R. W. (1995). *Masculinities*. Cambridge, MA: Polity Press.

Cuban, L. (2001). *Oversold and underused*. Cambridge, MA: Harvard University Press.

du Toit, M. (2002). Framing volksmoeders. In P. Bacchetta & M. Power (Eds.), *Right-wing women* (pp. 57–70). New York: Routledge.

Enders, V. (2002). And we ate up the world. In P. Bacchetta & M Power (Eds.), *Right-wing women* (pp. 85–98). New York: Routledge.

Fraser, N. (1989). *Unruly practices: Power, discourse, and gender in contemporary social theory*. Minneapolis: University of Minnesota Press.

Giugni, M. (1999). How social movements matter: Past research, present problems, and future developments. In M. Giugni, D. McAdam, & C. Tilly (Eds.), *How social movements matter* (pp. xiii–xxxiii). Minneapolis: University of Minnesota Press.

Godwin, M. (2003). *Cyber rights*. Cambridge, MA: MIT Press.

Gottlieb, J. (2002). Female "fanatics." In P. Bacchetta & M. Power (Eds.), *Right-wing women* (pp. 29–41). New York: Routledge.

Green, J. (2000). The Christian right and 1998 elections. In J. Green, M. Rozell, & C. Wilcox (Eds.), *Prayers in the precincts* (pp. 1–19). Washington, DC: Georgetown University Press.

Green, J., Rozell, M., & Wilcox, C. (2000). *Prayers in the precincts*. Washington, DC: Georgetown University Press.

Hakken, D. (1999). *Cyborgs@Cyberspace*. New York: Routledge.

Hardisty, J. (1999). *Mobilizing resentment*. Boston: Beacon Press.

Huerta, L. (2000). Losing public accountability: A home schooling charter. In B. Fuller (Ed.), *Inside charter schools* (pp. 177–202). Cambridge, MA: Harvard University Press.

Jordan, T. (1999). *Cyberpower.* New York: Routledge.

Kessler-Harris, A. (2001). *In pursuit of equity.* New York: Oxford University Press.

Koven, S., & Michel, S. (Eds.). (1993). *Mothers of a new world: Maternalist politics and the origins of the welfare state.* New York: Routledge.

Ladd-Taylor, M. (1994) *Mother-work.* Urbana: University of Illinois Press.

McAdam, D. (1999). The biographical impact of activism. In M. Giugni, D. McAdam, & C. Tilly (Eds.), *How social movements matter* (pp. 119–146). Minneapolis: University of Minnesota Press.

Meyer, D. S. (1999). How the Cold War was really won: The effects of the antinuclear movements of the 1980s. In M. Giugni, D. McAdam, & C. Tilly (Eds.), *How social movements matter* (pp. 182–203). Minneapolis: University of Minnesota Press.

Moore, K. (1999). Political protest and institutional change. In M. Giugni, D. McAdam, & C. Tilly (Eds.), *How social movements matter* (pp. 97–115). Minneapolis: University of Minnesota Press.

Rozell, M., & Wilcox, C. (1996). *Second coming.* Baltimore, MD: Johns Hopkins University Press.

Schwartz Cowan, R. (1983). *More work for mother.* New York: Basic Books.

Slevin, J. (2000). *The internet and society.* Cambridge, MA: Polity Press.

Smith, C. (1998). *American evangelicalism.* Chicago, IL: University of Chicago Press.

Stevens, M. (2001). *Kingdom of children.* Princeton, NJ: Princeton University Press.

Strasser, S. (1982). *Never done.* New York: Pantheon.

Wilcox, C., & Rozell, M. (2000). Conclusion: The Christian right in campaign '98. In J. Green, M. Rozell, & C. Wilcox (Eds.), *Prayers in the precincts* (pp. 287–297). Washington, DC: Georgetown University Press.

3

Can the Subaltern Act?

African American Involvement in Educational Voucher Plans

THOMAS C. PEDRONI

> If you're drowning and a hand is extended to you, you don't ask if the hand is attached to a Democrat or a Republican.... From the African American position—at the bottom, looking up—there's not much difference between the Democrats and the Republicans anyway. Whoever is sincere about working with us, our door is open.
>
> Wisconsin State Representative Polly Williams, the "mother of school choice" in Milwaukee (in Carl, 1995, p. 259)

The white educational left is missing something essential in its inattention to considerable support among marginalized communities for market-based educational reforms. My interest in more fully understanding and theorizing African American advocacy for vouchers in Milwaukee, the subject of this chapter, is an outgrowth of this concern. While critical educational researchers have demonstrated the particularly negative impact of educational marketization on those already disenfranchised (e.g., Lauder & Hughes, 1999; Whitty, Power, & Halpin, 1998), not enough attention has been paid to the crucial role the dispossessed have actually played in building these otherwise conservative reforms. Understanding this role as a manifestation of situated and subaltern agency within a moment of postwelfarism[1]—and not as naïve submission —will be critical to a larger project of *progressive modernization* of the increasingly fragmented relationships among those blocs of social actors in the American social formation most likely to protect previous socially democratic victories from further erosion.

Arguments by critical educational theorists and researchers Michael Apple and Anita Oliver concerning the role of identity formation in conservative movement-making have helped my intuitions about voucher supporters in Milwaukee take more concrete form. Reading their work, I began to consider how identity formation also played a significant role in the Milwaukee voucher context, but not in quite the ways that their analysis of a small-town textbook controversy had uncovered (Apple, 1996; Apple & Oliver, 2003). Although the conceptual tools they developed have become the foundation of my ability to imagine a more compelling theorization of the dynamics I have perceived in Milwaukee, significant conceptual, not to mention empirical, work remains to be done.

In this chapter I will renovate elements of Apple and Oliver's argument concerning identity formation in conservative modernization, making them more resonant with dynamics around African American support for vouchers in Milwaukee. If subalternly negotiated alliances in Milwaukee are a harbinger of a direction that conservative modernization might increasingly take, this renovation should assist critical educators, along with other critical cultural workers and social actors, in better understanding and contesting postwelfarism.

I begin with an assessment of the utility and limitations of Apple and Oliver's theory of rightist political formation for explaining the mobilization among working-class and poor African Americans for "parental choice" and vouchers in Milwaukee, one of the centers of voucher use in the United States. As I engage in this task, I will identify and problematize conceptual binaries embedded in this theory that do not adequately account for significant dynamics within market-based educational reform in Milwaukee (and presumably elsewhere). Given this problematization, I then retheorize the pro-voucher coalition of African American political representatives, community leaders, and poor and working-class families as representative of a *third force* in conservative formation, and assess the pivotal role played by such groups in conditional alliances enabling the success of other rightist projects in education and beyond. Employing the concepts of subaltern agency and identity formation in relation to the discursive constructions of African American voucher supporters manifested in interviews, I then argue that the alliances negotiated in such mobilizations are much more fleeting and ephemeral than the concept of "hegemonic alliance," standing in isolation, might imply. Significantly, the retheorization that this analysis suggests—that conservative modernization at least initially relies on subaltern negotiations—leaves the door more open than white critical educators might have thought for rearticulating marginalized families' educational concerns to ultimately more effective, meaningful, and democratic educational reform projects.

I turn now to a discussion of the theory of conservative movement formation proposed by Apple and Oliver.

Political, State, and Subject Formation

In their groundbreaking essay "Becoming Right," Apple and Oliver examine a controversy in a semirural western community over the local school district's adoption of a new and, according to some parents, strange textbook series.

Their purpose is to better understand the ways in which rightist educational movements are formed at the everyday, local level (Apple, 1996; Apple & Oliver, 2003). What they find significantly disrupts previous analyses of how the educational right grows, which "too often assume a unitary ideological movement, seeing it as a relatively uncontradictory group rather than a complex assemblage of different tendencies many of which are in a tense and unstable relationship to each other" (Apple, 1996, pp. 44–45). For Apple and Oliver, the right is not simply an already existing "massive structuring force that is able to work its way into daily life and into our discourses in well-planned ways" (Apple, 1996, p. 44). Rather, the right grows through a complex series of "accidents" and interactions between individuals' "elements of good sense" and the intransigence of a bureaucratic state (Apple, 1996; Apple & Oliver, 2003).

In documenting and analyzing how vaguely socially conservative but largely nonpoliticized concerns over a new textbook series led to the growth of the right, Apple and Oliver draw upon Apple's earlier theorization of the process of conservative modernization. At the core of this process, Apple (1996) has identified four powerful groups that together constitute what he calls a hegemonic alliance within the social order of the United States: neoliberals, neoconservatives, authoritarian populists, and a fraction of the new middle class (p. 7). Stated most simply, neoliberals are those social actors who essentially regard unregulated markets as a panacea for all social and economic ills. They therefore advocate the marketization or even privatization of all public sector services as a palliative for perceived state inefficiency and social inequity. Neoconservatives, on the other hand, call for the recentralization of knowledge and values embedded in the "Western" cultural tradition as an antidote to the social balkanization, moral deterioration, and economic decline they perceive in American society. Authoritarian populists—the third group—demand and assert forms of localized control, which they believe will insulate their families from the sinister forces and secular humanism that increasingly pervade public schools. Finally, members of the managerial and professional middle classes, while often not overtly aligning themselves with any of these tendencies, supply the technical expertise and professional knowledge in matters of efficiency, measurement, and management upon which rightist social and educational reforms depend (Apple, 2001).

Taken together, these groups are hegemonic in that they are able to sustain leadership and advance a particular agenda largely through winning consent for their social vision. Groups within the hegemonic alliance accomplish this in two ways—by compromising with each other over what the elements of that vision are to be, and by (re)shaping the terrain of common sense within the larger culture so that it increasingly resonates with their cultural messages and interpretations (Apple, 1996, p. 15).

Because it is formed and sutured through compromise, the social vision of this hegemonic alliance is never unitary—rather it exists always in a somewhat fragile tension, fraught with contradictions that constantly threaten to undo its continued success (Apple, 1996, p. 15). As the rightist alliance sutures over its internal contradictions and infuses the everyday discourses of American public life with its sense-making constructions, it also, at least potentially, grows.

For Apple, this hegemonic bloc is dynamic (that is, always in formation) in three important ways. First, it is dynamic temporally, in that it can and must respond to changing historical conditions, shifting alliances, the introduction of new technologies, the birth of new social movements, and larger economic trends. Second and third, this conservative modernization is dynamic spatially, discursively speaking, in both a horizontal and vertical fashion. Horizontal dynamism is present in the suturing that takes place as different dominant groups gather together in tense unity under a single "ideological umbrella" (Apple, 1996, p. 15); vertical dynamism is present as the discourses of these dominant groups

> act in creative ways to disarticulate prior connections and rearticulate groups of [largely ideologically unformed] people into this larger ideological movement by connecting to the real hopes, fears, and conditions of people's daily lives and by providing seemingly "sensible" explanations for the current troubles people are having. (p. 45)

In short, this is a process of horizontal *suturing* and vertical *articulation*.

The politically formative process of disarticulation and rearticulation does not occur, however, in a seamless manner directly governed by the dominant groups' political will. Instead, as Apple and Oliver demonstrate in their study of conservative formation in the textbook controversy mentioned earlier, "ordinary people" become articulated to larger conservative social movements through a complex series of "accidents" and interactions with the state (Apple, 1996, p. 45).

For Apple and Oliver, it is not just the hegemonic alliance and the subjectivities of those who might be articulated into it that are always in flux—the state, too, is dynamic in an analogous manner; the state "grows" in response to its interactions with assemblages of social movements that constantly seek to reshape it to their vision. Although this growth occurs through a variety of potential responses (e.g., by adopting, mediating, and/or resisting the demands of social movements), families in Apple and Oliver's study who were concerned about what they perceived as culturally unfamiliar and disturbing materials in the textbook controversy primarily encountered a defensively postured state resisting further challenges by what it impatiently concluded were the organized forces of right-wing censorship.

> Nearly every [concerned] parent ... stated that their original introduction
> to the textbooks began when their child came home and was made upset
> by a particular selection in the texts.... [Parents] were more than a little
> surprised to read stories in their children's books that seemed inappro-
> priate, and were even more surprised and dismayed by what they felt
> was the board's and the administration's "heavy handed" response.
> (Apple, 1996, p. 58)

The state, as enshrined in the bureaucratic offices of the local school district,
responded to the concerns of ideologically relatively unformed[2] and heterogeneous groups of parents by making available to them only two subject positions through which they might be seen, heard, and understood: that of the
responsible parent who supported the "professional decision making" of
school district officials and teachers regarding curriculum, and that of the
irresponsible right-wing censor. Forced into the latter subject position as a
result of their unmet and persistent concerns, many politically unformed
parents became quite ideologically formed as they turned to right-wing
national organizations for help in overcoming the intransigence of the school
bureaucracy. In the process of this "accidental" and highly mediated subject
formation, in which the agency of concerned parents became articulated to
the agency of the broader right, the right grew (Apple, 1996, p. 64).

Possibilities and Limitations: The Battle over "Parental Choice" in Milwaukee

In their study of conservative formation within a small-town textbook controversy, Apple and Oliver have clearly disrupted received and unhelpful notions
of a unitary right growing seamlessly, in isolation, and through strict inten-
tionality. In many ways reminiscent of Apple's earlier interventions concerning
reproduction in schools (Apple, 1982), the researchers have provided us with a
rich account of the complex, mediated, and contradictory ways in which the
hegemonic alliance actually grows through articulations with the real hopes,
fears, and good sense of ordinary people rebuked by the state.

In this section I explore the ways in which this approach to conservative
formation both enables and limits our understanding of another moment in
which processes of conservative modernization have significantly altered public policy—the construction of the voucher alliance and the resulting voucher
program in Milwaukee. After identifying and analyzing some of the possible
limitations of Apple's framework, I will propose some substantive alternatives.

Jim Carl (1996), in an article entitled "Unusual Allies: Elite and Grass-roots
Origins of Parental Choice in Milwaukee," adopts a theoretical framework for
understanding events in Milwaukee that resonates with Apple and Oliver's
own theoretical constructions. However, as we shall see, some elements of the
history that Carl narrates seem to fit less comfortably within their framework.

Carl begins his analysis of factors leading to the rise of the "parental choice" debate in Milwaukee by describing the emergence nationally of a hegemonic alliance in the early 1980s, which he calls the conservative restoration (a term also used by Apple in earlier works). Within this alliance, in relation to issues of parental choice, Carl depicts the tensely intersecting agendas of two of the dominant groups delimited by Apple—neoliberals and neoconservatives. According to Carl (1996), local neoliberal education reformers, on the one hand, believed that the extension of private markets into the state's education systems would bring improvement in educational attainment as well as profitability. On the other hand, local neoconservative educational reformers privileged private schools for their supposed traditional academic curriculum, religious training, and strict discipline (p. 268). Although Apple is much less cursory in describing the complexity of these positions and interactions (Apple, 1996, pp. 27–31), the parallels are quite clear and, as will be shown below, useful for understanding certain dynamics within the Milwaukee context.

However, Carl also acknowledges that "not all proponents of vouchers in Milwaukee can be described as agents of the conservative restoration" (1996, p. 268). Rather, he outlines a "conditional alliance" between state-level neoliberal reformers and Milwaukee-based supporters of a handful of independent community schools. According to Carl:

> Five factors generated this conditional alliance: dissatisfaction among many black Milwaukeeans with a school system that failed to deliver acceptable educational outcomes for disproportionately high numbers of black students; the existence of community schools whose multicultural supporters had sought public funding for two decades; the growth of black political representation in Milwaukee during an era when government policies tilted rightward, as personified by state representative Polly Williams; the efforts of Governor Tommy Thompson's administration to craft neoliberal and neoconservative social policy; and the rise of Milwaukee's Bradley Foundation as the nation's premier conservative grantmaker. (p. 268)

In analyzing the conditional alliance that Carl describes, Apple and Oliver's model seems to offer two possible inroads for making sense of African Americans in Milwaukee who have supported publicly financed vouchers as a means of enrolling their children in Milwaukee's independent community schools. The first possibility—one that Apple would presumably not endorse given his discussion of race and class as central dynamics in unequal power relations —is that we see the Milwaukee-based voucher supporters under the leadership of African American state representative Polly Williams as becoming part of an alliance of dominant groups. In such a scenario, we would read Polly Williams's group as having horizontally sutured itself together, through compromises, with neoliberals and neoconservatives, thereby sharing in the (always partial) exercise of hegemonic control over education debates in Milwaukee. The second possibility, again experimenting with Apple and Oliver's framework, is that we see Polly Williams's group as vertically articulated to right-wing movements in the manner of the ideologically relatively unformed "ordinary people" of the textbook controversy, a possibility that Apple would presumably reject given the many decades of educational activism by African American families in Milwaukee.

Although these seem to be the two theoretical spaces conceptually available in Apple and Oliver's framework for interpreting the conditional alliance around vouchers in Milwaukee, in what follows I will show the partial inadequacy of both. In fairness, Apple and Oliver do mention that "rightist policies are often compromises both between the Right *and other groups* and among the various tendencies within the conservative alliance" (italics added; Apple, 1996, p. 45). However, if the compromises "between the Right and other groups" are to be understood as a conceptual category outside the two possibilities I have mentioned, Apple and Oliver have not yet adequately described or theorized this possibility.

Before analyzing the ways in which each of the two theoretical possibilities described above partially explains and partially misconstrues the reality of the conditional alliance in Milwaukee, I want to introduce a set of binaries that underlie Apple's conception of rightist formation. Later I will problematize these in hopes of opening up a *third theoretical space* for analyzing the conditional alliance in Milwaukee, and by extension similar alliances in other settings.

At least temporarily, and within the Milwaukee context, despite our contrary intuitions, Polly Williams's pro-voucher faction embodies characteristics that seem to locate it within Apple and Oliver's framework as a dominant member of the alliance. For example, Williams's explicit recognition of the limitations of historical alliances with white liberals (Carl, 1996, p. 274) clearly indicates carefully formed and sophisticated tactical ideology in response to political experience. Her often expressed realism and lack of naiveté regarding both the political climate of the late 1980s and the self-interestedness of neoliberals willing to ally with her is further indication of this; it is also indicative of the suturing nature of her relationship with neoliberals, in which neoliberal language concerning competition and markets became fused with her own vision of community control. As Carl notes, "Unlike her New Right allies, who argued that the social safety net ought to be lowered or dismantled, Williams believed that blacks needed to take control of publicly funded programs and institutions that targeted their communities" (1996, p. 274). In short, Williams had not allowed her vision to be subsumed into that of the right, as in the case of the concerned parents by the end of the textbook controversy; neither she nor her faction "became right" in any way that would preserve the normal stability of that terminology.

While Williams's faction resonates with certain characteristics of membership within an alliance of dominant groups as described by Apple and Oliver (and as depicted in the scenario 1 column in Table 3.1), it falls far short in other respects. It is very difficult to conceive of Williams's faction and its poor and working-class Latino and African American supporters as a dominant group within the political landscape of Milwaukee. The most cursory examination of social and material conditions that frame the everyday lives of low-income African American and Latino families in Milwaukee renders this a conceptual impossibility, as does the long and frustrating experience African American parents and community leaders, including Williams, have had in failing to gain greater responsiveness from the Milwaukee Public Schools (MPS) bureaucracy (Carl, 1995; Fuller 1985).

This marginalization, then, seems to point us away conceptually from locating African American supporters of vouchers in Milwaukee within the alliance of dominant groups (scenario 1 in Table 3.1), and toward scenario two, resonant with the experiences of the ordinary, ideologically relatively unformed parents described by Apple and Oliver in the "Becoming Right" piece. Immediately we are struck by the parallel between the encounter of the concerned parents in the textbook controversy with an unresponsive state bureaucracy, on the one hand, and the experiences of Williams and her followers as they sought redress with MPS, on the other. Williams and her followers were clearly pushed toward rightist social movements because of the perceived intransigence of state actors. Furthermore, within this educational struggle, it is easy for most progressives to identify the "real hopes and fears" of Williams's faction with which we presumably are highly sympathetic. Finally, as mentioned previously, Williams's faction in the conditional alliance rests much more comfortably, relative to power, on the side of the "not-yet-dominant" in Table 3.1.

Nevertheless, as alluded to earlier, aspects of Williams's faction are more than a little incongruous with the "ordinary people" formulation of scenario two. To argue that her group remained ideologically largely unformed or characterized in its ideas by common sense understandings would be to deeply insult the decades of struggle around education in which groups of African Americans in Milwaukee (and elsewhere) have engaged (Carl, 1995; Fuller, 1985; Holt, 2000). Furthermore, the relationship of Williams's faction to the neoliberal groups with which she worked was not simply vertical; again, the sophisticated manner in which Williams was able to negotiate her interests with those of neoliberals demonstrates a significant degree of "horizontal" relationship between the two.

If the conditional alliance described by Carl does not fit conceptually into the two available scenarios, how then should it be theorized? And if this practical example and its theorization apply in other settings, what are the

Table 3.1 The Two Scenarios (or 'Spaces') of Conservative Formation in Apple and Oliver

Category	Scenario	
	1. Part of the alliance of dominant groups	2. Ordinary people who become Right
Example	Neoliberals, neoconservatives, etc.	Parents in textbook controversy
Relationship to power	Horizontal	Vertical
Connection to power	Suturing compromises	"Good sense" articulated to conservative project
Quality of ideology	Formed	Unformed
Nature of ideas	Ideology	Common sense
Relative power	Dominant	Not-yet-dominant
Character of ideas	Elements of good sense which appeal to ordinary people	Real hopes and fears to which progressives are sympathetic
Relative spatial metaphor	Above	Below
Relationship to state	Attempt to affect the direction of the state through an assemblage of social movements	Pushed toward rightist social movements when rebuked by an unresponsive state

implications for our understanding of the right's success in the present moment in other contested spheres?

Toward a *Third Space* in Conservative Formation

In the battle over publicly financed private school vouchers in Milwaukee, as I have shown, Williams's group of African American voucher supporters cannot properly be theorized as either a dominant group sutured within a hegemonic alliance, or as a group of ideologically relatively unformed, ordinary people articulated into the right as a result of the state's unresponsiveness. Despite its theoretical elusiveness, Williams's faction was absolutely central both to the emergence of parental choice programs in Milwaukee, and to the claims to respectability and legitimacy that voucher programs have since attained in national and even global educational debates. Given this, a further theorization of African American supporters of vouchers in Milwaukee is crucial to the project of more fully understanding and contesting the right's continued success in dismantling key vestiges of the American social democratic accord.

As the Milwaukee parental choice case suggests, the hegemonic alliance was not able to impose voucher programs in Milwaukee or elsewhere until the birth of a more fleeting conditional alliance, in which dominant groups were nevertheless the major and exponentially more powerful players. Although Carl does not "unpack" his use of the term conditional alliance as much as we might hope, his usage, especially in relation to the Milwaukee example, seems to imply an alliance that is much more fleeting and ephemeral than a stand-alone hegemonic alliance restored over thirty years, successfully suturing new compromises among its dominant members while articulating ideologically relatively unformed, ordinary people into its ranks (see Apple, 1996, p. 61; and endnote 2 in this chapter).

In theorizing the qualities of the nondominant but ideologically more formed groups that join with dominant ones in order to build successful conditional alliances, a useful approach might be to envision the opposite poles of the qualities of scenarios one and two in Table 3.1 as horizons, with the parent textbook activists as described by Apple and Oliver largely encapsulated within the descriptors in the column of scenario two. Dominant groups, such as neoliberal forces, on the other hand, would largely align with the characteristics in the column of scenario one. Different "third space" groups with which the right formed conditional alliances, such as pro-voucher African American families in Milwaukee, would occupy various points along each of the eight categorical horizons.

In accordance with the sketch presented earlier, African American voucher families in Milwaukee, as an example of a social force implying a third scenario, or third space tendency in conservative formation, should be located along the respective horizons in Table 3.1 as relatively *formed, ideological*, and *suturing* in a *horizontal* manner with dominant groups (all descriptors on the left side of the table). At the same time they remain largely *not-yet-dominant, pushed toward rightist social movements by an unresponsive state*, and constituted by *real hopes and fears to which progressives can be sympathetic* (as encapsulated more within the right side of the table).

Just as we need to realize the heterogeneous qualities of groups that are sutured and articulated to the hegemonic alliance in conditional alliances, we also need to think clearly about the quality of the conservative victories implicit in such alliances. Whereas the first two scenarios of the right's growth—through horizontal suturing and vertical articulations—represent fairly unequivocal victories for the rightist project, the third scenario involving subalternly negotiated alliances presents a more nuanced, ambiguous, and contradictory sense of victory. Is the political success of the Milwaukee Parental Choice Program simply a monolithic loss for those supporting radically democratic reform in education, or is it also a partial victory? More will be said about this in relation to African American tactical mobilizations for vouchers later.

Identity Formation and Subaltern Agency: A Reconceptualization

In order to develop a more nuanced conceptualization of the importance of such third space groups in conservative formation, it will be useful to further sharpen our focus upon the process of what Apple and Oliver (along with other theorists) have called *identity formation* (Apple, 1996; Apple & Oliver, 2003). In the voucher example, identity formation occurs as various factions of the conservative alliance, African American educational activists, and low-income families in Milwaukee suture their interests together within tensely constructed and maintained alliances. In the earlier years of the Milwaukee Parental Choice Program, discourses circulating through the Milwaukee Public Schools system, as well as through the voucher alliance, positioned African American families and offered identities in particular ways. Primary among the subject positions in circulation among teachers, administrators, and other professionals in the Milwaukee Public Schools were those predicated on culturally based, racially based, and/or biologically based deficit models. African American families fleeing public schools and embracing the proposed voucher system frequently cited instances in which public school failure was blamed on the supposed culturally rooted unruly behavior of students of color. Similarly, families complained about the regularity with which their children were pathologized and abandoned to special education programs and "alternative" schools after being marked with disability labels (Corporation for Educational Radio and Television, 1993).

In contrast to this, school marketization efforts in Milwaukee seemed to offer much more dignified subject positions to disenfranchised parents and guardians, perhaps most significantly that of *rational consumer*. Rather than pathologizing "black" cultural forms through racist social scientific normative discourses, market-oriented voucher advocates first positioned parents and guardians as ideal consumers whose sole constraint consisted of artificially limited, market-defined choice. While positioning low-income parents and guardians of color as rational educational consumers empowered to make the best choices for their children dehistoricizes their agency by largely failing to see it as emerging within unequal material and discursive relations of power, neoliberal discourse at the same time allows parents and guardians to be seen, heard, and understood, and perhaps most importantly to act, in ways that are often simply not possible within the everyday life of urban public schools.

An analysis predicated on questions of identity formation allows for the possibility of a microlevel examination of the tactical choices groups of parents and guardians make in negotiating their sets of perceived educational options on a terrain that is not largely of their own choosing. Rather than focusing only on the structural dynamics around educational marketization, which will likely further marginalize low-income urban communities of color (Lauder & Hughes, 1999; Whitty, Power, & Halpin, 1998), I wish to follow Apple and Oliver's lead in taking seriously the everyday dilemmas, consciousness, and agency of voucher families as they attempt to negotiate educational structures, which intentionally and/or functionally, have not been designed with their best interests in mind (Apple, 1996; Apple & Oliver, 2003). Thus, while I am deeply concerned about the likely outcomes of market-oriented educational reforms in Milwaukee and elsewhere, I also want to take utterly seriously a consideration of how conservative educational mobilizations succeed by seeming to speak to marginalized people's very real fears and desires.

It is through understanding this articulation, as a matter of identity formation and subaltern agency, that the process of conservative formation will perhaps most effectively be interrupted and supplanted with a more socially democratic (and ultimately more effective) educational vision.

Thus, seen from "below," from the vantage point of poor and working-class families of color, free market educational discourses seem to open a space to African American parents and guardians in interesting and contradictory ways (and in a manner not always present in the often pathologizing discourses of urban public schools). To approach this question of how offered subject positions are tactically "taken up" and "inhabited" by parents and guardians, we are aided by the work of critical cultural theorist Michel de Certeau. Although de Certeau problematically posits a monolithic sense of "power structure" (after all, in the case under examination it is impossible to comfortably attribute the status of power structure to only either MPS and its allies or the pro-voucher forces), a further engagement with his ideas will prove useful in examining the forms of agency with which African American parents and guardians negotiate their best interests.

In characterizing the mechanisms of power operating within the modern social formation, de Certeau (1984) endorses French theorist Michel Foucault's "microphysics of power," in which one finds "'miniscule' technical procedures acting on and with details, redistributing a discursive space in order to make it the means of a generalized 'discipline' (*surveillance*)" (p. xiv). Nevertheless, de Certeau faults Foucault's analysis for once again "privileg[ing] the productive apparatus" in failing to discover "how an entire society resists being reduced to [discipline]," and particularly "what popular procedures (also 'miniscule' and quotidian) manipulate the mechanisms of discipline and conform to them in order to evade them" (p. xiv).

De Certeau uses the term *strategy* to identify a deployment of power to promote or maintain the interests of a power structure, and *tactics* to refer to the operations by which the less powerful defend or promote their interests. De Certeau's project is to make Foucault's analysis of power more complete, specifically by discerning an "anti-discipline" in the "ways of operating" that "constitute the innumerable practices by means of which users reappropriate the space organized by techniques of sociocultural production" (1984, p. xiv).

In the Milwaukee example, some disenfranchised African American "users" (that is, parents) negotiated the space of two powerful competing alliances —MPS and pro-voucher conservatives—deciding for tactical reasons, that at least for some, and at least in the short term, a conditional alliance with conservative forces represented greater opportunity than previously largely failed alliances with sympathetic forces within Milwaukee Public Schools. De Certeau would argue that parents and guardians are never passive or without agency within this process of alliance building and subject formation. They, to use another one of his terms, "make do" within the identity options that are made available to them, turning subject positions as much as possible to purposes they feel will best serve their educational and social interests (Apple, 1996; De Certeau, 1984).

Such a focus on identity formation as a component of subaltern agency allows us to discern that the articulations and alliances formed around vouchers in Milwaukee are much more transient, ephemeral, opportunistic, and unstable than current literature, including Apple and Oliver's "Becoming Right" piece (Apple, 1996; Apple & Oliver, 2003), implies (Apple & Pedroni, in press). Nevertheless, despite the often transient nature of such conditional alliances, crucial and lasting gains are in fact won by educational conservatives as a result of the reforms that these alliances are able to engender. The effect of voucher mobilizations on legislation and on the global currency of private vouchers is not nearly as ephemeral as the conditional alliances that undergird and enable their initial success.

Therefore, as I argued earlier, a more nuanced theorization of groups such as the grassroots supporters of vouchers in Milwaukee (which cannot be adequately posited either as dominant elements within a hegemonic alliance, or as relatively ideologically unformed and ordinary individuals articulated into the right as a result of the state's intransigence) is crucial to the project of a more full understanding of the right's continued success in dismantling key vestiges of the American social democratic accord.

The current underemphasis on the importance of subaltern agency in hegemonic successes might result from our inclination to theorize elements within conservative modernization as "groups" unproblematically embodying "ideal types," rather than as "discursive tendencies." While some individuals and organizations can be more or less correctly categorized into one of Apple's four elements, there are also (almost) always contradictory tendencies within these groups and individuals. The fact that these tendencies are not embodied as ideal types (e.g., few groups or individuals are monolithically neoliberal or neoconservative), but rather are mediated in contradictory ways, actually expands conceptually the spaces for progressive rearticulation within the formation of these subjectivities.

Since we still want to foreground the ways in which these discourses construct and are constructed by real social actors, thus sidestepping the disposition of some poststructural theorists to see the world as made up only of competing discourses that somehow exist beyond history and human agency (Pedroni, 2005), we may want to refer to Apple's four elements as *embodied tendencies*. To not do so restricts our likelihood of apprehending the importance of subaltern groups in hegemonic successes because subaltern groups, unlike those closely aligned with more powerful embodied tendencies, often act tactically, in a manner suggested by de Certeau, and often not through the deployment of largely internally cohesive discourses that seek to (re)narrate a set of relationships between elements such as the state, the economy, individuals, and the social formation (De Certeau, 1984). The ability to materialize elaborate and cohesive intellectual discursive production is more typically a privilege of the powerful, who as de Certeau suggests, shape and control the terrain upon which ideological and material battles over such things as access to education are fought. On the other hand, subaltern yet politically savvy groups, such as the African American and Latino supporters of private school vouchers in Milwaukee, quite often operate in a tactical relationship to power, sensing the need to act within the spaces that the powerful provide, sometimes in ways that creatively turn the strategic deployments of the powerful back against the powerful, and other times in ways that are ultimately self-defeating for subaltern groups, as powerful groups accomplish their objectives precisely *because of* tactical "poaching" by subaltern groups. This latter scenario, I would argue, is the far more likely long-term outcome of African American support of private school vouchers in Milwaukee.

In fact, my analysis of data gathered in a series of interviews and observations of parents and guardians, as well as other African American voucher advocates in Milwaukee, indicates that this is indeed the case (Pedroni, 2004). African American articulation to neoliberal interventions including voucher programs seems to be largely tactical and opportunistic, rather than strategic and ideologically disciplined. As shall also be evident in my brief analysis of interviews (in the next section) conducted by a conservative videographer supported by the Bradley Foundation, African American voucher advocates rarely offer "intact" neoliberal or neoconservative discourses as underpinning their investment in vouchers. Although their discourses include occasional neoliberal and neoconservative elements, they also contain other elements that run significantly counter to each of these discourses. Because of their tactical relationship to dominant groups, and because of their investment in other mobilizations that are in clear opposition to the project of conservative modernization, African American supporters of vouchers in Milwaukee (and I believe this will manifest itself more broadly) do not typically "become right" in terms of identity formation, despite their tactical investment in neoconservative and neoliberal subject positions (Apple, 1996; Apple & Oliver, 2003). One brief example from Milwaukee will help illustrate this point, though many examples surfaced during my research and have been analyzed elsewhere (see Pedroni, 2004).

Listening to African American Voucher Families in Milwaukee

Laura Fordham (pseudonym) is an African American parent of a child utilizing vouchers provided through the Milwaukee Parental Choice Program to attend a participating nonsectarian private school. The interview from which I draw this brief analysis was recorded in 1998 shortly before the Wisconsin Supreme Court upheld the constitutionality of the Milwaukee

Parental Choice Program, thus lifting an Appeals Court injunction predicated on issues of separation of church and state.[3] The interview, conducted by a Bradley Foundation–supported European-American professional videographer closely affiliated with neoconservative Catholic educational organizations in Milwaukee, took place in Madison, Wisconsin, shortly after a well-publicized speak-out and rally among voucher proponents protesting the injunction (phone interview with videographer, April 22, 2000).

The daughter of the interview subject, Laura Fordham, attends a private nonsectarian elementary school in which her mother also works as the admissions chairperson. For Ms. Fordham, the overriding factor in using a voucher to choose this particular school is its proximity to the family's home. In Milwaukee, this is not an inconsequential issue. With the advent of busing, many public neighborhood schools in the urban core were closed. This has presented significant difficulties related not just to the daily transportation of children; distance has also formed a significant obstacle to parental involvement in the public schools, particularly when many families do not own cars. This, in turn, has exacerbated the sense that public schools are frequently out of touch with the communities they serve.

As Ms. Fordham explains, "If she has to go back to the public schools, then she would be bused possibly across town. Well, I would not allow for her to be bused across town. First thing's, she's a chronic asthmatic kid. And for her to be bused, it would be impossible." Ms. Fordham's decision to relocate her child to a neighborhood private school came only after considerable effort to make the public school option work. "I could not transport her to school back and forward every day. I did that for her first year ... that was seventeen and a half miles away. So when she become more chronically ill, and my husband becomes ill, she had to stop going to school there, because I couldn't take her to school. Plus we couldn't afford it."

Ms. Fordham is nostalgic for a time "when the schools were so much better than they are now, the public schools at least.... You could go to school down the street and meet your neighbors." That is, public schools were also important centers of life within the community. "Now, the way the [public] schools are going, they tell you where your kid can go. Where with the Choice program, you're able to put your kid ... where you want them to go.... And you're able to afford it." Today in Milwaukee, private voucher–accepting neighborhood schools are often called upon by parents and guardians to fulfill the community role the neighborhood public schools once played. "And that's important, because we find that our private schools are closer around in the circle than public schools are."

Beyond the absence of public schools within some Milwaukee urban neighborhoods, Ms. Fordham also characterizes the experiences of many public school children in the following way: "They are in the classroom, and they're crowded. And if a kid is a little slower learning he [doesn't] have the time to take ... so after a while he'll just stop going to school, or he'll miss school because he didn't know his lesson, or he had nobody to pay attention to him."

Fordham's characterization of the public school beset by overcrowding contrasts markedly with the figure of the public schoolteacher in the interviewer's own narrative, in which public schools are seen as failing not because of overcrowded classrooms, but because of their monopolization by teachers' unions, which protect unworthy teachers while sheltering bloated and inefficient school bureaucracies from market discipline (Creative Media Services, 1998). An indictment of overcrowded classrooms, rather than union monopolies and a lack of competitive educational markets, points to a diagnosis and prescription for urban public schools that can only sit awkwardly within the neoliberal frame of "market efficiency/inefficiency." The awkwardness of this articulation is tempered only by considerable work, which allows for a type of hegemonic suturing (Apple, 1996) that never resolves the inhering contradictions.

This divergence of assumptions between Ms. Fordham and the interviewer is further evident as they negotiate the content of the interview. For example, in relation to the issue of consumer choice within educational markets, he asks, "Why should that be your choice? As a parent, or as a grandparent, or as a family member, why should you have the right to [choose] that?" While the interviewer positions Ms. Fordham as a consumer within an educational marketplace, she answers from a very different subject position—that of a member within a community and society: "One of the things I feel is going to improve our society is if we can educate our kids better." Again, Ms. Fordham's position as "parent/community member" sits awkwardly with the interviewer's own position as "parent/consumer."

Disarticulation and Rearticulation

These brief excerpts represent, at the microlevel, an important instantiation of the tense, contradictory, and often successful process of articulation and conditional alliance building within the movement for vouchers. While the tensions and contradictions in such articulations are vividly evidenced in the differing purposes, resources, and identities that the interviewer and the interview participant bring to the interview, clearly they also share a limited common purpose that allows them to stand together "in the same room," however awkwardly. Both the interviewer (as a neoliberal and neoconservative advocate of educational marketization and Catholic schools) and the interview subject (as a parent concerned about her child's education) are interested in furthering at least a specific, limited version of parental choice in Milwaukee. One can imagine that this parent and others similarly positioned, in contrast to the interviewer, are unlikely to favor "choice" beyond the low-income parameters within which it was initially established.

In significant ways, then, the subaltern and tactical agency that Ms. Fordham and other African American parents, guardians, and community leaders have demonstrated within the contested terrain over vouchers is a testament to the strength of their potential political agency, rather than, as is sometimes suggested, an indication of naïve submission to hegemonic conservative educational and economic discourses. This remains true even if these parents, guardians, and community leaders are ultimately proven wrong, as I believe they will be, in their assertions that their actions will be of maximum benefit in the long run not just for their children but also for other children left behind in newly market-disciplined urban public schools. And I believe this tactical agency will in all likelihood be further instantiated in future mobilizations, quite possibly around other traditionally conservative themes, many of which have long been issues of concern for large numbers of African American families, including support for school prayer and "religious freedom," as well as antipathy toward abortion and the interests of sexual minorities.

Reflecting on the pivotal role played by subaltern groups, I want to suggest that the conservative hegemonic alliance in the late 1980s recognized that it *almost* wielded the power to get vouchers through. Although by itself the hegemonic alliance was not able (yet) to successfully realize its marketization agenda concerning education and vouchers, the right could "stretch" its power by bringing parts of a traditional liberal constituency (a portion of African American low-income families) on board. Articulating the privatization agenda in education to these parents and guardians' "good sense" and perceived interests would enable the right to tip the scales of educational power away from an alliance of liberal groups including teachers' unions, other trade unions, the American Civil Liberties Union, People for the American Way, the National Association for the Advancement of Colored People, the Urban League, and feminist and environmental organizations and toward the amalgamation of groups pursuing conservative modernization in education. Given the Wisconsin political climate of the late 1980s, in which progressives wielded very little power, coupled with a long and historic movement among African American families in Milwaukee for community-controlled schools that would protect their children from the sometimes reprehensible racial practices of the Milwaukee Public Schools, Milwaukee presented itself as an ideal battleground upon which the conservative alliance might win crucial ideological battles over the character, form, and funding of education in the United States (Carl, 1996). Such a victory would also have promising implications for farther-reaching conservative goals involving the broad privatization of the public sphere and the deresponsibilization of the state.

In the process, the immediate and long-term conservative agendas around privatization in education and elsewhere would not be the only part of the hegemonic project that would be served. It will be useful here to reinvoke the conceptualization Michael Apple has proposed of the conservative hegemonic alliance as constituted through a series of tensely negotiated and maintained compromises among disparate but overlapping powerful interests (Apple,

1993, 1996, 2001), or what I have proposed calling discursive tendencies. In regard to the contestation of such a tense alliance, critical theorists in education and elsewhere have correctly argued that one strategy to forward the agenda of a radically democratic social and educational project might be to carefully discern these fault lines within the hegemonic alliance so that potential tensions among the different positions might be exacerbated, thereby pushing the project of conservative modernization in the direction of crisis. Just as progressives hope to strategically promote their interests through capitalizing on these points of suture on the right, so too the right has an interest in continuing to capitalize on and subvert tensions among real and potential progressive allies.

For many African American urban leaders who have, sometimes even tepidly, supported vouchers, the reaction of some progressive whites has been quite illuminating. It is characteristically a reaction that, previously content to see blacks as "wisely" coalescing with predominantly white progressive initiatives, now sees these same blacks as foolishly allying themselves with dangerous forces. A tacit message appears to be that blacks don't know the real dangers of allying with "reprehensible" conservative people; only white liberals know that. It smacks of a feeling of the "white man's burden," where liberal white educators are now angry at the "black children" who they had gathered under their umbrella, because those children are showing independence of mind.

Toward a Theory of Subaltern Agency and Identity in Educational Research

Public school has a lot of changes that I felt that needed to be made. I'm not knocking public schools. Public school has a lot of good things to offer. But public school also on the other hand has a lot of improving to do. And I resented that being African American—and of course I live in one of the poorer neighborhoods—my children were stigmatized by that. And they felt like they were giving you something. I'm a working mother. I pay taxes.... And my taxes help pay for public education. So as far as I was concerned, it was a paid education. You know, and I didn't appreciate the stigma like you have to take whatever I give you, you know. It's free. You ain't paying for nothing. And you know, that was the stigma. And it was so hard to get anything done. I was always.... It was always a fight. And I was looking in search of *something different.*

Sonia Israel, mother whose two daughters attended an Islamic voucher school (in Pedroni, 2004, p. 156)

In this chapter I have utilized a conceptual and empirical discussion of the discursive overlaps, tensions, and power differentials among constituents of the Milwaukee voucher alliance to suggest the importance of subaltern agency and identity formation within the process of conservative formation. Based on the conceptual and empirical juxtapositions in which I have engaged, I have argued for an expansion and reconceptualization of the theories of conservative modernization offered by Apple and Oliver in their essay, "Becoming Right." The modifications that I have proposed incorporate processes of identity formation and subaltern agency among third space groups as key components of the fragile and uneven process through which conservative educational mobilizations experience varying degrees of success or failure.

I have argued that the success and maintenance of such educational projects is predicated neither on a direct imposition of a conservative educational agenda onto unwitting and passive subaltern populations (e.g., voucher parents and guardians), nor on the "welling up from below" of a reified (parental) identity that somehow fits seamlessly into conservative educational mobilizations. Rather, utilizing but also expanding Michael Apple's theories of conservative modernization, I have pointed to the formation of fleeting and conditional alliances among differently empowered and socially situated actors. Within this process of subalternly negotiated alliance building there is always a highly structurally and discursively limited agency on the part of the dispossessed who are mobilized over the issue of their consent, as well as a contested discursive space within which potentially more socially democratic articulations and educational visions might be formed.

While the empirical and conceptual work conducted in this chapter provides critical educators with new understandings of the significance of participation among the marginalized in conservative educational reform (and therefore assists us in building more meaningful and effective urban educational reform movements), this work also suggests significant theoretical revisions of notions of subaltern agency and identity as these transact with more dominant structures and discourses within particular historical moments and sociocultural fields.

We can no longer assume that the subaltern simply "become right" in the process of conservative educational formation. Much like Sonia Israel's strategic use of the subject position *consumer* or *taxpayer* in the quote that opened this section, the forms of agency that voucher parents and guardians manifest frequently demonstrate a creative "inhabiting" of the very educational structures and discourses that would seemingly contain and further marginalize them. That is, a discussion of the discourses and subject positions that are "on offer" by various social movements and institutionalized educational forms only tells us part of the story. Such subject positions are not simply offered—they are also inhabited. And it is this latter part of the formulation of identities that has been inadequately theorized and sometimes even neglected within critical education theory.

Stuart Hall has accomplished much in helping critical theorists become more aware of this conceptual "blind spot." In essence, he argues, the successful construction of a theory of identity that is simultaneously nonessentializing yet politically possibilitarian has remained elusive. Current attempts at this project:

> offer us a formal account of the construction of subject positions within discourse while revealing little about why it is that certain individuals occupy some subject positions rather than others.... Discursive subject positions become *a priori* categories which individuals seem to occupy in an unproblematic fashion. (Hall & Du Gay, 1996, p. 10)

He continues (and I quote him here at length, finding his thoughts immensely relevant to the tensions around identity formation explored in this chapter):

> What I think we can see [in one of the seminal works on identity cited by critical and post-structural theorists—*Discipline and Punish*] is Foucault being pushed, by the scrupulous rigour of his own thinking, through a series of conceptual shifts at different stages in his work, towards a recognition that, since the decentring of the subject is not the destruction of the subject, and since the "centring" of discursive practice cannot work without the constitution of subjects, the theoretical work cannot be fully accomplished without complementing the account of discursive and disciplinary regulation with an account of the practices of subjective self-constitution. It has never been enough—in Marx, in Althusser, in Foucault—to elaborate a theory of how individuals are summoned into place in the discursive structures. It has always, also, required an account of how subjects are constituted; and in this work, Foucault has gone a considerable way in showing this, in reference to historically-specific discursive practices, normative self-regulation, and technologies of the self. The question which remains is whether we also require to, as it were, close the gap between the two: that is to say, a theory of what the mechanisms are by which individuals as subjects identify (or do not identify) with the "positions" to which they are summoned; as well as how they fashion, stylize, produce and "perform" these positions, and why they never do so completely, for once and all time, and some never do, or are in a constant, agonistic process of struggling with, resisting, negotiating and accommodating the normative or regulative rules with which they confront and regulate themselves. (pp. 13–14)

Hall faults critical and poststructural theories of identity for deferring the question of how the subject is constituted. That is, the subject is "hailed" and interpellated through discourse, through the limited number of subject positions that are offered, and by the constraints embedded in each—but what is it in the subject that allows it to be hailed in the first place? For Hall, this question is only likely to be advanced "when both the necessity and the 'impossibility' of identities, and the suturing of the psychic and the discursive in their constitution, are fully and unambiguously acknowledged" (Hall & Du Gay, 1996, p. 16).

While a comprehensive and satisfactory response to Hall's concerns lies well beyond the purview of this chapter—and perhaps the intellectual capabilities of this author as well—I want to suggest that the empirical and conceptual work conducted in this essay points to both the necessity and the possibility of a more adequate theorization of this "latter part" of identity formation. Clearly, pro-voucher African American parents, guardians, and community leaders, to again use Hall's words, do not occupy offered subject positions "in an unproblematic fashion." As I argued earlier, and as my empirical work (see Pedroni, 2004) helps demonstrate, parents, guardians, and community leaders adopt, resist, and/or mediate these subject positions in complex, contradictory, and creative ways. These discursive "performances" are products of a subaltern agency that is clearly rooted in and formed through the raced, classed, and gendered collective and individual experiences and struggles of working-class and poor African American women and men. That is, identities offered through educational discourses and structures are offered not to blank and amorphous subjects-in-waiting.

Conservative educational discourses and their concomitant structural forms instead offer subject positions to lived identities that are already in formation. These identities, formed and in formation, which are the shifting ground upon which conservative educational discourses must seek to become rooted, are themselves the product of individual and collective histories and struggles. In Milwaukee, the genealogy of this agonistic process of agency and identity has included the decades of raced, classed, and gendered struggle over issues of educational access and self-determination among the city's communities of color, as well as related struggles within other relatively autonomous political, cultural, and economic spheres (McCarthy & Apple, 1988, pp. 67–69).

As this chapter has argued, subaltern identities do not "naturally" fit into either conservative or radically democratic educational forms and discourses. Nor are such forms and discourses ever simply imposed upon the subaltern. Along with Ernesto Laclau and Chantal Mouffe, I want to emphasize the necessity of reworking Gramscian and other neo-Marxist conceptualizations of the social, so as to remove what these theorists have called the "epistemological obstacles" to the full realization of neo-Marxism's radical political and theoretical potential (Laclau & Mouffe, 1985). They write:

> It is only when the open, unsutured character of the social is fully accepted, when the essentialism of the totality and of the elements is rejected, that this potential becomes clearly visible and "hegemony" can come to constitute a fundamental tool for political analysis on the left. These conditions arise originally in the field of what we have termed the "democratic revolution," but they are only maximized in all their

deconstructive effects in the project for a radical democracy, or, in other words, in a form of politics which is founded not upon dogmatic postulation of any "essence of the social," but, on the contrary, on affirmation of the contingency and ambiguity of every "essence," and on the constitutive character of social division and antagonism. (pp. 192–193)

In this chapter, Laclau and Mouffe's "unsutured character of the social" is realized in a refusal to ensnare the agency of black voucher advocates within a paternalistic binary of "false consciousness," on the one hand, and its transcendence through black realization of the "correctness" of an anti-voucher stance, on the other. Instead, using conceptual tools borrowed from de Certeau, the acts of parents, guardians, and community leaders as they tactically navigate a complex educational terrain that is not of their own choosing is retheorized as *subaltern agency*. This notion of subaltern agency has the conceptual advantages of being discursively produced, nonessential in regard to "the social," yet cast within relations of power (De Certeau, 1984).

It is my hope that understanding the acts of pro-voucher black working-class and poor families in this way builds upon Apple and Oliver's crucial work in helping critical educators envision strategies for rearticulating these families' educational concerns to ultimately more effective, meaningful, and democratic educational reform. Hopefully the conceptual modifications that evidence, such as the interviews with voucher parents and guardians suggest (in this chapter, but also much more extensively in Pedroni, 2004), will assist researchers in other contexts in discerning similar subaltern processes and trajectories and their centrality to processes of conservative modernization. We can imagine that tactical investments in fleeting conservative alliances and subject positions among marginalized communities will play an increasingly significant role both in the United States and elsewhere.

Endnotes

1. Theorists such as Gewirtz (2002) have noted the displacement in many postindustrial democracies of the welfare state by a new state form—the postwelfarist state—which emphasizes efficiency in the delivery of services to clients and privatization of the public sphere over public sector fulfillment of its obligations to citizens.

2. Apple and Oliver characterize the parents in the textbook controversy as initially having political intuitions that were "not fully formed in any oppositional sense" (Apple, 1996, p. 61). In this chapter I use the phrase *ideologically unformed* or *ideologically relatively unformed* to refer to this quality of parents' ideology as conceptualized by Apple and Oliver. By *unformed* ideology I do not mean *without* ideology. Rather, I am trying to capture Apple and Oliver's sense of their ideology as not (yet) explicitly cohering to a singular ideological stream within conservative thought and conservative discourse in the United States. Their ideology is less "worked out"; they are less overtly politicized, at least initially.

3. Audiovisual copies of this interview were given to the author directly by the videographer. Complete transcripts of the interview upon which the analysis here is based, as well as copies of the original audiovisual interview, are available from the author upon request.

References

Apple, M. W. (1982). *Education and Power.* Boston, MA: Ark.

Apple, M. W. (1993). *Official knowledge: Democratic education in a conservative age.* New York: Routledge.

Apple, M. W. (1996). *Cultural politics and education.* New York: Teachers College Press.

Apple, M. W. (2001). *Educating the "Right" way: Markets, standards, god, and inequality.* New York: RoutledgeFalmer.

Apple, M. W., & Oliver, A. (2003). Becoming Right: Education and the formation of conservative movements. In M.W. Apple et al., *The state and the politics of knowledge* (pp. 25–50). New York: RoutledgeFalmer.

Apple, M. W., & Pedroni, T. C. (in press). Conservative alliance building and African American support of voucher reforms: The end of *Brown's* promise or a new beginning? *Teachers College Record.*

Carl, J. (1995). *The politics of education in a new key: The 1988 Chicago School Reform Act and the 1990 Milwaukee Parental Choice Program.* Unpublished doctoral dissertation, University of Wisconsin, Madison.

Carl, J. (1996). Unusual allies: Elite and grass-roots origins of parental choice in Milwaukee. *Teachers College Record, 98,* 266–285.

Corporation for Educational Radio and Television. (Producer). (1993). *Liberating America's schools* [Videotape]. United States: PBS Video.

Creative Media Services. (Producer). (1998). [Videotape interview segments]. Unpublished raw data.

De Certeau, M. (1984). *The practice of everyday life.* Berkeley, CA: University of California Press.

Foucault, M. (1977). *Discipline and punish: The birth of the prison.* New York: Vintage Books.

Fuller, H. (1985). *The impact of the Milwaukee Public Schools system's desegregation plan on black students and the black community (1976–1982).* Unpublished doctoral dissertation, Marquette University.

Gewirtz, S. (2002). *The managerial school: Post-welfarism and social justice in education.* London: Routledge.

Hall, S., & Du Gay, P. (Eds.). (1996). *Questions of cultural identity.* Thousand Oaks, CA: Sage Publications.

Holt, M. (2000). *Not yet "free at last": The unfinished business of the Civil Rights Movement—Our battle for school choice.* Oakland, CA: Institute for Contemporary Studies.

Laclau, E., & Mouffe, C. (1985). *Hegemony and socialist strategy.* London: Verso.

Lauder, H., & Hughes, D. (1999). *Trading in futures: Why markets in education don't work.* Buckingham: Open University Press.

McCarthy, C., & Apple, M. W. (1988). Race, class and gender in American educational research: Toward a nonsynchronous parallelist position. *Perspectives in Education, 4* (2), 67–69.

Pedroni, T. C. (2004). Strange bedfellows in the Milwaukee "parental choice" debate: Participation among the dispossessed in conservative educational reform. *Dissertation Abstracts International, 64* (11), 3946A. (UMI No. 3113677)

Pedroni, T. C. (2005). Can post-structuralist and neo-Marxist approaches be joined? Building composite approaches in critical educational theory and research. Unpublished manuscript, Utah State University.

Whitty, G., Power, S., & Halpin, D. (1998). *Devolution and choice in education: The school, the state, and the market.* Buckingham: Open University Press.

II
The Subaltern Speak
National Contexts

4

"In My History Classes They Always Turn Things Around, the Opposite Way"

*Indigenous Youth Opposition to
Cultural Domination in an
Urban High School*

GLENABAH MARTINEZ

Indigenous youth in urban, public high schools in the southwest are faced with daily challenges to their individual and collective existence as Indigenous peoples. While the argument could be and is made that all youth and teachers face challenges to some degree in public high schools, the challenges that Indigenous youth face in urban high schools are different. They are different because of the history of tense relations between Indigenous peoples and colonizers of Spain and the United States that precedes them as they enter high school for the first time. They are different because of their cultural ties to their aboriginal homeland, which calls for them to fulfill community and cultural obligations throughout the year. They are different and unique, as Indigenous legal scholar David Wilkins (2002) reminds us, because Indigenous peoples are the original inhabitants of the Americas. As descendents of the original inhabitants, we possess cultural distinctiveness, property rights, and political sovereignty. Oftentimes, however, the unique position that Indigenous peoples occupy is not consistently recognized in public education. Instead, the interests of the colonizing state are dominant in determining, for example, what counts as knowledge.

The intensity of cultural hegemony in the schools is symptomatic of a larger educational crisis that has prevailed in the historical and contemporary experiences of Indigenous peoples.[1] Graham Hingangaroa Smith's (1990) examination of the crisis of Maori education is particularly useful in making this point. According to him, the crisis must be "analyzed within a theoretical framework of context power relations" where power is determined by numbers.

In New Zealand the state education system embraces the social, political and cultural structures of Pakeha (white New Zealanders; non-Maori) dominant society. A converse position is also true, that wider Pakeha dominant society endorses the structures of the education system. Within the New Zealand democratic context the numeric advantage, approximately 7:1, of the Pakeha population ensures the maintenance of Pakeha *control* and *influence* over almost all political, economic, and social resources. It is therefore the cultures and the interests of dominant Pakeha society that are endorsed as "the culture" and "the interests" of the state structures, including the education system. Pakeha cultural capital is firmly embedded in the structures of schooling and education. ... It is the dominant cultural group or selected members from within the group who are able to influence what is to count as valid, acceptable knowledge, culture, and language at every level, from the majority of teachers at the classroom level, to the majority of members on Boards of Trustees at the organization level. Acceptable knowledge is maintained and protected by a variety of visible and hidden gate-keeping strategies. (pp. 79–80)

Hingangaroa Smith's analysis of power and education is critical to the approach taken in this chapter in two ways. First, the analysis explains how numeric advantage bolsters the power of dominant interests in policy and instruction at the school level. In the case of Mountain View High School (MVHS) where data for this chapter was collected in a 2.5-year-long critical ethnographic study, the dominant cultural groups consisted of whites and Latinos.[2] Cultural dominance at MVHS existed in these two groups exercising their power of position to influence curricular decisions, school policies, and aspects of school life such as schoolwide assemblies and the articulation of concepts such as *diversity* in the yearbook.[3] Second, Hingangaroa Smith's analysis is useful in examining how dominant interests are served at the school district level. In this chapter, I will present the voices of youth who face challenges to their individual and collective existence as Indigenous peoples on a daily basis in an urban, public high school located in the southwestern region of the United States.

The first section is a discussion of the aftermath of a districtwide controversy centered on graduation attire. In that discussion, I contend that the interests of the state prevailed, as the school board (acting on behalf of the state) maintained its power by placing a condition on the exercise of one's pride in an Indigenous identity. The second section is a discussion of how Indigenous youth at MVHS made curricular decisions. I will argue that although the students were cognizant of the value that dominant interests placed on the core curriculum, they also recognized the intrinsic value of Native American studies to their own intellectual and cultural growth as Indigenous people.

**People say the American way is to be white.... If you want to show
your true colors, screw the cap and gown. (ALNA)**

In the spring of 1997, graduating seniors requested permission to wear traditional cultural Native attire instead of the cap and gown for commencement at five of the eleven comprehensive high schools. Their requests were
denied and the students, along with their supporters (parents, relatives,
tribal leaders, and grassroots organizations), appealed the decision to the
district school board. At one meeting, one graduating senior spoke on behalf
of the students: "There are so few of us graduating that wearing our traditional clothes would make us stand out," he said. "Many of us are the first
members of our families to graduate and it's a big accomplishment for our
culture. But the cap and gown, the ties and the dress shoes—those represent
the white culture" (Santillanes, 1997, p. D1). A spokesperson for the school
district delivered the following statement as a rationale for denying the
students' request. "Everyone wears a cap and gown. It's been the policy
forever." This official continued:

> It's a legal dilemma. If you allow one, you have to allow all. The signifi-
> cance of the graduation becomes *convoluted* when you have so many
> ethnic and religious groups expressing their own way.... Public educa-
> tion is for all. Once we allow one religious or cultural group to express
> itself during ceremony, there could be some legal ramifications.
> (Saltzstein, May 5, 1997, pp. C5–6; italics added)

The official response of the district was released in a statement that was
prepared by the district's attorneys. It reads in part: "The district's policy of
requiring traditional academic dress at graduation ceremonies is intended to
recognize and preserve the academic character of the ceremony, as well as the
dignity and solemnity of the occasion." The use of the word *dignity* set the
stage for a number of responses by Indigenous leadership from the region.
Dressed in a turquoise blue ribbon shirt, a leader from one of the Pueblo
Nations stated, "We consider ourselves—the way I'm dressed—very dignified"
(Gallegos, 1997, A5).[4] The editor of a local daily newspaper also responded to
the district's use of the term *dignity*. While acknowledging the symbolic nature
of the cap and gown as a hegemonic cultural marker of graduating from high
school (modeled after "this country's European inheritance"), the editorial
concluded with the following thought:

> School officials who are coping with these honest requests must be
> sensitive to what they are dealing with and remember that terms like
> dignity are relative. Dignified dress is not merely that determined by
> Western standards. It includes traditional and ornamental clothing from
> all cultures. (Graduation, 1997, p. A8)

At the final meeting before commencement exercises in the district, the school board voted (four to three) to allow Indigenous students to wear their traditional dress under their caps and gowns. The district's superintendent asked the board to clarify the policy change by adding the statement that "full regalia" is allowed but "not below the hemline" and for "Native American students" only.

Graduating seniors and their supporters expressed mixed feelings about the outcome of the vote. The student spokesperson stated, "It was a small victory for Native American rights. We have to fight for everything. Tonight we won" (Saltzstein, May 19, 1997, p. D10).

Although the school board's decision appears to be a victory for the graduating seniors and a loss for the school administrators, I view it as a symbolic gesture of compromise. Michael Apple's (1995) scholarship on the relationship between power and schooling addresses the nature of compromise:

> The state itself is a site of conflict among classes and class segments and among gender and racial groups as well. Because it *is* the site of such conflict, it must either force everyone to think alike (a rather difficult task that is beyond its power and would destroy its legitimacy) or generate consent among a large portion of these contending groups. Thus, to maintain its own legitimacy the state needs gradually but continuously to integrate many of the interests of allied and even opposing groups under its banner. This involves a continual process of compromise, conflict, and active struggle to maintain hegemony. (pp. 26–27)

Graduation ceremonies and all that they stand for were not convoluted with the exercise of cultural pride in one's Indigenous identity. Rather, the exercise of cultural pride was *covered* with caps and gowns. In other words, much like the assault on cultural identity that occurred at Santa Fe Indian School and Carlisle Indian School in the late nineteenth century, Indigenous youth in the late twentieth century were told to "leave your Indian at home."[5] Adams (1995) discussed at length the historic assault on cultural identity, which is worth quoting:

> From the policymakers' point of view, the civilization process required a twofold assault on Indian children's identity. On the one hand, the school needed to strip away all outward signs of the children's identification with tribal life, that is to say, their savage ways. On the other, the children needed to be instructed in the ideas, values, and behaviors of white civilization. These processes—the tearing down of the old selves and the building of new ones—could, of course, be carried out simultaneously. As the savage selves gave way, so the civilized selves would emerge. (pp. 100–101)

In effect, the school board's decision communicated two messages to the graduating seniors and to the larger collective of Indigenous peoples in the area. First, not much had changed over a one-hundred-year period. The policy of the white man's schools continued to be founded on the racist assumption that Indigenous peoples are "savages" and are destined to be saved by "white civilization." Second, the school board's decision was a symbolic act of "giving in" to the requests of the Indigenous students and their supporters, but the school board (acting on behalf of the state) maintained its power and supported school administrators by placing a condition on exercising one's pride in Indigenous identity. In other words, the state will tell Indigenous men and women when it is okay to be Indian and how an Indian should dress and behave.

The messages were not ignored. They were stored in the collective memory of the graduating seniors and their younger relations who still had years to finish high school. As I will demonstrate in the remainder of this chapter, oppression continues to affect the daily experiences of Indigenous youth who attend an urban, public high school. However, the perspectives offered by Indigenous youth reveal daily resistance to cultural domination. In an interview one year after the graduation attire controversy, the response of one student, Sara, to my question about being Diné at MVHS encapsulates that spirit of resistance.

GM: What does it mean to be Native American or what does it mean to be Diné in this school?

Sara: I think it's real important.... It makes you feel special or something because you're Indian. Like Mexicans will say "Our home is just right there across the border." But we're like "Ours is right here! You're standing on it." And that makes you feel real proud. People, they express their culture but that's like far away. Ours, we're just right here. It's real important to tell people and let them know that this place that you're in, people have lived here before. It's real important that you know where you are ... and know the people who live here so you can respect it. Let them know to respect where we're coming from.

GM: How do non-Native people feel when you express that?

Sara: Sometimes we argue because they wonder, white people, they're like all "How come you get all the special benefits and how come you get this?" And it's like, "You don't understand" and they get all hurt. And it's like, or they'll have these stereotypes, you know. I remember one year, this guy was all "Do you guys have witchdoctors?" (laugh) And I'm like "Where did you get that from?" or like when we're telling them about our dress, this guy was all, "Oh, I can see how it would be hard to sit in, during the commencement because you've got to deal with all those feathers." And we're all, "Whatever."

> GM: Oh, was that last year when you guys were dealing with the attire and stuff?
>
> Sara: And people would ask us about that. It was not fair, like the black people; it's not fair. I never see them wearing their dress, you know, and for us, it's part of our everyday stuff. Like my jewelry, a lot of us wear jewelry. I don't see them wearing it everyday. (Interview with Sara)

From Sara's point of view, the graduation attire was one of many points of tension that existed in her classes. Correcting inaccurate perceptions of what it means to be an Indigenous person in today's society was part of her daily interactions with non-Native students.

Well, the one I don't really like is Spanish, but I have to take it to get into college. (Interview with Yolanda, Diné)

The data presented in this portion of the chapter comes from interviews that I conducted with Indigenous youth at MVHS.[6] I asked students to talk about their conceptions of an educated Native American and educational experiences at MVHS. While the responses yielded a number of themes for my examination, I will focus on one specific theme here: Students recognize the politics of what counts as knowledge.

Students in general reported that their schooling was helping to prepare them to meet their goals to continue their education after graduating from high school or to enter the job market. I approached this issue by asking questions about the relationship between the high school curriculum and their current lives and plans for the future. For the most part, the students viewed their classes as being useful because they provided them with skills for employment or post-secondary education.

Learning skills and knowledge for the future were consistently communicated to the students at MVHS in their course description books, registration workshops, parent newsletters, and in the daily discourse of teacher talk. In other words, the message—*knowledge is power*—was all around them from the time they entered the school to the time they left school. Yolanda (Diné), a ninth grader, talked about her perspective on the core curriculum.

> GM: Do you think the classes that you're taking this year, are they useful to you?
>
> Yolanda: Yeah. I'm taking algebra and I know it's going to be useful in the future if I'm going to be working in a bank or something. English, like if I want to be a writer when I grow up, it helps me be prepared. Just be prepared so I don't make any mistakes. Stuff like that. (Interview with Yolanda)

In a group interview with two juniors, Laura (Pueblo) and Ned (Diné /Northern Plains), their responses provided different perspectives on the useful nature of their classes.

GM: Are the classes that you've taken so far, are they useful to you?

Laura: I think so because I'm thinking about going into the medical field and taking the health occupations class. It gives me a chance to experience what it's like to be in the medical field. So that way I can decide whether or not that's really what I want to do.

GM: Ned, how about you?

Ned: Well, I haven't really took any classes except for the normal classes. Maybe math, that might be it. You always have to use math. (Interview with Laura and Ned)

Ned's characterization of his classes as "normal" is significant in two ways. First, it demonstrates the central role that hegemony plays in the high school curriculum. Ned's perception of math as one of his normal classes demonstrates how an ideological form (math) appears to be neutral. It becomes something close to an unquestioned truth or an embodiment of what Raymond Williams (2001) calls the "selective tradition." Absent from the course descriptions of the various math classes, math textbooks, and math instruction are political discussions of answers to questions like "What counts as math?" and "Whose interests are served with math?" and "What role does math have in social stratification?" Instead the focus of Ned's instruction in math is on content (e.g., numbers and operations) and process (e.g., problem solving, reasoning, and proof) only.

Iris's (Northern Plains) response to my question about the usefulness of her classes is additional evidence to consider in a discussion of selective tradition.

GM: Do you think your classes so far are useful to you?

Iris: I think they're useful to me. Like my Spanish class, I don't think it'll be useful to me in the future; but it's required for college. But it's useful for me because I'm learning another language. And well, geometry and biology, I think that's, because I'm learning a lot of stuff that applies to the regular world so I think they're useful. (Interview with Iris)

In *Official Knowledge*, Apple (2000) discussed the central role that textbooks have in "organizing that vast universe of possible knowledge." He characterized the embodiment of curriculum content and form as "what Raymond Williams called the *selective tradition*: someone's selection, someone's vision of legitimate knowledge and culture, one that in the process of enfranchising one group's cultural capital disenfranchises another's" (p. 46). References to particular classes such as math and science as "regular" or "normal," such as the responses provided by Iris and Ned, are significant within the context of a discussion of selective tradition and official knowledge in a high school setting.

The entire project of determining the core curriculum and establishing state requirements (e.g., setting the minimum number of credits, identifying specific courses that count toward graduation, and developing and administering standardized assessments) for high school graduation is political. At some point between the conflicts at the school board meetings and the distribution of course-offering books to high school students, the political nature of curriculum gets lost or essentialized.[7] Consequently, students like Ned and Iris are unaware of the political processes at work to create the illusion that math and science are normal or regular. In short, a void exists where there should instead be a forum for interrogating deeper epistemological issues.

There is a connection between the selective tradition and hegemony (Apple, 1990). It is relevant to the larger issue of how students draw distinctions between what counts as knowledge to be successful in high school and in the future.

> The educational institutions are usually the main agencies of transmission of an effective dominant culture, and this is now a major economic as well as cultural activity; indeed it is both in the same moment. Moreover ... there is a process which I call the *selective tradition*: that which, within the terms of an effective dominant culture, is always passed off as "the tradition," *the* significant past. But always the selectivity is the point; the way in which from a whole possible area of past and present, certain meanings and practices are neglected and excluded. Even more crucially, some of these meanings are reinterpreted, diluted, or put into forms which support or at least do not contradict other elements within the effective domain. (p. 6)

For this segment of the discussion, two points are significant in their relevance to the ways that these students recognize the politics of what counts as knowledge in high school.

First, it is important to recognize the processes that exist in the high school that neutralize or naturalize particular constructions of knowledge. In order for ideological forms to appear neutral, a process must exist that gives them legitimacy. Second, it is crucial to remind ourselves that the process (of neutralizing and naturalizing) is not necessarily one of imposition where the relationship is one-way, as social reproduction theories might have us believe. Instead, selective tradition, as it is embodied in the form of a national standard, state curriculum benchmark, or district content objective is "reinterpreted, diluted, or put into forms which support or at least do not contradict other elements within the effective domain."

Ned's classification of a particular set of classes as normal is also significant, especially when we consider Hall's (1997) analysis of racialized discourse as being structured by a set of binary oppositions. The concept of *binary oppositions* is an analytical tool for understanding how cultural representations and signifying practices from the mainstream affect how Indigenous youth and their teachers construct an educated Native person.[8] I see two sets of binaries operating here: (1) white/normal and red/exotic and (2) white/core (required) knowledge and red/peripheral (elective) knowledge. Hall addressed binary oppositions as they affect distinctions:

> There are the rich distinctions which cluster around the supposed link, on the one hand, between the white "races" and intellectual development—refinement, learning and knowledge, a belief in reason, the presence of developed institutions, formal government and law, and a "civilized restraint" in their emotional, sexual and civil life, all of which are associated with "Culture"; and on the other hand, the link between the black "races" and whatever is instinctual—the open expression of emotion and feeling rather than intellect, a lack of "civilized refinement" in sexual and social life, a reliance on custom and ritual, and the lack of developed civil institutions, all of which are linked to "Nature." (p. 243)

As indicated in my interviews with Indigenous youth at MVHS, they recognized distinctions between the courses that were either required for graduation or that looked good on the transcript for college applications, *and* courses that were classified as electives and were consequently viewed by some as peripheral to their education and by others as central to their identities as educated Indigenous people. For example, in one interview with Antonio (Diné), I asked him about what he was thinking when he selected his classes for the upcoming school year. He said, "I want to experience everything like French. It'll look good on your transcript." I asked him to explain the importance of certain classes appearing on his transcript and he said, "I guess [the] French language, the more you have, the more colleges will accept you." Later, in my questions about constructions of the educated Native person, I asked Antonio:

GM: Do you consider yourself an educated Native American?
Antonio: In a way, yeah.
GM: Not fully?
Antonio: Not yet, 'cause I haven't, I haven't experienced enough.
GM: When do you think you will be an educated Native American?
Antonio: When I learn Navajo. (Interview with Antonio)

In this brief but telling exchange, I found that students like Antonio not only recognized the white/core (required) knowledge and red/peripheral (elective) knowledge binary, but they also acted on it by electing to take French because it added cultural capital to a transcript. Yet when students such as Antonio engaged in dialogue for critical consciousness, the opposite (learning the language of the Diné people, Navajo) was viewed as essential to being an educated Native American. In the end, what is reflected on the transcript is a flat record of a student's educational experience without the conflicts, tensions, and compromises that Indigenous youth contend with throughout their high school years.

Cognizant of the tension created by the binary—white/core (required) knowledge and red/peripheral (elective) knowledge—Indian education faculty worked diligently to develop and teach Native American studies at several middle and high schools that served a significant number of Indigenous youth. The objectives of the course (Albuquerque Public Schools, 1998) were to provide Indigenous youth with an opportunity to: (1) understand and appreciate their tribal culture; (2) identify their role in the preservation of their culture; (3) build skills that will assist them to be successful in their futures; (4) increase knowledge of other cultures; and (5) respect the rich heritage and contributions of their tribes. The course outline was designed to provide "culturally relevant experiences, build curriculum standards and student performance levels, and give teachers activities and resources to assist students in reaching course objectives" (p. III).

During academic year 1998–99, I worked as a resource teacher and curriculum writer for the district as a representative of the Indian education unit. My job consisted of working with the district's curriculum coordinators and four other resource teachers on curricular issues (e.g., writing district objectives in content areas that matched state benchmarks and national standards; working with teachers during textbook adoption). My main job, however, was to work with the Native American studies teachers in completing unit plans and creating instructional lessons for both middle school and high school levels. As I recall that experience, a critical element of my work was to ensure that district objectives, state benchmarks, and national standards were addressed in the unit plans and lessons. The experiences, political socialization, and commitment to Indigenous youth empowerment were at the foundation of our work. As both professional educators and Indigenous men and women, we were aware of the binaries that students faced because we had faced similar challenges in our own academic lives. We envisioned the pedagogical project of Native American studies as one that advocated for cultural self-esteem, cultural preservation, sovereignty, and support of the students in their quest to satisfy graduation requirements.[9]

Mountain View High School was one of three high schools in the district that offered Native American studies (NAS) during the time I collected data. The course was presented in two parts: Native American Studies I and Native American Studies II. Waylon and Owen worked exclusively with Indigenous youth at MVHS. Waylon taught both NAS courses while Owen worked as the home-school liaison. In addition to providing financial support for the instruction of both NAS courses at MVHS, the Indian education unit also provided money and support for an after-school program for cultural enrichment and tutoring. The NAS classroom at MVHS was a popular site for Indigenous youth during breaks throughout the school day and after school. The Native American Club conducted their meetings in, and coordinated their activities from, the NAS classroom.

Of the twenty-nine students interviewed, seventeen had taken a Native American studies course at MVHS, were enrolled in the course at the time of the interview, or had formerly taken the course at another school. With the exception of one student, the twelve students who had not taken an NAS course at MVHS stated that they were planning to take the course before graduation.[10] I asked the students to share their reasons for taking NAS courses early on as opposed to later in their high school careers. Four major factors shaped their decisions, including the desire to: (1) take the "harder" classes first and take NAS later in their high school careers; (2) satisfy "core" curriculum requirements; (3) take NAS as a means of dignifying and honoring the knowledge of Indigenous peoples; and (4) exercise "Native pride" via research projects and community-based learning.

In the excerpt below, Yolanda (Diné) pointed out that her interest in delaying NAS to her junior and senior years was based on taking the "harder" classes first.

GM: Have you ever taken Native American studies here at Mountain View High School?

Yolanda: No. I probably will in my junior and senior year.

GM: Why do you want to wait until then?

Yolanda: Because right now, I'm trying to get my hard stuff, hard classes gone so that during my junior and senior year, I won't have to struggle as much. Plus, it makes it easier because if I have problems in the [required] class, I can always retry next year; and if you're a senior, you can't really do that. Plus, yeah, I'm just trying to get my hard stuff gone with so that in my junior and senior year, I can do more stuff that are more easier and more fun.

GM: Do you think Native American studies is easy and fun?

Yolanda: I don't know. From my friends, they speak a lot. They have presentations and for me that will probably help me in the future because like I said, I get nervous talking in front of people. I think it will be a good experience for me. (Interview with Yolanda)

Similar to Yolanda, a group interview with three sophomores—Amy (Diné), Ursula (Pueblo), and Carolyn (Diné)—revealed student concerns with satisfying the core requirements before taking NAS. It is important to note that when Ursula stated that she might not take NAS, the other two expressed their discontent.

GM: Do you think you'll take Native American studies Amy or Ursula?

Amy: I signed up for it (laughter) next year.... I signed up for it next year because I'm interested in it.

Ursula: I don't think I will.

All: Oh! Ah! Shhhh! (laughter)

Ursula: Because I'm trying to get all my core classes so that next year all I'll have are the hardest classes in the world.

GM: How about when you're a senior?

Ursula: Yeah! Probably then!

GM: So it's not that you have something against it....

Ursula: No! (laughter) I just want to get over with the hardest subjects first and then.... (silence) (Interview with Amy and Ursula)

Although the students expressed interest in taking Native American studies at some point in their high school career, they viewed it as the type of course that could wait. Their priority, as demonstrated above, was to take the *harder* classes first. It is also important to note that when Yolanda talked about taking NAS as a junior or senior, she focused on public speaking as a skill that would help her in the future.

For other students, Native American studies provided them with opportunities to dignify and honor the knowledge of Indigenous peoples. Students like Edwin (Pueblo) spoke fondly of their teacher, Waylon Gates, and his instructional style. Waylon's approach to Native American studies, in their opinion, merged new information presented from a variety of sources (videos, guest speakers, Internet, media) with their experiences as members of distinct Indigenous nations.

GM: Let's talk about Native American studies. Why did you like it so much?

Edwin: Mr. Gates is a nice guy, a good guy plus the whole thing of learning about different tribes and it's real interesting. That way you don't know about your tribe and your tribe only. You get to know about the customs, just how different people are, where they're from, where they're located. And I'd go out and hear somebody say "Yeah, I'm from this place" and I know where that was. So that really helped me out a lot. (Interview with Edwin)

In addition to taking advanced courses in preparation for college, Edwin had leadership roles in interscholastic sports, the Native American Club, and in youth empowerment organizations at the local, state, and national levels. For Edwin, the knowledge that he acquired in Native American studies at MVHS enhanced his ability to work with Indigenous youth in and outside of his familiar surroundings. For example, the Native American Club worked with other Indigenous youth organizations from five high schools in the district to sponsor communitywide activities. Similar to organizing that takes place among Indigenous peoples outside of school, prior knowledge of the geography, culture, and issues of specific nations establishes a sense of solidarity (as Indigenous peoples) while honoring diversity. Developing alliances and working collectively for political and cultural solidarity was an important theme addressed by Waylon in his classes.

I worked with Waylon Gates (Northern Plains) on projects during school and planned districtwide activities for the Indigenous community in and near the city. Waylon was relatively new to the district, although he had years of experience as an educator and guidance counselor in other districts. I asked him how he got to MVHS.

> One of the elements that I've always been interested in is this idea of *urban Indian* and some of the issues that they are confronting. Some of the Native Americans that are within the city that may or may not have the cultural pride and background that I feel is necessary to succeed and feel good about yourself, first of all, and then succeed. So, the decision was made for me, but when I found out it was Mountain View High School that I was going to be stationed at, I thought this is almost a dream come true because if I had a choice of any high school, if my supervisor said, "Waylon, pick a school," I would have picked Mountain View High School. So when that happened, I said, this is too good to be true. So, that's how I ended up here. (Interview with Waylon)

In recognition of the range of cultural experiences that were represented among his students, Waylon believes that success is closely linked to cultural pride.

Waylon is not alone in his approach to teaching Indigenous youth. In the summer of 1997, a group of Indigenous peoples of Hawaii, North America, New Zealand, and Australia met in New Mexico to identify ways that support learning experiences of Indigenous peoples. Benham and Cooper (2000) recorded the events of the gathering and described the philosophy that was collectively shared by the participants:

> We began by asking the two questions: "What is it that we want for our Native children and youth?" and "In light of this what ought to be the goals of Native education?" … We wanted our children to articulate a Native self-identity, be centered in their unique Native ways of knowing, and live as a proud Native people. Pride and knowledge of one's culture, history, and language meant our children would respect their ancestors and take care of their homeland. Finally we wanted our children to negotiate confidently the boundaries between their Native and non-Native worlds and make choices that maintained self and cultural integrity. (p. 14)

One of the ways that Indigenous youth acted on their desire to dignify the knowledge of Indigenous peoples was to exercise their pride, what they called *Native pride*, through research projects.

I asked students to talk about their research projects in Native American studies. They identified their topics, which included: Native American athletes, gaming, veterans (Vietnam, World War II), Indian health services, specific Indigenous nations, and art. Edwin (Pueblo) talked about his project.

> It gave me a chance to express myself the way I wanted to. If it was about a Native issue, I'd write about a Native issue. And I was willing to do it. We had a project to do. You just kind of decide what you want to do rather than the teacher giving you a topic to do like in other classes.... The topic I chose was Vietnam veterans from [student's pueblo nation]. That was real interesting for me. I got to meet a lot of people just interviewing them. A lot of stuff came out from them, real interesting stuff. I can imagine like thirty, forty years from now, when the Vietnam War would be a long time ago. I can say, "He used to talk about that" or "He told me how it was out there." (Interview with Edwin)

Oral tradition is a key element of learning and teaching among Indigenous peoples who have maintained their language and cultural traditions. For Edwin, the project merged oral history of elders in his home community with an assignment at school. In addition to learning about the impact of the Vietnam War on Indigenous peoples—something that was not addressed in the official curriculum of U.S. history—he valued the project for allowing him to honor his elders by listening to their stories. Finally, he viewed himself as fortunate for learning the history at the present time and teaching or sharing that knowledge with others in the future.

At the end of the semester, the students presented their research using posters and audio-visual resources. Their posters were prominently placed throughout the classroom for students and visitors to the class to view. Students from the class often received invitations to present their research at other schools.[11] They seemed to enjoy this element of the project. The research project was the culminating activity for the semester-long course.

David (Diné) was a junior at the time of the interview. I asked him to talk about his courses. As he shared his account of U.S. history (a graduation requirement usually taken in 11th grade), David compared the perspective he was presented with in U.S. history to the perspective offered in a Native American studies class.

David: In my history classes they always turn things around, the opposite way. They always try to make the white people or the Spaniards better than the Native Americans.... It's all written up like that in the history books. And here in our Native American studies class, we learn about things in the past.

GM: So how does that make you feel?

David: It got me mad and I was about to go up in front of the class and about to show them the information I got was the opposite way

... but I didn't want to make a fool of myself. I thought they might just kick me out or something. (Interview with David)

From David's perspective, the content that he received in two classes—U.S. history and Native American studies—was, at times, contradictory. According to David, he learned that "they always try to make the white people or the Spaniards better than the Native Americans" in his U.S. history textbook, and in Native American studies the opposite takes place. At the same time that David was faced with a history that subordinated the status of Indigenous peoples in the interest of elevating the experiences of the colonizers (United States and Spain), a similar struggle was taking place outside of the school.

In 1997 a proposal was presented to the city council to use city funds to build a sculpture commemorating the arrival of Juan de Oñate to New Mexico in 1598.[12] The proposal was introduced in 1997 and was put to a vote in early March 2000. The public was invited to comment on the issue before the city council voted on the proposal. I attended the city council meeting on the evening of the final vote on the proposal.

The city chamber was filled to capacity. The pro-Oñate group—mostly Hispanic or Nuevo Mexicanos—sat together in one section wearing red shirts. The other three-fourths of the room was filled with anti-Oñate people—mostly Indigenous peoples. The public was invited to give comments on the proposal. One pro-Oñate person said, "To not build this monument is to deny Hispanics their place in history." Speaking directly to one of the city council members who wanted to scale down the monument and work on a compromise, he continued, "How dare you, an Anglo, cut back funding for a statue for Hispanics." Another pro-Oñate person said, "If your family is of Spanish descent, this is a personal attack on you, your family, and your heritage." Several elders from Acoma testified in their native language for fairness and peace. One said, "There are so many ways we can recognize Hispanic history without putting up a statue of Oñate." One young Laguna woman said, "If I could take the hate from the hearts of everyone here tonight, that is what I would do." Many of the city residents who were in favor of the Oñate statue prefaced their testimonial with the phrase "as a tax-paying citizen of this city," such as one who said, "These Indians want their sovereignty, but they want to tell us what to do. Unless you live in Albuquerque and pay taxes, don't come here and tell us what to do because I do not intend to come to Acoma and tell them how to run their business."[13]

After nearly two hours of emotional testimony and heated debate, the city council voted seven to two to keep Juan de Oñate in the monument, but not in the park named for Indigenous peoples. Instead the monument would be set up on the grounds of a city museum. The design was a collaboration of three artists that included one well-known woman artist from a pueblo nation in the north. The monument also changed from one that focused on Oñate to one that depicted a grouping of cattle, dogs, sheep, Spanish settlers (including Oñate), and Pueblo Indians. The pro-Oñate group viewed the vote as a victory, while the anti-Oñate group left the meeting disappointed. Similar to the "compromise" reached in the graduation attire controversy of 1997, the interests of Indigenous peoples were set aside to appease a numeric majority and to maintain hegemony.

Relevant to understanding both the struggle over the monument and David's response to the lessons in his U.S. history class is Apple's (2000) reminder that "We cannot assume that what is 'in' the text is actually taught. Nor can we assume that what is taught is actually learned" (p. 58). It is the case, rather, that multiple readings are always possible and that readings of all texts, whether books or monuments, will be shaped by one's historical and cultural biography as well as one's class, race, and gender. Although David did not challenge the historical interpretations presented in his U.S. history class for fear that he might make a "fool" of himself or that he might get "kick[ed] out or something," he was not willing to let the official knowledge and meanings of the textbook replace his own construction of the past.

Similar to David, other Indigenous youth whom I interviewed were actively engaged in constructing meanings of education and challenging dominant knowledge. People or students (in this particular case), according to Apple (2000), potentially respond to text in three ways: dominant, negotiated, and oppositional.

> In the dominant reading of a text, one accepts the messages at face value. In a negotiated response, the reader may dispute a particular claim, but accept the overall tendencies or interpretations of a text. Finally, an oppositional response rejects these dominant tendencies and interpretations. The reader "repositions" herself or himself in relation to the text and takes on the position of the oppressed. These are, of course, no more than ideal types and many responses will be a contradictory combination of all three.... We must always remember [too] that there are institutional constraints on oppositional readings. (p. 58)

Unlike David, Edwin (Pueblo) seemed to be actively engaged in challenging the canon of English literature and history through the construction of oppositional readings. When asked if his teachers were aware of how important his identity as an Indigenous man was to him, he responded with the following explanation.

GM: Do you think your teachers are aware of what your identity means to you?

Edwin: Some aren't but I kind of make it known to them, like my English teacher, my history teacher, I'll make it known to them that I am, I do value my culture.

GM: How do you do that? Do you just tell them?

Edwin: Like for English ... she'll tell me to write an essay about a topic and sometimes I just don't agree with it. Like for instance she told us to write about *The Odyssey* and how Odysseus traveled ... and conquered different lands and try to tell how that story would set values for a civilization. I didn't agree with it. I said, "He really didn't set values for me. I disagree, being Native American. Look what the white man did to the Native Americans is no different than what Odysseus is doing in that story. He went from land to land conquering people without sympathy. Just only had himself in mind. He didn't really care about who he killed." I made certain points out of that. So that's how I felt. She kind of got the idea that I was being smart or something so throughout my essay there were a lot of question marks as to why I think like this. That's the first thing that came to my mind, "This ain't no hero story." I can understand from my perspective that this is the same thing that white man did to us. (Interview with Edwin)

The English class that Edwin was taking at the time of the interview was an advanced placement (AP) course for seniors. Edwin's statement that the story of Odysseus was "no hero story" for him demonstrated his frustration with a curriculum that had little or no relevance to his experiences as an Indigenous man. Edwin was not alone in his frustration with the selective tradition that occurred in his AP English class.

Sara (Diné) challenged a classmate to critically analyze the selective tradition in history and language arts where discussions of the Holocaust had occurred solely in relation to Jewish people and the horrors of the historic genocidal campaigns waged against them.

Sara: I remember our class was reading *The Diary of Anne Frank* and it so happens the following day that they were remembering the Holocaust. We came to a clash there when the girl was saying, "I'm Jewish and I don't think any other culture has experienced the holocaust." And I sat there, you know me, I don't say much ... but I told her, "Do you realize that you are standing on this land. This land that you're standing on, thousands and thousands of my ancestors were killed just so you could be here." I told her "We had our own holocaust and it didn't happen just like that within a few years.... It's lasted for hundreds of years. And people are still getting killed." I said, "1973, AIM [American Indian Movement] ... those years, during AIM, people were getting killed. It still goes on." We both had our holocausts and it was kind of emotional and like, I cry when I think of the Long Walk (Trail of Tears). I wrote a poem about that one time and I was just crying when I wrote about it. (Interview with Sara)

Sara was engaged in a struggle to disarticulate a link between the Jewish experience and the concept of holocaust. At the same time, she was attempting to rearticulate the discourse of holocaust to the experiences (historical and contemporary) of Indigenous peoples.

We need a real hard core Native American film … something that's from the people rather than from some anthropologist or some researcher. (Interview with Edwin and Orlando)

The premise of the analysis put forward throughout this chapter is based on the conviction that the intensity of cultural domination faced by Indigenous youth in urban, public high schools in the present time is symptomatic of a crisis that has prevailed over the past five centuries. Indigenous youth at MVHS are engaged in a struggle against two forms of colonization—one undertaken by Spain and the other by the United States. The discourse of Spanish colonial imperialism is as alive in the text that glorifies the colonizing expeditions of early Spanish conquistadores as it is in the actions of city government to propose the expenditure of public funds for a monument that commemorates the exploits of Oñate. The discourse of white or U.S. colonial imperialism is also present in policies such as the graduation attire ruling that, in effect, conveyed a message to "leave your Indian at home" or cover it up with a gown. However, as demonstrated by the insight provided by students such as Edwin, David, and Sara, daily challenges to the cultural integrity of Indigenous peoples were not always passively received. Instead, they were and continue to be met by resistance. As indicated by Edwin, Indigenous youth at MVHS see the need for a "hard core" Indigenous perspective to be incorporated into all elements of the curriculum, instruction, and policy.

Endnotes

1. The crisis here refers not only to indicators in achievement and retention, but also to the policies and practices that directly challenge the sovereignty of Indigenous peoples. For further discussion of sovereignty, see Wilkins (2002), Deloria (1979), and Coffey & Tsosie (2001).
2. Mountain View High School (pseudonym) is a large (2000 plus students) comprehensive public high school located in a metropolitan area of the southwest in the United States. During the 2.5 academic years that I collected data (1997–98, 1998–99, and 1999–2000), the white student population ranged between 36.2 and 33.8%, the Latino/a population ranged between 40 and 41.3%, the black population ranged between 7.6 and 8.3%, the Asian population ranged between 4.5 and 5.1%, and the Indigenous student population ranged between 10.2 and 10.5%. In the current school year (2004–05) 46% of the students are Latino/a, 32% are white, 9% are Indigenous, 7% are black, and 4% are Asian.
3. For further discussion of cultural dominance, see this author's upcoming publication *Native Pride: The politics of curriculum and instruction in an urban, public high school* (Cresskill, NJ: Hampton Press).
4. Throughout this article, I use the term "Pueblo Nations" to refer to the nineteen Indigenous nations. While the term "pueblo" is a Spanish word for village, it continues to be used by Indigenous peoples and others to describe the entire collective (e.g., All Indian Pueblo Council, Eight Northern Pueblo Agency). However, it is important to note that when introducing oneself, the specific homeland of the Pueblo person is usually indicated.
5. For an outstanding essay on the effects of schooling on Pueblo youth, see Suina (1992).

6. I interviewed students who volunteered to participate in the research project. In total, I interviewed twenty-nine students (grades 9–12) at least once. For the most part, I interviewed small groups because that was within the comfort level of the students. After the group interview, I invited students to be interviewed on a one-to-one basis. Five of the twenty-nine students agreed to be interviewed a second time. I also conducted follow-up interviews with two groups of students. The first one occurred when they were freshmen and the second interview took place when they were juniors. The interviews were ethnographic in design. They were audio taped, and I transcribed them. The transcripts were returned to the students for their review. They had the option of removing any statements or passages from the transcript. They were also given an opportunity to restate or explain statements if they saw the need. Only two students edited their comments by providing more explanation. No one asked for the removal of any passages or statements. The interviews were conducted at the school during the class day and after school.

7. Numerous accounts of tensions at the state level (e.g., Minnesota's social studies wars and California's math wars) around what should and should not be included in the curriculum are evidence of the political nature of curriculum and instruction, yet by the time the curricular documents are published and purchased, the controversies are absent from or barely visible in the classrooms. See Ansary (2004).

8. In the larger study, students and Indigenous faculty talked about the positive outcome of being an educated Native person by "proving them wrong." Specifically they talked about how their existence as sober, educated Native Americans subverted the stereotype of the "drunken Indian."

9. We were constantly reminded of the declining rates of school completion coupled with the low achievement on standardized tests by our students in district meetings, staff meetings, and in the media.

10. I found out later that the one student who expressed no interest in taking an NAS course not only registered for both NAS courses, but also served as an officer in the Native American Club during the student's senior year at MVHS.

11. In a recent newsletter distributed by the district's Indian Education office, I read about students from MVHS who traveled to another high school (predominantly white and high socioeconomic status) in the district to present their research. In the article, "Mountain View High Native Pride," the author wrote: "We are especially proud of the MVHS Native American Studies students that presented Native American history and culture to over 800 students at Smith High School. They demonstrated that Native pride and academic achievement work hand-in-hand" (p. 10).

12. In 1595, Juan de Oñate was awarded a contract from the Spanish crown to lead a colonizing expedition into New Mexico. After years of preparation, Oñate arrived in northern New Mexico (near the present-day pueblo nation of San Juan). Spanish officials had demanded that pueblo people pay tribute to the Spanish crown by working for *encomenderos*. (An encomendero was a proprietor of a grant called encomienda. Such a proprietor was privileged to collect an annual tribute from a specified town or number of Indigenous people, who were expected to pay in the form of corn or cotton blankets. The encomendero exercised trusteeship over his "subjects," a system that functioned in New Mexico from 1600 to 1680, when the Pueblo Revolt occurred.) At the same time, Spanish priests established missions on pueblo lands and demanded that the pueblo people abandon their own religion in favor of Christianity. Meanwhile, Oñate searched throughout the lands of present-day New Mexico for gold and other precious metals. Relations worsened when Juan de Oñate received word in December 1598 that his nephew, Zaldívar, was killed in a skirmish with Acoma pueblo people. Upon hearing of his nephew's death, Oñate led Spanish troops to Acoma with the purpose of punishing them. Oñate and his brother, Vicente de Zaldívar, arrived at Acoma on January 21, 1599. The pueblo atop the mesa was the site of a battle that lasted four days. On January 24th it ended with the Acomas yielding to the Spanish military force. Of the six thousand Acomas, eight hundred were killed. Eight Acoma girls were forcibly taken to Mexico. In February 1599, a trial for those who had been taken prisoner announced sentences in accordance with sixteenth century Spanish law. All Acoma males over twenty-five years of age were condemned to have one foot cut off and to give twenty years of personal service; all males between the ages of twelve and twenty-five were to give twenty years of personal service. All females above the age of twelve were to give twenty years of personal service.

13. At the meetings where the Oñate sculpture and the paved road through the petroglyphs (a sacred site for Indigenous peoples in the region) were on the agenda, individuals who testified for the Oñate sculpture and for the paved road began to preface their testimony with phrases like "as a tax-paying citizen of this city" or "as a city resident who owns property in this city." Clearly, the purpose was to show the city legislators that they had more of a right to speak because they paid taxes, insinuating that the Indigenous peoples who were testifying did not pay taxes and therefore did not have a voice in city government. Proponents of the Oñate sculpture and the paved road through the petroglyphs may have also been displaying their ignorance by acting on an old stereotype that Indians do not pay taxes. In fact there were a number of city residents and property-owning Indigenous peoples who testified and, they too, began to preface their statements with the same phrases. Some added the phrase, "as a descendant of the original inhabitants of this land," which was met with applause (by Indigenous peoples and their supporters) every time it was uttered.

References

Adams, D. W. (1995). *Education for extinction*. Lawrence, KS: University Press of Kansas.

Albuquerque Public Schools. (1998). Native American studies curriculum. Unpublished manuscript.

Ansary, T. (2004). The muddle machine: Confessions of a textbook editor. *Edutopia, November/December*, pp. 31–35.

Apple, M. W. (1990). *Ideology and curriculum* (2nd ed.). New York: Routledge.

Apple, M. W. (1995). *Education and power* (2nd ed.). New York: Routledge.

Apple, M. W. (2000). *Official knowledge* (2nd ed.). New York: Routledge.

Benham, M., & Cooper, J. (2000). *Indigenous educational models for contemporary practice: In Our mother's voice*. Mahwah, NJ: Lawrence Erlbaum Associates.

Coffey, W., & Tsosie, R. (2001). Rethinking the tribal sovereignty doctrine: Cultural sovereignty and the collective future of Indian nations. *Stanford Law and Policy Review, 12* (2), 191–221.

Deloria, V. (1979). Self-determination and the concept of sovereignty. In R. Dunbar-Ortiz (Ed.), *Economic development in American Indian reservations*. Albuquerque, NM: Native American Studies.

Gallegos, G. (1997, April 17). APS looks into Indian graduation attire. *Albuquerque Tribune*, A5.

Graduation is cap and gown event. (1997, April 19). *Albuquerque Journal*, p. A8.

Hall, S. (Ed.). (1997). *Representation: Cultural representations and signifying practices*. Thousand Oaks, CA: Sage Publications.

Saltzstein, K. (1997, May 19). Students win right to traditional dress under cap & gown. *Indian Country Today*, p. D10.

Saltzstein, K. (1997, May 5). Albuquerque schools fight traditional dress: Seniors, parents, attorneys planning protest. *Indian Country Today*, pp. C5–C6.

Santillanes, V. (1997, April 17). Indians plead for native dress. *Albuquerque Journal*, p. D–1.

Smith, G. H. (1990). The politics of reforming Maori education: The transforming potential of Kura Kaupapa Maori. In Lauder & Wylie (Eds.), *Towards successful schooling* (pp. 73–87). London, UK: Falmer Press.

Suina, J. (1992). And then I went to school: Memories of a pueblo childhood. In B. Bigelow & B. Peterson (Eds.) *Rethinking Columbus: Teaching about the 500th anniversary of Columbus's arriving in America* (pp. 34–36). Milwaukee, WI: Rethinking Schools.

Wilkins, D. (2002). *American Indian politics and the American political system*. Lanham, MD: Rowman & Littlefield.

Williams, R. (2001). *The long revolution*. Orchard Park, NY: Broadview Press.

5
Rethinking Grassroots Activism
Chicana Resistance in the 1968 East Los Angeles School Blowouts

DOLORES DELGADO BERNAL

The 1960s was an era of social unrest in American history. Student movements that helped shape larger struggles for social and political equality emerged from street politics and mass protests. A myriad of literature discusses the social and political forces of the 1960s, particularly the liberal and radical student movements. Yet as Carlos Muñoz (1989) argues, there is a paucity of material on 1960s nonwhite student radicalism and protest. He outlines various explanations that have been provided by white scholars for their failure to incorporate nonwhite student radicalism into their work: that the black student movement was not radical enough and that Mexican students were simply not involved in the struggles of the 1960s. However, though Muñoz points to the omission of working-class people of color in the literature on 1960s student movements, he neglects to include a serious analysis of gender in his own examination of the Chicano movement and the politics of identity.

[margin note: not much, small amount]

In March 1968, well over ten thousand students walked out of the mostly Chicano schools in East Los Angeles to protest the inferior quality of their education. This event, which came to be known as the East Los Angeles School Blowouts, has been viewed through a variety of analytical historical perspectives, including those of protest politics, internal colonialism, spontaneous mass demonstrations, the Chicano student movement, and as a political and social development of the wider Chicano movement (see Gómez-Quiñones, 1978; Muñoz, 1972; Negrete, 1972; Puckett, 1971; Rosen, 1973). None of these historical accounts, however, include a gender analysis. Even contemporary depictions, such as the important documentary series *Chicano: A History of the Mexican American Civil Rights Movement*, continue to marginalize women's activism; part three of the series, "Taking Back the Schools," fails to tell the stories of young Chicanas and the roles they filled in the East Los Angeles Blowouts (Ruiz & Racho, 1996).

[margin note: Never knew this]

[margin note: Why is gender important in this?]

As an educational researcher and a Chicana, I am interested in the women's voices that have been omitted from the diverse historical accounts of the "blowouts"—particularly those women who were key participants.[1] The blowouts provide an opportunity to rediscover a history that has been unrecognized and unappreciated. In addition, a historical analysis that focuses on the blowout participation of women allows us to explore how women offered leadership and how that leadership, while different in form and substance from traditional interpretations, was indeed meaningful and essential (for related works on Chicana activism, see de la Torre & Pesquera, 1993; Mora & Del Castillo, 1980; Ruiz, 1987).

Through the oral history data of eight women, I provide an alternative perspective to the historical narratives of the 1968 blowouts, which have thus far only been told by males with a focus on males.[2] At the same time, I will use the oral history data to examine the concept of leadership in community activism. I propose that a paradigmatic shift in the way we view grassroots leadership not only provides an alternative history to the blowouts, but also acknowledges Chicanas as important leaders in past and present grassroots movements.[3]

The Women

All eight women are similar insofar as they are second- or third-generation Chicanas, first-generation college students, and grew up in working-class neighborhoods on the east side of Los Angeles. However, these women are not a homogeneous group, nor does their composite lend itself to a "typical Chicana" leader or activist. Two of the women grew up in single-parent households with only two children, while the other six come from two-parent families with four or more children. Four of the women come from families that had been involved in union organizing or leftist political movements since the 1940s. Three women state that they come from strong Catholic families, while three other women state they were raised in families in which their parent(s) had abandoned the Catholic Church. Though six of the eight women are bilingual in Spanish and English today, only one of the women grew up in a predominantly Spanish-speaking home. Three of the women come from mixed marriages and are half white, Jewish, or Filipina. Finally, during high school, six of the women maintained an exceptional academic and extracurricular record as college-tracked students.

Despite the similarities, the notable differences in the women's family and personal histories reflect the complexity and diversity of Chicanas' experiences in 1968 and today. Indeed, there are also similarities and differences in the type of participation and leadership each woman contributed to the East L.A. Blowouts. While this chapter is an interpretation based on the personal perceptions and experiences of these women, knowing the historical circumstances of the time provides a clearer picture of the 1968 East L.A. School Blowouts.

The 1968 East Los Angeles School Blowouts [and continues today in 2018]

Chicanos' struggle for quality education and the right to include their culture, history, and language in the curriculum is not a phenomenon of the 1960s, but instead predates the 1968 blowouts by a number of decades. In fact, many of the concerns and issues that were voiced by participants and supporters of the 1968 blowouts—implementation of bilingual and bicultural training for teachers, elimination of tracking based on standardized tests, improvement and replacement of inferior school facilities, removal of racist teachers and administrators, and inclusion of Mexican history and culture into the curriculum—were very similar to those voiced in Mexican communities in the United States since before the turn of the century (for different interpretations of blowout demands, see McCurdy, 1968b; Muñoz, 1974; Puckett, 1971; Rosen, 1973; see also González, 1990). [Doesn't seem like unreasonable requests]

For years, East Los Angeles community members made unsuccessful attempts to create change and improve the education system through the "proper" channels. In the 1950s the Education Committee of the Council of Mexican American Affairs, comprised of educated Mexican professionals, addressed the failure of schools to educate Mexican students through mainstream channels. They met with legislators, school officials, and community members and attended hearings, press conferences, and symposia to no avail (Briegel, 1974). In June 1967 Irene Tovar, commissioner of Compensatory Education for the Los Angeles district, explained to the U.S. Commission on Civil Rights that a long list of recommendations to improve the inferior schooling conditions had been presented to the Los Angeles Board of Education in 1963, but that "few of those recommendations were accepted and even fewer reached the community" (California State Advisory Committee [CSAC], 1968). In the years immediately preceding the blowouts, students and parents participating in one East L.A. high school's PTA specifically addressed the poor quality of education and requested reforms similar to those demanded by the blowouts two years later (Rosalinda Méndez González, interview, October 8, 1995). Nonetheless, formal requests through official channels went unanswered. [Typical]

In 1963, the Los Angeles County Commission on Human Relations began sponsoring an annual Mexican-American Youth Leadership Conference at Camp Hess Kramer for high school students. These conferences were important to the development of the 1968 blowouts because a number of students who participated in the conference later became organizers in the blowouts as well as in other progressive movements. Given these outcomes, it is ironic that the camp held an assimilationist perspective, stating that the official goal of the camp was to improve self-image and intergroup relations so that Mexican American students "may be free to develop themselves into the mainstream of Anglo-American life" (Mexican-American Youth Leadership Conference, 1967). Students were encouraged to be traditional school leaders, run for school offices, and go on to college. The student participants were selected by either a school, a community person, or an organization based on their ability to contribute to the group as well as on their ability to return and create progress in their own communities. The weekend camps were held at Camp Hess Kramer in Malibu, California. The student participants were assigned to cabins, and college students served as camp counselors and workshop leaders. Four of the women in my study participated in at least one of the leadership conferences prior to their involvement in the 1968 blowouts. They remember the camp as a beautiful place where they were given a better framework to understand inequities and where they developed a sense of community and family responsibility. As one woman put it, "These youth conferences were the first time that we began to develop a consciousness." Rachael Ochoa Cervera (interview, December 10, 1995) discusses her memories of the camp:

> It was a nice experience because you'd get away for a whole weekend and the environment, the atmosphere was quite beautiful, very aesthetic. Being by the ocean, yet you felt you were in the mountains.... It was very affirmative. That's where you began to have an identity. You weren't with your schoolmates; you could be more open. You could say what you wanted to.

While the camp fostered civic responsibility and school leadership, many students left motivated to organize around more radical and progressive issues. Rosalinda Méndez González describes how the conferences motivated students to organize:

> Well, when we started going to these youth conferences, there were older Mexican Americans. Now we were high school kids, so older was probably twenties and early thirties. They would talk to us, and explain a lot of things about what was happening, and I remember they were opening up our eyes. After those youth conferences, then we went back and started organizing to raise support for the farmworkers, and things like that. (Méndez González interview)

As a direct result of youth participating at Camp Hess Kramer, the Young Citizens for Community Action (YCCA) was formed. The YCCA (which later became Young Chicanos for Community Action and then evolved into the Brown Berets) surveyed high school students' needs, met with education officials to discuss problems, and endorsed potential candidates for the board of education. YCCA members, still following official channels to bring about improved educational conditions, supported and helped elect the first Chicano school board member, Julian Nava (Rosen, 1973).

Also influential in the development of the blowouts was the fact that by 1967 a relatively larger number of Chicano students began entering college, though still a small representation of the Chicano population. In that year, one of the first Chicano college student organizations in the Los Angeles area, the Mexican American Student Association (MASA), was formed at East Los Angeles Community College (Gómez-Quiñones, 1978). Student organizations rapidly formed throughout college campuses in California, including United Mexican-American Students (UMAS) at the University of California, Los Angeles; California State University, Los Angeles; Occidental College; and Loyola University. The primary issue of these organizations was the lack of Chicano access to quality education.

Historians have also noted the importance of the community activist newspapers *Inside Eastside* and *La Raza* to the rise of the blowouts (Briegel, 1974; Rosen, 1973). *Inside Eastside* had an emphasis on social, cultural, and political activities relevant to students, and for the most part was written and edited by high school students. In fact, two women in this study wrote articles for *Inside Eastside* and *La Raza*. *La Raza*, aimed at the Chicano community as a whole, was concerned with a spectrum of political activities focusing on the schools, police, and electoral politics. The newspapers provided a forum in which students and community members were able to articulate their discontent with the schools, and frequent themes were the poor quality of East Los Angeles schools and the cultural insensitivity of teachers. The newspapers, the increased number of Chicano college students, and events such as the Camp Hess Kramer conferences were influential in bringing attention to the poor educational conditions of East Los Angeles schools.

During the 1960s, East Los Angeles high schools had an especially deplorable record of educating Chicano students, who had a dropout/pushout rate of well over 50% as well as the lowest reading scores in the district. In contrast, according to a survey undertaken by the Los Angeles City School System, two west side schools, Palisades and Monroe, had dropout rates of 3.1% and 2.6%, respectively in 1965–1966 (California State Advisory Committee to the United States Commission on Civil Rights [CSAC], 1968). According to the State Department of Education's racial survey, Mexican American students were also heavily represented in special education classes, including classes for the mentally retarded and the emotionally disturbed (CSAC, 1968). The classrooms were overcrowded, and most teachers lacked sensitivity to or understanding of the Mexican working-class communities in which they taught. Rosalinda Méndez González recalls:

[handwritten: that is crazy what a difference]

[handwritten: Why are minorities so quickly labeled SpEd?]

There were teachers who would say, "You dirty Mexicans, why don't you go back to where you came from?" So there was a lot of racism we encountered in the school. We had severely overcrowded classrooms. We didn't have sufficient books. We had buildings that were barrack-type buildings that had been built as emergency, temporary buildings during World War II, and this was in the late 1960s, and we were still going to school in those buildings. (Méndez González interview)

[handwritten: ohh wow!]

[handwritten: sounds familiar to AA education & NA]

As a result of the poor educational conditions and the fact that numerous attempts to voice community concerns and secure school reforms were ignored, school strikes took place during the first week of March 1968. Though the blowouts were centered at five predominantly Chicano high schools located in the general east side of Los Angeles, other schools in the district also participated, including Jefferson High School, which was predominantly African American.[4]

The school boycott began on different days during the first week of March and lasted a week and one-half, with over ten thousand students protesting the inferior quality of their education. Though there had been weeks of discussions and planning, the first impromptu walkout was sparked by the cancellation of the school play, *Barefoot in the Park*, by the administration at Wilson High School. Paula Crisostomo (interview, November 16, 1995), a student organizer at Lincoln High School, comments on the atmosphere at her school preceding the walkout:

> I know tension had heightened, activity had heightened districtwide, a lot of schools were talking about it, everyone knew it was going to happen, everyone was waiting for the sign. But I remember the atmosphere was absolutely tense, I mean it was just electric in school. This had been building for so long, and everyone knew it was going to happen and everyone was just waiting and waiting.

Though there was coordination between the schools, the planning and actual implementation of each school walkout took on a distinct character. High school students, college students, Brown Beret members, teachers, and the general community took on different roles and provided different kinds of support.

Vickie Castro, a Roosevelt graduate, was a college student who played a crucial role in organizing and supporting the blowouts. Vickie recalls that while she was at Roosevelt trying to help organize students, she was recognized by a teacher and escorted to the gate. The teacher told her, "If I see you on campus again, I'll have you arrested" (interview, June 8, 1995). Vickie later used her old Mazda to pull down the chain-link fence that had been locked to prevent high school students from leaving: "I remember having to back my car and put chains on and pull the gates off." In contrast, her key role at Lincoln was to set up a meeting with the principal and detain him while other college students came on campus to encourage high school students to participate in the walkouts. Vickie recalls the strategy she used at Lincoln, pretending to be a job applicant to get an appointment with the principal:

> I remember we had a whole strategy planned for Lincoln, how we were going to do it. And who was going to be in the halls to yell "walkouts" at the various buildings. And my role was to make an appointment with

the principal to meet him, to talk to him about either employment or something. I'm in his office and my job is trying to delay him. He kept saying, "I'll be right with you, I'll be right with you." So I was to just keep him distracted a little bit. Then when the walkouts came, of course, he said, "I have to leave." And then somehow, I don't even recall, I got out of the building too.

Just as the planning and actual implementation of each school walkout took on a distinct character, so did the response by each school administration and by the police. While the student walkouts on other campuses could be characterized as ranging from peaceful to controlled with mild incidents of violence, the students on Roosevelt's campus experienced a great deal of police violence. Police, county sheriffs, and riot squads were called. With a number of students and community members injured and arrested, the student protest turned into a near riot situation (for a history of police brutality in East Los Angeles, see Morales, 1972). Tanya Luna Mount, a student organizer, points out that even though the students were following the legal requirements of a public demonstration, the situation with the police escalated to the point of senseless beatings with school administrators trying to stop the police:

> They [the Los Angeles Police Department, LAPD] were treating it like we were rioting and tearing everything up, which we weren't. We weren't breaking, destroying anything. Nobody was hanging on school property and tearing it apart. Nothing, nothing like that happened. And we were told to disperse, we had three minutes. Everybody kept yelling that we had a right to be there.... All of a sudden they [the riot squad] started coming down this way. They start whacking people. Now they're beating people up, badly, badly beating people up. Now people, administrators are inside yelling, "Stop, my God. What are you doing?" Once you call LAPD, the school no longer has any jurisdiction. They couldn't even open the gate and tell the kids to run inside because the police were telling them, "Remove yourself from the fence and go back, mind your own business." That's when all of a sudden they [the administrators] realized, "My God." (Tanya Luna Mount interview, January 31, 1996)

The student strikers, including those at Roosevelt who were subjected to police violence, were not just idly walking out of school. They proposed that their schools be brought up to the same standards as those of other Los Angeles high schools. The students generated a list of grievances and pushed for the board of education to hold a special meeting in which they could present their grievances. The official list of student grievances to be presented to the board of education consisted of thirty-six demands, including smaller class size, bilingual education, more emphasis on Chicano history, and community control

Literally all they want is better education

of schools (McCurdy, 1968b). Many of the grievances were educational reforms previously proposed by concerned parents, educators, and community members, and all of the demands were supported by the premise that East Los Angeles schools were not properly educating Chicano students.

The blowouts generated the formation of the Educational Issues Coordinating Committee (EICC) by parents, various community members, high school students, and UMAS members. With pressure from the EICC and the student strikers, the blowouts also generated at least two special board of education meetings in which students, the EICC, and supporters were allowed to voice their concerns. By Friday, March 9, the school strikes had not ended, and the board of education scheduled a special meeting to hear the students' proposals. At this meeting it was decided that another meeting would be held at Lincoln High School and that the board would grant amnesty to the thousands of students who had boycotted classes (McCurdy, 1968a). *an official pardon*

Approximately 1,200 people attended a four-hour board meeting that was held at Lincoln High School, yet the board of education made no commitments. Students walked out of the meeting in response to the board's inaction. The sentiments of the board were captured by an article in the *Los Angeles Times* stating that "school officials deny any prejudice in allocation of building funds and say that they agree with 99% of the students' demands—but that the district does not have the money to finance the kind of massive changes proposed" (McCurdy, 1968b). At this meeting, the board went on record opposing the discipline of students and teachers who had participated in the boycott. Yet in the late evening of June 2, 1968, thirteen individuals involved in the blowouts were arrested and imprisoned on conspiracy charges. Though female students were involved in organizing the blowouts, the L.A. 13 were all men, including Sal Castro, a teacher from Lincoln High School. With a focus on males, especially those who looked the militant type, females avoided arrest. Though the charges were later dropped and found unconstitutional, Sal Castro was suspended from his teaching position at Lincoln High School. For many months students, community, and EICC members rallied in support of the L.A. 13 and then focused organizing efforts on the reinstatement of Sal Castro.

A Reconceptualization of Leadership

In exploring how and when women participated in the blowouts, it is important to outline a reconceptualization of leadership that places women at the center of analysis and does not separate the task of organizing from leading. The reconceptualization I put forth comes out of a women's studies tradition that in the last twenty years has produced an impressive body of new knowledge, and has contributed to the development of new paradigms on leadership. Rather than using traditional paradigms that view leaders as those who occupy a high position in an organization, feminist scholars have developed alternative paradigms that more accurately consider gender in the analysis of leadership (see Brodkin Sacks, 1988a, 1988b; Astin & Leland, 1991).

In the area of science, Thomas Kuhn's (1970) influential work *The Structure of Scientific Revolutions* presents a model for a fundamental change in theories and scientific paradigms, arguing that without major paradigm shifts we may never understand certain scientific phenomena. He gives the example of how Joseph Priestley, one of the scientists said to have discovered the gas that was later found to be oxygen, was unable to see what other scientists were able to see as a result of a paradigm revision. Similarly, a paradigm shift in the way that we understand and study leadership allows us to see how women—specifically the women in my study—emerge as leaders. Perhaps there is something faulty in the previous leadership paradigms that have not allowed us to understand and explain the lived experiences of Chicanas.

[margin note: Meaning we need to redefine what exactly leadership entails?]

Karen Brodkin Sacks (1988a) indicates that the traditional paradigm of leadership implicitly equates public speakers and negotiators with leaders and also identifies organizing and leading as two different tasks. She challenges this notion of leadership by placing working-class women at the center of analysis. Leadership in this perspective is a collective process that includes the mutually important and reinforcing dynamic between both women's and men's roles. Leadership as a process allows us to acknowledge and study a cooperative leadership in "which members of a group are empowered to work together synergistically toward a common goal or vision that will create change, transform institutions, and thus improve the quality of life" (Astin & Leland, 1991, p. 8). This paradigm of cooperative leadership, along with the inclusion of women's voices, allows an alternative view of the blowouts and different dimensions of grassroots leadership to emerge.

[margin note: leaders are not always loud]

Dimensions of Grassroots Leadership

In previous work, I have identified five different types of activities that can be considered dimensions of grassroots leadership in the 1968 blowouts: networking, organizing, developing consciousness, holding an elected or appointed office, and acting as an official or unofficial spokesperson (Delgado Bernal, 1997). The distinction between these activities is not meant to be a rigid and impermeable one, nor are these activities inclusive of all dimensions of grassroots leadership. Not every leader need participate in every dimension of leadership, and I argue that there is no hierarchical order assigned to the different dimensions. The activities can be envisioned as locations on a moving carousel, each location being of equal importance. There are many entry points at which one can get on and off, and once on the carousel one is free to move about to different locations.

Writing about black women involved in the civil rights movement of the same period, Charlotte Bunch points out that "while black male leaders were the ones whom the press called on to be the spokesmen, it was often the black women who made things happen, especially in terms of organizing people at the community level" (in Astin & Leland, 1991, p. xiii). Likewise, when I initially described my research proposal to a male Chicano colleague of the movement generation, he sincerely encouraged me to pursue the topic, but unassumingly warned that there were no female leaders in the blowouts and that few women were involved. Perhaps because he views the blowouts from a traditional leadership paradigm, he overlooked Chicanas as leaders and failed to recognize their important contributions to the blowouts. Yet in distinct ways and to varying degrees, the women I interviewed participated in these different dimensions of leadership. Their participation was vital to the blowouts, but because a traditional leadership paradigm does not acknowledge the importance of those who participate in organizing, developing consciousness, and networking, their leadership remains unrecognized and unappreciated by most historians.

In the following sections, I will discuss each of the five identified, interrelated dimensions of leadership, exploring the ways in which the oral histories of the women in this study further our understanding of the blowouts and of women's activist leadership.

Participation and Implementation of Meetings, Events, and Activities: Organizing

Organizing includes attending meetings and planning or implementing events and activities that were directly or indirectly related to the blowouts. There were numerous meetings, events, and activities that took place prior to and after the blowouts in which students, teachers, parents, and community members raised concerns about the quality of education in the East L.A. high schools. All eight of the women discuss attending and actively participating in PTA meetings, school board meetings, blowout committee meetings, or community planning meetings that were held in such places as the Cleveland House, the Plaza Community Center, and the home of Tanya Luna Mount's parents.[5]

In an attempt to address and remedy school inequities, activists in these organizations implemented a number of strategies before resorting to a school boycott. For example, Vickie Castro, Paula Crisostomo, and Rachael Ochoa Cervera were intimately involved in YCCA, a community youth group formed by former Camp Hess Kramer participants that took up issues of education. Members of this group met regularly, talked to other youth at government-sponsored Teen Posts, and conducted a needs assessment survey to find out what was going on in the schools. Vickie discusses her and others' organizing efforts in the years prior to the blowouts:

And we even had like a questionnaire that we had made. I wish we had kept all these things. We wanted to compile complaints and I guess we were trying to develop, even in our simple perspective, like a needs assessment. We would talk to kids: What do you think about your school? Do they help you? Do they push you out? Are you going to college? ... I know that we compiled quite a bit of complaints and that's where during the walkouts when you hear about the demands, a lot of that was based on these complaints. So we had a process in mind. (Castro interview)

After the surveys were returned and tallied up, Vickie, Paula, Rachael, and other YCCA members decided to actively support and work on Julian Nava's school board campaign. Paula remembers how their organizing efforts progressed:

Got student perspectives

So it was interesting when we got it [the surveys] back and we tallied it up and again it strengthened our belief of how inadequate we saw the schools to be. Well, of course, the next question was, "Okay, now what do we do?" We got involved in a campaign, my first political campaign that I worked in, for Julian Nava, the first Latino to run for school board. It was an at-large position before the board was broken up into districts or regions, and he courted us. We worked with him, we worked for him, thinking that this was the way, this was an answer. (Crisostomo interview)

When Tanya Luna Mount speaks of her organizing efforts, they range from the antiwar movement she helped organize at Roosevelt just prior to the blow-outs to the work she did against police brutality in her community. In addition, Tanya remembers participating in the planning of what would be presented in discussions with the board of education: "I was on the committee that would decide what would be said at the board of education meetings. And we'd elect who would do it." She also speaks of the many blowout organizational meetings that were held at her home and how "we were open all night ... [and] people would come over our house during the walkouts." She remembers that her home even made the news when George Putnam, a conservative news commentator, said that there was a house at "126 South Soto Street in East Los Angeles, in Boyle Heights that is notorious for being commies, rebel rousers, and anti-government." *Baffling that historians did not consider her a leader*

In fact, an important component of organizing the blowouts was the active participation in meetings that helped to develop or support the demonstra-tions. Mita Cuaron (interview, January 23, 1996) remembers actively partici-pating in many community meetings prior to and during the blowouts in which "we set up a list of demands on various topics and issues that we felt we were being deprived of," and community members decided that these concerns had to be brought before the board of education. Rosalinda Méndez González describes the school board meetings in which she and others protested the suspension of teacher Sal Castro and demanded that the board return him to his teaching position at Lincoln High School. Though the police employed various intimidation techniques, she and others continued to organize and actively participate in these meetings:

> I mean there would be so many hundreds of us that would show up—students, elderly people, some professionals, all kinds of people that would show up to these meetings that we couldn't even fit inside the board room. I mean people were out in the courtyard and they had to have the PA system.... But I remember also at these meetings all of the intimidation. The police were going around literally, aisle by aisle, snapping, snapping, snapping, snapping pictures of everybody who was there. I mean it was pure intimidation. If you're here to testify and you're here to demonstrate, we're going to have you on file. *wow! That is intimidating*

No! Probably not. Without the organizing efforts and persistence of these and other young Chicanas the blowouts probably would not have taken place, and the attention needed to expose poor educational conditions may not have been garnered. By organizing community people, the women in this study demonstrate the dynamic process and complex set of relationships that comprised the leadership of the 1968 blowouts. Indeed, this reconceptualization of leadership allows us to consider organizers as leaders in various grassroots movements, including the Chicano civil rights movement.

From Behind the Scenes: Developing Consciousness — *Raising awareness*

A second dimension of leadership is developing consciousness, the process of helping others gain awareness of school and social inequities through discussions or print media. Developing the consciousness of individuals is crucial to generating and maintaining the momentum needed for any social movement. Yet just as organizing is separated from the task of leading, consciousness shaping is often overlooked as part of the dynamic process.

Each of the women I talked with participated in raising consciousness through informal dialogues with peers, family members, or community members. As young women they challenged others to think about and consider the inequities they confronted on a daily basis. Rachael Ochoa Cervera put it bluntly, "You raised consciousness in any way that you could do it, subtly or outright." Often one of the most difficult and least rewarding tasks of leading, developing consciousness requires one to help others see and understand things like they never have before. Cassandra Zacarías (interview, December 7, 1995) reflects on the difficulty of the task:

This is definitely a behind-the-scenes task

> I was talking to students and trying to explain to them, and I remember that was really hard for me because I was a really shy person at the time. I was a real introverted person and this was really difficult to have people actually say, "Oh you're nuts. What the hell is wrong with you?" And I remember feeling sometimes—what have I gotten myself into?

In addition to holding informal discussions about school conditions or social inequities, these women used print media to raise consciousness. Both Tanya Luna Mount and Mita Cuaron's families had mimeograph machines that they used for mass duplication of informational leaflets and flyers, which were then distributed throughout the communities and schools. Furthermore, all the women I interviewed were somehow connected to the community activist newspapers *Inside Eastside* and *La Raza*. Celeste Baca worked in the *La Raza* office as a volunteer, Tanya Luna Mount and Paula Crisostomo wrote for and distributed newspapers, and the other women all read and encouraged others to read these newspapers. As high school students, Tanya Luna Mount and Paula Crisostomo contributed to building consciousness by writing articles specifically addressing the poor educational conditions in East Los Angeles schools. Paula recounts her involvement with the community activist newspapers:

> I typed and did layouts, and wrote ghost articles about the schools. I would also go to the [Whittier] Boulevard to sell *Chicano Student Movement* or *Inside Eastside*.... I would bring a whole stack to school and I would give a few to people, and they would pass them out to their friends. And then the school said we couldn't do it anymore, so I'd get to school early and I'd leave them around the campus. I would go into the bathroom and I would put them in the bathroom, the cafeteria, where I knew kids hung out, and I would tell people where they could find them. People would find them, but I wasn't actually distributing. *Sneaky & risky*

Developing consciousness, whether through verbal or written communication, is less public than tasks normally associated with traditional interpretations of leadership. Like organizing and networking, it is work that is done from behind the scenes, often unrecognized and unappreciated. By placing working-class females at the center of analysis, we are able to see this behind-the-scenes work and appreciate its importance in the leadership of the 1968 East L.A. Blowouts.

A Need for a Wide Base of Support: Networking

A third dimension of leadership, networking, refers to activities that link diverse groups in building a base of support. During the time of the blowouts it was important to have support from community members as well as from those outside the community who could lend some legitimacy to the students' efforts. Thus, networking involved both transforming community and familial ties into a political force and building a supportive political front by reaching those outside a comfortable social network. As Brodkin Sacks (1988a) found in her study of workplace networks at Duke Medical Center, the networks formed during the blowouts functioned as a sort of "telegraph system, carrying a collective message of protest against unfairness" (p. 81).

What! How?!

Students who were involved in the walkouts were continuously accused of being communist, being organized by outside agitators, or just wanting to skip school. Networking within the community was a way to develop an awareness of the school inequities and develop a political force. Cassandra Zacarías remembers having to defend her own and other students' actions while trying to gain support from teachers, peers, and some family members:

> The issue would come up, well, it's all outside agitators, it's all communists coming in and riling up the little Mexicans and these little teenagers and we'd say, "No it's not. It's within our community." ... I remember feeling like most of the kids didn't really like us and they'd say, "Oh, you know you guys are communists and you're crazy."... I'd tell my family, "No, I'm not a communist," and then start to tell them that there's all these inequities in the system.

Similarly, Vickie Castro, a college student at the time, comments on how important it was that high school students not cause a disturbance or skip school without understanding the issues:

> I remember something that was very important to all of us is that we just didn't want disturbance for disturbance sake. And we were really talking to kids saying, "We want you to know why you're walking out."... There was a purpose so that we did meet with groups in the park, in the schools, on the corners and we tried to say, "This is why we're doing this and we need your support."

Cassandra and Vickie's statements exemplify how networking (transforming community ties into a political force) is closely interrelated with raising consciousness—helping others gain awareness of school and social inequities.

During my interview with Sal Castro (February 6, 1996), he discussed networking strategies that involved students connecting with individuals outside of the communal or familial social networks. He knew that an endorsement from the church, César Chavez, or politicians would lend legitimacy to the students' cause: "I constantly wanted people of the cloth to support the kids. I was never able to get any support from the Catholic Church. We had to steal a banner of the Our Lady of Guadalupe because we couldn't get any priest." Finally, after a number of phone calls and some pleading, "a major coup" was set in place: Bobby Kennedy agreed to talk to the students and make a statement of support. Kennedy was on his way back to Washington, D.C., from a visit with César Chavez in Delano, California. He had to make a stop at the Los Angeles airport, where he agreed to meet with a group of students that included Paula Crisostomo and Cassandra Zacarías. A picture of Kennedy with the students appeared in local East Los Angeles papers, and Kennedy's endorsement proved to be a helpful networking strategy that increased support for the blowouts.

During the actual week and a half of the blowouts, Paula Crisostomo was involved with other students who were building a base of support throughout the city with groups such as the Jewish organization B'nai B'rith and Hamilton High School on the west side. Through speaking engagements, students voiced their concerns and discussed school inequities with others who could offer support and advocate on the students' behalf. Crisostomo recalls:

> We were also doing speaking engagements. I remember we spoke to the B'nai B'rith in West L.A. And we went to Hamilton and they had a rally for us in a park. During that week we were hot items, and a lot of groups were asking us to come and speak, and we were getting more support, so the board had to [listen].

In light of the widespread communist and outside agitator accusations, it was especially crucial to develop a network of individuals and organizations that could sanction and endorse the students' actions and demands.

Less Focus on More Visibility: Holding Office   makes sense

Holding an elected or appointed office is a fourth dimension of leadership. Four of the women I talked with held an elected or appointed office in direct or indirect relationship to the blowouts. Vickie Castro was the first president of YCCA, the youth organization that focused on education and was a precursor to the blowouts. Shortly after the school walkouts, Mita Cuaron and Cassandra Zacarías were elected student-body officers. Their Freedom Candidate slate was made up of Garfield Blowout Committee members and was based on the ideal of "instituting an educational system in our school which is based on equality, justice and first-rate education for all" (Garfield Blowout Committee, 1968). Months after the blowouts, Rosalinda Méndez González was one of the youths appointed to the Mexican American Education Commission, which was originally an advisory board to the school board.

Though these positions probably accorded these women slightly more visibility than other young female participants, the positions seemed to be secondary to their other leadership activities. For the most part, women casually mentioned these positions during their interviews. They spent much more time recalling and talking about the more private tasks that I have included under the dimensions of networking, organizing, and developing consciousness. In other words, they seem to identify their role in the blowouts more in relation to these dimensions of leadership than to the elected or appointed positions that they held. Though these women gave less focus to the more visible and public roles, documenting this dimension of leadership is important in that it demonstrates that young Chicanas also contributed to the blowouts (and to other social movements) within the more prevalent notion of leadership that equates elected officers and public speakers with leaders.

A More Public Space: Acting as Spokesperson

The fifth dimension of leadership is acting as an official or unofficial spokesperson. During the blowouts male participants usually took on this role and were found in front of the camera, quoted in the *Los Angeles Times*, or heard speaking before crowds. However, there were occasions in which a female student who was active in other dimensions of leadership also took on the role of spokesperson. Rosalinda Méndez González and Paula Crisostomo were both asked to act as official spokespersons by providing testimony about Mexican Americans in education based on their experiences as students. Each of them testified before the United States Commission on Civil Rights at hearings held in Los Angeles. As a recent graduate of Lincoln High School, Rosalinda felt that the school curriculum was primarily responsible for the failure of many Chicano students. The following is an excerpt of Rosalinda's comments before the United States Commission on Civil Rights in June of 1967:

> From the time we first begin attending school, we hear about how great and wonderful our United States is, about our democratic American heritage, but little about our splendid and magnificent Mexican heritage and culture. What little we do learn about Mexicans is how they mercilessly slaughtered the brave Texans at the Alamo, but we never hear about the child heroes of Mexico who courageously threw themselves from the heights of Chapultepec rather than allow themselves and their flag to be captured by the attacking Americans.... We look for others like ourselves in these history books, for something to be proud of for being a Mexican, and all we see in books and magazines, films, and T.V. shows are stereotypes of a dark, dirty, smelly man with a tequila bottle in one hand, a dripping taco in the other, a serape wrapped around him, and a big sombrero. But we are not the dirty, stinking wino that the Anglo world would like to point out as a Mexican. (CSAC, 1968)

[handwritten marginal note: powerful]

In an effort to return Sal Castro to the classroom, Rosalinda also testified before the Los Angeles School Board, as did Vickie Castro and other young Chicanas.

Though most young women involved in the blowouts did not fill roles as official spokespersons, several of the women I interviewed described instances in which they spontaneously addressed a group of students or the media in relation to the blowouts. Mita Cuaron reconstructs a situation in which she was an unofficial spokesperson:

> It was just so spontaneous. And I remember picking up an orange cone from the street, and began talking about, we are protesting and this is what's happening. And I don't remember exactly what I said, but I remember physically standing on a car and talking out loud. And for

two minutes there was quite a group of students not going back into school and then the police were called and they began to chase us.

Thus, although acting as a spokesperson is a dimension of leadership that was more often filled by males, these examples show that some women did participate in this dimension of leadership while also participating in other dimensions. Glad this was noted

The Multidimensional Influence of Gender

How is it that these eight women came to participate in the 1968 blowouts in the ways they did? What influenced and shaped their participation? This study provides evidence suggesting that the dimensions of leadership are not necessarily gender specific, and the same individual may engage in several dimensions (see also Brodkin Sacks, 1988b). While young women were more likely to be found participating in the first three dimensions of leadership— networking, organizing, and developing consciousness—it is important to look at the factors that shaped their participation rather than assume that these are gender-specific dimensions of leadership that are only filled by females. In a study of traditional and nontraditional patterns of Chicana and Mexicana activism, Margaret Rose (1990) concedes that personalities have shaped female participation in the United Farm Workers of America (UFW). However, she argues that the pattern of participation is more greatly influenced by complex factors such as class, cultural values, social expectations, and the sexual division of labor. Indeed, the eight women I interviewed discuss similar factors that appear to have shaped their participation in the school boycotts. In this final section, I will present the oral history data that speaks to the multidimensional influence of gender. uazy

The influence of gender was perceived in a somewhat nebulous way by the women in this study. Women made statements ranging from, "Nobody ever said that you couldn't do this because you were a girl," to "I know that the females were not the leaders," and from, "Being a female was not an issue, it was just a nonissue," to "I'm sure I knew that there was sexism involved ... but we probably didn't talk about it." This diversity of statements, both within interviews and between interviews, leads to a conclusion that these women held no single distinct and precise viewpoint on the influence of gender. Rather, the women's individual and collective thoughts on gender represent the indeterminate and complex influence of gender within a system of patriarchy —a system of domination and unequal stratification based on gender. Though the way that boys and girls were socialized may have reinforced the gender differences in how they exercised leadership in the school blowouts, the women's diverse comments reflect the complexity of gender's influence while also attributing their participation in various leadership roles to sexism, role compatibility, choice, and expectations.

The social, cultural, and temporal milieu all contributed to what was expected of young women in 1968. And though most of these women ventured from these expectations, they were very aware of them. For example, Vickie Castro stated, "So I think that my home life, in one sense, brought me up very traditional. And I definitely knew what the female role was suppose to be. And that it wasn't college, and it wasn't this and that." Paula Crisostomo also comments on the way that gender expectations, "how it was then," and her personal agency shaped the ways in which she participated in the blowouts:

> Boys were more outspoken and I think that's just because of, that's how it was then. They were given the interviews more than the girls were. When we would talk about the division of who was going to speak to what group, it was the boys who were chosen and the girls who sort of stayed back. And I think that's just how it was.... And I was happy, as I still am today, to be in the background. I'll do what you want me to do, but I'll do it back here. Don't have me stand in front of a mike, or in front of a group of people, I just don't want to do that.

Vickie points out that patriarchy and her own agency were complex forces that interacted to shape her participation. She believes there was a "big gender issue in the family." She grew up in a "traditional" family with a very strong and dominant father who expected her to get married and have children. Her father was an inspiration through his own strength and leadership, yet he often held traditional gender expectations and tried to place limitations on Vickie. On the other hand, her older brothers were always encouraging and supportive, and they urged Vickie to go on to college. Her family's influence gave her the strength to combat the sexism she and other young women found in some of the student organizations:

> Maybe my male friends at the time, in the organization, would try to put me in female roles. Like be the secretary, make the sandwiches, do that. But I think that I had such a strong male influence in my household, you know, four brothers and my father, that among my brothers I was equal. So I always challenged. And when I would see that there were no women involved, boom, I made myself right there. (Castro interview)

Rosalinda Méndez González also offers comments that demonstrate how the influence of gender interacted with various structures and social systems to offer a multidimensional influence. First, she acknowledges that few people raised the question or offered a critique of patriarchy in the early part of the Chicano movement (a point with which most of the women concur), yet Rosalinda experienced sexism in a personal relationship. Second, she points to the fact that it was older males involved in Camp Hess Kramer and other organizations, rather than females, that encouraged her and other young women to become involved in blowout-related activities:

I think that when we participated in things initially, there wasn't a consciousness of patriarchy. If you were a young man or young woman and you saw injustice, whether in regards to the farmworkers or in regards to our college, you spoke out and got involved. Now in my case, I very early on began to encounter some patriarchal hostilities from my own boyfriend, who very much criticized me for taking an active role and speaking out. But he didn't convince me nor did he succeed in holding me back. I was just very hurt by it, but I didn't accept his arguments or his reason. I encountered it at a very personal level. At the same time there were a lot of men, older men that were encouraging me to speak out and participate.

He was probably threatened.. —

Rosalinda explains that after the blowouts, as the movement began to gain momentum, she encountered increasing evidence of sexism and that women began addressing patriarchy as a system of domination. In fact, she argues that in many cases it was the female students who were at the forefront of the movement and that male students tried to hold young women back and move into the more visible leadership positions.

Typical

Though sexist gender expectations were prevalent within the existing patriarchal relations, Vickie Castro also points to how she and other female and male students were conscious of gender stereotypes and used them to their advantage. They would strategize the roles that students would take based on individual characteristics and resources. For her, that meant different things at different times. At one point it meant using her car and a set of chains to pull open the gates around Roosevelt High School; at other times it meant using her "goody-two-shoes image":

So we knew that if we needed someone who didn't look threatening, that looked like a nice person, I was to go in. I was the, you know, I'm a little bit more guera. I didn't really dress, I didn't really look chola. If we wanted somebody to be aggressive and very vocal then that was David's [Sanchez] role.... I always had the look to get out of it. I always looked real straight laced. And I knew that. And I used it. I never looked the militant type, the chola type.

In other words, she did not embody what some school officials feared most in Mexican American students. As a fair-complexioned female who dressed "appropriately," she was not threatening to the white mainstream community nor to the older or more conservative Mexicans in her own community. Vickie's physical appearance influenced the type of participation and leadership she offered to the blowouts, and she used it to gain support for the blowouts.

use what you have

Gender interacted with sexism, patriarchal relations, personal agency, and the family to shape the participation and leadership of young women in the blowouts. And while the women in this study acknowledge the impact gender expectations had on their participation, they link their participation in the blowouts to the discrimination and oppression of the community as a whole rather than to that of women. Mita Cuaron (interview, December 3, 1994) stated, "I felt as a whole, in terms of my peers and I, we were being discriminated against, but, personally, as a woman, I didn't feel that there was a differentiation."[6] This echoes the findings of Mary Pardo's (1990) study of the Mothers of East L.A. in which she points out that working-class women activists seldom opt to separate themselves from men and their families. As the women in my study reflect back, they too view their participation in the school blowouts as a struggle for their community and quality education.

Conclusion

The oral history data I present challenges the historical and ideological representation of Chicanas by relocating them to a central position in the historical narrative. Through a cooperative leadership paradigm that recognizes diverse dimensions of grassroots leadership, we are able to move beyond the traditional notion of leadership and identify ways in which women offered leadership in the blowouts. Though their stories are often excluded in the writing of history, I confirm that Chicanas have been intimately involved with and have offered leadership to the ongoing struggle for educational justice. The experiences of Celeste Baca, Vickie Castro, Paula Crisostomo, Mita Cuaron, Tanya Luna Mount, Rosalinda Méndez González, Rachael Ochoa Cervera, and Cassandra Zacarías rebuke the popular stereotypes of Mexican women as docile, passive, and apathetic, and demonstrate that women's leadership in events like the 1968 East Los Angeles School Blowouts has often been unrecognized and unappreciated.[7]

Through the oral history data of these eight women, I illustrate that looking at grassroots leadership within a cooperative leadership paradigm leads us to an alternative history of the 1968 East Los Angeles School Blowouts—a history that makes the invisible visible. This alternative history of women's participation and leadership also pushes us to consider how we can redefine the categories for studying and participating in community activism. By redefining the leadership paradigm, we may be able to break through dominant ways of thinking and doing and reclaim histories that have been silenced in our communities, as well as shape our future histories to be more inclusive of traditionally silenced voices. Indeed, there is something faulty in previous leadership paradigms that have not allowed us to acknowledge Chicanas as leaders in the 1968 blowouts, the Chicano movement, and in other grassroots movements. A cooperative leadership paradigm allows us to address the erroneous absence of Chicanas as participants and leaders in history and contemporary life.[8]

Endnotes

1. In this paper *Chicana* is used when referring to female persons of Mexican origin living in the United States—irrespective of generational or immigration status. *Chicano* is used when referring to both male and female persons; I specifically indicate when the term refers only to males. Terms of identification vary according to context and it should be noted that during the period of interest in this paper (1968), these terms were especially prominent within the student population as conscious political identifiers. The term *Chicano* was not prominent prior to the 1960s and is therefore used interchangeably with *Mexican* when referring to pre-1960s history.
2. I am indebted to the eight women who allowed me to transform their lived history into a written one—*muchisimas gracias.*
3. The oral history interviews I conducted took place between June 1995 and January 1996. Following a network sampling procedure, I interviewed eight women who were identified by other female participants or resource individuals as key participants or leaders in the blowouts. I followed an interview protocol with open-ended questions in order to elicit multiple levels of data. Although I took interview notes, each interview was also recorded and transcribed. In addition to conducting an oral history interview with each participant, I also conducted a focus group interview that included seven of the eight women together for one interview. Finally, I provided each woman with a transcription of her individual interview so that she had a chance to reflect and comment on her responses to questions. I did so prior to the focus group interview, allowing the women the opportunity to bring up concerns at the group interview. During the group interview, I also shared my preliminary analysis with the women and asked for their reaction and input to the themes I had identified from their oral history interviews. Their comments have helped me to better understand the roles they played in the blowouts and the ways in which we might look at grassroots leadership differently. Throughout my investigation, I utilized a theoretical and epistemological perspective grounded in critical feminisms that are strongly influenced by women of color (e.g., see Delgado Bernal, 1998b). For more on the methodology of this study, see Delgado Bernal, 1998a.
4. Based on the Los Angeles Unified School District's "Historical Racial Ethnic Data 1966–1979," the percentage of Hispanic students in each of the five schools in 1968 was as follows: Garfield, 96%; Roosevelt, 83%; Lincoln, 89%; Wilson, 76%; and Belmont, 59%.
5. Tanya Luna Mount's parents had a long history of labor, civil rights, and peace activism. Her mother, Julia Luna Mount, was actively involved in a labor resistance movement at one of the largest food processing plants in Los Angeles, which included a massive walkout and a twenty-four-hour picket line to end deplorable working conditions. See Ruiz (1987).
6. This particular interview with Mita Cuaron was conducted by Susan Racho.
7. For snapshots of where the eight women are today, see Delgado Bernal (1998a).
8. A longer version of this chapter was originally published in *Frontiers* (Delgado Bernal, 1998a).

References

Astin, H. S., & Leland, C. (1991). *Women of influence, women of vision: A cross-generational study of leaders and social change.* San Francisco, CA: Jossey-Bass.

Briegel, K. (1974). Chicano student militancy: The Los Angeles High School Strike of 1968. In M. P. Servin (Ed.), *An awakened minority: The Mexican-Americans* (2nd ed.) (pp. 215–225). New York: Macmillan Publishing.

Brodkin Sacks, K. (1988a). *Caring by the hour: Women, work, and organizing at Duke Medical Center.* Urbana: University of Illinois Press.

Brodkin Sacks, K. (1988b). Gender and grassroots leadership. In A. Bookman & S. Morgen (Eds.), *Women and the politics of empowerment* (pp. 77–94). Philadelphia, PA: Temple University Press.

California State Advisory Committee to the United States Commission on Civil Rights, "Education and the Mexican American Community in Los Angeles County," CR 1.2: Ed 8/3 (April 1968), 16.

De la Torre, A., & Pesquera, B. M. (Eds.). (1993). *Building with our hands: New directions in Chicana studies.* Berkeley: University of California Press.

Delgado Bernal, D. (1997). Chicana school resistance and grassroots leadership: Providing an alternative history of the 1968 East Los Angeles Blowouts. Unpublished doctoral dissertation, University of California, Los Angeles.

Delgado Bernal, D. (1998a). Grassroots leadership reconceptualized: Chicana oral histories and the 1968 East Los Angeles Blowouts. *Frontiers, 19* (2), 113–142.

Delgado Bernal, D. (1998b). Using a Chicana feminist epistemology in educational research. *Harvard Educational Review, 68* (4), 555–582.

Garfield Blowout Committee. (1968). Election campaign materials.

Gómez-Quiñones, J. (1978). *Mexican students por la raza: The Chicano student movement in southern California, 1967–1977.* Santa Barbara, CA: Editorial La Causa.

Gonzalez, G. G. (1990). *Chicano education in the era of segregation.* Philadelphia, PA: Balch Institute Press.

Kuhn, T. S. (1970). *The structure of scientific revolutions* (2nd ed.). Chicago, IL: University of Chicago Press.

McCurdy, J. (1968a, March 12). School board yields on some student points. *Los Angeles Times,* 1, 3.

McCurdy, J. (1968b, March 17). Frivolous to fundamental: Demands made by East Side High School students listed. *Los Angeles Times,* 1, 4–5.

Mexican-American Youth Leadership Conference. (1967). Conference Fact Sheet: Fifth Annual Mexican-American Youth Leadership Conference, Malibu, CA.

Mora, M., & Del Castillo, A. R. (Eds.). (1980). *Mexican women in the United States: Struggles past and present.* Los Angeles: Chicano Studies Research Center Publications, University of California.

Morales, A. (1972). *Ando Sangrado/ I am bleeding: A study of Mexican American police conflict.* La Puente, CA: Perspectiva Publications.

Muñoz, C., Jr. (1972). *The politics of Chicano urban protest: A model of political analysis.* Unpublished doctoral dissertation, Claremont Graduate School, California.

Muñoz, C., Jr. (1974). The politics of protest and Chicano liberation: A case study of repression and cooptation. *Aztlan, 5* (1/2), 119–141.

Muñoz, C., Jr. (1989). *Youth, identity, power: The Chicano movement.* New York: Verso.

Negrete, L. R. (1972). Culture clash: The utility of mass protest as a political response. *Journal of Comparative Cultures, 1* (1), 25–36.

Pardo, M. (1990). Mexican-American women grassroots community activists: "Mothers of East Los Angeles." *Frontiers, 11* (1), 1–7.

Puckett, M. (1971). *Protest politics in education: A case study in the Los Angeles Unified School District.* Unpublished doctoral dissertation, Claremont Graduate School, California.

Rose, M. (1990). Traditional and nontraditional patterns of female activism in the United Farm Workers of America, 1962 to 1980. *Frontiers, 11* (1), 26–32.

Rosen, G. (1973). The development of the Chicano movement in Los Angeles from 1967–1969. *Atzlan, 4* (1), 155–83.

Ruiz, V. L. (1987). *Cannery women, cannery lives: Mexican women, unionization, and the California Food Processing Industry, 1930–1950.* Albuquerque: University of New Mexico Press.

Ruiz, L. (executive producer), & Racho, S. (segment producer). (1996). "Taking Back the Schools," part 3 of *Chicano: A history of the Mexican American civil rights movement* [Documentary]. Los Angeles: National Latino Communications Center & Galan Productions, Inc.

6

Detraction, Fear, and Assimilation
Race, Sexuality, and Education Reform Post–9/11

KEVIN K. KUMASHIRO

Over the past few years, my experiences in the fields of educational research and advocacy suggest that many people, while interested in seeing race- and sexuality-based oppressions in schools challenged, are willing to challenge only so much. I was once told by a leader in a major educational organization that they could advocate for policies and programs to stop the bullying and harassment that target differences in sexual orientation and gender identity, but not curriculum that raises awareness of heterosexism and gender privilege. I was once told by a member of a team of researchers on and advocates for students of color that their work would focus on developing programs and curriculum to close the measurable gaps in academic achievement between groups of students based on race and ethnicity, but not on raising critical questions about what is being measured as achievement, how it is being measured, and why such standards and assessments of learning might themselves privilege certain racial groups. I was even told, by colleagues of leading scholars on race and leading scholars on sexuality, to be careful when writing about intersections of differences because my analyses of the heterosexism in race studies and the racism in sexuality studies have already caused me to lose favor among those who see me as a traitor to their cause. At times, anti-oppressive education seems willfully partial.

There are many possible reasons why researchers and advocates who are intentionally and explicitly working against race- and sexuality-based oppressions in education might be willing and able to go only so far. In this chapter I offer one such reason—that assumptions framing anti-oppressive education reforms are often, at their core, assimilationist. I begin by examining several events and changes in the United States following September 11th, 2001, some with more apparent connections to K–12 education (including attacks on civil liberties and harassment of certain groups) and some without (including the abuse of Iraqi prisoners). I do so to illustrate two lenses—a lens of detraction and a lens of fear—that lead us to understandings and responses that often fail to interrupt the racially and sexually oppressive status quo in society and in schools. Given the assimilationist demand of even anti-oppressive assumptions of "progress" and "reform," I argue that educational research and advocacy must do more to trouble their tendency toward willful partiality. Perhaps nowhere in post–9/11 society is this willful partiality more stark than in the abuse of Iraqi prisoners and the scandal that ensued, and thus it is there that I begin my analysis.

Orientalism and the Lens of Detraction

In the spring of 2004, images of naked brown bodies in sexualized situations flashed on television and computer screens across the United States and the world. More and more photographs and personal testimonies had surfaced of abuse inflicted on Iraqi prisoners by members of the U.S. military. Some of the abuse involved a mockery or forced abdication of religion, as when prisoners were compelled to denounce their Islamic beliefs, thank Jesus, consume prohibited foods and drinks, abstain from prayer and worship, undress in front of others, and simulate or engage in prohibited sex acts (Fay, 2004). This was perhaps not surprising: The September 11th tragedies were largely understood as constitutive of a religious or holy war (i.e., a *jihad*) against the United States. Although not all in the Arab region are Muslim (and vice versa), and not all Muslims subscribed to this anti–United States war, many in the United States embraced the discourse perpetuated by political leaders and the media that conflated race, religion, and political ideology into the category of "Arab-Muslim terrorist" (Chon & Yamamoto, 2003).

Significantly, this racialization of the Arab Muslim, along with a newly rationalized fear toward this group as "terrorist," resulted not merely in abuse that targeted religion. Much of the abuse was also sexual in nature, which is, again, perhaps not surprising. Within the United States, racialized oppression has long operated alongside a queering of sexuality and sex for men of color, as in the post–Civil War lynching of black men that involved physical castration (Pinar, 2001). Even stereotypes and representations of men of color have long involved some queering of the male body, as with black American men stereotyped as oversexed and oversized, or Asian American men stereotyped as asexual and small (Kumashiro, 2002).

In Iraq, for the most part, male guards were forcing male prisoners to undress for others to see for extended periods of time. Prisoners were placed in human pyramids or other positions in which their naked bodies were in contact, and some were forced to simulate or even engage in same-sex sexual activity with one another. Some guards themselves were perpetuators of forced sodomy with foreign objects and of various forms of rape. Such abuse should not be considered homoerotic by mere coincidence, and should not be dismissed as the acts of sadistic homosexuals. As has been known to happen in college fraternity initiations, straight-identified men often subject other straight-identified men to homoerotic situations as a gendered enactment of power, as a way to feminize another group, sometimes playfully but sometimes not (Sanday, 1990).

It was here, in the sexual aspects of the Iraqi prisoner abuse, that we saw manifest on a physical, visceral level a new articulation of Orientalism (Said, 1979). Orientalism can be traced back 2000 years when European explorers of Asia and the Middle East began crafting tales of a mystical Orient, a place where the landscape, the food, and even the bodies of the human inhabitants were fundamentally different than (and inferior to) their own. By subordinating Asia and the Middle East within an imagined patriarchal relationship between the feminized East and the masculinized West, Europeans convinced themselves that they had a moral responsibility to make the Orient more civilized. According to Said, this relationship took on physical and sexual symbolism as a male Europe was to arouse, penetrate, and possess the "Eastern bride," and the impact went beyond the symbolic as Europeans colonized different parts of the East and profited from their natural and human resources.

While the abuse of Iraqi prisoners could have been portrayed as the newest manifestation of Orientalism and of the history of gendered racism in the United States, such was not the case. Political leaders were quick to denounce the abuse and joined the public outrage against the individuals whose (presumably) singular sadism or irresponsibility made such abuse possible. People seemed surprised that Americans could inflict such abuse, even in a time of war. The abuse was not seen as indicative of the colonialist, racist, or (hetero) sexist relations that the United States has long developed with Asia and the Middle East (Lee, 1999). Rather, the abuse was seen as an anomaly—a detraction from what is otherwise a mutually beneficial relationship. In fact, the public discourse of oppression seemed to focus entirely on the graphic images of abuse, on the spectacle of soldiers gone bad, making possible a willful ignoring of less overt and more systemic forms of oppression. Ironically, the abuse, while a physical manifestation of Orientalism, was exactly what helped the United States to willfully ignore its role in Orientalism. That is, the Iraqi prisoner abuse was a spillage of the United States' Orientalist relationship with the East, but one that detracted attention from that very relationship.

It is important to ask, then, what it would mean for the public to learn to read these spillages in counterhegemonic ways, that is, in ways that interrupt complicity with the oppressions from which they originated. There are many ways to frame or understand or respond to the spillages of oppression. Not all understandings need to be detracting.

The mental image of a white U.S. soldier raping a brown-bodied prisoner out East reminded me of a short story titled "The Shoyu Kid" (Kaneko, 1976), about a group of young boys in a Japanese American internment camp during World War II. In this story, the spillage of Orientalism is the molestation of a Japanese American boy by a white U.S. soldier. As with the Iraqi abuse, the molesting of a Japanese American boy (in which the boy pleasures the soldier) embodies the gendered language of West–East relations that is symbolic of Orientalism. But unlike the press coverage of the Iraqi abuse, the short story does not create a spectacle of the boy's molestation. In fact, the reader does not learn about the molestation except through implication because the boy who observed the molestation refuses to describe what he observed. By not capturing in language or graphic detail, and thus instantiating the molestation, the story prevents the reader from feeling that the event is now known, and in doing so, prevents the reader from feeling outraged at only the individuals responsible. The silence around the act of molestation keeps that act from becoming known as only a singular occurrence, thus helping to drive the story around a deeper meaning of molesting relations.

Therein lies the pedagogical potential of the framing of this spillage. The boys who learn of the molestation do not direct their frustration at the individual soldier alone. To them, the soldier and the molested boy symbolize how "everyone's" queer. As the boys commiserate in silence, one of them throws rocks at but misses the sign that names the camp in which they are being interned, physically acting out and demonstrating their frustration at things beyond their reach (Eng, 2001). And there the story ends, inviting the reader to ask troubling questions about the meaning of the molestation in the context of the Japanese American internment. The story does not frame the molestation as a detracting spillage or spectacle. Rather, it frames the molestation as something that we could not bear to know, and that in our struggle to come to know, we are compelled to interrupt our complicity with that from which it spilled.

Admittedly, there are formidable challenges to learning to read in ways that ask troubling questions about the contexts of such spillages. Today, perhaps one of the greatest challenges to anti-oppressive readings can be seen in the climate of fear that has been cultivated in the United States post–September 11th—a fear that compels only certain hegemonic readings. Thus, I turn to the second lens of analysis in this chapter—the lens of fear.

Hegemony and the Lens of Fear

I note elsewhere (Kumashiro, 2004) that I was sitting in my office on the morning of September 11, 2001, when a colleague rushed to my door to tell me that she had just heard that an airplane had crashed into one of the World Trade Center towers in New York City. As the hours passed, more airplanes crashed, both of the towers collapsed, a part of the Pentagon in Washington, DC, was destroyed, and all attention seemed to turn to the terror that had hit U.S. soil. Thousands were presumed to have died, forthcoming tragedies were not ruled out, and the nation seemed paralyzed with grief, fear, and uncertainty. Classes were cancelled at the college where I was teaching, so

I headed home, glued to the radio, and then the television. I, too, was overcome with sadness. I wept as I saw many die and heard many witnesses tell their stories of panic and loss. I, too, was overcome with fear. Some of the attackers passed through the airport not far from where I was then living, in Maine. I had friends and relatives living in New York City and Washington, DC. I hoped that they were safe. And I hoped that I was safe.

Many people wanted answers. These were not tragic coincidences. These were planned attacks. Why would people want to attack "us?" How could people be so evil? Who is responsible? How will we punish "them?" Mixed in with grief, fear, and uncertainty was a profound sense of anger. I remember not being able to eat very much that day. My nausea was but one of the indications that I was, indeed, overcome with great emotion. But unlike many others, my feelings of sadness and fear resulted not only from acknowledging the attacks on U.S. soil and the deaths left in their wake. My feelings derived increasingly from how I suspected many in the United States would respond. News commentators were speculating that this was an act of terrorism by Muslim extremists, and political leaders were promising to use all resources at their disposal to punish those responsible for this "worst act of terrorism on U.S. soil." People wanted revenge. And I feared that in the name of revenge, many would be unwilling or even unable to recognize the oppressiveness of their responses. I feared that many would respond in terribly oppressive ways. My fears were justified.

As U.S. intelligence agencies gathered evidence that "Muslim extremists" were responsible for these attacks, the responses were swift. Abroad, the United States sent more and more military forces to find and punish those responsible. Political leaders called for a war on terrorism that would span not only the Middle East, but the entire globe in an effort to eliminate those who sought to attack freedom and democracy. Within the United States, more and more individuals seemed to think this war was against anyone who "looked Muslim" or "looked Arab," including those who wore a turban or head wrap or simply had darker skin. Such Muslim- or Arab-looking people were treated as potential criminals. They were carefully, even aggressively scrutinized when trying to board airplanes and were subject to harassment and abuse. In the months that followed September 11th, the reports of hate incidences and hate crimes against individuals who looked Muslim or Arab increased dramatically in the United States (Coen, 2001).

Although political leaders were quick to denounce such racial and religious scapegoating, they themselves were guilty of similar acts of harassment and discrimination. As agencies responsible for fighting terrorism began arresting or harassing many they suspected of being connected to the attacks or to future attacks and were denying many of them their constitutional rights, political leaders were granting more and more powers of surveillance to these agencies to fight terrorism (American Civil Liberties Union, 2001). In fact, in an eerie parallel to the Japanese American internment during World War II, hundreds upon hundreds of people, including Muslim Americans and Americans of Middle Eastern descent, were rounded up and interned. More and more initiatives were launched to expand the abilities of the government to gather information on how we spend our money, what we read in the library or on the Internet, where we travel and when, what we do in our spare time and with whom—and this information could come via our neighbors and private companies in ways we were not even aware. These increased powers may have conflicted with our constitutional and civil rights, but polls indicated that the majority of the people in the United States supported such a compromise (Taylor, 2001).

This was, after all, a time for the nation to come together. We should stand behind our political leaders and present ourselves as a strong, united nation. We should be proud to be part of the United States and display this pride with flags on our shirts and our cars and our desks and our lawns. After all, the United States was said to symbolize freedom and democracy, and to attack the United States was to attack these institutions as well. The pressure to conform to these convictions was significant, as was the penalty for failing to do so. The sole congresswoman who voiced dissent for the president's war policies received death threats (Carlson, 2001). Even in my own neighborhood, news that individuals were being attacked verbally and physically for being "anti-American" prompted a woman and her partner to take down a sign from their apartment window that read, "Give peace a chance." Being "American" required acting in only certain ways and wanting only certain things.

People were afraid, and were kept in a state of fear as the government constantly raised and lowered and raised again the terror alert. The media constantly reminded us that the terrorists were still out there, planning their next attacks, and although U.S. intelligence was successful in thwarting one attack after another, the terrorists continued to evade capture. So long as the enemy was out there, the American public would continue to turn to what it perceived to be a source of strength: strength in our sense of national identity and unity; strength in our president and his ability to fight back. We are now learning that the president might have been lying about reasons to go to war, and with whom, and where, and when (Moore, 2004). It might have been the case that the United States was not as much the innocent victim as the media would have had us believe, given our actions around the world in the past century. It might be the case that the fear we feel is generated in part by those who profit most when we support paying more for greater security, including contractors and businesses with ties to the Bush administration (Moore, 2004). Or perhaps that is the point: Much can be overlooked and, more importantly, accomplished when people are afraid. From the financial benefits of business contracts to the social benefits (for those already privileged) of a reduced welfare state to the political benefits of increased unity and conformity, there is great profit in the business of fear.

Within education, fear similarly drives reform. For over two decades, the public has been told to fear that we are a "nation at risk" of problems. Domestically, large percentages of students are failing, especially in poorer communities with less resources and presumably (or perhaps, consequently) more crime. Abroad, students from some countries are outperforming our students on standardized tests. Critics argue that students in our nation's schools are failing to learn what is needed to succeed in the workplace and the global market, forcing the nation to devote more of its resources to addressing social ills while compromising its position as a world leader in military strength, scientific achievement, democratic values, and political influence.

If we believe that the United States is faltering, and if we believe that things were better in some mythical past, some golden age, then we are likely to want things to be as they were then. And if we believe that education back then was better and is faltering because of the various trends in educational reform, then we are likely to revert to commonsensical notions of how schools were and should be. We will want schools to be teaching primarily the academic subjects, like the "three Rs" of reading, writing, and arithmetic; we will want standardized curricula that level the playing field by teaching everyone the same thing; we will want to see high test scores as proof that students have learned; and we will want teachers to use instructional methods that we know "work" for students. Current reforms (via the No Child Left Behind Act) are following these romanticized ideals by making explicit what and how teachers are supposed to teach through learning standards, scripted curricula, high-stakes tests for student promotion and graduation, and instructional methods that are "scientifically proven" to be effective (United States Department of Education, 2002).

Such reforms are financially profitable. Scripted curricula require textbooks, worksheets, teacher guides, and other materials to be purchased by schools or districts. High-stakes tests require testing sheets, scoring services, study guides, and other materials, also to be purchased by schools or states. Defining only certain methods to be "scientifically proven" privileges only certain kinds of research in competitions for funding, publishing, and other forms of support. Even the delineation of learning standards is profitable, perhaps not financially, but socially and politically, because it privileges only certain knowledge, skills, and perspectives, or perhaps more accurately, the knowledge, skills, and perspectives of only certain groups in society—those defining the standards (Apple, 2001).

We can agree that there are problems in education. However, we need to appreciate that there are many ways to understand the problems, and consequently, that what we are fearing, and how we go about addressing it, are necessarily framed by only partial understandings. We need to recognize that there are always multiple ways of understanding and addressing problems in education, each with its own strengths and weaknesses.

Detraction and Fear in Education Initiatives

This brings me back to my opening argument that education communities are often willing to address only certain problems in only certain ways, thereby going only so far in challenging oppression. Consider, for example, the issue of sexual orientation and gender identity in schools. Mainstream society seems committed to ensuring the safety of all students in schools, including students who are lesbian, gay, bisexual, transgender, and queer (LGBTQ). However, beyond the issue of school safety, disagreement persists over whether any other lesson or even conversation around queer sexuality belongs in school, including discussions to raise awareness of sexual diversity, students' identities, and especially the privileges of heterosexuality and gender conformity. Some people choose not to pursue such lessons or conversations out of fear of criticism that they are encouraging students to think differently than their parents or religious communities, or that they are encouraging students to become queer, either in their behavior or their desires. This fear of being seen as promoting homosexuality helps to explain why many are willing to respond to homophobia, but not to address the underlying dynamic of heterosexism. Of course, without interrupting heterosexism, the oppression of queers will continue to find ways to slip out, perhaps in more subtle forms of harassment or perhaps in ways that, by their extremism or apparent singularity, continue to detract attention from the root of the problem.

Consider, as another example, issues of race in schools. Much attention in research and the popular press has centered on the gap that persists between the academic achievement of some groups of students and that of others, especially black American and Latino/a students in working-class communities in comparison to white American students. One explanation for this problem centers on money—black American and Latino/a students tend to sit in schools with crumbling walls, outdated resources, and underprepared staff, the implication being that with better resources, these students too can learn and achieve. However, not often debated among policy makers and educational leaders are problems with the definitions and measures of achievement that frame this gap. People are not often asking whether we need to significantly change what we are trying to teach or how we are measuring what students are learning, as if the core curricula and the standardized tests are not themselves problematic. The focus remains on how to get all students to learn what white American students are learning, and to perform as they perform. The fear that they will be seen as dismissing the educational inequities experienced by certain racial groups helps to explain why many people are willing to respond to the disadvantaging of students of color, but not the privileging of whiteness that engenders these gaps.

Significantly, such fears have much to do with containing various racial and sexual "problems," that is, with limiting the extent to which racial and sexual differences can and should matter in schools. This is especially apparent when examining the politically convenient way that some groups—such as the "model minority" Asian Americans and the gender-conforming or "properly" gendered LGBTQ students—are positioned against or outside of the victims of these problems. Asian American students (with aggregated achievement scores as high as or higher than those of white American students) and gender-conforming LGBTQ students (who do not draw attention to their sexual differences) help to make it possible to overlook racial or sexual privilege precisely because their differences are not considered the cause of problems that draw public outrage (e.g., statistical gaps in achievement, widespread bullying and harassment). Despite research showing the problems experienced by even the high-achieving Asian American student (Osajima, 1993) and the gender-conforming LGBTQ student (Friend, 1993), stereotypes persist that these groups model how racially and sexually different students can and even should fit into schools.

My point, here, is that educational reforms targeting race- and sexuality-based oppressions in schools seem to seek balance: balance between pushing the envelope but not pushing too far, between addressing some forms of oppression but not others, between responding to some fears but not responding to others—and in seeking this balance, we often filter out the very things that can bring about systemic change. Thus we need to ask: What is it that drives us to seek this balance in the first place?

Covering and the Lens of Assimilation

I argue that much of current educational reform that attempts to challenge race- and sexuality-based oppressions centers on a demand to assimilate. This is, of course, ironic: The protection of those who are different comes in the form of demanding that they downplay those differences, which means the "protection" is really a guise for assimilationist demands. But this irony is exactly what frames much of contemporary discourse on anti-oppression in broader society.

According to Yoshino (2002), society often measures its progress against various forms of oppression by the degree to which it prohibits—legally and culturally—overt forms of discrimination. In particular, it views as progress the moves from demanding that differences be changed (*converted*), to demanding that differences be hidden (*passed*), to allowing differences to coexist so long as they are downplayed (*covered*). This progression from the demands to convert to pass to cover characterizes dominant views of the history of progress for LGBTQ people in the United States. The thinking goes something like this: Whereas LGBTQ people were once expected to be converted or cured, they are now being asked to pass, as with the military's "don't ask, don't tell" policy, and are in some contexts even allowed to be out as LGBTQ if they do not make obvious their LGBTQ-ness, such as by refraining from cross-dressing, or public displays of affection, or mention of their same-sex partners or longings.

This model of progress sets up hierarchies not only among the different forms of assimilation (with conversion being the most severe) but also among the different groups in society targeted by these assimilationist demands. In particular, those groups that experience discrimination because of traits considered to be immutable or necessarily visible—including people of color and women—have been deemed more in need of legal protection from discrimination than groups that can more easily pass or cover. As Yoshino (2002) argues:

> The American legal antidiscrimination paradigm has been dominated by the cases of race, and, to a lesser extent, sex. The solicitude directed toward racial minorities and women has been justified in part by the fact that they are marked by "immutable" and "visible" characteristics—that is, that such groups cannot assimilate into mainstream society because they are marked as different. The law must step in because these groups are physiologically incapable of blending into the mainstream. In contrast, major strands of American antidiscrimination law direct much less concern toward groups that can assimilate. Such groups, after all, can engage in self-help by assimilating into mainstream society. (p. 771)

Of course, the distinction between groups that are visibly marked and those that are not is not always very clear. Racial and gender differences are not always apparent (as with people of color who "look white"), and sexual orientation is not always hidden (as when LGBTQ people "act gay" through dress, mannerism, and affiliation). Perhaps more important, not all forms of discrimination target the differences that we cannot change or hide. In fact, Yoshino argues that discrimination today often targets what we *can* change. Like LGBTQ people, people of color and women are demanded to cover all the time, as when expected to lose an accent, wear only certain clothes, style the hair in only certain ways, behave properly feminine, and so forth:

> [C]ontemporary forms of discrimination to which racial minorities and women are most vulnerable often take the guise of enforced covering. A member of a racial minority cannot be sanctioned for failing to convert or to pass without having a Title VII employment discrimination claim. But he can be sanctioned for failing to cover—for wearing cornrows, for lapsing into Spanish, or for speaking with an accent. Similarly, a woman generally cannot be burdened for failing to convert or to pass. Yet it is still true that for constitutional purposes, state actors can burden pregnancy without triggering a sex discrimination analysis. (Yoshino, 2002, p. 781)

Antidiscrimination laws that protect against demands to convert or pass often fail to protect against demands to cover.

While these subtle forms of discrimination may seem less severe than demands to convert or pass, demands to cover can impact as severely as the other demands on the very core of a person's identity. That is, the demand to cover can be a demand to downplay those things that are central to one's sense of self. This becomes clear when we recognize that our identities and differences are not embedded in our bodies, but rather, are developed in relation to other identities and differences. Who we are has much to do with how people relate to one another and view our relations to one another, which means that a person's sense of self has much to do with how others read that person, from the immutable bodily traits to the mutable acts and ways of being. By failing to protect such constitutive acts of self (or more accurately, by failing to protect us from discriminatory responses to *transgressive* constitutive acts), antidiscrimination laws are indirectly requiring that differences be assimilated —because only with assimilation will we avoid discrimination. This is certainly the case with LGBTQ students who are told that they would not experience bullying and harassment if they would not be so obviously gay. It is here that we can see educational reforms advancing assimilation: when compelling LGBTQ students to look straight and behave as do straight students; when compelling students of color to learn what white American students are supposed to be learning and perform as they perform.

Both legally and culturally, we need to trouble the assumption that the demand to cover is less severe. This requires changing our assumptions about what should be protected, and perhaps more important, about who should be the one to change:

> Civil rights practice, after all, is fundamentally about who has to change: The homosexual or the homophobe? The woman or the sexist? The racial minority or the racist? Yet the current paradigm errs prescriptively in extending greater protections to those who cannot change, and errs descriptively in characterizing identities like race and sex as being incapable of any kind of change. I believe that it could not err in either of these ways if it more closely examined the ubiquity of assimilation. When we see how much we all can and do change along every axis of our identity, we should apprehend that any account of discrimination that does not take assimilation into account is fundamentally impoverished. (Yoshino, 2002, pp. 938–939)

What needs protection is not our *inability* to change, which by implication, means that those things that can be changed should be changed. Rather, what needs protection is our *ability* to change so that we are free to be different than what mainstream society says we ought to be. What needs to change are not the differences among us, as if assimilation were the cure to all social ills, but rather the ways we read those differences, the demands we make of those differences, and our complicity with their assimilation.

Troubling the demand to assimilate requires shifting the questions that education reforms seek to address: from, "how do we get all students to learn as white American students learn?" to "how do the very things that students are currently learning (and the very ways we assess those learnings) themselves disadvantage certain groups, and how do we change such things?" Or from, "how do we protect LGBTQ students from encounters that oppress sexual difference?" to "how do we protect all students from encounters that privilege particular brands of sexual normalcy?" Until such shifts occur, educational reforms will continue to push only so far toward anti-oppressive change.

Reading "Problems" in Anti-Oppressive Ways

In this chapter, I examined how the lenses of detraction, fear, and assimilation can help to complicate the ways we think about problems surrounding racial and sexual difference in schools and society. Educational research should continue to use these lenses to examine other problems in education, not only in terms of safety or differences in levels of academic achievement, but also in terms of inclusion, recruitment and retention, equity of funding, and so forth along the various dimensions of diversity in society (i.e., gender, social class, religion, language, disabilities, and so on). With any problem, we need to be asking: Does the problem detract from a more fundamental recognition of oppression or relations of unequal power? Does our reading of the problem demand assimilation of some dimension of diversity or difference? Does some form of fear prevent us from reimagining the problem and possible solutions to it?

The lenses do not offer a panacea to our problems. In fact, more than proposing solutions, the lenses invite us to read problems in different ways—in troubling ways—as when uncovering insidious demands to assimilate (and our complicity with such demands). Anti-oppressive education requires constantly complicating our understanding of what makes for oppression and anti-oppressive change.

References

American Civil Liberties Union. (2001). *Surveillance under the USA PATRIOT Act* [On-line]. Available: http://www.aclu.org/SafeandFree/SafeandFree.cfm?ID= 12263 &c=206.

Apple, M. W. (2001). *Educating the "right" way: Markets, standards, God, and inequality.* New York: RoutledgeFalmer.

Carlson, P. (2001, September 23). California's Barbara Lee under attack for opposing war powers resolution. *Pittsburgh Post-Gazette*, 4.

Chon, M., & Yamamoto, E. K. (2003). *Resurrecting Korematsu: Post–September 11th national security curtailment of civil liberties* [On-line]. Available: http://www1. law.ucla.edu/~kang/racerightsreparation/Update__Ch__8/update__ch__8.html.

Coen, J. (2001, October 9). Hate-crime reports reach record level. *Chicago Tribune*, 11.

Eng, D. L. (2001). *Racial castration: Managing masculinity in Asian America.* Durham, NC: Duke University Press.

Fay, G. R. (2004). *AR 15-6 Investigation of the Abu Ghraib Detention Facility and 205th Military Intelligence Brigade* [On-line]. Available: http://www.yuricareport.com/PrisonerTorture-Directory/GeneralFay82504rpt.pdf.

Friend, R. A. (1993). Choices, not closets: Heterosexism and homophobia in schools. In L. Weis & M. Fine (Eds.), *Beyond silenced voices: Class, race, and gender in United States schools* (pp. 209–235). Albany: State University of New York Press.

Kaneko, L. (1976). The shoyu kid. *Amerasia Journal, 3* (2), 1–9.

Kumashiro, K. K. (2002). *Troubling education: Queer activism and antioppressive pedagogy.* New York: Routledge.

Kumashiro, K. K. (2004). *Against common sense: Teaching and learning toward social justice.* New York: RoutledgeFalmer.

Lee, R. G. (1999). *Orientals: Asian Americans in popular culture.* Philadelphia, PA: Temple University Press.

Moore, M. (Producer & Director). (2004). *Fahrenheit 911* [Film]. Available: Columbia Tristar Home Entertainment, 10202 W. Washington Blvd, Culver City, CA 90232.

Osajima, K. (1993). The hidden injuries of race. In L. A. Revilla, G. M. Nomura, S. Wong, & S. Hune (Eds.), *Bearing dreams, shaping visions: Asian Pacific American perspectives* (pp. 81–91). Pullman: Washington State University Press.

Pinar, W. F. (2001). *The gender of racial politics and violence in America: Lynching, prison rape, and the crisis of masculinity.* New York: Peter Lang.

Said, E. (1979). *Orientalism.* New York: Vintage.

Sanday, P. R. (1990). *Fraternity gang rape: Sex, brotherhood, and privilege on campus.* New York: New York University Press.

Taylor, H. (2001). *Overwhelming public support for increasing surveillance powers and, in spite of many concerns about potential abuses, confidence that these powers would be used properly* [On-line]. Available: http://www.harrisinteractive.com/ harris_poll/index.asp?PID=260.

United States Department of Education. (2002). *PL 107–110 The No Child Left Behind Act of 2001* [On-line]. Available: http://www.ed.gov/policy/elsec/leg/esea02/ index.html.

Yoshino, K. (2002). Covering. *Yale Law Journal, 111,* 769–939.

III
The Subaltern Speak
International Contexts

7

Subaltern in Paradise
*Knowledge Production in the
Corporate Academy*

STANLEY ARONOWITZ

Introduction

In her widely disseminated article "Can the Subaltern Speak?" written more than twenty years ago, Gayatri Spivak (1988) urged her interlocutors to consider the condition of postcolonialism. While so-called third world nations are formally independent, their economies remain tied to global capitalism. Within these countries, the poor and especially women remain silent, unrepresented, or underrepresented. In any case, they rarely represent themselves and remain under the domination of men; in the first place their husbands and their fathers. Spivak argues that Westerners cannot speak for those driven to silence by repression; despite good intentions, the ability of the subaltern to speak for themselves is hampered by liberal concern. Yet new struggles against global capitalism have produced a new discourse of human rights in which the universal has once more taken its place in the lexicon of emancipation. While Spivak's admonition remains salient to our times, it must be mediated by new conditions. While people historically excluded from participation, at any level of the national state, must, in the end, engage in self-activity to overcome the burdens of domination and exploitation, the repressive structures of state and patronymic control, especially in rural areas of Asia, Africa, and Latin America, require a response from those privileged to acquire a global vision.

Subalternity is a euphemism for the excluded, the *other*, the despised, the wretched of the earth. For better or for worse, the subaltern has been identified with the poor peasant classes, including the urban reserve army of labor, of what used to be termed the third world, and now, more accurately, the developing world. In the so-called advanced capitalist societies (where the adjective refers to the level of development of both the forces of production and the generally high standard of living), we have been visibly touched by subaltern peoples due to the great waves of immigration that have been experienced by nearly all of them. Like the turn-of-the-twentieth-century immigration from eastern and southern Europe, the current wave brings to the shores of the United States people who have been displaced from the land or, in the case of Jews, were unwilling to fight the Czar's wars.

We are now engaged in a great international debate about immigration, a vital aspect of globalization. What is happening in Africa, China, India, and Latin America constitutes nothing short of new enclosures. Hundreds of millions of people who once held some form of land tenure are being driven from their ancestral homes into the cities of the developing world and into the cities of the developed world by the force of arms, law, technological innovation in agriculture, or hunger. There they find poorly paid industrial jobs, and are condemned to casual labor or none at all. They are not welcomed as potential citizens of their new habitats. Human rights advocates have argued that the old national boundaries are, to say the least, archaic, and the political economy of the developed world demands the importation of cheap, vulnerable labor to overcome the worldwide plague of falling rates of profit. Consequently, some argue the movement of capital and, consequently, movements of labor across national borders make urgent a redefinition of citizenship. Many, especially in Western Europe and Israel, have been classified as guest workers, a designation that subjects them to expulsion at any time. In developing countries they have little chance of attaining legal status.

The disenfranchisement is not confined to immigrants. Despite their formal status as citizens within a nation-state, many native-born lack the basic elements of actual citizenship; they rarely, if ever, participate in the institutions of civil society, such as parent-teacher associations, civic organizations, and trade unions. Even when they are employed, circumstances such as long working hours, multiple jobs, and for women the double shift, conspire to exclude them from even the most informal institutions of democratic life. The United States—always the innovator in the abrogation of labor's rights and historically dependent not only on prohibitions of strikes and boycotts, but also on the rank exclusion of blacks from the industrial workplace except in times of war—is a pioneer in introducing a new dimension of subalternity. Millions of workers, white as well as black, have been driven from the industrial workplaces, victims of the relentless cost-cutting policies of large and smaller corporations alike. Technological displacement, outsourcing, and capital flight have together reduced the quantity and quality of industrial jobs. For example, faced with fierce global competition, mainly from developed societies, the once mighty and seemingly invulnerable United States–based car industry is shedding some of the best jobs, at least in monetary terms, in the American economy. The textile and apparel industries, once the largest employers of industrial labor, are shadows of their former selves having yielded, in turn, to the blandishments of Latin America and east Asia (mostly China), whose wages are between 5 and 15% of their already low-waged U.S. counterparts. As the safety net rapidly disappears they are forced into the informal economy—not only working off the books in industrial workshops, but into drug dealing and other demeaning sources of contingent work.

But we are experiencing a new phase of subalternity. In nearly every sector of intellectual labor, a system is being constructed that establishes several classes within an increasingly clear hierarchy. From computer engineering and programming to academic labor, some are awarded "real" jobs, while many are relegated to the status of part-time, contingent, and temporary labor. The computer professional is as likely to be a freelance repair and maintenance worker as a full-time employee. As with all freelancers, she has little time for recreation and certainly none for participation in the life of the community. Another case in point: Adjunct teachers in colleges and universities are often anything but part-time. These positions are no longer the province of people whose day jobs in law, business, journalism, and highly specialized technical areas allow them to accept an occasional course when the host institution cannot afford to employ full-timers to teach courses that are best filled by experienced professionals who bring to the classroom rich practical experiences. The new adjunct professor is likely to be a full-time wage slave whose teaching load exceeds that of the full-time tenured faculty members by two or three times. Teaching five to seven courses in two or three different institutions, the adjunct professor hardly has time for intellectual work, let alone participation in political or civil society. These workers have become veritable prisoners of the flawed American dream: Get a good education (or at least a credential) and you can live the life of the mind, secure in your job, with full benefits and periodic sabbaticals for writing and spiritual refreshment. Instead they are situated at the bottom of the educational pyramid, and their lives consist of work without end.

I.

The twentieth-century history of American higher education was periodically punctuated by allegations that its institutions had been seriously compromised by corporate and state influence in the conduct of academic inquiry, and by administrative infractions against the traditional aspiration of shared governance. Thorstein Veblen's *Higher Learning in America* (1918) and Robert Lynd's *Knowledge for What?* (1939) were prescient indictments of a not-yet-mature corporate university. Asking whether higher learning should serve the public good or private gain, Veblen and Lynd's rants were regarded with considerable skepticism even as the authors were accorded the status of respected cranks. At the moment of their interventions, mainstream America was preoccupied with each of the two World Wars and was seriously considering mobilizing its intellectual resources, including the universities. Under these circumstances, appeals to academic freedom and autonomy tended to fall on deaf ears. Indeed, in contrast to some European countries where scientific and technological research was conducted by independent institutes rather than universities, President Franklin D. Roosevelt's science advisors recommended that a handful of elite public and private schools, such as Berkeley and Princeton, be charged with the responsibilities associated with scientific and technological aspects of the war effort. Although the decision was made to outsource the bulk of weaponry production to private firms rather than producing most material in government-owned plants (the components of the atomic bomb were a major exception), the government remained the client of nearly all research products. Still, war and the Cold War that followed generated not only a massive arms industry, but resulted in the vast expansion and diversification of the chemical, electronics, and transportation industries, which were collectively the engines of economic expansion until the 1970s.

By 1960 under the imperatives of the Cold War, military/corporate power over nearly every aspect of U.S. society had so increased that no less a conservative than President Dwight D. Eisenhower warned against the "military-industrial complex," already discussed at great length by C. Wright Mills in his magisterial *The Power Elite* (1956) four years earlier. Veblen went so far as to argue that because the Morrill Act in 1863, by which Congress for the first time committed the federal government to support public higher education (primarily with land grants), the main business of the university was to provide knowledge and a trained cadre for private industry, especially in science and the technology of agricultural production. The burden of his claim is that the concept of an autonomous university, revered since the Enlightenment, remained an ideal that was far from the existing situation. More than two years before the entrance of the United States into World War II changed the landscape of the relation of higher education to the federal government, Lynd raised the disturbing question: Should the university serve the public rather than the private interest?

These were chiefly works of social criticism that pointed to corporatist tendencies within universities, even as most institutions of higher education promulgated the fiction that their faculty were dedicated to the disinterested pursuit of knowledge. Of course the decision of the Roosevelt administration (in the context of preparations for a world war) to invest its primary war research in a handful of leading universities had already raised doubts that scientists could remain free to perform their work independent of the influence of the military or the imperatives of the Cold War. Throughout the Cold War era, these doubts occupied the work of social critics and scholars such as I. F. Stone, Michael Klare, Noam Chomsky, and Edward Herman, among others. But the argument that the national security interests of the United States overrode the concerns about their autonomy, and the increasing centralization of funds available for scientific and technological research in the military establishment, persuaded many scientists to collaborate with the federal government's military program, especially because the Department of

Defense provided significant support to basic research not directly linked to the war effort. One of the most important functions of the defense contracts was to support the university-based liberal arts, especially the humanities and social sciences. In fact, absent alternative sources of funds, national defense contracts were frequently the vehicle through which natural and social scientists were able to do theoretical research or work not directly connected to the war imperatives.

By the 1980s writers like Martin Kenney discovered the "University-Corporate complex," focused not on government contracts but university/business partnerships. In *Academic Capitalism*, Slaughter and Leslie (1997) drew similar conclusions that the pursuit of knowledge as a public good, let alone for its own sake, was no longer a shared value of the academic community, if it ever was. The collapse of the Soviet Union and the demise of its successor states as military superpowers and political rivals to the United States raised profound issues for the scientific establishment. How could the high level of research within U.S. universities be sustained in the post–Cold War era? The meticulous empirical research of Slaughter and Leslie demonstrated that in the wake of stagnation of federal financing (in the 1980s and 1990s) of basic and applied research in the sciences, leading research universities added to their dependency by entering into partnerships with large pharmaceutical, chemical, and electronic corporations. A 1992 conference attended by the presidents and other key officials of leading research universities was dedicated to responding to the challenge. According to conference organizer Jonathan Cole, Columbia University's provost, they had only one main option: turning to private industry for support. Under these arrangements, corporations provided significant funds to the university in exchange for joint patents, and "early access and review of all proposed publications and presentations by faculty members whose work the company supported" (Walsh, 2004). While research in the so-called *policy sciences*, associated with branches of sociology and especially political science, has not been as subject to direct corporate control and influence, these subdisciplines have long been adjuncts of the state (Fisher, 1993). These relationships have prompted critics to ask whether the decline in terms of real dollars of the federal government's allocations to basic, disinterested research was primarily a reflection of the conservative program of privatization of knowledge rather than budgetary constraints. Put another way—are the decades of "budget crisis" an ideological and political mask for an attack against public goods, framed in purely fiscal terms?

Moreover, the privatization of scientific knowledge has led to widespread secrecy. Scientists who would otherwise have unswervingly accepted the doctrine that it is in the nature of their work to share knowledge were now, by contract, sworn to secrecy. The emergence of partnerships has had a chilling effect on the tradition of scientific transparency, shared knowledge, and open debate about scientific discoveries. It is not uncommon for presenters at scientific meetings to purge their papers of information that might violate the patent rights of their corporate sponsors. Because the reward systems of research universities are results driven, and in a fiercely competitive global market, corporate partners demand that researchers keep ahead of the competition, the erosion of the ethic of honesty has led to frequent instances of fraud in reporting evidence. Additionally, some scientists have invested in or received lucrative consulting contracts from the corporations that support their research, often reaping substantial dividends. That such practices are condemned as unethical by leading spokespersons for the American Association for the Advancement of Science and other institutions is a measure of how widespread they are within scientific circles.

But there is barely a murmur about the underlying fact of the commodification of knowledge that has become the main consequence of the end of the bipolar world created by the Cold War. If knowledge is subject to market forces—that is, it can be bought and sold like any other commodity—what follows is that scientific knowledge has become private property and the research university is sustained by its ability to sell its wares to the highest bidder, in which case it becomes, itself, a corporate entity. Holding trade secrets is common practice among corporate competitors, but contradicting one of the first principles of the seventeenth-century scientific Enlightenment—that in the interest of encouraging criticism and revision, scientific knowledge should be widely shared—commodification signifies the reverse: To the degree that the university remains a key producer of scientific knowledge it may no longer be a bastion of open inquiry. Whether we determine that the subordination of knowledge to the commodity form is in the public interest is a complex question. If the fund of fundamental knowledge upon which technological innovation depends is deemed adequate for a multiplicity of applications, many corporations decide that a high volume of basic research is not only unnecessary but unproductive. Federal agencies such as the National Science Foundation may allocate some funds for these projects, but policymakers, absent a compelling case, such as was provided by the race to develop a nuclear weapon during World War II or during the Cold War, have concurred with drug and electronics firms that new science must take a back seat to product development that can facilitate the investment, circulation, and profitability of capital. In short, as long as knowledge is viewed as a commodity, the concept of "disinterest" in research is bound to suffer eclipse.

II.

But perhaps the most serious challenge to the independence of the academic system of American society is the effect of these practices upon the most fundamental right still possessed by the professoriate: academic freedom. That federal agencies such as the National Science Foundation and the National Institutes of Health, charged with dispensing research funds, have increasingly privileged proposals dedicated to producing knowledge that can be readily translated into products is by now almost commonplace. Since the Clinton administration, the purpose of federal science policy has been to encourage dedicated rather than basic research. The relative decline of funding for theoretical physics, for example, may be attributed to the long period of transition between basic science and practical consequences. Since the transformation of biology into a technoscience, where the fundamental molecular paradigm is intimately linked to applications, funds have become scarce for those who persist in working in the field of evolutionary science or in the old functionalist perspective. Today, if the university is not prepared to support such research, and private foundations, whose scientific sensibility is not far from the mainstream consensus, are not favorably inclined, the evolutionist as well as practitioners of some older biological disciplines find themselves without the laboratory facilities, travel funds, and assistants to facilitate their work. In the life sciences, money is available virtually exclusively for research in molecular biology and biophysics, where knowledge can be rapidly transformed into commercial biotechnological applications (especially for genetically modified organisms in food), and pharmaceuticals. These deprivations do not appear as a violation of academic freedom because no authority is telling biologists they cannot engage in the fascinating work associated with finding the origin of our species or others, any more than physicists are prohibited from addressing the building blocks of matter or the history of the universe. However, if money is no longer available save for a tiny corps of investigators, the priorities themselves are tantamount to refusing such projects, and scientists who wish to stay "relevant" are well advised to fall into line.

Of course, during the period of war emergency (not yet ended) the federal government, in the interest of national security, claims the right to establish priorities in scientific research and deploys fiscal incentives to enforce its position. This approach is particularly effective at a time when the costs of scientific research, specifically in technology needed to perform experiments, have led to the distinction between *big science* and *little science*. The exemplars of big science are well known: groups engaged in applications of physics and engineering to space travel; the huge accelerators needed for experiments in high energy particle physics; the massive biophysics programs at the Massachusetts Institute of Technology and at various University of California campuses, especially Berkeley, Los Angeles, Davis, San Diego, Irvine, and Santa Barbara. But even at centers of so-called little science, such as New York's Mount Sinai School of Medicine where, during the 1980s, the focus was sharply limited to finding molecular biological solutions to problems of brain research, funding opportunities drove the research program of the entire school, and there is no reason to believe that any significant research institution today would take a different approach. Under such circumstances, leading theoretical physicists such as the late Richard Feynman or Steven Weinberg, or evolutionists and biologists such as Stephen J. Gould and Richard Lewontin, are important to the university as ornaments signifying their commitment to intellectual excellence. Meanwhile, in the knowledge factories of lucrative research, most of the work that the university needs for its financial sustenance gets done.

But with rewards go punishments. Immediately after September 11th, among the many reconfigurations of civil liberties and of academic freedom, the Bush administration launched a program of harassment of professors, mainly of Middle Eastern background, who were not U.S. citizens. Some state universities collaborated with the Justice Department by dismissing them or permitting the government to implement a program of surveillance. As serious as these acts of political repression were, the government justified them on national security grounds and as a result, save for the objections registered by human rights and civil liberties organizations, went largely unchallenged. More recently, again based on national security justification, the administration is floating a proposal to enable the federal government to intervene more directly in monitoring curricula offered by American universities to foreign students. But a recent case at the prestigious University of California-Berkeley raises far more serious issues for our conceptions of the core mission of higher education. In fall 2003 the university administration denied tenure to Ignacio H. Chapela, an assistant professor of ecology, overriding his department's unanimous recommendation and that of the faculty senate to grant him tenure. In November 2001 Chapela, and a graduate student, David Quist, published an article in the British scientific journal *Nature* that "claimed that native corn in Mexico had been contaminated by material from genetically modified corn." Six months later the journal received a number of letters contesting the research and it issued an editorial note acknowledging that the evidence was not "sufficient to justify the original paper." As the controversy brewed, Chapela said that he suspected the journal had been pressured by scientists working with the biotechnology industry and noted that he had been a critic of a 1998 deal between the University of California-Berkeley and Norvartis, a Swiss biotechnology company from which the university receives $5 million each year for five years "in exchange for giving the company information on faculty publications and presentations" (Walsh, 2004).

The Chapela affair is only one of the more blatant instances where the administration of a leading research university is strongly suspected of invoking nonacademic criteria for turning down a candidate for tenure. During the 1960s, academic dissent was frequently met with retributive contempt by university authorities. While some stood up to government pressure to discipline recalcitrant professors, Columbia University's administration took pains to create an inhospitable environment so that even some prominent tenured professors felt obliged to leave; at the same time it became an open secret that after 1968, when the entire campus was rife with student demonstrations, the administration, which held the right to grant tenure tightly in its hands, routinely denied that status to radicals, even as it claimed that it was free of prejudice because most assistant professors were denied tenure. Of course, the principle and practice of academic freedom is at the heart of the matter, but alongside the capacity of the institution to tolerate criticism, especially of its own corporate relationships, lurks the long-contested issue of the role of the faculty in academic governance at a time when higher education is increasingly privatized. During the past fifteen years, the professoriate has stood by as the allegiances of administration have, with the encouragement of state governments, shifted from their commitment to higher education as a public good to becoming contract players in the theater of capitalist hegemony. With the exception of a few relatively privileged departments and elite institutions, the humanities and social sciences have suffered near-crippling cuts or stagnation, even as the science and technology programs are funded in order to prepare them to seek private money.

The Chapela tenure case was at first hardly controversial, either in his own department or at the level of the faculty as a whole. That the administration made the decision to override a consensual judgment in Chapela's favor by his peers, underscores a problem that has bedeviled advocates for decades regarding what has been termed *shared governance*. Although they have acknowledged the governing role of university administration—mistakenly I would argue—they have insisted on the equal role of the faculty, especially on academic matters such as tenure and promotion. Indeed the establishment of promotion and tenure committees, which in most instances are composed exclusively of peers, perpetuates the perception of shared governance. Yet in all public universities and colleges and the large majority of private institutions, decisions of promotion and tenure committees and deans have the standing of being recommendations to a sovereign administration, which according to its own rights may, with impunity, turn down the recommendations of lower bodies. In fact, the arbitrary authority of the president and his office is frequently challenged by candidates, faculty senates, and unions. Many schools have established appeals tribunals that hear cases of faculty discharge, discrimination in salary issues, refusal of tenure and of promotion. In some schools where unions have bargaining rights, the case is subject to a formal grievance procedure. But in many instances candidates are obliged to go to court in order to obtain restitution and, in general, courts are extremely reluctant to intervene in what they believe are purely academic decisions.

If the broad application of tenure, won after decades of agitation and struggle, signifies that the faculty is free to pursue channels of inquiry that may be unpopular and unprofitable for the university and its partners, then there is reason to believe that its short sixty-year reign is under siege. That both public and private universities and colleges have, in the wake of budget constraints and their own priorities, adopted the practice of employing adjuncts and graduate students to teach the bulk of introductory courses is fairly well known.

Many adjuncts and graduate students are superb teachers. In any case they are no worse than the full-time faculty. In pedagogical terms the difference resides primarily in the fact that the part-timer is rarely paid for the time required for student academic advisement or for class preparation. Beyond these egregious conditions, the spread of a vast, contingent workforce in academe threatens both tenure and academic freedom. It undermines tenure because the overwhelming majority of part-time adjuncts are hired for a semester or for the academic year; the condition of their reappointment militates against their participation in free intellectual inquiry. Lack of freedom may be ascribed not so much to policy as to their uncertain situation. Any conflict with a department chair—personal, intellectual or political—can be, and often is, an occasion for termination of even a long-standing relationship to the institution. And recently, many schools have hired faculty on one- to five-year nontenure-track contracts, some of which are renewable at the discretion of the administration, while others not. At Harvard, Yale, and other elite institutions, these appointments may become steppingstones to permanent jobs elsewhere. However, in ordinary third-tier, four-year colleges and universities, after finishing their stint, faculty members often migrate to another temporary assignment.

We are at the beginning of an era where tenure is rapidly becoming a privileged status reserved for a relatively small minority of faculty members. When this or the next generation of tenured faculty retires from active service, unless the professoriate as a collectivity is better organized and mobilized than at present, we may experience a return to the situation that prevailed from the nineteenth century to the first four decades of the twentieth century. At that time, tenure was rarely granted by boards of trustees at private institutions, and the situation was no better at public colleges and universities. For example, one of the leading literary scholars and critics of the post–World War II period, Lionel Trilling, received tenure at Columbia after more than ten years on one-year contracts during which he held the rank of instructor, despite having earned a Ph.D. and having published a major biography of Matthew Arnold and innumerable articles in leading cultural journals. Similarly, although one or two professors in Columbia's anthropology department were tenured, important figures such as Ruth Benedict and Margaret Mead never held a permanent position.

The presumption of tenure for qualified scholars and intellectuals was achieved by determined and dogged advocacy by the small but prominent American Association of University Professors (AAUP). Founded in 1915 as a national organization dedicated to academic freedom at a moment when college and university presidents (most of whom were politically conservative) wielded almost unlimited power, AAUP advocated (1) institution of tenure for all qualified faculty, (2) the ability of faculty to engage in free inquiry and speak and write dissenting opinions without facing discharge and other forms of discrimination, and (3) shared governance—its three key objectives. While the association's efforts were crucial in the post–World War II adoption and routinization of tenure by most schools, fears of a postwar recession must be awarded equal credit. From an academy attended by some 1.5 million students in 1941, nine years later the number had doubled, largely due to the enactment by Congress in 1944 of the Servicemen's Readjustment Act (popularly known as the GI Bill of Rights), which sanctioned tuition-free school attendance for returning veterans and provided them with financial support and housing during the transition between service in the armed forces and paid work. It was, next to social security, the most comprehensive New Deal reform.

But the Cold War was no less beneficial to higher education. The dramatic increase of enrollments combined with federal funding through the Department of Defense for student loans as well as graduate assistantships continued almost unabated for twenty-five years until the end of the Vietnam War. From the Depression era, when the relatively small number of teachers with doctorates constituted a glut on the academic market, to the first twenty years after the war during which graduate programs expanded as fast as they had public funds to do so, but were still woefully behind the demand (according to one popular saying, all one needed to get an academic teaching job was a Ph.D. and a heartbeat), many academic institutions hastened to institute tenure, chiefly as a motivation to attract qualified applicants. While pay was modest, at least in comparison to other opportunities for educated workers in the rapidly expanding service and industrial sectors, the prospect of lifetime job security was attractive to many who still had vivid memories of Depression hardships and may have experienced the effects of the postwar recessions of 1954, 1958, and 1960 to 1961 (Aronowitz, 2000).

Only the rise of academic unionism between the late 1960s and the 1980s, which witnessed the organization of more than 30% of faculty and staff in colleges and universities, and growing enrollments that increased by a factor of 500% from 1950 to 2000, temporarily saved tenure from a powerful counterattack. Yet as many institutions, beleaguered by fiscal constraints and shifting priorities, met their curricular and pedagogical needs in the human sciences with part-time and contingent labor, the routine practice among nonelite institutions of granting tenure to faculty who met certain informal publication, teaching, and service requirements came under scrutiny. Of course the claim of some educational economists and leaders of academic disciplines that graduate schools had saturated the market by overproducing Ph.D.s was a fallacy born of their naïve acceptance of administration claims. For if the various constituents of the higher education industry had insisted that colleges and universities replace retirees, the deceased, and others who left university employment on a one-to-one basis, indexed the number of full-time hires to enrollments, and enforced limits on faculty/student ratios, we might still suffer from a shortage in some fields. In any case, the concept of *glut* is a corporate ideological construct whose success is attributable not to natural market causes, but to the prevailing relationship of political forces within the academy. If the "handwriting is on the wall," it is not fated to come to pass. As long as professors refuse to deconstruct the ideology of overproduction, they are likely to transfer blame from the institution to themselves. In the beleaguered disciplines of language study, emulating the building trades, prominent professors began to call for limiting the supply of Ph.D.s by raising admissions standards or, as two progressives argued, institutionalizing a two-tier professoriate by establishing a special "teaching" credential (Berube & Nelson, 1995).

III.

Why has the collective higher education administration been so compliant with pressures to join the mainstream of the U.S. labor market in the relentless drive toward casualization of a considerable portion of academic labor? After all, most middle-level administrators and most top officials were and remain recruited from the professorial ranks despite a powerful push from a variety of sources to install high level corporate bureaucrats into leading academic administrative positions. The common explanation for the capacity of administrators to adjust to the new market-driven realities of their "industry" relies heavily on two detours from the historical experience of expanded public funding. Under the weight of federal and state tax cuts and recessionary conditions that combined to reduce state revenues, state legislatures throughout the 1980s and 1990s (which were years of official prosperity) have sharply reduced funding for education as a whole, but particularly in the northeast and on the West Coast, they have been harsh on state colleges and universities. In the past three years even some southern and historic Midwest land-grant universities, which were previously protected by the fact that many legislators are their graduates, have suffered some funding cuts. According to this wisdom, higher education got a bad name because of student and faculty dissent from the 1960s to the present, but began to suffer when many state governments were captured by the right. Under these conditions, it is argued, administration, which is after all a professional bureaucracy and not a political party, has little choice but to adjust its strategies to the new realities—privatization of the sciences and technologies, outsourcing many services such as building maintenance, food, and bookstores, and unrelieved cost cutting in the least economically viable branches: the arts, humanities, and "soft" social sciences such as anthropology, which do not raise large amounts of outside money.

To these I would add a third transformation, which helps explain why we have seen so little resistance within the top echelon administrators. Historically, presidents, provosts, and deans were, and still are, mainly recruited from faculty ranks and accepted these posts as an entailment of academic citizenship. After six, or at most nine or ten years, they looked forward to returning to the ranks of the professoriate. If they were serious intellectuals—scholars, social critics or scientists—administration was considered a duty like the armed services, not a career. However, with the advent of the corporate university, teaching and research are now regarded by many as a prelude to a much more lucrative career as an administrator. The corporatization of the academy requires the formation of a cadre whose loyalty is no longer to their erstwhile colleagues, whose main duties are teaching, research, and writing, but to the new institutional mission of making the university relevant to the dominant forces within the political economy. The measure of a successful administrative career is no longer academic leadership—indeed many deans and presidents seem curiously indifferent to what goes on in the classroom or in the public life of the college or university. What counts is the size of the endowment, the quantity of research funds, and in the public universities, success in holding the line against legislative budget cuts. How can a "team" be consolidated at the top of the corporate university whose loyalty is firmly ensconced in the institution and its corporate partners?

The major requirement is to reconfigure the institution on the model of the American corporation. The corporate hierarchy has a chain of command where, in contrast to the old collegial university or even the small family firm, the boundaries between executives and line employees are fairly rigid and the division between intellectual and manual labor is strictly enforced. In the private corporation these tiers are rarely porous. Executives are rarely recruited from the professional ranks and manual workers may rise only to the level of line supervision. As previously mentioned, the trend in colleges and universities is to recruit presidents and vice presidents for finance, administration, and other posts from the ranks of corporate chief executives, financial operating officers, and top military commanders. In the old regime, those who came from these ranks may have earned as much as 50% over their base pay, but search committees cannot offer such pittances to Chief Executive Officers (CEO), Chief Financial Officers (CFO), and generals. The solution gradually put in place over the past decade or so is the executive pay plan.

This plan replaces the former practice of offering a 50% stipend and 10 to 25% stipends to vice presidents, deans, and provosts over their professorial pay, which terminated when they returned to academic ranks. Now the president is considered to be a CEO, and as university executives and corporate executives have become increasingly interchangeable, their salaries tend to become more competitive, although by no means identical. In 2004 some presidents of leading universities were earning $500,000 to $750,000 a year plus stipends for housing, a car and driver, and unlimited travel funds. In addition, many of them sit as paid directors of corporate boards, even those with whom the university has relationships. The sticky position is the academic affairs vice president or provost for which tradition still demands a genuine academic. The executive pay plan for the top academic officer tends to separate them from the professorial ranks. It is not uncommon for provosts and academic vice presidents in private universities to earn twice the top rate of the elite professoriate or three times the median rate of full-time faculty members. At most public universities, the ratio of provosts' to top professors' pay has risen to 1.5 to 1. It is not likely that these individuals would appreciate term limits or, more to the point, look forward to returning to the classroom.

What has resulted from the adoption of the corporate model in higher education? The interests of the institution are now everywhere separate from those of the collegium, and we have seen the formation of a professional/managerial class whose relationship to the intellectual life of the institution is increasingly remote or, to be more exact, tends to reduce faculty and staff to employees in both the private and public sectors. The administration is charged with "management," not merely of buildings and grounds, services and finances, but also of its core activities: teaching and learning. In many of the 4,100 institutions of post-secondary education, provosts, under presidential direction, no longer depend on faculty initiatives to undertake innovative programs or to devise new curricula. Academic planning has become the province of the administration and, under the rubric of "service to the university," faculty are invited—or assigned—to do the basic work needed to put their ideas into practice. At community colleges, which enroll half of all students in post-secondary learning, mandates from above ordinarily entail prescription of certain textbooks and even pedagogies. Because many two- and four-year degree programs are undertaken in partnership with private corporations, the curriculum may be packaged by the company. In this case, faculty members are relegated to positions as transmitters of received knowledge, and this is no longer a symbolic act, but becomes a literal mandate.

In first- and second-tier research institutions, top officials, ever sensitive to market forces, have embarked on a determined effort to recruit top nationally recognized scholars. Given the exigencies of public finance, many public universities find themselves outbid by the leading private institutions whose endowments and investments enable them to attract the top talent. Consequently, the privileged few among the professoriate are in a position to earn salaries that are double the median salaries of even the highest paid of these institutions. For example, while in 2004 full professors at Columbia, Yale, and Harvard earned an average annual salary in excess of $125,000 to $150,000, it was not uncommon for superstars in the humanities or social and natural sciences to enter these universities at $250,000 plus generous travel funds, housing allowances, and several assistants. In some instances their teaching loads are half those of the average faculty member. The small circle of superstars tends to regard their appointments as sinecures from which to pursue their private interests. Some continue to perform research and writing while others become public figures. But, with exceptions, they remain fairly remote from the festering problems of their own universities: They stand idly by while graduate assistants struggle for better pay and benefits, they are often impervious to the fate of their less anointed colleagues whose salaries have remained relatively stagnant for years, and they tend to ally with administration in the struggles over faculty governance. Needless to say, few are in contact with undergraduates and have few ideas about education.

What Are the Implications for the Future of Higher Learning?

Jacques Derrida has issued a strong but gentle plea to protect and defend academic freedom and the autonomy of the university against the nefarious consequences of corporate takeover and the consequent subordination of academic knowledge to private interests. We have added the dangers of the formation of a distinct administrative class whose economic and ideological interests are tied to the corporate order and of an increasingly intrusive state in everyday academic affairs, especially abrogating faculty's control over hiring, tenure and promotion, curricular matters, and its own production of knowledge. But we have learned that the system of higher education in the United States has been, for almost 150 years, partially integrated into the state, and as if to belie its image of an ivory tower, has become a practical adjunct to the scientific and technological basis of both the production and administration of things as well as people.

If these theories are true (and one's evaluation will depend almost entirely on her or his standpoint) the task of preservation, let alone restoration, of what remains of academic freedom is nothing less than monumental. Plainly, the starting point must be to challenge the professoriate to recognize the assault upon free inquiry, the autonomy of the faculty as a collective, and on its most powerful weapons, especially tenure. Those who would defend academic freedom are obliged to recognize that a substantial portion of the faculty has been so bludgeoned by recent developments that it has lost hope. Another much smaller segment may be afflicted with unease at the measure of how much they have become complicit with corporate and government funders who dictate the nature and direction of much scientific research, including most of the social scientific disciplines and education. A third group lacks all reflexivity because it has been formed in the era when the concept of partnership—read faculty subordination to corporate control—seems a thing of nature and, more to the point, the royal road to academic and financial reward.

Who is left? Philosophers (most of whom are not in philosophy departments, especially in the research universities), social theorists, humanists, unrepentant liberals and radicals, and a tiny fraction of libertarians who bridle at corporatization because they realize that it has little to do with the free market. Many are to be found in faculty senates and councils, among academic union activists, and in the tiny band of public intellectuals. Needless to say, in the main, their voices remain muted in the avalanche of crises that have afflicted higher education. If Derrida's call to arms is to be heeded, his interlocutors will require strategic acumen to enter the fray. Where they start will depend on what issues arouse a powerful minority to focused outrage.

The experience of social movements, especially the labor movement, tells us that those grievances that induce a group to take action are, from the standpoint of analysis, often not the most consequential. At a time of war mobilization, faculty may not pay heed to the blatant violations of the rights of alien professors, and under pressure of fiscal constraint, may shrug off the evidence of creeping privatization. But will they rationalize administrative refusal to heed faculty recommendations for tenure and promotion? They might take umbrage at administrators who never tire of invoking the doctrine of sacrifice in a time of emergency, treating themselves to huge salaries while imposing a salary freeze on the faculty and staff, and relentlessly pursue the program of casualization of large chunks of the teaching labor force. At public universities and colleges they might bridle against the state's effort to subvert the faculty's prerogatives by imposing mandates—funded as well as unfunded—on the curriculum. In short, what gets the professoriate to act is indeterminate in advance, but one thing we do know: The more abstract the appeal, the less likely it will be to provoke practical activity. Phrases like academic freedom, corporate university, and shared governance retain ideological resonance. It is more difficult to find the concrete instances by which these ideals are violated. Such is the task of a good organizer.

As Swedish writer and ethnographer Goran Palme once claimed, we must "dig where we stand." In solidarity, progressives and radicals have an obligation to support struggles against global capital, racism, and violence perpetrated against women wherever they are called to action. Acts of solidarity in one place, especially in the advanced industrial societies, only strengthen the movements of the subaltern everywhere. But the real test of a determined struggle for freedom and democracy is whether intellectuals and activists are prepared to fight to preserve and to establish the elements of citizenship in their own communities and institutions. For in the final accounting, the assault against the subaltern is directly proportional to the level of understanding and mobilization in both the developed and the developing world, as they share a common foe: global capital. The precipitous decline of the labor movements and political forces of opposition in all western European countries and those of North America has largely left people in the developing world to fend for themselves. Whether they can secure their survival and advancement alone is doubtful, but the chief obstacles to the emergence of a truly transnational movement to match transnationalization of capital resides right here.

If we understand the concept of the subaltern in a new way—not only as a concept calling attention to the situation of economic deprivation, but one that describes the absence of social and political freedom—then there is a basis for rescuing movements for solidarity with the "other" from the throes of abstract moralism and moving them toward achieving our own freedom. It is true that our condition of servitude is, even after more than thirty years of deterioration of living standards for most workers in advanced capitalist countries, more subtle and elusive. Perhaps we are the subaltern in "paradise." Among other things, we have a substantial professional managerial class of which large sections of the professoriate are a part. There is a loose and ultimately disastrous credit system to sustain many over the bumps of frictional unemployment, steep deductibles for hospital care, and the high costs of energy and post-secondary education of our children or ourselves. Many of us have become so accustomed to defeat that we have come to believe that domination is an inherent human condition—something that may be easier to believe when our relative lack of freedom is compared with oppressive conditions elsewhere. We become bystanders in our own oppression, and in the wake of global warming, which threatens the very existence of life on the planet, fret rather than take decisive action.

We can no longer be content to repeat the outworn truism that living standards, even for the poor, are much higher in the West than elsewhere. For those suffering the insecurities of the new restructuring of labor conditions, and those who have witnessed the erosion of their capacity to play a crucial role in the governance of society in general and their own neighborhoods, cities, states, and workplaces in particular, to be reminded of relative privilege is neither solace nor an incentive to action. For people only engage in acts of solidarity when their own situation is being addressed by collective organization and action, and higher education is no exception. If current arrangements continue, all but a tiny minority will be rendered subaltern. And if that occurs, the whole promise of education as the road to freedom will have been crushed.

References

Aronowitz, S. (2000). *The knowledge factory: Dismantling the corporate university and creating true higher learning.* Boston, MA: Beacon Press.

Berube, M., & Nelson, C. (Eds.). (1995). *Higher education under fire.* New York: Routledge.

Fisher, D. (1993). *Fundamental development of the social sciences.* Ann Arbor: University of Michigan Press.

Lynd, R. S. (1939). *Knowledge for what?* Princeton, NJ: Princeton University Press.

Mills, C. W. (1956). *The power elite.* New York: Oxford University Press.

Slaughter, S., & Leslie, L. L. (1997). *Academic capitalism.* Baltimore, MD: Johns Hopkins University Press.

Spivak, G. (1988). Can the subaltern speak? In C. Nelson & L. Grossberg (Eds.), *Marxism and the interpretation of culture* (pp. 271–313). Urbana: University of Illinois Press.

Veblen, T. (1918). *The higher learning in America.* Chicago, IL: B.W. Huebsch.

Walsh, S. (2004). Berkeley denies tenure to ecologist who criticized university's ties to the biotechnology industry. *Chronicle of Higher Education, 50* (18), A10.

8

Struggling for Recognition

The State, Oppositional Movements, and Curricular Change

JYH-JIA CHEN

Introduction

In recent years, the role that cultural struggles have played in interrupting dominance, be it rooted in the field of education or in broader society, has become part of a wider intellectual agenda in critical scholarship (see, e.g., Apple, 1995, 1996, 2003). In this regard, demands for the recognition of cultural difference may significantly undermine the very legitimacy of symbolic injustice, an injustice rooted in cultural domination, nonrecognition, or the misrecognition, disrespect, and devaluation of particular societal patterns of representation, interpretation, and communication (Fraser, 1997, pp. 11–39). Research shows that various fronts of collective actors strive, inside and outside schools, for a winning of symbolic recognition, for a reevaluation of social identities, and for a transformation of cultural structure, all of which suggest the effects of diversified social antagonisms and oppositional movements on educational change (e.g., Chen, 2003; Nozaki, 2005).

The struggle over cultural incorporation and identity formation was a distinguishing facet of the politics of educational policy in Taiwan as far as the production and change of legitimate knowledge were concerned. Cultural policy in postwar Taiwan involved an episodic process of "nationalizing Chinese culture." Through this process, "Chinese tradition had been invoked, icons and narratives of Chineseness had been constructed, history and civilization had been reinvented, and rituals and etiquette had been domesticated, impeding subordinated ethnic groups' equal participation in the making of culture and curriculum" (Chun, 1994, p. 55).[1] Over the past two decades, the emergence and the unfolding of curricular reform have revealed an ongoing process in which different versions of Taiwan-related knowledge in historical, geographical, cultural, and linguistic terms, have intertwined with the quest for cultural recognition and change. In particular, ideological articulations that have centered on issues of nativization and

197

indigenous education reveal the presence of intricate relationships involving state power, cultural orientations, social relations, consciousness, and curricular change.

Existing accounts of state-education relationships, while tending to view the state as an absolute regulator, give the collective action of educational reform groups short shrift, let alone grasp the nettle of oppositional movements. In this chapter, I attempt to incorporate a sharper awareness of the role of oppositional movements into the analyses of both state formation and the pedagogic device. A key question addressed in this chapter is: To what extent do oppositional movements mediate the link between the state and curricular change?

My orienting assumption is that social movements and ethnic struggles operate as central motors of symbolic change and pedagogic reform with respect to the creation of official knowledge. I argue that oppositional movements mediate between the state and education and that the state in formation must be seen as a set of agencies and projects that, for the winning of consent, are institutionalized responses to oppositional movements of the past. The following pages will demonstrate that in the context of crafting a more liberal-democratic, native-led state, curricular change in Taiwan involves mass struggles over the control of ideological institutions such as schools, the appropriation of culture and language, and the construction of collective identity. The overall trends toward nativization in both political and educational spheres are, in effect, the result of struggles over the cultural politics of recognition.

This chapter begins with an introduction to a more dialectical approach, one that is derived from the perspective of New Social Movements (NSMs) and that draws the role of oppositional movements back into analyses of the state-education connection (see appendix for acronyms used in this chapter). I then elucidate the rebuilding of a settler state in Taiwan and how changes in political, economic, and cultural conditions have modified the boundaries of the state system itself. Finally, I shall examine three cases of struggle against symbolic injustice—the struggles over interpretations of history, representations of sovereignty, and the production of localized curricula—and illustrate how these struggles constitute vital and insistent efforts to win recognition and to define identity within the context of state formation.

Bringing the Oppositional Movement Back In

Researchers' theorizing of state-education relationships has forcefully demonstrated that the specificities of the state's role in education are embedded in different historical trajectories of state formation, ideological struggle, and cultural context, thus embodying different logics of state intervention in schooling (Ball, 1990; Carnoy, 1989, 1992; Carnoy & Levin, 1985; Carnoy & Samoff, 1990; Curtis, 1988, 1992; Green, 1997). Relatively little of the dialogue among theorists has centered on the impact of oppositional movements on the linkage of the state to education.[2] As Bernstein (1990, 1996) argues, the dominant group tends to control the pedagogic device that serves as the dominant principle of symbolic control, and that regulates the production, reproduction, and transformation of culture. Yet the pedagogic device is never a stable set of rules imposed on the ruled, but an arena of struggle where the agents and agencies of civil society and the state compete with one another for the appropriation of the device. Indeed, the struggle for the appropriation of the pedagogic device among rival forces surfaces over time and exposes the unstable equilibrium structuring the state-education nexus, suggesting that various collective actions play a central role in the intermediary relationship between the state and curricular change (Chen, 2003).

Some insights arising from the perspective of NSMs are significant to one's consideration of the cultural and cognitive factors of oppositional movements and their relations to the production and the transformation of official culture and knowledge. First, the NSMs have been emanating from and aiming to expand civil society where hegemonic apparatuses (schools, cultural institutions, voluntary associations, and so on) are located and where ideology, identities, cultural codes, and social relations of domination and resistance are created and transformed. Second, a certain segment of the NSMs is involved in counterhegemonic struggles that contest or undermine structures of domination by reorganizing people's cognitive structures in ways that support alternative ways of perceiving the world (Charles, 2000, pp. 3–53; Cohen, 1985).

The framing theory in NSM research furthers a focus on the role of culture in social change. A frame is defined as a shared interpretative schema that not only makes sense of a reality, but also operates as the articulation principle by which social movements identify problematic situations, who or what is to blame, and alternatives that bring about desired change. The *frame alignment processes* of collective action involve acts of cultural appropriation through which movement organizers seek to articulate resonant cultural values with the cognitive frameworks of the masses in order to galvanize protest activity. Master protest frames—that is, shared cultural or ideological understandings legitimating collective action—thus serve as the sources that movement actors draw deeply on in order to mobilize potential participants and to expand cultural opportunities (Hunt, Benford, & Snow, 1994; McAdam, 1994). Finally, the identity dimensions of the NSMs bring our attention to symbolic issues and belief systems associated with "sentiments of belonging to a differentiated social group; with the members' image of themselves; and with new, socially constructed attributions about the meaning of every-day life" (Johnston, Larana, & Gusfield, 1994, p. 7). The construction of ethnic identities is therefore viewed as the initial kick that prompts movement participants to "name themselves" in ethnic or nationalistic movements.

NSM concepts contribute to a deeper understanding of collective action, mass mobilization, ethnic struggles, and social change, which are at the center of state formation and pedagogic reform. The intermediating between the state and educational transformation hinges on social antagonisms in which ethnicity has been a fundamental axis of nation building, political representation, and cultural meaning, as has been the case in postwar Taiwan. In the 1980s and 1990s, political and social opposition movements proliferated as attempts to politicize civil society and to appropriate master protest frames fueled the development of oppositional education reform. It is particularly worthy to note that the demands of oppositional movements eventually bring about policy and curricular change through the generating of new entitlements, the legitimating of subordinate culture, the creating of collective identities, and to a certain degree, the incorporating of the perspectives of the oppressed into curriculum. It is thus crucial to show *how* the process of institutionalizing cultural recognition really works. To provide some context for exploring this process, I first turn to a brief discussion of the history of state formation in postwar Taiwan.

The State in Formation

After World War II, China assumed control over Taiwan as a result of a complete transfer of power from the Japanese government to the Chinese Nationalist Party (the Kuomintang, or KMT). The KMT introduced into Taiwan's political structure an explicit preference for mainlanders who governed Taiwan as a colony. The vast majority of government posts were staffed by mainlanders, and the lowest positions by Taiwanese. Given the financial difficulties underlying the KMT's war against the Chinese Communist Party (CCP), Taiwan's government agencies emphasized the importance of exporting state-owned resources to China. Mainlander dominance in Taiwan, coupled with fierce economic inflation, rising unemployment, and declining living standards, soon resulted in Taiwanese demands for self-governance and the opening up of state-owned enterprises (Zhang, 1988). During the February 28 Massacre in 1947, which followed an islandwide revolt against KMT mismanagement, thousands of civilians were slaughtered by mainland troops. The traumatic February 28 Massacre and the notorious mass-scale purge in the ensuing decade have since symbolized the ethnic cleavage in postwar Taiwan.

While at war with the CCP, the KMT enacted the Temporary Provisions in 1948 to substitute for the Constitution of the Republic of China (ROC). Decades of emergency orders had legitimized the exercise of emergency presidential powers, restricted the establishment of new political parties and newspapers, and outlawed demonstrations. The KMT later fled to Taiwan and declared martial law when the CCP gained control of the mainland.[3] Among other policies, the KMT established a *fa tong* regime (literally, ruling the nation by means of the constitution) in order to stabilize its hold on the island. First and foremost, the KMT declared itself the sole legitimate government of all China while treating the CCP as a rebel regime. Taiwan was thus viewed as a temporary seat of the ROC state for the mission of *mainland recovery*. Second, regional elections were prohibited so as to prevent the emergence of native authorities. Another aspect of the *fa tong* regime was a mainlander-dominated Congress. Elections for the three chambers of the parliament were suspended in order to indefinitely extend the tenures of representatives who had been elected in China, until they could return to their constituencies. The mainlander-dominant Congress had long been criticized by the opposition as the *perennial parliaments*.

External threats, such as diplomatic setbacks in the 1970s, prompted opposition forces to question the legitimacy of the KMT's rule. In turn, the KMT modified itself by instituting a Taiwanization policy,[4] economic upgrading, and cultural reconstruction. The convergence of international and domestic crises in the 1980s forced the KMT to further transform itself by moving toward democratization—a political liberalization framed from a Chinese nationalist perspective. In line with the liberalization trend was a proliferation of social movements and a dramatic expansion of civil society. Segments of many social movements sought to appropriate counterideologies, offer alternative identities, and advance needs claims. Issues addressed included campus democracy and university reform (a student movement), academic autonomy (the teachers' rights movement), the use of native languages in media and schools (the Hakka rights movement), to cite only the most relevant to educational reform. Highly sensitive issues, such as the February 28 Massacre, were no longer taboo topics of discussion and were greeted with sympathy by the public.

The late 1980s and early 1990s saw a transition from an authoritarian, mainlander-dominated state to a somewhat more liberal-democratic, native-dominated one. The KMT reconstructed itself under the leadership of Lee Teng-hui, who succeeded to the presidency in 1988 after the death of President Chiang Ching-kuo. Lee Teng-hui soon confronted challenges from mainlander elites who were still in power and who resisted popular demands for political liberalization. Additional challenges arose from mounting oppositional movements that exposed the contradictions of several state policies and discourses, including the state's corporatist mode of domination, the *fa tong* regime, and Chinese nationalism (Wang, 1993, pp. 21–60). The legitimacy of the new ruling groups thus required not only capital accumulation, but also representative democracy and a unified national identity. Lee Teng-hui's reformist faction and the oppositional party, the Democratic Progressive Party (DPP), aimed to nativize state power and to democratize the *fa tong* regime, with the former adhering to an ROC framework, and the latter advocating Taiwan independence. Consequently, several political events concerning the democratization of the *fa tong* regime sparked conflicts between the divided KMT and the opposition.

Lee Teng-hui's approach to parliamentary reform—in particular, his designation of a certain number of delegates as both nationwide representatives and overseas Chinese representatives in order to maintain the *fa tong* regime—galvanized the opposition in its efforts to mobilize street demonstrations, the principal function of which involved a complete reelection of the perennial parliaments and the compulsory retirement of their aged members. Later, the illegitimacy of the presidential election, which the National Assembly had manipulated, angered university students and civilians, inciting them to demonstrate in the streets. In March 1990, once docile university students staged a large-scale sit-down protest and hunger strike to vigorously urge the KMT to dismantle the National Assembly and to abrogate the Temporary Provisions. Discontent among the masses soon exploded across the island and more than 20,000 protesters rallied in Taipei, staging what became known as the March Student Movement. The militancy of the March Student Movement pressed the newly elected president Lee Teng-hui to completely reconstruct three national representative bodies through popular elections.

The opposition's wrath increased when President Lee Teng-hui appointed a mainlander military strongman to the position of prime minister. University students, professors, social groups, and the DPP mobilized a massive antimilitary government movement. The number of demonstrators rose to 10,000 when the appointment gained the approval of the Congress. In May, Lee Teng-hui declared that the Temporary Provisions would be abrogated and the Constitution amended. The aim underlying this move was possibly to convert popular resentment of conservative mainlander forces into a reform agenda of greater nativization and political liberalization. The abolishment of the Temporary Provisions in 1991 was of particular importance to the termination of the "civil war" with the CCP. Domestically, decades of "emergency situations" that had legitimized the existence of the *fa tong* regime were ultimately over. Internationally, a pragmatic China policy began to prevail. The National Unification Guidelines promulgated in the same year officially recognized the People's Republic of China (PRC) as a legitimate political entity and suggested a long-range process of rapprochement with the PRC, viewed as the "one China, two political entities" formula.

Lastly, the quest to replace the Chinese nationalist constitution with a constitution geared toward a native-dominated state was inevitably intersected with the building of a new, independent state. Constitutional reform thus became a pivotal topic, on the basis of which the ruling groups and the ruled contended with each other in order to legitimize their own version of the nation-state in Taiwan. The opposition decided to take their protest to the streets, and organized a new constitutional drive to promote an independent Taiwan, known as the New Constitution Movement. During the 1991 extraordinary session of the First National Assembly, a university student-professor coalition and the DPP staged a two-day protest march. More than 30,000 protesters demonstrated their opposition to the aging representatives who had a hand in the constitutional revisions (Wakabayashi, 1994, p. 240). The KMT under Lee Teng-hui managed to secure the cooperation of the DPP and passed constitutional amendments in 1992. These amendments, which were finalized over the subsequent two years, provided a legal basis for the holding of direct elections for the presidency, the provincial governorship, and two municipal mayorships. A liberal democracy was set in motion, and the KMT reconstructed itself into an election-oriented party that demanded the consent of "the people."

Contesting the Official Narrative and Constructing Countermemories

With greater freedom of expression and freer access to media, the opposition brought the long-prohibited, unrecognized memory of the February 28 Massacre into a public forum of debate in order to contest the official version of the past. In February 1987, 41 social groups established the 2-28 Peace Day Promotion Association. The association staged a nationwide campaign to mobilize a public call on behalf of several symbolic and practical goals: the designation of February 28th as Peace Day; the establishment of a commemorative monument to those killed; material compensation for the victims; an official apology for the repressive measures taken; and finally, an investigation of the massacre itself. Over the following years, concerned scholars and writers continued to battle the KMT over the narration and interpretation of the notorious massacre. They supported the declassification of official archives, held symposiums on the massacre, and published research reports and oral histories of victims' family members. The establishment of a research team in 1991 by a group of intellectuals associated with the opposition epitomized the maneuver of bringing the standpoint of Taiwanese people back into the construction of the collective memory of the massacre (Chen, 1989).

Together with both the emerging countermemories of the massacre and the intensified struggles against mainlander dominance in politics, opposition forces turned their attention to the relationship between this formerly taboo subject and curricula. Beginning in 1988, DPP legislators demanded that the massacre receive treatment in textbooks in the hope that students would learn an important lesson from the event (Legislative Yuan, March 2, 1988). Encouraged by calls for reform in the legislature, university students also voiced their outrage, burning history textbooks to protest government censorship in general and the government's treatment of the massacre in particular (Shi, 2000).

By the 1990s, the massacre was still recorded in the annals of the ROC as a shameful rebellion organized by communist-controlled conspirators, and all official archives related to the massacre remained classified. In contrast, the PRC claimed that the resistance, attributed to the corruption of the "American-Chiang

Kai-shek gang," received its inspiration from the "New Democratic Revolution" led by Mao Ze-dong (Hsiau, 2000, p. 168). The official discourse on the massacre underwent a dramatic transformation throughout this process of nativization, which involved a fundamental shift in the distribution of power from mainlander elites to Taiwanese situated within the state. In 1990, soon after the establishment of a timetable for the reconstruction of three national representative bodies, the National Institute for Compilation and Translation (NICT) announced that a reference to the February 28 Massacre would be included in high school history textbooks as follows (Ministry of Education [MOE], July 31, 1990):

> At the very beginning of Taiwan's retrocession, social problems were severe owing to the fierce wartime destruction, the [social] disorder and economic inflation after the war, the increased unemployment, and people's loss of a normal means of livelihood. The administrative regime of Taiwan Province was special when Chen Yi served as the Governor-General of Taiwan Province. [He was appointed] not only as the Governor-General but also as Garrison-Commander, possessing both military and civilian authority.... This delivered a great blow to the hopes of Taiwanese compatriots who had been longing for [Taiwan's] retrocession and a return to their motherland. People felt even more discontent with the military abuse and the political abuse stemming from the Office of the Governor-General, the implementation of economic regulations, government officials' corruption, and military misbehavior. The conflict between the government and civilians coincidentally broke out when [official investigators] were confiscating the vending of untaxed cigarettes, resulting in the "February 28 Accident" of 1947. Innocent civilians were targeted, some of whom were wounded and killed. Mr. Chiang Kai-shek, then chair of the Nationalist Government, was informed [of this revolt] and ordered Chen Yi to prevent clashes that could follow the massacre. Otherwise, [Chen Yi] would face the charge of rebelling [Chiang Kai-shek's order]. [Chiang Kai-shek] immediately replaced Chen Yi, reorganized the Office of the Governor-General into Taiwan Province, reformed the general administration, and pacified the people. In order to alleviate the pain brought on by this accident and in order to recognize its historical legacy, the Executive Yuan appointed the "February 28 Massacre Accident ad hoc team" in November 1990 to investigate the truth of the accident. President Lee Teng-hui apologized to family members of victims. The government compensated [family members of victims] and established the February 28 [Accident] monument in order to comfort the victims of [the massacre]. (NICT, 1996, pp. 165–166)

Unfortunately, the new textbooks failed to mention who was ethically responsible for giving the order to send nationalist soldiers to quash the revolt. Other telling omissions and lapses involved the estimated number of victims and how they were jailed or murdered, the sufferings of victims' family members, and the opposition's struggles against the official interpretation of the massacre.

Hsiau (2000) pointed out that:

> the narration of history was contested because it was of central importance to the formation, maintenance, and redefinition of collective memories. A distinct form of collective identity hinged in part on the specific construction of a collective memory—on the interpretation of who "we" are, of what it is "we" have experienced, and of what, therefore, "we" share. (p. 150)

Suffice it to say that the countermemories of dissidents and survivors posed a challenge to the official interpretation of the massacre. As a consequence, the Taiwanese KMT attempted to control the unthinkable by closely regulating access to classified government archives. The KMT also attempted to control perceptions by manufacturing a safer pedagogic narrative of the massacre. During the early 1990s, the opposition was less capable of translating unrecognized knowledge of the massacre into the public memories represented in the textbook, given the relatively low autonomy of agents in the pedagogic recontextualizing field mainly composed of institutions, such as universities, schools, the media, and civic and cultural foundations. The state-authored textbook policy ensured a stronger official recontextualizing field (mainly composed of the state and its subagencies) and again became the major point of contention for the opposition when the issue of the sovereignty of China, as represented in textbooks, emerged.

Negotiating the Representation of Contested Sovereignty

The reduction of restrictions governing the contacts between Taiwan and China complicated the possible transformation of the themes of anticommunism and mainland recovery in curricula. In 1987, a group of former mainlander soldiers, who had fled to Taiwan with the KMT and who had expected to return before long to their mainland homes, organized a campaign demanding the right to visit their homes in order to reestablish contact with their families on the continent. In October, the KMT approved their requests for the right to visit their homes in China. Tourist visits to, and civilian contacts with, the mainland were further granted to the residents of Taiwan the following year.

The increasing cross-Straits (Taiwan Straits) contacts through family reunions, tourism, and trade called into question the CCP's fictitious pronouncements regarding the character of Taiwan. Similarly, the KMT's propaganda on mainland China lost its power to convince, as communication between the two peoples expanded. The CCP had redefined its territory and borders after 1949 and recognized the sovereignty of Outer Mongolia, independent since 1932 and now known as the Mongolian Republic, separate from the PRC. The administrative regions of the PRC thus included 22 provinces, 3 metropolises, and 5 autonomous regions. By contrast, the KMT insisted that Outer Mongolia remain part of the ROC, which had 35 provinces, 14 metropolises, and 2 autonomous regions. As a result, the maps of China used on both sides of the Taiwan Straits were astonishingly different from each other. Taiwan's map formed the outline of a begonia leaf and included part of Outer Mongolia, while the mainland resembled an old mother hen, owing to the exclusion of Outer Mongolia. The metaphor of *begonia leaf* versus *old mother hen* vividly expressed the constructed and contested nature of textbook knowledge about China's sovereignty.

Notwithstanding the home visiting and the growth of investments between Taiwan and China, the KMT was reluctant to acknowledge the superstructure in China under the rule of the CCP. For the KMT, any recognition of the redefined PRC territory would delegitimize the ideology of the ROC as the sole legitimate government of all China. Scholars and legislators appealed to the Ministry of Education (MOE) to update humanities textbooks in order to "teach kids the truth." They argued that the National Curriculum's dominant themes, such as One China, anticommunism, and reconquering the mainland, needed to cede place to perspectives that could reflect the real circumstances of the mainland and the ipso facto relationships between China and Taiwan (Legislative Yuan, December 14, 1988).

When the KMT approved the home-visiting policy, the NICT announced its decision to revise the textbook's description of the mainland. Starting from the 1988 school year, test-free supplementary aids concerning the CCP's changes to China's sovereignty, territory, and borders after 1949 appeared in appendices of high school geography textbooks. Regarding the map of China used in textbooks, the PRC's territory and administrative regions were noted along with a remark that indicated the ROC's lack of recognition of the "illegal" change (Legislative Yuan, November 22, 1988).

It was the expected termination of the Temporary Provisions that created the necessary structural conditions for the rewriting of the China–Taiwan relations represented in textbooks. A call for Taiwan's de facto sovereignty by the opposition did, to some extent, accelerate the process of textbook revisions. In October 1990, as a reaction to the KMT's emerging unification policy, the DPP passed a resolution claiming that the ROC's sovereignty extended neither to the mainland nor to Outer Mongolia. The constitutional regime of the ROC was to be built upon its effective jurisdiction (Wakabayashi, 1994, p. 244). Dismissing the de jure sovereignty of the ROC, which had been constructed in the textbooks as "against the facts," the DPP and independent legislators proposed a resolution to press the MOE to revise the narration of China's sovereignty in geography textbooks (Legislative Yuan, October 10, 1990).

Debates over the gap between the reality of the CCP-ruled mainland and the school text of the KMT-imagined mainland effectively challenged the dominant principle wherein the ROC was the sole legitimate government of China—a principle that had been regulating the production of the National Curriculum for decades. In January 1991, the MOE invented the principle of *factual recognition* for political and societal changes in post-1949 China. However, there was disagreement among ministries over the extent to which the factual recognition principle should be applied if textbook narratives concerning the mainland were revised. The Interior Ministry took a relatively conservative stand of "no change in the ROC-claimed sovereignty, territory, and administrative regions" because the divided KMT was confronting intensified struggles over national identity during the period of constitutional reform. The Transportation Ministry favored recognizing the mainland's post-1949 city and county names and its post-1949 rail and road construction, a preference that was in accordance with the needs of the contacts between Taiwan and China and the new cross-Straits relations (Da lu, 1991). The MOE recommended that school textbooks be removed from the list of government publications so as to include the PRC's administrative regions in textbooks, but its proposal was disregarded. With the official acknowledgment of the PRC as a political entity as revealed in the draft of the National Unification Guidelines, the NICT announced a new textbook policy permitting the updating, in geography textbooks, of China's city and county names and its rail and road construction (MOE, February 28, 1991).

The ideology and the practice of "one China, two political entities" could be viewed as the initial stage of the process of native-led state-building. The selective tradition of the old KMT—a nationalist version of Chinese traditional culture—was articulated from a nativist perspective of *Taiwan experience*, modifying the rule for the creation of Taiwan-related knowledge in schools. In 1992, the MOE incorporated materials concerning the facts of Taiwan's separation from China, and of the Taiwan experience into social studies and humanities textbooks at all levels of education. Core elements of the Taiwan experience were identified in textbooks as follows:

1. Economic development: The most well known part of the Taiwan experience is the growth of the economy. In the past fifty years, Taiwan has evolved from a backward agricultural society to an advanced industrial one. Along with rapid economic development, consumer prices have remained stable and the distribution of social wealth equal. Therefore, all citizens can share in the fruit of national economic development. By solving the dilemma underlying a balancing of development, stability, and equality, the economic development of our country is complimented by the world as the "Taiwan Miracle."

2. Democratic development: Political democratization is an important and stable direction in the "Taiwan experience." In Taiwan, the simultaneousness of developing democracy and retaining social order is unique among developing countries.

3. Social structure: The basic living standards of the masses are high because rapid economic development did not result in the concentration of wealth. Anyone who is willing to work hard enough has access to success because the equal competition system in society allows for a high degree of social mobility. Consequently, Taiwan has become a stable and open society. (NICT, 2000, pp. 114–115)

By invoking the Taiwan experience, the KMT has intended to legitimize its version of a native-led nation-state. Curriculum development in the 1990s thus involved an ongoing process of politicizing the Taiwan experience, through which the past of Taiwan was selectively created, narratives of native identity were manufactured, and native languages and customs were restored. Indigenization education became a site of struggle over the cultural meanings and the social identities of ethnic groups, as we shall see in the introduction of nativization curricula.

Incorporating the Teaching of Localized Language and Culture

The process of de-Sinicizing education by the end of 1993 went hand in hand with the process of nativizing the KMT state. As discussed above, the idea of nativization was desirable both for Lee Teng-hui's reformist faction and the DPP when they both confronted reactionary resistance to the transformation of mainlander dominance. However, nativization assumed, in reality, different and even antagonistic meanings from one social group to another, since all had partially or totally different historical experiences, cultural interests, and ideological orientations. The KMT reformist camp tended to frame the ideology and practice of nativization on the basis of a more relaxed Sinocentrism, while the DPP referred to a Taiwanese identity. The conflict between the Mandarin-only policy (or *Sinocization education*) and the recognition of native languages (or *indigenization education*) thus represented the struggle for symbolic power in which the construction and the reconstruction of native identity were at stake.

The Invention of Xiang tu Curricula

Linguistic domination—the imposition of standard Mandarin as the official language—did not result in the total abolition of the oral use of "Taiwanese dialects." Native languages, Hoklo in particular, were used by dissidents as languages of opposition that expressed political discontent, and as languages of identity that mobilized support among ethnic Taiwanese. With the lifting of martial law and with greater freedom of expression, national television channels received permission to broadcast a Hoklo news program for 20 or 30 minutes every day beginning in 1987. Feeling marginalized by the mainlander-dominated KMT and the Hoklo-controlled DPP, Hakka groups, who comprised about 15% of the population, demonstrated on the streets to call for the Return My Mother Tongue objectives in 1988. Their immediate appeal was for equal access to the use of mass media and to a bilingual education. The Hakka rights movement had direct implications for the KMT's national language policy. The government-owned TV channel started to broadcast a 30-minute Hakka program on Sundays in 1989 (Hsiao, 1989, pp. 27–28).

Along with a more relaxed Mandarin-only policy in the cultural sphere, the opposition fought for native languages[5] to be recognized as languages of instruction. In the 1989 elections for county magistrates and city mayors, DPP candidates promoted platforms emphasizing indigenization education, which included the *xiang tu* (literally, hometown and soil) curricula and bilingual education at the primary and junior high levels. A greater advance in voter support for the DPP—6 seats out of 21 in mayoral elections—contributed to the shifting balance of power between the central and local governments, exposing contradictions in the contest over interpretations of native identity in educational domains. Independent and DPP county magistrates and city mayors created a formidable league and delegated I-lan County to pioneer the making of native-language teaching materials. The indigenization curriculum developed by nativist literary writers, university professors, and schoolteachers in I-lan County included subjects in the native language, history, and geography, and was meant to induce students to identify with their hometowns, native cultures, and languages (Youxikun, 1990).

Subject to the National Curriculum, which defined official knowledge in great detail, the local government adopted a strategy for the practicing of indigenization education. This strategy was based on a subject called *group activity*, which was conducted 80 minutes per week. According to the National Curriculum Standards, schools should offer weekly 80 minutes of activity in physical education, music, fine arts, language, and sciences on the basis of students' interests. Although the language category presupposed Mandarin-based teaching, non-Mandarin-mediated activities were justified by the local government through a category called *other* in a total of 89 items listed by the MOE. The multiplicity of interpretations of the standards thus provided a gray area for the implementation of indigenization education without confronting dominant ideologies embedded in the standards. Following the model of I-lan County, more and more local governments invested in the development of the *xiang tu* curricula in order to rejuvenate Taiwan's native cultures and languages in which, many Taiwanese believed, their native identity had roots.

In the face of militant struggles over the withering away of the *fa tong* regime in the early 1990s, the KMT insisted on the indispensability of the Mandarin-only policy in education in order to please mainlander elites still in power. The construction and the imposition of an official language, from the MOE's point of view, could decisively fashion the common consciousness of the people and cement the nation's spirit. Native languages were pejoratively defined as regional dialects, in opposition to the common language, and were better mastered, it was said, at home. Nevertheless, official curricula for regional dialects remained, for far too long, pitifully inadequate (MOE, July 31, 1990).

At the local level, the emergence of integrated bilingual education and the localized *xiang tu* curricula challenged not only the status of Mandarin as the normalized language of instruction, but also the myth of the National Curriculum as the sole legitimate selective tradition. At the national level, debates over indigenization education became one of the major contentions between the opposition and the divided KMT.

The Debates Over Indigenization Education

In the 1989 reelected Congress, DPP legislators continuously engaged in policy dialogue with the minister of education to press for increased native teaching materials. They questioned the Sinicized curriculum and the oppressive monolingualism that had been crafting an illusory Chinese identity in education. Students became rootless and were encountering an identity crisis partly because they grew up with little knowledge of their own hometowns, their own native languages and cultures, and the history of Taiwan. Opposition legislators demanded that the MOE implement bilingual education and increase indigenized content such as folksongs, aboriginal music, and Taiwanese literature and geography in national standardized textbooks (Legislative Yuan, April 24, 1991, October 24, 1992).

Beginning in 1993, the discourse of indigenization education was disarticulated from a Taiwan-centered framework that derived from the opposition and was rearticulated by the Taiwanese KMT under its ideological matrix, "Rooted in Taiwan, Mindful of the Mainland, Looking Out into the World," which culturally assumed a core-margin relationship between China and Taiwan. As discussed above, the total renewal of the perennial Congress in 1992 manifested the ascendancy of Taiwanese in politics. In particular, the DPP's securing of 51 out of 161 seats in the legislature made it a determinant minority that enjoyed veto power and influenced the legalization of national policymaking, profoundly transforming the power relations between the executive and legislative bodies. Furthermore, the resignation of the mainlander premier in 1993 signified the ultimate defeat of the KMT's hardliners. The dispute over indigenization education intensified in the reconstructed Legislative Yuan, which provided the conditions for a modifying of the

National Curriculum Standards still based on the old KMT's version of Chinese nationalism.

The facility in native languages in general and Hoklo in particular was gaining political significance. As competitive politics developed, not only Taiwanese elites but also mainlander political figures saw the inevitability of mastering and using "Taiwanese dialects" in political settings, or campaign activities, or both, for the winning of votes. Regulations covering the proportion of Taiwanese language television programming were no longer enforced after 1991 and were removed from the Broadcast and Television Law in 1993. Nevertheless, Taiwanese dialects, as an emerging linguistic capital, could be favored by the ruling groups as a "language of elections" in the political sphere or tolerated as a "language of media" in the realm of culture, but not as a language of instruction in the educational domain. Considering language to be the medium of cultural production and circulation, DPP legislators proposed an amendment called the Mother-Tongue Article in the Children Welfare Law in 1993 to delegate to the MOE both children's native-language education and the publication of related teaching materials (Legislative Yuan, March 17, 1993).

The legalization of native-language education called into question the remaining traditional rankings of language education in school. DPP legislators further demanded a multilingual education. Controversies over the KMT's Mandarin-only policy in education centered mainly on three points. The first point pertained to linguistic hierarchy—that is, national language versus dialect. The MOE continued to promote Mandarin as the official language—the lingua franca of communication—and the sole medium of instruction in school. Mandarin was coded as formal, literate, middle class, and an elevated means of communication. In sharp contrast, the properties adhering to native languages in Taiwan contained negative references such as dialect, informal, illiterate, working class, and coarse. DPP legislators increasingly denounced the pervasive devaluation and disparagement from which native languages had been suffering, and asked for multilingualism that officially recognized Hoklo, Hakka, and aboriginal languages as national or common languages. The second point of contention centered on the subordination of native-language education or mother-tongue learning versus multilingual education. The MOE, which viewed native languages as vernacular—not as true languages—disapproved of bilingual education but compromised on the practice of mother-tongue learning. That is, the teaching of Taiwanese dialects made it feasible for students to learn their mother tongue. This subordinate position of studying one's mother tongue as a dialect was in opposition to the multilingual education advocated by DPP legislators. The third point of tension was the status of native-language instruction as either voluntary or mandatory. The MOE intended to practice mother-tongue learning through extracurricular activities that were to be informal and voluntarily offered by local educational authorities. However, the opposition attempted to make native-language education part of national curricula and thus mandatory nationwide (Legislative Yuan, April 14, 1993, December 28, 1994).

The dynamics underlying the changes to educational Sinocization discourse were partly generated by the presence of a more conflicting official recontextualizing field (e.g., the DPP's securing of positions in the legislature) and of a more effective pedagogic recontextualizing field (e.g., numerous activities of educational reform groups and headlines in the media). When public calls for a nativization of the National Curriculum were mobilizing even wider public support, the dominant Sinocization principle in education was about to be transformed.

Rooted in Taiwan, Mindful of the Mainland

Along with the intensification of opposition nativization discourses were efforts by the Taiwanese KMT to modify its pedagogic discourse, as represented in the slogan "Rooted in Taiwan, Mindful of the Mainland, Looking Out into the World." On the basis of this principle, the MOE decided to invent the first-ever mandatory native curriculum. The new native curriculum included three separate subjects: Local Culture Teaching Activities from the third grade to the sixth grade and Folk Art Activities and Getting to Know Taiwan for the seventh grade. The implementation of the Local Culture Teaching Activities was based on the guideline "from near to far" (townships, counties, and cities), which aimed to "provide students the opportunity to learn dialects and to enhance their understanding of *xiang tu* culture." City and county governments, schools, and teachers would be in charge of the composition of decentralized teaching material (MOE, 1993, pp. 366–367). Furthermore, the purpose of Getting to Know Taiwan, a three-part series of junior high school textbooks that dealt with Taiwan's historical, social, and geographical studies, was to get students to better know and love the place where they were living, and to develop an awareness and confidence that all people in Taiwan had a shared identity, regardless of what ethnic group they belong to or where they come from (MOE, February 28, 1995). The nativization curriculum took effect in 1997.

The official indigenization subjects, to a certain degree, may have crystallized the pedagogic discourse of "Rooted in Taiwan, Mindful of the Mainland, Looking Out into the World" as a newly emerging principle in curricular production. However, the apparently more inclusive, official *xiang tu* curricula were primarily oriented toward a geographically hometown-based instruction that emphasized only the history, geography, customs, and folklore of a particular city or county in contrast to a culturally Taiwan-centered pedagogy as found in opposition discourses. The presentation of Taiwan was fragmented by administrative borders (townships and counties), and thus the connotation of *xiang tu* had more of an administrative sense than an ethnic or cultural one

(Mao, 1997). Suffice it to say that the official *xiang tu* curricula could practice depoliticized ethnic politics by applying them to the learning of psychology and of teaching methods (e.g., the notion of "from near to far") without confronting "dangerous" issues such as the complexity of interrelationships between political dominance, cultural oppression, language inequality, and ethnic assimilation.

Conclusion

The heart of this chapter focuses on the idea that a more integrative approach to the study of the state-education nexus requires attention to the formation of oppositional movements focused on ideological struggle, cultural change, identity construction, and social relations of domination and resistance, especially if the links between the state and education are to be understood as dialectical. This chapter examined how Sinocentric cultural norms were institutionalized in the state and how the restructuring of curriculum in Taiwan emerged as a bitterly contested site of cultural recognition and incorporation, with far-reaching ramifications for identity politics. Making sense of collective actions helps us to conceptualize oppositional movements as one of the driving forces behind educational transformation.

This chapter demonstrates that struggles over the silencing of the past, represented by the February 28 Massacre, have involved control not only over the unthinkable and the thinkable, but also over the construction of collective memories that have been invisible for decades. The period of political liberalization constituted the structural conditions for the emergence of protest frames and counternarratives that recognized the injustice of the massacre and enabled the grievances of victims' family members to be articulated. Shared wrongs and sufferings were interpreted and reworked by campaign adherents, constituting the cultural and ideological base for mobilization. Symbolized as the most profound ethnic cleavage in postwar Taiwan, the massacre thus served as a historical prototype that crystallized a tragic encounter between ethnically differentiated groups. What is at stake is how to render justice to history, both for the education of a democratic citizenry and through the building of a shared memory among different social groups. What should be acknowledged is that to reshape collective memories is to confront incessantly and imaginatively the difficulties underlying any attempted harmonization of the interests of diverse or fragmented groups (Wu, 2004).

This chapter also suggests that the collective framing effort for mobilization may arise from a contrast between official rhetoric and social practices. In the case of the contested representations of China's sovereignty in textbooks, the trend of cross-Straits contacts dramatizes a glaring contradiction between the imagination of KMT-claimed sovereignty and the reality of the CCP-ruled mainland. This ideological contradiction contributes to the emergence and the development of collective actions that fuel the modification of the dominant Chinese nationalist principle constructed over a period of decades as a means of cultural dominance and symbolic control.

Finally, the idea of nativization, operating as the master frame of oppositional movements, possessed a pervasive commonsense meaning for the people of Taiwan, but was inherently unstable and constantly being reconstructed. The construction of a native identity buttressed a popular sentiment for recognition—recognition, if not of Taiwan as a sovereign state, then of the Taiwanese people as possessing a lived presence (Yee, 2001). The chief articulations of curricular reform employ the nativization frame to invoke the support of a population that, in large part, suffered under the state's cultural domination and its suppression of indigenous cultural expression. The state nevertheless managed to incorporate the practice of nativization curricula into the ideological matrix "Rooted in Taiwan, Mindful of the Mainland." The struggle for the creation and the reproduction of de-Sinicized knowledge, as a major part of curricular reform in Taiwan, thus bespoke the significance of, to use Fraser's words, a "deep restructuring of the relations of recognition" in education (1997). This chapter suggests that the struggle for recognition is a complicated, ceaseless battle characterized by negotiations between, on the one hand, the state-in-formation and, on the other, the enduring collective action of oppositional movements.

Endnotes

1. This chapter adopts the pinyin system to transliterate Chinese characters and names (with family names preceding given names) into the Roman alphabet. However, if a name has a publicly known romanized form, the original form will be used to avoid confusion (e.g., Lee Teng-hui).
2. Exceptions to this are provided in Apple (1996, 2003) and Omi & Winant (1994).
3. The retreat of the KMT to Taiwan and the large-scale immigration of Chinese to the island changed its demographic composition—changes that constituted the base of constant constructions of ethnicity-related self-identification over the following decades. Up to the 1990s, Taiwan's population was conventionally classed into four ethnic groups according to origin, time of arrival in Taiwan, and language. The non-Han residents—the indigenous peoples—are of Malay-Polynesian origin and comprise slightly more than 1% of the population. The Han Chinese can be divided into islanders, who moved to Taiwan in line with the waves of Chinese migration that occurred over the preceding three hundred years, and mainlanders, who were born on the mainland and fled to Taiwan with the KMT government around 1949. Based on their languages, islanders themselves are usually referred to as Hoklo and Hakka, which together comprise about 85% of the population. See Wei-der Shu (1997/1998).
4. The Taiwanization policy was intended to enhance the role of Taiwanese in policymaking by selectively co-opting them into the upper echelons of the power hierarchy in the party and government.
5. Acknowledging that Mandarin had become the new mother tongue of the younger generations, linguistic activists used the term *native language* to refer to Hoklo, Hakka, and aboriginal languages.

List of Acronyms

CCP	Chinese Communist Party
DPP	Democratic Progressive Party
KMT	Kuomintang (Chinese Nationalist Party)
MOE	Ministry of Education
NICT	National Institute for Compilation and Translation
NSMs	New Social Movements
PRC	People's Republic of China
ROC	Republic of China

References

Apple, M. W. (1995). *Education and power* (2nd ed.). New York: Routledge.

Apple, M. W. (1996). *Cultural politics of education*. New York: Teacher College Press.

Apple, M. W., et al. (2003). *The state and the politics of knowledge*. New York: RoutledgeFalmer.

Ball, S. J. (1990). *Politics and policymaking in education: Explorations in policy sociology*. London: Routledge.

Bernstein, B. (1990). *The structuring of pedagogic discourse*. New York: Routledge.

Bernstein, B. (1996). *Pedagogy, symbolic control, and identity: Theory, research, critique*. London: Taylor & Francis.

Carnoy, M. (1989). Education, state, and culture in American society. In H. A. Giroux & P. L. McLaren (Eds.), *Critical Pedagogy, the state, and cultural struggle* (pp. 3–23). Albany: State University of New York Press.

Carnoy, M. (1992.). Education and the state: From Adam Smith to Perestroika. In R. F. Arnove, P. G. Altbach, & G. P. Kelly (Eds.), *Emergent issues in education: Comparative perspectives* (pp. 143–159). Albany: State University of New York Press.

Carnoy, M., & Levin, H. M. (1985). *Schooling and work in the democratic state*. Palo Alto, CA: Stanford University Press.

Carnoy, M., & Samoff, J. (1990). *Education and social transition in the third world*. Princeton, NJ: Princeton University Press.

Charles, N. (2000). *Feminism, the state and social policy*. New York: St. Martin's Press.

Chen, F.-M. (Ed.). (1988). *Er ba shi jian xue shu lun wen ji* [Essays on the February 28 Incident of 1947]. Irvine, CA: Taiwan Publishing.

Chen, J.-J. (2003). *State formation, pedagogic reform, and textbook (de)regulation in Taiwan, 1945–2000*. Unpublished doctoral dissertation, University of Wisconsin, Madison.

Chun, A. (1994). From nationalism to nationalizing: Cultural imagination and state formation in postwar Taiwan. *Australian Journal of Chinese Affairs, 31*, 49–69.

Cohen, J. L. (1985). Strategy or identity: New theoretical paradigms and contemporary social movements. *Social Research, 52* (4), 663–716.

Curtis, B. (1988). *Building the educational state: Canada West, 1836–1871*. Philadelphia, PA: Falmer Press/Althouse Press.

Curtis, B. (1992). *True government by choice men? Inspection, education, and state formation in Canada West*. Toronto, Canada: University of Toronto Press.

Da lu di tu, bian yi guan bu de shan gai [The National Institute for Compilation and Translation shall not change the map of the mainland]. (1991, February 2). Lian he bao.

Fraser, F. (1997). *Justice interruptus*. New York: Routledge.

Green, A. (1997). *Education, globalization and the nation state*. New York: St. Martin's Press.

Hsiao, H.-H. (1989). Taiwan xing xin she hui yun dong de pou xi: Zi zhu xing yu zi yuan fen pei [An analysis of the newly-emerged social movements in Taiwan]. In H.-H. Hsiao, et al. (Ed.), *Ling duan yu bo xue* [Monopoly and exploitation: The political economy of authoritarianism] (pp. 9–32). Taipei: Taiwan yan jiu ji jin hui [Taiwan Research Fund].

Hsiau, A.-C. (2000). *Contemporary Taiwanese cultural nationalism*. New York: Routledge.

Hunt, S. A., Benford, R. D., & Snow, D. A. (1994). Identity fields: Framing processes and the social construction of movement identities. In E. Larana, et al. (Ed.), *New social movements: From ideology to identity* (pp. 185–208). Philadelphia, PA: Temple University Press.

Johnston, H., Larana, E., & Gusfield, J. R. (1994). Identities, grievances, and new social movements. In E. Larana, et al. (Ed.), *New social movements: From ideology to identity* (pp. 3–35). Philadelphia, PA : Temple University Press.

Legislative Yuan. (1988–1994). *Li fa yuan gong bao* [Communiqué of the Legislative Yuan]. Taipei: Author.

Mao, C.-J. (1997). *Constructing Taiwanese identity: The making and practice of indigenization curriculum.* Unpublished doctoral dissertation, University of Wisconsin, Madison.

McAdam, D. (1994). Cultural and social movements. In E. Larana, et al. (Ed.), *New social movements: From ideology to identity* (pp. 36–57). Philadelphia, PA: Temple University Press.

Ministry of Education (MOE). (1990–1995). *Jiao yu bu gong bao* [Communiqué of the Ministry of Education]. Taipei: Author.

Ministry of Education (MOE). (1993). *Guo min xiao xue ke cheng biao zhun* [Curricula Standards for Elementary Schools]. Taipei: Author.

National Institute for Compilation and Translation (NICT). (Ed.). (1996). *Gao zhong li shi jiao ke shu di san ce* [Senior High School History, Vol. 3]. Taipei: Author.

National Institute for Compilation and Translation (NICT). (Ed.). (2000). *San min zhu yi di er ce* [Three Principles of the People, Vol. 2]. Taipei: Zhengzhong.

Nozaki, Y. (Ed.). (2005). *Struggle over difference: Curriculum, texts, and pedagogy in the Asia-Pacific.* Buffalo: State University of New York Press.

Omi, M., & Winant, H. (1994). *Racial formation in the United States: From the 1960s to the 1980s.* New York: Routledge.

Shi, C.-F. (2000, June). Construction of the public memory: A case of the 228 incident in Taiwan news media. Paper presented at the annual meeting of the North American Taiwan Studies Association, Harvard University, Cambridge, Massachusetts.

Shu, W.-D. (1997/1998). The emergence of Taiwanese nationalism: A preliminary work on an approach to interactive episodic discourse. *Berkeley Journal of Sociology, 42*, 84–85.

Wakabayashi, M. (1994). Taiwan: Fen lie guo jia yu min zhu hua [Taiwan: Divided nation and democratization]. Taipei: Yue dan.

Wang, J.-H. (1993). Zi ben, lao gong, yu guo jia ji qi [Capital, worker, and state apparatus]. Taipei: Taiwan.

Wu, N.-T. (2004, December). Transition without Justice, or justice without history: Transitional justice in Taiwan. Paper presented at the International Conference on Political Challenges and Democratic Institutions, National Taiwan University, Taipei, Taiwan.

Yee, A. C. (2001). Constructing a native consciousness: Taiwan literature in the 20th century. *China Quarterly, 165*, 83–101.

Youxikun yao qian yu yan zhuan jia, ding ding ben tu yu yan jiao cai [Youxikun invites linguists to invent indigenous language teaching materials]. (1990, February 12). Shou du zao bao.

Zhang, X.-C. (1988). Er er ba shi jian de zheng zhi bei jing ji qi ying xiang [The political background and effects of the February 28 Massacre]. In F.-M. Chen (Ed.), *Er er ba shi jian xue shu lun wen ji* [Essays on the February 28 Massacre] (pp. 93–112). Irvine, CA: Taiwan Publishing.

9

Creating Real Alternatives to Neoliberal Policies in Education

The Citizen School Project

LUÍS ARMANDO GANDIN

It is becoming increasingly difficult to listen to subaltern voices these days. Neoliberalism is capable of articulating encompassing policies, but it is as powerful for what it creates as new realities as for what it eliminates from our social imaginary. This is why it is so important to recuperate the voices and the stories of alternative creation. Silva helps us to understand this idea by pointing to the "process by which the neoliberal discourse produces and creates a 'reality' that ends up making it impossible to think and nominate another 'reality'" (1994, p. 16). Even though Silva's point seems a little too deterministic, the thrust of his argument points in the right direction: Subaltern and dissident discourses and practices are not unconditionally circulated or adopted as possibilities by those in power. It is not that the subaltern are not speaking; voices are being raised, but mainstream discourses have constantly overpowered them. This process produces the feeling that these voices are mere noise among the "real" sounds. Nevertheless, if we pay attention to this "noise" it has been sending a clear signal for a long time—there are other ways to organize education and it is far from impossible to implement them. When these voices come from peripheral countries, it is even more improbable that they will be heard. This chapter deals with one group of subaltern voices that has gained space in local state policy: the Citizen School project being implemented in Porto Alegre, Brazil.

The policy described in this chapter is not important because it represents a model of educational reform that can be replicated everywhere; it is important because it provides discursive and institutional weapons in a struggle against market-based one-size-fits-all models in education. The lesson that the Citizen School project teaches us all is exactly this one: There is no model that can be replicated everywhere. No progressive reform in education can be implemented in spite of the people involved. If this project is to be tried elsewhere, what should be undertaken is not a replication but rather a translation, which is always a rewrite of the original—one that makes sense in the new site.

It is with this spirit that I invite the reader to delve into this chapter. We have become overly skeptical of real educational transformations. I will describe and analyze one of these real transformations in the making. This proposal is far from complete and has flaws and contradictions, but it represents a new way of conceiving education and this alone deserves a close examination. It is a proposal that searches for responses to educational problems in places other than market-based policies that center their solutions in testing and economic accountability. In this chapter I will present the conception of the Citizen School project and the basic mechanisms created to implement it, and will evaluate its strengths and some of its contradictions. But first let me describe and analyze the context in which the Citizen School project is situated.

The Context—Local and Global

Porto Alegre is a city of almost 1.4 million people, situated in the southern region of Brazil. It is the capital of the state of Rio Grande do Sul, and is the largest city in the region. Since 1989, it has been governed by a coalition of leftist parties under the general leadership of the Workers' Party (Partido dos Trabalhadores, or PT), which was formed in 1979 by a coalition of unions, social movements, and other leftist organizations. PT has been reelected three consecutive times, thus giving it and its policies even greater legitimacy. Despite the recent electoral loss that will replace PT in 2005 after sixteen years in municipal administration, the fact that the winning coalition of parties (a centrist alliance) was elected promising not to change the major set of policies implemented by PT clearly means that these policies are already organic to the life of Porto Alegre.

Since its birth, the Workers' Party has been strongly opposed to the tradition of centralism in communist parties. The organization provided a "basis for an apprenticeship in democratic participation and decision-making and … also created an opportunity for new leaders to emerge from the ranks" (Keck, 1986, pp. 299–300). The creation of the Workers' Party represented a radical change in politics in Brazil. In a country where politics were always something to be left to the elite,[1] the creation of the Workers' Party was the materialization of the first political party (apart from the Communist Party, which was illegal for the majority of its history in Brazil) created to defend and promote the interests of the Brazilian working class (Pinheiro, 1989). This is an essential change of perspective. Workers and subaltern classes had to propose new forms of governing because the elites and the dominant groups in Brazil did not do it for them. Proposing a change in common sense was an important part of the Workers' Party platform, and ultimately part of the Citizen School project.

This new way of thinking about the state and its role soon appeared in Porto Alegre. According to one of the former mayors of Porto Alegre (a nationally respected member of the Workers' Party), the purpose of the government of the Popular Administration (as the PT is called in Porto Alegre) is to "recuperate utopian energies, to create a movement which contains, as a real social process, the origins of a new way of life, constructing a 'new moral life' (Gramsci) and a new articulation between state and society ... that could lead social activity and citizenship consciousness to a new order" (Genro, 1999, p. 9).

This is also the goal of the educational policy of the Popular Administration: to promote the real involvement of communities in the education of their children and to learn from the experiences of community organization. There is clearly a radical difference between this proposal and neoliberal ones. It is important, therefore, to understand the global context in which the Citizen School project is situated before we examine the practical elements of the proposal.

The rhetoric of neoliberalism insists on the importance of education to solve the problems of capitalism. Several reports show how education has failed to efficiently provide workers with the appropriate skills.[2] What is the proposed solution? Neoliberal proponents say that there is only one way to solve this crisis—to apply the logic of the market to the educational system. They say that just as in other spheres of society, the intervention of the state and the control of the unions over the workplace are disastrous for school efficiency. Competition is the only force that will end the historical inefficiency in schools, which are currently controlled by the corporatist power of the teachers' unions and the bureaucratic structure of school districts or local departments of education.

Neoliberalism also promotes a discursive movement that eliminates social causes from the equation and limits explanations to individual ability and effort. Silva (1996) claims that, "linguistic categories and concepts, by restraining and limiting the sphere of the possible, by allowing or disallowing certain things to be thought out, are a central part of any political project of social transformation" (p. 167). Categories such as *participation, democracy, collaboration*, and *solidarity*, which are all historically connected with progressive social movements in education, are disarticulated from their previous meanings and rearticulated in the educational arena using the language and practices of marketization (Apple, 1993). Those categories are now stripped from the meanings that linked them to specific struggles for justice and equality in society in general and in education in particular, and connected with categories like *efficiency, productivity*, and *knowledge as commodity*. As Gee, Hull, and Lankshear (1996) point out:

> Part of the way in which fast capitalist texts "grab us" is that they use words that name things which nearly all of us like but which, on reflection are seen to mean slightly (and sometimes *very*) different things in fast capitalist texts than they mean to many of us. (p. 29)

It is important to say, however, that this laborious discursive project is not one that can be done once and for all; it is always a process (rather than a state) where articulations have to be constructed, reconstructed, and struggled over in relation to the historical circumstances of each specific social formation.

The concept of articulation is central here because it helps us to understand the "work" that has to be done to connect ideas and practices. The examples above illustrate that to disarticulate a concept historically associated with counterhegemonic movements and rearticulate it to the hegemonic discourse actually requires heavy lifting.

Globalization: A Space of Contradictions

It is important to recognize here that although there is a clear global movement toward conservative modernization, which must be acknowledged in order to understand the constraints that alternative reforms face, specific realities in each society will pose different challenges to this hegemonic movement. When dealing with the conservative modernization movement, one is tempted to use the current discourse of globalization to assume that what happens in the Brazilian context is a mere transfer of the policies of the core countries to the ones on the periphery. However, what I encountered in my research of educational policy implementation in Brazil was not a monolithic implementation of conservative policies originally conceived in the core countries and transferred to Brazil, but rearticulations and hybridisms formed in the struggles between global and local hegemonic forces and between hegemonic and counterhegemonic forces.

Although globalization is a process that has been able to reach even remote locales, it has been generating very different consequences depending on the local realities. As Ball (1998) says, "the new orthodoxies of education policy are grafted onto and realised within very different national and cultural contexts and are affected, inflected and deflected by them" (p. 133). So when this adaptation of a global hegemonic discourse occurs at a local level, not only must it be reconfigured and rearticulated to make sense in the particular context, it also has to account for the opposition and resistance of local groups.

The Creation of the Preconditions for the Citizen School Project

How does this discussion apply to the case of the Citizen School project? Because neoliberal policies cannot merely be imposed but must also win the consent of the agents involved in education, spaces are created where it is possible to construct alternative practices. The Citizen School rearticulates these spaces and turns them into opportunities for its project. One of the problems with the idea of operating in the gaps is that the hegemonic forces set the agenda, and the progressive movements must operate within the field constructed by these forces. The difference in the Citizen School project is that it uses the spaces and gaps created by neoliberal policies and creeds to launch an alternative project—one that has a radical new logic. So rather than operating only in the gaps, the Citizen School proposes a field with different priorities and assumptions, and starts to foster a real alternative educational proposal. Rather than being merely tactical, this project builds a new strategy.[3]

When the discourse of conservative modernization reaches Brazil, and more specifically the city of Porto Alegre, some interesting rearticulations are forged. One of the ideas stressed by this discourse is the definition of education as the solution for capitalist crises. If *we* prepare students for the increasingly competitive new capitalism, *we* will be better prepared to excel in the globalized market, says the dominant educational rhetoric. Education is stressed as a targeted sphere for transformation in this hegemonic discourse.

The Popular Administration uses the space generated by this discourse to prioritize education in a country where education for the poor has been neglected. Once the space is occupied by rhetoric calling for more investment in education, the Citizen School can deploy its alternative project, with its realignment of priorities, and invest in a transformative project of education for the excluded. The Popular Administration can also start to recuperate, and at the same time reinvent, concepts such as *autonomy, decentralization,* and *collaboration,* currently advanced by neoliberals. These concepts had a completely different meaning in the popular movements in Brazil and now have to be disarticulated from neoliberal discourse and rearticulated to the Citizen School project.

Taking advantage of the hegemonic decentralization discourse expressed in Brazilian educational policy, the Popular Administration was able to construct a system that does not have to follow any federal curricular directives and can be structured in cycles of formation, an option anticipated in the educational law. While the governments of other state capitals only complained about the neoliberal effects of decentralization, which gave them more responsibility without more resources, the Workers' Party in Porto Alegre, while strongly protesting the lack of resources, explores every aspect of decentralization proposals and uses them to construct a real alternative. Rather than performing only the minimum that the federal legislation demanded from municipal systems, Porto Alegre created a democratic Municipal Council for Education, able autonomously to regulate education in Porto Alegre and to explore every possibility that the law allows to construct an alternative school structure and an alternative curriculum.

This does not mean that the battle has been won by the Popular Administration. New articulations are forged by hegemonic groups and education remains a site of struggle. But the important point is that no hegemonic action can block all spaces simultaneously, and even its own discourse can be rearticulated to favor counterhegemonic purposes. That is what the Citizen School project has done.

The process of disarticulation and rearticulation can also help us understand the terminology of citizenship. Certain concepts can acquire different meanings in different contexts. The concept of *citizenship*, central to the project in Porto Alegre, has a very specific meaning in contemporary Brazil. It is not a randomly chosen word; it actually symbolizes the struggles against attempts to introduce the market logic inside public spheres, such as education. Therefore, saying that you want to form citizens inside public schools must be read, in the Brazilian context, as a response to the neoliberal discourse. The term citizenship serves as a discursive weapon against rival notions involving *clients* or *consumers* introduced by neoliberal discourse. It provides very different subject positions for agency than those offered by the idea of the consumer in a set of market relations. The political meaning of citizenship has been rearticulated to a set of more socially critical ideas and practices, one that intends to construct a new common sense that is truly focused on collective as well as individual empowerment.

Speaking of citizen as opposed to client or consumer is a conscious move to insert political words in the discussion. There is an attempt to bring to the very center of the political debate the idea that impoverished communities, contrary to what the "experts" say, can participate in the definition of their social destiny. Thus, not only are concepts that were relegated to the margins being brought back to the public discussion, but entire groups of people that were marginalized and excluded from the economic, social, and political goods of society are affirmed as having the right to space, to voice, to social existence. Subaltern groups regain not only voice, but real space to be subjects of their own history.

Nonetheless, no progressive policy can be a real alternative without changing the structures that discourage the implementation of the new project. It is necessary to evaluate whether the Citizen School is able to construct a different structure, one that acts both as a stimulant for the intended change and as a real example of the alternative in action—a reality that can work as an anchor for new experiences.

The Citizen School Project

Historically, as a rule, schools in Brazil have had little autonomy. In the majority of states and cities, there are no elections for the city or state council of education (traditionally a bureaucratic structure with members appointed by the executive), let alone for principals in schools. The curriculum is usually defined by the secretariats of education in the cities and states. The resources are administered by the centralized state agencies; schools usually have very little or no financial autonomy.

Although Brazil has recently achieved a very high level of initial access to schools, the indices of failures and dropouts are frightening. This reality is where the central purpose of the Citizen School, and the entire educational project of the Popular Administration, begins. The field of education has become central to the Popular Administration's project of constructing new relations between the state, schools, and communities. The Citizen School is organically linked to and considered a major part of the larger process of transforming the whole city. The goal is to form citizens. According to the Municipal Secretariat of Education (SMED), citizens are the ones who have the material goods necessary for survival, the symbolic goods necessary for their subjectivity, and the political goods necessary for their social existence (Azevedo, 1999, p. 16).

Having learned from their participation in social movements and their engagement with democratic experiences in the teachers' union, the members of the SMED knew that they could not impose a proposal that was not created by those involved in the daily life of schools. The political origin of the coordinators of the Citizen School is an important factor in the democratic component of the proposal. Many of the participants have experienced years of struggle as leaders of teachers' unions. Their experience constitutes one of the reasons for a clear political will to construct participatory and democratic alternatives. In fact, although the SMED plays an essential role in coordinating the actions of the schools and pushing a democratic agenda, the principles that officially guide the SMED's actions were created collectively with the active participation of teachers, school administrators and staff, students, and parents in institutionalized forums for democratic decision making.

The main goals of the Citizen School project can be summarized in a quote from the secretary of education. He says that the project wants to create a school:

> where everyone has guaranteed access, that is not limited to transmission of content; a school that is able to articulate the popular knowledge with the scientific knowledge. A school that is a public space for the construction and experience of citizenship, that goes beyond merely delivering knowledge and transforms itself into a social-cultural space, with a pedagogical policy oriented toward social transformation, where the student is the subject of the knowledge and where the pedagogy takes place in a interdisciplinary perspective, overcoming the curricular fragmentation present in schools. A school that has the necessary material resources to implement this policy, where the participation of all in the community can lead to the construction of an autonomous school, with real democratic management, where all segments of the community have their participation guaranteed. (Azevedo, 1999, pp. 19–20)

The basic goals of the project—democratization of access to school, democratization of knowledge, and democratization of governance—were developed collectively through a participatory structure especially created for conceiving these goals: the Constituent Assembly. It had the goal of generating the principles that would guide the policy for the municipal schools in Porto Alegre.

The process of organizing the Constituent Assembly took a good deal of time. The whole process started in March 1994, lasted 18 months, and involved thematic meetings in the schools, regional meetings, the assembly itself, and the elaboration of the schools' internal regulation. The themes that guided the discussion were school governance, curriculum, principles for living together, and evaluation.

The Citizen School project was created using a process that does not separate the determination of the goals from the creation of the mechanisms to implement the goals. Generating the practical goals is an innovative mechanism that has been able to produce transformations in the relationships between the schools and the community. The idea was to foster a government that creates channels for real development of collectively constructed normative goals and that replaces the traditional relationship of distant government officials managing schools they know little about.

Democratization of Access to Schools

If the schools were to have an impact on the lives of the children living in the most impoverished neighborhoods of Porto Alegre—where the municipal schools are situated—the initial access to schools had to be a priority. For the Popular Administration, guaranteeing this access was, therefore, the first step in promoting social justice for communities historically excluded from social goods.

Granting access to all school-age children is not as easy as it might sound. Historically, Brazil has had an enormous number of children who did not attend school. National statistics show that this has been changing rapidly, but in 1991, when the Popular Administration was just starting, and even in 1994, when the Citizen School project had only been in existence for one year, the situation was grave in terms of initial access to schooling. Almost 17% of Brazilian school-age children were not being formally educated in 1991, and in 1994 this number dropped to almost 13%.

When the Workers' Party was elected in 1988, the city of Porto Alegre had only nineteen K–8 schools (fundamental education, as it is called in Brazil), with 14,838 students and 1,698 teachers, curriculum coordinators, and educational supervisors. Under the Popular Administration the number of students grew at a remarkable rate. Between 1988 and 2000, the number of students in fundamental education increased by 232%. This shows how profound the impact of the SMED's actions has been in Porto Alegre. And although the comparison is not between identical circumstances, it is worth pointing out that between 1991 and 1998 the number of school-age children in Brazil increased by only 22.3% (National Institute for Studies and Research in Education [INEP], 2000, p. 53).

The number of fundamental education schools increased by 126% under the Popular Administration government. If we consider all the schools under the municipal government, including the schools geared toward early childhood, adolescents and young adults, and special education, the increase is actually 210%. It is important to point out that these schools were all constructed in very impoverished areas of the city, and that the majority of new schools were actually built inside or around *favelas* (slums). This means that the schools are not only bringing back students who drop out of state schools, but they are also creating a space for many children who never attended school and possibly never would have were it not for the new municipal schools.

But guaranteeing initial access to school does not guarantee that these children will benefit from school. In order to really democratize access to schools, the SMED proposed a new organization for the municipal schools in 1995. Instead of keeping the traditional structure of grades over the duration of one year (1st to 8th in fundamental education), the idea was to adopt a new structure called Cycles of Formation. It is important to note that the idea of reorganizing the curriculum and the space-time of the schools in cycles instead of grades did not originate in Porto Alegre. What the Citizen School implemented was not new per se, but a new configuration that, according to the SMED, would offer a substantially better opportunity for dealing with the need for democratization of access and knowledge.

The idea is that by using a different conception of the equation learning/time, the Citizen School would not punish students for allegedly being slow in their process of learning. In this new configuration, the traditional deadline (the end of each academic year), when the students had to prove that they had learned, was eliminated in favor of a different organization of time. The establishment of the cycles is a conscious attempt to eliminate the mechanisms in schools that perpetuate exclusion, failure, and dropouts, as well as the blaming of the victim that accompanies these.

How do the cycles of formation actually work in the Citizen School? The schools now have three cycles of three years each, something that adds one year to fundamental education (as one year of early childhood education inside the schools expands fundamental education to nine years). This makes the municipal schools responsible for the education of kids from 6 to 14 years of age. The three cycles are organized based on the cycles of life: each one corresponds to one phase of development—childhood, preadolescence, and adolescence. The idea is to group together students of the same age in each of the years of the three cycles. This aims at changing the reality in the majority of public schools in Brazil, which cater to popular classes and the one the SMED faced when the Popular Administration started to govern the city: students with multiple failures in classrooms intended for much younger children. By having students of the same age in the same year of the cycle, the SMED claims to remotivate the kids who have failed multiple times.

In the schools using these cycles, students progress from one year to another within one cycle; the notion of failure is eliminated. Despite this victory, the SMED understood that the elimination of mechanisms of exclusion was not enough to achieve the goal of democratization of knowledge. Because of this, the Citizen School created several mechanisms that aim at guaranteeing the inclusion of students. It established Progression Groups for the students who have discrepancies between what they have learned and where they should be in the standard Brazilian school based on their age. The idea is to provide students who have experienced multiple failures in the past with a stimulating and challenging environment where they can learn at their own pace and fill the gaps in their academic formation. The Progression Groups are also a space for students who come from other school systems (from other city or state schools, for example) and have experienced multiple failures to be given closer attention so that they are ultimately integrated into the cycles according to their age. The idea here is that the school has to change its structure to adapt to the students, and not the reverse, which historically has been the case (Souza et al., 1999, p. 24–25).

This idea of creating a new structure to better respond to students' needs led to the creation of another entity: the Learning Laboratory. This is a space where students with more serious learning problems get individual attention, but also a place where teachers conduct research in order to improve the quality of the regular classes. For students with special needs, there are the Integration and Resource Rooms, which "are specially designed spaces to investigate and assist students who have special needs and require complementary and specific pedagogic work for their integration and for overcoming their learning difficulties" (SMED, 1999a, p. 50).

With all these mechanisms, the Citizen School project not only grants initial access, but also guarantees that the educational space occupied by subaltern children is a space that treats them with the dignity, respect, and quality necessary to keep them in school and educate them to be real citizens.

Democratization of Knowledge

Curriculum transformation is a crucial part of Porto Alegre's project to build active citizenship. It is important to say that this dimension is not limited to access to traditional knowledge. What is being constructed is a new epistemological understanding about what counts as knowledge as well. It is not based on a mere incorporation of new knowledge within the margins of an intact "core of humankind's wisdom," but a radical transformation. The Citizen School project goes beyond the mere episodic mentioning of cultural manifestations or class, race, sexual, and gender-based oppression, and includes these themes as an essential part of the process of constructing knowledge.

In the Citizen School project, the notions of *core* and *periphery* in knowledge are made problematic. The starting point for the construction of curricular knowledge is the culture(s) of the communities themselves, not only in terms of content, but in terms of perspective as well. The whole educational process is aimed at inverting previous priorities and instead serving the historically oppressed and excluded groups. The starting point for this new process of knowledge construction is the idea of thematic complexes. This organization of the curriculum is a way of having the whole school working on a central generative theme, from which the disciplines and areas of knowledge, in an interdisciplinary effort, structure the focus of their content.

The schools are encouraged to follow 10 steps for the construction of the thematic complex and for the translation of the macrodiscussions into curriculum. These steps—nicknamed by some in the SMED and in the schools as the *decalogue*—are the following:[4]

1. acknowledgment and study of the context [where the school is situated] through participatory research conducted by the school collective in the community;
2. reading and problematization of the [findings of the] research; selection of the statements gathered in the research that are significant and representative of the aspirations, interests, conceptions, and cultures of the community;
3. definition of the complex in the collective of the cycles; determination of a phenomenon that gives organization to the most significant information and angles of the researched reality;
4. elaboration of the principles in the knowledge areas;
5. collective selection of a conceptual matrix; broadening of the conceptual matrix in the areas;
6. creation of a graphic representation of the complex;
7. elaboration of work plans in every knowledge area, cycle, and year inside the cycles;
8. circulation of these plans among all the participants; composition of interdisciplinary strategies among and within cycles;
9. evaluation and periodic replanning through systematic meetings by cycles, years in the cycle, and area;
10. problematization of the lived thematic complex, aimed at finding the focus of the next thematic complex. (Gorodicht & Souza, 1999, p. 82)

As we can see, through research (a process performed by teachers in the communities where the schools are situated), the themes that interest and/or concern the community are gathered. After gathering the statements of community members, the most significant statements will be selected by the collective of teachers through discussions that specifically center on this and guide the construction of the thematic complex. This thematic complex provides the whole school with a central focus for the curriculum for a period of time that can be one semester or an entire academic year.

After having determined the principles, the larger contribution of each knowledge area to the discussion of the thematic complex, and the conceptual matrix (a web of concepts from the knowledge area rather than isolated facts or information, which the teachers understand as essential when dealing with the thematic complex), the teachers have meetings organized by their knowledge areas and by each year in the cycles to elaborate and plan the curriculum. Teachers must study their own knowledge areas and elect the concepts that would help to problematize the thematic complex. They also have to work collectively with teachers of other areas in order to assemble a curriculum that is integrated and dense enough to simultaneously address the issues listed in the thematic complex.

According to one of the creators of this conceptualization, in the context of the Citizen School project, "the thematic complex brings about the perception and comprehension of reality and makes explicit the worldview that all those involved in the process have" (Rocha in SMED, 1999a, p. 21). Because the thematic complex is closely related to social problems, the process makes teachers search for the relation of their discipline to social reality as a whole. Finally, because the starting point for the thematic complex is popular knowledge or common sense, teachers are also forced to think about the relationship between official knowledge and this common sense. Therefore, this approach deals simultaneously with three problems of traditional education: the fragmentation of knowledge, the "apparent" neutrality of school content, and the absolute supremacy that traditional schools grant to scientific/erudite knowledge over local knowledge of communities, especially very impoverished ones as is the case in Porto Alegre.

The Citizen School project conceives the organization of the curriculum around a thematic complex not only as a means for generating alternative knowledge inside the curriculum, but also as a form of political intervention.

> To teach using thematic complexes not only generates the possibility of selecting knowledge that is significant to students but also presents us with the perspective of having a tool for analysis that can help students to organize the world they live in, so that they can understand it and act upon it through a critical, conscious, and collective social practice. (Gorodicht & Souza, 1999, p. 78)

The traditional rigid disciplinary structure is broken and general interdisciplinary areas are created. These areas of study are termed social expression; biological, chemical, and physical sciences; sociohistoric; and logic-mathematical.

To give a concrete example of how this works, I now describe how the sociohistoric knowledge area proceeded, in one school of Porto Alegre, to organize its curriculum. After carrying out research in the community, the school elected "the quality of life in the *favela*" as its thematic complex. The sociohistoric knowledge area had to construct the principle of that area—that is, the contribution of this area to dealing with the elected thematic complex. This area expressed its possible contribution as "the individual and collective transformation of the citizen, in his/her time and space, recuperating his/her origins, aimed at improving the quality of life, taking into account the ideas of the community where this individual is situated."[5]

From the major thematic complex (the quality of life) three subthemes were listed by the teachers in the sociohistoric area: rural exodus, social organization, and property. In the rural exodus subtheme, the issues reflected the origin of the community—living now in a *favela*, but originally from the rural areas. This is a common story in the *favelas* where people who had nothing in the rural areas came to the cities only to find more exclusion. In this subtheme, the issues discussed were migration movements, overpopulation of the cities, "disqualification" of the working force, and marginalization. In the social organization subtheme, the issues were distributed in terms of temporal, political, spatial, and sociocultural relations. The issues, again, represent important questions in the organization of the community: the excessive and uncritical pragmatism of some in the neighborhood associations, and cultural issues such as religiosity, body expression, African origins, dance groups, and samba schools. In the third subtheme, property, the issues were directly linked to the situation of families in the *favela*—living illegally in lots with no title; having to cope with the lack of running water, basic sanitation, and other infrastructure problems, and attending to the history of this situation and the struggles around the legalization of the lots in which they live; the right to have basic public goods in the neighborhood; and the duties of citizens (such as understanding the importance and the social function of taxation). Starting with this understanding of their social context, students will approach school matters such as Brazilian and world history, geography, math, language, and social studies not as a disconnected corpus of knowledge, but as tools necessary to operate in and transform their realities.

This example shows the real transformation that is occurring in the curriculum of the schools in Porto Alegre. The students are not studying history or social and cultural studies through books that never address their real problems and interests. Through the organization of thematic complexes, the students learn history by beginning with the historical experience of their families. They study important social and cultural content by focusing on and valorizing their own cultural manifestations. It is important to note that these students still learn the history of Brazil and the world, including the so-called high culture, but these will be seen through different lenses. Their culture will not be forgotten in favor of learning high status culture. Rather, by understanding their situation and their culture and valuing it, these students will be able to simultaneously learn *and* will have the chance to transform their situation of exclusion. By studying not only the problems (rural exodus, living in illegal lots, etc.) but the strengths of self-organization (in neighborhood associations and in cultural activities and groups), and connecting these issues to school knowledge, such as geographical notions of space, historical events, mathematical competence, and much more, the Citizen School helps to construct real knowledge and alternatives for communities with terrible living conditions.

This shift of what is considered the core or the center of knowledge affects not only the pedagogical conception that guides daily life in the classrooms; it also transforms how the school itself functions as a whole. This conception of knowledge is now spreading throughout the entire school system. The project not only serves the excluded by generating a different formal education for students, but also serves them by creating an innovative structure that makes it possible for historically excluded communities to regain their dignity (both material and symbolic).

Democratization of Governance

The first mechanism that guarantees the democratization of governance is the Constituent Assembly. It not only provided a space to decide on the administration of the project, but also allowed for real participation in defining the goals of the Citizen School.

Among the mechanisms created to democratize the governance of the educational system in Porto Alegre, the school council is a central element. Its role is to promote the democratization of the decision-making process and governance in education in Porto Alegre. A product of the political will of the Popular Administration and the demands of social movements involved in education in the city, the school councils (established by a municipal law in December 1992 and implemented in 1993) are the most important institutions in the schools. They are formed by elected teachers, school staff, parents, students, and by one member of the administration, and they have consultative, deliberative, and monitoring functions.

The school council reserves 50% of its seats for teachers and staff and 50% for parents and students. One seat is guaranteed to the administration of the school, usually the principal, who is elected by all members of the school.

The task of the school council is to deliberate about the global projects for the school and the basic principles of administration, to allocate economic resources, and to monitor the implementation of the decisions. The principal and her team are responsible for the implementation of the policies defined by the school council.

In terms of resources, it is important to say that before the Popular Administration took office, there was a practice (common in Brazil) of centralized budgeting. Every expense (even the daily ones) had to be sent to the central administration before it was approved, and then the money was sent to the school or a central agency would purchase the necessary product or service.

In such a system, the school council would have its hands tied, with no autonomy at all. The SMED changed this structure and established a new policy to make an amount of money available to each school every three months. According to the SMED, this was the measure that instituted the financial autonomy of the schools, as it allowed the schools to manage their expenditures according to the goals and priorities established by the school council. At the same time that it creates autonomy, this measure gives parents, students, teachers, and staff who are council members a social responsibility for administering public money, and it teaches them to prioritize their investments with solidarity in mind (SMED, 1999b).

The school council also has the power to monitor the implementation, through the principal and his team, of its decisions (SMED, 1993, p. 3). In fact, the school council is an empowered structure in the schools. It is the main governing mechanism inside the schools, and it is limited only by educational legislation and policy collectively constructed in democratic forums. Decisions about the curriculum can be part of the deliberation, and the inclusion of parents, students, and teachers (or even staff, if we consider the traditional school) in this process is a great innovation.

Along with the school council, another structure guarantees democratic spaces in the Citizen School; in the municipal schools of Porto Alegre, the whole school community elects the principal by direct vote. As the one responsible for the implementation of the decisions of the school council, the principal is elected based on his or her defense of a particular project of administration for the school. There is a legitimacy born of this fact. The principal is not someone who necessarily represents the interests of the central administration inside the school councils, but someone with a majority of supporters inside that particular educational community. Principals have a great degree of embeddedness, which (the SMED feels) avoids having an individual not connected with the project be responsible for making concrete the deliberations of the school councils. But the responsibility of the community does not stop there: Through the school council, the school community has a way of monitoring the activities of the principal and holding that person responsible for implementing its democratic decisions. One example of where this control is exercised involves the pressure that parents put on the schools to make sure their children are not given a watered-down version of curriculum.

The direct election of the one responsible for implementing the directives of the school council creates a mechanism that honors the principle of democratic management at the local level of the school.

Evaluating the Success of the New Educational Structures

The democratization of access is certainly an important aspect of the Citizen School project and the SMED was able to advance substantially in this area. The SMED knew that it would have to attack the problem of dropouts if it really wanted to democratize access to schools. It recognized that the dropout problem is not an accident, but something structural in the society, as pointed out by Apple (1996, p. 90). By drastically reducing the number of students who abandon school and therefore dramatically increasing their chances of having better opportunities, the Citizen School project attacks a central problem. The students who stay in school are able to experience the alternative educational program designed by the Citizen School and will be able to learn about and, it is hoped, fight against the circumstances that led so many of them to drop out of school in the first place. The data speaks for itself: The dropout rate fell from more than 9% in 1989 to around 1% in 2003 (SMED, 2003).

Together with the cycles, another practice that has served to radically reduce the number of dropouts is the close monitoring of student attendance. By employing an aggressive policy of visiting parents at the homes of students who fail to show up at school after a number of days and explaining to them how harmful it is to their children not to attend school, the Citizen School was able to reduce the dropout rate significantly. Involving the whole community and the neighborhood associations in this monitoring has been another successful strategy. In fact, the drastic reduction of dropouts also appears to be related to the involvement of the communities with the school.

The care that the communities dedicate to the schools is readily apparent as well. While state schools are constantly damaged, robbed, and vandalized, the municipal schools are usually not targeted in this manner. These schools do not have such significant problems, and even the older ones are in very good shape. This is not something to be taken for granted. All over the country, and even in the state schools in Porto Alegre, there are complaints from teachers, students, and parents about the material conditions.

By valuing teachers, changing the whole environment of the schools, involving the community with the school as a public institution, and insisting that every student counts, the Citizen School project clearly attained its goal of democratizing access to school. In doing so, the Citizen School made possible a level of access to public benefits that are not usually available to students of public schools in Brazil. The numbers show this clearly: The number of students tripled between 1989 and 2000.

In order to evaluate the degree to which the project has succeeded in democratizing knowledge, several elements must be examined. One of these elements is the organization of the school in cycles of formation rather than traditional grades. As I showed before, there is a political conception of knowledge and learning behind the choice of radically changing the organization of the schools. The SMED has been investing heavily in teacher education and teacher salaries in order to make sure the priority of education in its schools is the learning process of the students. The elimination of repetition is only one of many measures, integrated in a whole new conception of schooling that involves a deep discussion of what is valued as knowledge and what is *real* democratization. Therefore, the lack of repetition does not mean the lack of evaluation and monitoring of the learning process of the students.

There is, nevertheless, another mechanism created by the SMED that is directly connected with the democratization of knowledge: the thematic complex. The thematic complex is a methodological technique constructed to deal with a serious challenge. The problem that the Citizen School project creators faced was how to simultaneously value and work with the knowledge and culture of the community, and to make the accumulated body of human knowledge available and accessible to the students. The question did not exactly end there because the Citizen School project also wanted to help students (and teachers) to construct new knowledge in the process of dialogue between, and problematization of, local and official knowledge. For the Citizen School project, only knowledge that is emancipatory is knowledge worth pursuing in schools—that is, knowledge that helps the students to establish relationships among phenomena and between their own lives and the larger social context.

Nevertheless, the Citizen School project does not claim that the schools should abandon traditional school knowledge. The creators of the Citizen School project know that this knowledge is absolutely necessary for the advancement of students in the school system. They also insist that the students who attend the municipal schools should not be denied the "accumulated knowledge of humankind." There are several educational programs for poor students that end up offering them a poor education, claiming that they will not need a better education because they will end up in jobs that only require basic skills. This is something that the Citizen School strongly fights against in its programs with teachers. It is necessary to break with the dominant cultural models that say that students who live in *favelas* have deficits because they are poor (Paes da Silva & Vasconcelos, 1997).

While insisting that students from the *favelas* should have access to the same quality of education that wealthier students have in Brazil (and, as I described above, the material conditions the schools offer for these students are in fact similar to those of some lower-middle-class students in some of the private schools), the Citizen School also wants to question the notion that the knowledge offered to these students should not be scrutinized and criticized. Every kind of knowledge should always be submitted to criticism. This can be better understood by Santos's notion of "double epistemological rupture." Santos claims that:

> the double epistemological rupture represents a work of transforming both common sense and science. While the first rupture is essential to the constitution of science—something that does not change common sense as it was before science—the second rupture transforms common

sense based on science. With this double rupture the goal is to achieve an enlightened common sense and a prudent science ... a configuration of knowledge that being practical is still enlightened and being wise is still democratically distributed. (1989, p. 54)

This is a notion that can help the municipal schools in Porto Alegre to use traditional school knowledge with students, but not simply teach it as if it were neutral. Both Santos and Freire contribute to understanding the need to be critical of such knowledge and not act as if there were some "stock of knowledge out there, not problematic at all, about which there is a general accord" (Silva & McLaren, 1993, p. 43).

This position seems to foster a real dialogue between the knowledge of communities and traditional school knowledge; this is a dialogue that does not reduce one to the other but establishes a dialogue to overcome the limitations of both. The fact that this is one of the visions being discussed by teachers when they are constructing the thematic complex is a very positive aspect of the project.

The epistemological rupture that plays such a major role in the Citizen School is a sign that the project has been successful in the construction of a real progressive alternative in education. The challenge to what counts as knowledge, to what counts as core and periphery, represents the essence of the democratization of knowledge. Instead of creating isolated multicultural programs or centering content that has little efficacy in the context of a largely dominant structure, the Citizen School project has been creating an environment, with popular participation, in which the question of diversity of cultures has space to flourish. The Citizen School has created spaces where multicultural practices are organically integrated, not merely added superficially to a bureaucratically determined structure that is averse to "difference." To construct a powerful and democratic set of multicultural experiences, the whole institutional structure was changed.

In this sense, the Citizen School advances beyond the mainstream notion of multiculturalism. In fact, "multiculturalism is too easily depoliticized" (Pagenhart, 1994, p. 178). It is exactly this depoliticization that the Popular Administration wants to avoid. The project seems perfectly to fit what Giroux (1995) calls an "insurgent multiculturalism," one where "all participants play a formative role in crucial decisions about what is taught, who is hired, and how the school can become a laboratory for learning that nurtures critical citizenship and civic courage" (pp. 340–341).

In terms of the democratization of governance, the Constituent Assembly is a core element. The major policy directives formulated by the SMED derive from this assembly. This marks a significant departure from the traditional model, in which decisions are handed down from above while implementation is left to the schools. Through their elected delegates, schools and their communities are actively involved in the construction of the major educational policies in Porto Alegre. This is a unique aspect of the Citizen School project. Fung (1999), who studied the local school councils in Chicago and classified them as highly positive, nevertheless suggests that "centralized interventions, themselves formulated through deliberation, would then further enhance the deliberative, participatory, and empowered character of otherwise isolated local actions" (p. 26). This combination, suggested by Fung as ideal, is exactly what has been achieved in Porto Alegre.

As I have shown above, the Citizen School truly has been a project for the excluded. Not only students, however, have benefited from the quality education they receive. Parents, students, and school staff, usually mere spectators of the processes in the traditional school, are now part of the structure of governance inside the school council and bring their knowledge to the table. In fact, the whole process challenges the cultural model that says that poor and "uneducated" people should not participate because they do not know how to do so.

Some Contradictions and Potential Problems

Thus far my evaluation of the experiment in Porto Alegre has been very positive. The project, in fact, has been making real progress in its goals of democratizing the schools and the educational system as a whole. Nevertheless, any project that tries to accomplish the broad range of innovations that the Citizen School has tried will inevitably face challenges and will certainly have contradictions. As Hargreaves (1997) says, "restructuring is not an end to our problems but a beginning" (p. 352). This section of the chapter will deal with some of these challenges and contradictions.

In interviews with senior administrators at the SMED about possible difficulties in the implementation of the proposal, there was, at times, a characterization of teachers as "conservative," as the ones who resist changes to the mainstream model of structuring schools. This has serious implications. In treating all resistance from teachers as a conservative response, the SMED creates problems for the project. Those teachers who are in fact somewhat leaning toward a conservative position—one that literally wants to conserve the traditional structures of power inside schools—can be pushed even further toward this position by the lack of consideration for their issues. As Apple and Oliver (1996) show in their research, a state agency that is unresponsive and quick to see resistance as conservative might end up leaving only this subject position as an option for those who are resisting. Moreover, those who are not conservative and who have an active alternative view and practice might become disillusioned. By treating all resistance as conservatism, the SMED runs the risk of losing allies among the most active schools and of losing input from the teachers who are implementing the proposal in daily life.

The insistence on labeling teachers as conservative because they resist aspects of the project may also be linked to a simplistic Marxist view among some members of the SMED. Teachers—ironically especially after the salary increases promoted by the SMED—are considered middle class, while students and their parents belong to the working class. If it is true that the working class will conduct the "revolution" or the real transformations, then teachers are only responsible for igniting the "revolutionary consciousness." If teachers resist, the tendency for those operating within this simplistic notion is to characterize their actions as conservative because they are not acting in favor of the revolutionary project. Although this is an oversimplification of such reasoning, I identified traces of this cultural model in several members of the SMED. This ambivalence toward teachers ("They are necessary, but the real targets of our actions are the communities, where real revolution will happen") is problematic. There are no problems in concentrating efforts on the communities, but teachers run schools and bypassing them in an effort to build alliances only with communities seems like a bad strategy—one that can backfire. Teachers are the ones implementing the project, and if they are not treated with respect and as allies, a great deal may be lost in the Citizen School project.

Another contradiction of the implementation of the project is the role of common sense. I quoted above Santos's points about the need for a double epistemological rupture, one that deals with the transformation of both common sense and science in the construction of new emancipatory knowledge. This very sophisticated vision does not seem to prevail, however, among all the senior members and advisers of the SMED.

Analyzing documents and the texts of interviews, I was able to identify a discourse that stresses the need for replacing common sense with more politicized or critical thought. The words used by many SMED people in the interviews were "overcome," "question," and "challenge" when talking about common sense. These statements suggest a discourse that is not informed by Santos's insights. They presuppose the existence of a discourse that already overcame common sense (that of the teachers) with a discourse that still operates within the boundaries of common sense (among members of the community). But teachers, according to these members of the SMED, might also be operating from the standpoint of common sense. As one senior member of the SMED, talking about the construction of the thematic complex, said: "The problem is that many times rather than questioning and challenging the common sense of the community, teachers actually agree with it." The rationale here is something like this: How can teachers agree with the statements of the community? How can they participate in this distorted vision?

Such words, used by members of the SMED, emphasize the negative connotation of common sense and suggest that it needs to be replaced by a more enlightened and critical view. The use of these terms actually indicates that the speakers are operating within a discourse based on the Marxist tradition of defining ideology as *false consciousness*. This is *one* tradition within Marxism—one that does not represent the whole body of Marxist thought. The contributions of Gramsci, Hall, and Apple have stressed the need to see common sense as practical knowledge and to understand the good sense in it. Nevertheless, the statements of the members of the SMED seem to put them at odds with these contributions.

There is a flagrant contradiction between using the notion of false consciousness to characterize common sense and, at the same time, insisting that one must start from it and connect with it in order to construct knowledge in the school. If common sense is always filled with false consciousness, why bother starting with it? One could suppose that this would be a valuable exercise for the students to learn how they should *not* think. The problem with this line of reasoning is that it directly contradicts the entire Citizen School project emphasis on the need to use the culture of the students in the learning process. It would make no sense to use the culture of the students only to denounce it as problematic. This would have deleterious consequences rather than being beneficial.

Finally, a potential problem of the Citizen School project is the issue of sustainability. Is it possible to maintain this mechanism and to generate beneficial results (e.g., through participatory decision making) over time? In the current context where PT lost the municipal election and will no longer be in power in 2005, this issue is even more crucial. Will the culture of inclusion and the discussion on the nature of knowledge still be a part of municipal school life even without PT in the government? Which spaces will be closed and which will be opened by a new city administration? These are core questions that new research on the Citizen School project will have to explore.

The problem of sustainability in the case of the Citizen School refers not only to the ability to continue bringing people to participate in the mechanisms that were created, but also refers to the quality of participation. If the mechanisms continue to have members from all segments (parents, students, staff, and teachers) making decisions while a rigid hierarchy remains among these segments, then the mechanism will not function properly. Because the goal of the Citizen School project is not only to have parents and students participate in the decision-making process, but to do so actively and in a democratic way, the nature of the participation is a fundamental question in the evaluation of the goals of the project. Hence, discussing sustainability in the context of the Citizen School project also involves discussing how to preserve active and engaged participation among all the segments.

In the case of the school councils, there is a serious risk that teachers, who have the technical knowledge of the institution, will dominate the decisions. Some teachers may even feel that this is only natural, because they are the ones who understand educational issues, but this contradicts the goals of the school councils. These sites should be places where teachers, students, parents, and staff learn together how to better manage a school, not only financially but pedagogically. Apparently this is not yet happening to a full extent in the schools of Porto Alegre, and this should certainly be addressed by the administration.

There is certainly a need for attention to the challenges the schools face. As I stated above, the difficulties and contradictions can jeopardize the whole project if not taken seriously. There is, however, a sign that should be viewed with optimism. In all of the schools there are very active groups of teachers who are critical and who look for better ways to deal with the problems of the proposal and how to reinvent it in daily life.

The kind of environment that the Citizen School fosters—where critical thought and action are valued as assets, where teachers have spaces to talk and to look for better ways of constructing projects that continue the radical democratization proposed in the first congress of education and the collective of the schools—is something that is now deeply rooted in the schools. The active criticism of the SMED by the schools and the understanding that conflict should not be suppressed because it is the source of new ideas, are signs that the schools are headed in the right direction; in other words, they are producing the critical citizens about which the proposal talks. Because schools are spaces where the proposal is implemented, it will be there, in the interactions of teachers, students, parents, and directive teams, that these contradictions and problems will have to be faced.

Final Remarks

In the municipal schools of Porto Alegre, I encountered teachers with a renewed hope in the possibility of constructing a school radically different from the ones they attended. I witnessed teachers actively creating a curriculum for their school by interacting with communities and meeting regularly at times specially allocated and institutionally guaranteed for dialogue about their methodology and their goals with the specific network of concepts they are developing with their students. Rather than being pressured for a kind of accountability that only looks at test results, these teachers are socially, politically, and culturally responsible for providing quality education for their students. Quality in this context is not reduced to the accumulation of information, or even the ability to establish connections among concepts; it is also linked to the schools' capacity to generate a culturally embedded curriculum that engages students in creative thinking and, to a certain extent, in actions that could lead to social transformation in the future.

While the worldwide emphasis is on testing, economic accountability, and blaming the victims, Porto Alegre is showing that it is possible to create an alternative space, where articulations can be forged and where a new common sense education can be created. The Citizen School project has been serving as a viable alternative to neoliberal market-based solutions for the management and monitoring of the quality of public schools in Brazil. Involvement of the parents and of the students in important decisions (not merely peripheral decisions) and active monitoring in the school gives them a real sense of what *public* means in public school. At the same time, because the SMED has been able to involve teachers actively in the transformations (as well as help improve their qualifications and their salaries) instead of merely blaming them and their unions for the problems in education (common practice in neoliberal-driven reforms), the Popular Administration has been able to include every segment of the schools in the collective project of constructing a quality education in the impoverished neighborhoods where the municipal schools are situated. Thus, instead of opting for a doctrine that merely treats parents as consumers of education (and treated education as a commodity), the Citizen School became an alternative that challenges this idea. Parents, students, teachers, staff, and administrators are responsible for working collectively, each contributing their knowledge and expertise to create better education. In this way, the Citizen School has defined itself as a concrete and effective alternative to the market logic that offers only competition and exit as solutions.

The greatest distinction of the Citizen School is the real change in the source of solutions for problems in education, such as lack of responsiveness of the schools to students and parents or absence of real and meaningful learning. Rather than looking to the market as the model site for positive influence and change, or to expert knowledge as the only foundation for promoting education, the Citizen School project sees community involvement and valorization of local knowledge as the starting points for a transformative learning experience. The solution will not reside in an expert telling the dwellers of the *favelas* what to do, but in a real dialogue between so-called popular knowledge and scientific knowledge.

It is when the subaltern speak that the real problems begin to be addressed. When subaltern groups are able to combine the strengths of their cultures with key elements of scientific knowledge, forming a newly empowered knowledge, their voices are amplified and gain space in the arena of educational solutions. The Citizen School project is one of these cases and we should pay attention to what is being tried there. There are important lessons to be learned from the voices of the subaltern, lessons that there are real alternatives in a world where alternatives are increasingly difficult to implement.

Finally, I end with the words of a teacher in one of the schools:

> The kind of transformation we are doing is not one that can easily be measured by statistical data. We can show the increase in enrolled kids, the sharp reduction in dropouts from the schools, but we cannot easily

show data about the radical change in the way teachers, parents, and students perceive the role of education and the nature of knowledge. These are not easily quantified, especially in reports and in the media that expects numbers.

Perhaps the Citizen School project has to come up with a creative way of constructing new common sense around how we understand and assess successful schools. This would be an even greater contribution in these days of testing and outcome-based evaluation.

Endnotes

1. For more on this, see Keck (1986).
2. More information about this can be found in Gee, Hull, and Lankshear (1996), and Molnar (1996).
3. For more on this discussion of tactics and strategies, see Certeau (1984).
4. These steps have changed slightly through time and among schools, but this description summarizes the core of the SMED's proposal for the schools.
5. The research that generated this chapter was mainly conducted in 2000. During two months, I interviewed teachers, parents, students, and administrators involved with the Citizen School project. I also analyzed official documents which expressed the rationale behind the policies being implemented by the SMED. These are the sources of the quotes from actors of the project.

References

Apple, M. W. (1993). *Official knowledge.* New York: Routledge.

Apple, M. W. (1996). *Cultural politics and education.* New York: Teachers College Press.

Apple, M. W. & Oliver, A. (1996). Becoming right: Education and the formation of conservative movements. *Teachers College Record, 97* (3), 419–445.

Azevedo, J. C. (1999). Escola, democracia e cidadania. In C. Simon, D. D. Busetti, E. Viero, & L. W. Ferreira (Eds.), *Escola Cidadã: Trajetórias* (pp. 11–33). Porto Alegre, Brazil: Prefeitura Municipal de Porto Alegre—Secretaria Municipal de Educação.

Ball, S. J. (1998). Cidadania global, consumo e política educacional. In L. H. Silva (Ed.), *A Escola Cidadã no contexto da globalização* (pp. 121–137). Petrópolis, Brazil: Vozes.

Certeau, M. (1984). *The practice of everyday life.* Berkeley: University of California Press.

Fung, A. (1999). *Deliberative democracy, Chicago style.* Unpublished manuscript. John F. Kennedy School of Government, Harvard University.

Gee, J. P., Hull, G., & Lankshear, C. (1996). *The new work order: Behind the language of the new capitalism.* Boulder, CO: Westview Press.

Genro, T. (1999). Cidadania, emancipação e cidade. In L. H. Silva (Ed.), *Escola Cidadã: Teoria e prática* (pp. 7–11). Petrópolis, Brazil: Vozes.

Giroux, H. (1995). Insurgent multiculturalism and the promise of pedagogy. In D. T. Goldberg, (Ed.), *Multiculturalism: A critical reader* (pp. 325–343). Cambridge, MA: Blackwell.

Gorodicht, C., & Souza, M. C. (1999). Complexo temático. In L. H. Silva (Ed.), *Escola cidadã: Teoria e prática* (pp. 76–84). Petrópolis, Brazil: Vozes.

Hargreaves, A. (1997). Restructuring restructuring: Postmodernity and the prospects for educational change. In A. H. Halsey, H. Lauder, P. Brown, & A. S. Wells (Eds.), *Education: Culture, economy, society* (pp. 338–353). Oxford, UK: Oxford University Press.

National Institute for Studies and Research in Education (INEP). (2000). *Education for all: Evaluation of the year 2000.* Brasilia, Brazil: INEP.

Keck, M. E. (1986). *From movement to politics: The formation of the Workers' Party in Brazil.* Doctoral dissertation, Columbia University, New York.

Molnar, A. (1996). *Giving kids the business: The commercialization of America's schools.* Boulder, CO: Westview Press.

Paes da Silva, I., & Vasconcelos, M. (1997). Questões raciais e educação: Um estudo bibliográfico preliminar. In S. Kramer (Ed.), *Educação infantil em curso* (pp. 38–66). Rio de Janeiro, Brazil: Escola de Professores.

Pagenhart, P. (1994). Queerly defined multiculturalism. In L. Garber (Ed.), *Tilting the tower* (pp. 177–185). New York: Routledge.

Pinheiro, P. S. (1989). Prefácio. In R. Meneguello (Ed.), *PT—A formação de um partido, 1979–1982* (pp. 9–13). Rio de Janeiro, Brazil: Paz e Terra.

Santos, B. S. (1989). *Introdução a uma ciência pós-moderna.* Porto, Portugal: Afrontamento.

Silva, T. T. (1994). A nova direita e as transformações na pedagogia da política e na política da pedagogia. In T. T. Silva & P. Gentili (Eds.), *Neoliberalismo, qualidade total e educação: Visões críticas* (pp. 9–29). Petrópolis, Brazil: Vozes.

Silva, T. T. (1996). O projeto educacional da nova Direita e a retórica da qualidade total. In T. T. Silva & P. Gentili (Eds.), *Escola S.A.—quem ganha e quem perde no mercado educacional do neoliberalismo* (pp. 167–188). Brasília, Brazil: CNTE.

Silva, T. T. & McLaren, P. (1993). Knowledge under siege: The Brazilian debate. In P. McLaren & P. Leonard (Eds.), *Paulo Freire: A critical encounter* (pp. 36–46). New York: Routledge.

SMED (Municipal Secretariat of Education). (1993). *Projeto Gestão Democrática—Lei Complementar no. 292.* Unpublished text.

SMED (Municipal Secretariat of Education). (1999a). Ciclos de formação—Proposta político-pedagógica da Escola Cidadã. *Cadernos Pedagogicos, 9* (1), 1–111.

SMED (Municipal Secretariat of Education). (1999b). *Official homepage of the SMED.* Retrieved December 15, 1999, from http://www.portoalegre.rs.gov.br/smed

SMED (Municipal Secretariat of Education). (2003). Boletim informativo—informações educacionais. Year 6, No. 11.

Souza, D. H., Mogetti, E. A., Villani, M., Panichi, M. T. C., Rossetto, R. P., & Huerga, S. M. R. (1999). Turma de progressão e seu significado na escola. In S. Rocha, & B. D. Nery (Eds.), *Turma de progressão: A inversão da lógica da exclusão* (pp. 22–29). Porto Alegre, Brazil: SMED.

10
Toward a Subaltern Cosmopolitan Multiculturalism

KRISTEN L. BURAS AND PAULINO MOTTER

The Boy without a Flag

"The American nation is a dangerous neighbor," wrote an editorialist in 1894 in *La Democracia*, a Puerto Rican newspaper (Sunshine & Menkart, 1999, p. 121). By 1898, the United States had acquired control of Puerto Rico through the Spanish-American-Cuban War. Nelson Miles, commander of the U.S. Army, had a different view of the American nation. "This is not a war of devastation," he asserted in a proclamation, "rather one that seeks to give to all those under control of army and naval forces the advantages and blessings of an enlightened civilization" (p. 122). While teaching 11th grade U.S. history in a public school, one of us (Kristen) used these documents to introduce students to debates on imperialism, constructions of nationalism, and the political, economic, and cultural history of globalization—then and now.

Students also considered a speech delivered in 1936 by Pedro Albizu Campos who headed the Puerto Rican Nationalist Party. Reflecting on Puerto Rico's colonial history, he said:

> We stand as a nation surrounded by industry, but with little of it belonging to our people.... The result is exploitation and abuses ... resulting in poverty for our people and wealth for the United States.... The intellectual, spiritual, and moral advancement of our race will be jeopardized as we are made to be more "North American." ... What will we have when we have nothing but dependency on those who destroyed us? (in Santiago, 1995, p. 28)

The Puerto Ricans: Our American Story, a film (WLIW, 1999) that highlights the "tangled roots" of Puerto Ricans in the United States, was also viewed and discussed by students. The class was even presented with details on the 1998 general strike during which over 500,000 Puerto Ricans mobilized to stop the sale of the government-owned Puerto Rico Telephone Company to a consortium based in the United States. Pedro Rossello, Puerto Rico's governor at the time, supported privatization as a means to statehood, inspiring some 80,000 Puerto Ricans the previous year to protest, "We Are a Nation" (Gonzalez, 1998).

But the pinnacle of our work focused on a story written by Abraham Rodriguez (in Santiago, 1995) called "The Boy without a Flag." This narrative is about an accomplished but poor Puerto Rican boy born in the United States, who twice refuses to salute the American flag at school. Schooled by his father on imperialism, the adolescent refuses to pledge "Because I'm Puerto Rican. I ain't no American" (p. 36). After his second refusal he is confronted by a teacher who questions, "This country takes care of Puerto Rico, don't you see that?" Quoting Albizu Campos, the boy responds, "Puerto Rico is a colony," then asks, "Why I gotta respect that?" (p. 42)

Based on these studies, students were asked to write an essay that provided an account of the history of Puerto Rico in relation to the United States, analyzed the story in light of this history, and explained their viewpoint on the actions of the boy. The following excerpts illustrate some perspectives shared by students—honors students predominantly of European American, middle-class background—during a final class dialogue based on their essays:

> The United States is an imperialistic nation. We fought with Mexico to gain land and power. We moved westward, overtaking the Native Americans. We took Puerto Rico from Spain. The boy realized that America is a country with a lot of power and no ethics.

> I can see how Puerto Ricans could feel apprehension about the development of their culture, considering the infliction of American culture. However, I believe the boy in the story was completely wrong. He may not like the United States, but until he exits the States, he should show respect to our flag and the opportunity of occupancy it has provided him.

These statements raise complicated questions. To what degree did imperialist and antiimperialist forms of nationalism shape students' understanding of history and the boy's actions? In what ways did students understand notions of identity and allegiance, and formulate these based on multiple sites of historical and contemporary evidence? Did this lesson challenge students to think about the national and transnational formations of unequal power that have shaped oppressive conditions or to consider possibilities for transformation? This lesson—with all its absences, simplifications, complexities, and contradictions—represents one teacher's attempt, under actually existing educational conditions in a specific classroom context, to move toward a curriculum that might be conducive to *subaltern cosmopolitan multiculturalism*.

The Argument for Subaltern Cosmopolitan Multiculturalism

In the spirit of the above pedagogy, we want to argue that in order to become a genuinely transformative and emancipatory project, multiculturalism must cross national borders and assume a global dimension. This requires us to reject the rather arbitrary distinction that has been drawn between *multicultural education* and *global education*, linking the former to diversity within the United States and the latter to the peoples and cultures of other lands (Diaz, Massialas, & Xanthopoulos, 1999; Tye & Tye, 1992; Ukpokodu, 1999).

Multiculturalists have been preoccupied with differences within the nation-state. We do not want to say that this order of priorities is all wrong. Rather, we contend that such a focus is insufficient. Most multicultural theories and practices, whether premised on conservative or liberal understandings of cultural diversity, are based on a vision that is historically and territorially bound by the state, and that frequently ignores cross-border inequalities. If multiculturalism is to be something more than the recognition of difference and harmonization of competing interests within the nation-state, it must go global.

Under conditions of accelerated and uneven globalization (Brecher, Costello, & Smith, 2000; Pieterse, 2004) such a compartmentalized education is problematic for many reasons. Our chief argument in this chapter is that multiculturalism cannot deliver what it promises unless it partly embraces a global perspective from below, which we will call *subaltern cosmopolitanism* following Santos (2001, 2002a). Emancipatory struggles today, whether aimed at recognition, redistribution, or both, are not solely contained within nation-states. Instead, they are increasingly transnational. As Santos (2002a) notes, hegemonic neoliberal globalization:

> while propagating throughout the globe the same system of domination and exclusion—has created the conditions for the counter-hegemonic forces, organizations and movements located in the most disparate regions of the globe to visualize common interests across and beyond the many differences that separate them and to converge in counter-hegemonic struggles embodying separate but related emancipatory social projects. (p. 446)

We think Cheah (1998b) asks a question that captures the spirit of this cosmopolitanism: "In an uneven neocolonial world, how can struggles for multicultural recognition in constitutional-democratic states in the North be brought into a global alliance with postcolonial activism in the periphery?" (p. 37)

In the end, we believe that a range of affiliations is possible. The choice is not between localized multiculturalism or globalism; rather the challenge is to nurture the kind of relationship between the two that most advances the democratic interests (sometimes in conflict) of subaltern communities.

In education there is an emerging recognition that the multicultural and the global must be brought together (Abowitz, 2002; Merryfield, 1996). Mass schooling is a strategic site where the relationship between multiculturalism, cosmopolitanism, citizenship, and democracy should be acknowledged and continuously reworked (Burbules & Torres, 2000; Torres, 1998). The sort of subaltern cosmopolitan multiculturalism we will advocate may not be immediately achievable and certainly does not require that the nation-state be dismantled. It is an educational project aimed at building new affiliations and challenging hegemonic globalization in all its forms—political, economic, and cultural. It is our hope that schools can contribute not only to the promotion of justice in immediate spheres, but facilitate the emergence of a global imaginary.

This educational proposal implies a range of complex questions. For example, what is the emancipatory potential of subaltern cosmopolitan multiculturalism in societies where even basic human needs and rights are neglected? Is it possible to nurture a cosmopolitan disposition within the bounds of a *national* schooling system? Why should one become a "citizen of the world" when there are so many problems in the immediate community? Considering the distributions of power both within and across national borders, is a *subaltern* cosmopolitan multiculturalism possible? Perhaps the way to begin getting at these and related questions is to engage in a more nuanced discussion regarding *which* of many multiculturalisms, nationalisms, cosmopolitanisms, and subalternities are implicated in the vision of education we are charting.

The Politics of Multiculturalism

Emerging from mid-century social movements in the United States that sought to transform the non/misrecognition of particular differences (e.g., race, gender), multiculturalism has become a slogan under which a great variety of interests and concerns, some oppositional, have been pushed forward. Torres (1998) emphasizes, "Given the ebbs and flows of social struggles in the United States, multiculturalism has not been a homogeneous social movement. Nor is it represented by a single theoretical paradigm, educational approach, or pedagogy.... Multiculturalism means different things to different people" (p. 180; see also Banks, 1995).

Grant and Sleeter (2003) have mapped various approaches to multicultural education since its inception. For instance, those embracing a "human relations" approach call for multicultural education to serve *interpersonal* ends, such as the promotion of mutual respect between individuals belonging to various race, gender, class, and religious groups. In contrast, advocates of "multicultural and social reconstructionist" education center the analysis of *systems* of unequal power and oppression, and encourage social action aimed at altering conditions that sustain inequality. Clearly, these approaches to multiculturalism are premised on different understandings of how diversity relates both to education and the collective life of the nation.

From across the political spectrum, in fact, there have been various articulations of multiculturalism as well as responses to competing paradigms. A good starting point is to acknowledge that "liberalism has been at the heart of the multiculturalism movement, and sometimes is portrayed as the mainstay ideology of multicultural education" (Torres, 1998, p. 185). Problematically, liberal multiculturalists—affiliated with a classic tradition that stresses individual autonomy—celebrate plurality without exploring the ways that difference is implicated in unequal relations of power or recognizing the need to distinguish between kinds of difference and their compatibility with democratic ends.

Conservatives, on the other hand, "argue that multiculturalism is a plot against the dominant cultural canon and a crusade for the fulfillment of key demands of ethnic groups" (Torres, 1998, p. 190). For instance, E. D. Hirsch—an influential figure within the neoconservative bloc—has deemed a shared common culture to be the foundation of cohesive nationhood (see Buras, 1999). And although Hirsch denies the cultural politics behind this vision, the Eurocentric mark is unmistakably present. Schlesinger (1992) blatantly asserts:

> It may be too bad that dead white European males have played so large a role in shaping our culture. But that's the way it is. One cannot erase history. These humdrum historical facts, and not some dastardly imperialist conspiracy, explain the Eurocentric slant in American schools. Would anyone seriously argue that teachers should conceal the European origins of American civilization? (p. 122)

Despite hostility toward the multicultural project, the desire to maintain hegemony has compelled cultural conservatives—confronted with ongoing struggles by oppressed groups for recognition—to respond to and even appropriate multiculturalism in strategic ways (Buras, 2005).

Hirsch (1992) warns, "Multiculturalism comes in different guises.... There's a progressive form that will be helpful to all students, and a retrogressive kind that ... tends to set group against group" (p. 1). The first form, which Hirsch calls "cosmopolitanism," is based on a universalistic view that rejects ethnicity as a major definer of identity. He labels the second form "ethnocentrism" and explains that this particularistic version stresses loyalty to one's local or ethnic culture. To highlight the differences between these two conceptions of multiculturalism, Hirsch asserts that "cosmopolitanism means being a citizen of the world, a member of humanity as a whole," whereas ethnic loyalism promotes parochialism and separatism by claiming that "accommodating oneself to a larger cosmopolitan culture means giving way to cultural imperialism, and a consequent loss of identity" (p. 3). In the end,

Hirsch's multiculturalism means living in a culturally monolithic cosmopolis where difference is policed for the good of "humanity."

Multiculturalism has also been taken up, criticized, and reenvisioned by the left. From a postcolonial perspective that centers cultural ambiguity, translation, and hybridity, Dimitriadis and McCarthy (2001) point to the "logics of containment," which preside over much of the multiculturalism inscribed in school curriculum. When guided by these logics, multiculturalism is aimed at normalizing, framing, and managing difference:

> It has become a set of propositions about identity, knowledge, power, and change in education, a kind of normal science, which attempts to "discipline" difference rather than be transformed by it. Multiculturalism has become a discourse of power that attempts to manage the extraordinary tensions and contradictions of modern life that have overtaken educational institutions. Multiculturalism has succeeded in preserving to the point of petrification its central object: "culture." (p. 113)

In opposition to insular and essentializing views that sometimes shape mainstream perspectives on culture, including Huntington's (1997) "clash of civilizations" thesis, Said (2000) points out that all cultures have had long and intimate contacts with each other. We live, he emphasizes, in a world of "mixtures, of migrations, of crossing over … [where] there are no insulated cultures or civilizations" (p. 587). These critiques underscore how multiculturalism often treats cultures as stable and pure. At the same time, however, we must acknowledge that mixing does not imply an even exchange. As Pieterse (2004) stresses, "Relations of power … are inscribed and reproduced *within* hybridity for wherever we look closely enough we find the traces of asymmetry in culture, place, descent. Hence, hybridity raises the question of the *terms* of mixture, the conditions of mixing" (p. 74). Considering our proposal for subaltern cosmopolitan multiculturalism and the national–transnational exchanges that we envision, it will be crucial to think through how global inequities might potentially inflect these associations.

Another related aspect of mainstream multiculturalism that has been criticized by the left includes the additive approach. Dimitriadis and McCarthy (2001) explain that "this hegemonic approach … attempts to hold the Eurocentric and establishment core of the curriculum in place, inoculating it by simply adding on selected, nonconflictual items from the culture and experiences of minority and subaltern groups" (pp. 117–118). Apple (2000) has referred to this tendency as the politics of cultural incorporation, meaning that subaltern groups are mentioned without substantively challenging the narratives of powerful groups. Here again, we contend that the circulation of knowledge between subalterns in unequally related nations means that knowledge in core nations will not simply be supplemented, but will need, more than likely, to be dramatically reconstructed as a result of globally marginalized epistemologies.

Perhaps the most strident challenge to liberal and conservative traditions of multiculturalism, however, has been articulated by critical theorists. Centering critiques of power, the experiences of subaltern groups, and emancipatory struggle, this tradition has assumed a variety of labels, including "pedagogy of the oppressed" (Freire, 1993), "insurgent multiculturalism" (Giroux, 1995a), and "revolutionary multiculturalism" (McLaren & Farahmandpur, 2001). Criticizing liberals who have "used multiculturalism to denote a pluralism devoid of historical contextualization and the specificities of relations of power" and conservatives for whom "multiculturalism has come to signify a disruptive, unsettling, and dangerous force," Giroux (1995a) insists: "Multiculturalism is too important as a political discourse to be exclusively appropriated by liberals and conservatives" (p. 336). He argues that:

> A critical multiculturalism means more than simply acknowledging differences and analyzing stereotypes; more fundamentally, it means understanding, engaging, and transforming the diverse histories, cultural narratives, representation, and institutions that produce racism and other forms of discrimination. (p. 328)

Giroux goes on to suggest that this kind of multiculturalism expands opportunities for reflection, exchange, and identity work among an array of dominant and subaltern groups. Most importantly, insurgent multiculturalism is constituted by critical praxis, or efforts to link reflection "to struggles over real material conditions that structure everyday life" (p. 340).

In advocating a subaltern cosmopolitan *multiculturalism*, we mean to invest in the possibilities of critical, insurgent, and emancipatory multicultural traditions—with due respect for the dangers of essentializing and the risks associated with privileging particular axes of oppression to the exclusion of others (e.g., see Farahmandpur, 2004). At the same time, we earlier argued that *at best* the multicultural project (in even its more critical guises) can contribute to reshaping *national* identity to accommodate the claims for recognition of different groups by the state, and to challenging forms of unequal power that exist within territorial borders. Multicultural theories in circulation are not designed to deal with issues related to cosmopolitanism. There is a latent contradiction, however, arising from the territorialized politics of multiculturalism in an age of increasingly deterritorialized culture and economy (Bauman, 2001; Tomlinson, 1999). A cosmopolitan multiculturalism ought to challenge inequalities deepened by the ravages of globalization. Giroux (1995a) seems to have this relationship in mind when he states that "insurgent multiculturalism should serve to redefine existing debates about national identity while simultaneously expanding its theoretical concerns to more global and international matters" (p. 341).

We think that such a relational and multidimensional effort can be enriched by entering into conversation with the resurgent debate on cosmopolitanism, especially from a subaltern perspective (Mignolo 2000a, 2000b; Santos 2002a), and by critically analyzing the development of various schools of thought in global education. But before examining the cosmopolitical dimensions of this project, we need to first say a bit more about multiculturalism and its relationship to the state, nationalism, and national identity.

Nationalisms, National Identity, and Multiculturalism

We need to speak not of nationalism in the singular, but of nationalisms. European nationalism has been informed by ideas of superiority, civilization, and progress. Considering its long, bloody history, many contemporary thinkers on the left have come to see it as the *only* ideological form that nationalism can take. For Said (2000), this Eurocentric outlook should be eschewed as it facilitates disdain for anti-imperialist nationalism, which spread throughout the third world after World War II. Some critics, he points out, have tended to see in this latter form of nationalism the repetition of Western nationalism: statism, chauvinism, and reactionary populism. Said warns against a wholesale condemnation of third world nationalism, highlighting its importance during anticolonial struggles for legitimate self-determination and independent statehood. A similar position is supported by Immanuel Wallerstein (in Nussbaum et al., 1996), who draws a sharp distinction between the "nationalism of the oppressed" and the "nationalism of the oppressor."

This does not mean that decolonizing nationalism rooted in struggles for liberation is immune from degeneration into ethnocentric discrimination, oppressive political identity, or murderous forms of chauvinism. Said (2000) draws a clear distinction between authentic nationalist resistance against colonialism as opposed to "nativism that would turn nationalism into a reductive and diminishing rather than a truly liberating effort" (p. 426). One should bear in mind that postcolonial states in Latin America, though drawing their constitutions upon liberal principles, kept intact political practices that had served the colonial order, condoning slavery and intensifying the genocide of Indigenous peoples (Santos, 2002b).

In light of all this, can nationalism still provide energy for liberatory struggle? Many critical and postcolonial theorists have argued that nationalism and national identification remain powerful sources for resistance against *neocolonial globalization*. Reflecting on the work of Samir Amin—one of the stronger voices to claim that nationalism remains valid in the third world—Cheah (1998b) explains that he "suggests that popular nationalism in the periphery is a necessary step toward socialist cosmopolitanism because we live in an uneven capitalist world-system that largely confines the most deprived masses of humanity to national-peripheral space" (pp. 33–34). It is essential to recognize that the rejection of nationalism in an era of uneven globalization may only weaken the ability of states in the periphery to counter neoliberalism. In a related vein, Bello (2002) calls for an alternative system of global governance that he suggestively names "deglobalization" or "the re-empowerment of the local and national" (pp. 23–24). His proposal, along with others (Brecher, Costello, & Smith, 2000; Stiglitz, 2002), emphasizes the need for democratizing decision-making processes presently controlled by publicly unaccountable, nontransparent, northern-dominated institutions such as the International Monetary Fund, World Bank, and World Trade Organization, through genuine participation and representation of peripheral states and civil society groups from below.

As the foregoing discussion reveals, nationalism can serve many agendas. Viewing the nation as central to symbolic politics, Verdery (1996) argues that one "should treat nation as a symbol and any given nationalism as having multiple meanings offered as alternatives and competed over by different groups maneuvering to capture the symbol's definition and its legitimating effects" (p. 228). In our view, it thus seems significant to ask: If the meanings of nationhood and nationalism are contested and malleable, then what are the possibilities for constructing new and potentially liberatory forms? We must recognize that nationalism remains a force in the molding of collective identities—one that must be addressed by progressives if it is not to be used and abused by demagogues (see Giroux, 1995b).

There exists a world of difference between dominant conceptions of national identity premised on a monolithic common culture (or even liberal tolerance) and insurgent multicultural visions based on the recognition of diversity through ongoing negotiations over collective identity and the transformation of structures of power. In examining the relationship of diversity to the nation-state, many commentators have drawn a clear distinction between state and nation, linking the former to the sphere of politics and the latter to the sphere of culture (e.g., see O'Byrne, 2001). As a matter of fact, a single state can actually encompass many nations or culturally affiliated minorities—what Kymlicka (1995) calls a "multination state" (p. 11). Yet it is clear that states have only uneasily accommodated diversity and competing identifications. Canada is often cited as an example of a multination state that has sought to recognize group claims and rights—those of Francophones, First Nations, and immigrants—without endangering a universal national identity. But political compromises premised on alleged state neutrality, tolerance, and even affirmation have not erased problems of identity and cultural difference, guaranteeing at best a fragile equilibrium (Ghai, 2000). The state has not yet learned to deal with its nations in a genuinely democratic way. At a fundamental level, we have yet to grasp that the democratic state is not solely a political concept, but an economic and cultural one as well.

Regarding issues of cultural recognition, Fraser (1997) asserts that cultural domination undermines the democratic project and suggests that the remedy lies, at the very least, in "upwardly revaluing disrespected identities and the cultural products of maligned groups" and "recognizing and positively valorizing cultural diversity" (p. 15). Yet this conceptualization of cultural democracy is antithetical to present notions of what it means to belong to a nation-state.

Much democratic theorizing is, in fact, plagued by the contention that the state must rest on a uniform cultural tradition. Dahl (1998) discusses what he calls "conditions favorable to democracy." He claims that democracy "is more likely to develop and endure in a country that is culturally fairly homogeneous and less likely in a country with sharply differentiated and conflicting subcultures" (pp. 149–150). In this view, multiculturalism is understood as a threat to the democratic experiment rather than being consti-tutive of it. Dahl goes on to explain assimilation as a possible solution to the multicultural "problem." Speaking of turn-of-the-twentieth-century immi-grants and their descendants, for example, he states in positive terms that assimilation "was mainly voluntary or enforced by social mechanisms (such as shame) that minimized the need for coercion by the state" (p. 152). What is striking is Dahl's belief that any democratic state could find justification—if necessary—for such coercion. When cultural differences cannot be reconciled, he concludes, the formation of independent political units in which cultural groups "possess enough autonomy to maintain their identity" is a solution (p. 155). Understood in this way, multiculturalism is the problem rather than undemocratic structures that fail to recognize diverse cultural forms.

Instead, it is imperative to recognize that diversity does not inherently undermine democracy or community—whether local, national, or global in scale. Fraser (1997) reminds us that there has always been a "host of compet-ing counterpublics," whether "elite women's publics, black publics, or work-ing-class publics" (p. 75). Moreover, she insists that "this need not preclude the possibility of an additional, more comprehensive arena in which members of different, more limited publics talk across lines of cultural diversity" (p. 84). For those who would argue that multiple publics undermine a broader sense of national community, it is important to remember that "people participate in more than one public, and that the membership of different publics may overlap" (p. 84). In this way, community is understood as something that consists of multiple belongings at multiple scales, with bonds at a plethora of levels creating all sorts of unities. Such a vision also allows for the kinds of spaces that have enabled "subaltern counterpublics" to develop oppositional discourses and strategies necessary for challenging dominance, with due recognition that not all subalternities are "virtuous" (pp. 81–82).

This reconceptualization of democracy may contribute to reshaping the kinds of nations and national identities that we imagine. To the extent, however, that insurgent multiculturalism attempts to imagine a democratic multicultural state, it still allies itself with the ideal of nationhood. From a political standpoint, one can reasonably argue that multiculturalists of most stripes share the same commitment to maintain and strengthen the nation-state, though each faction calls for a different understanding of what it means to be an "American." Even if the nation-state were to embrace a radically inclusive identity and polity that enables an ongoing deliberation over issues of recognition and redistribution, such an identity still remains territorially bound. Moving forward with our argument, we want to defend nationalisms of the oppressed as well as national identities and state formations that are radically democratic and critically multicultural. To extend the emancipatory horizons of multiculturalism, however, it is necessary to imagine the possibilities for connecting liberatory national efforts and identities with the cosmopolitical.

Which Cosmopolitanism?

In recent years, there has been a renewed interest in cosmopolitanism—a philosophical orientation generally attributed to the Stoics, then later revived by Immanuel Kant, which stresses a regime of universal affiliations and rights emanating from shared humanity. Writing in the 1790s at a time when the war between the French republic and the monarchical states of Europe was concluded and a treaty was established, Kant authored an essay on peace between nations. In *Perpetual Peace*, he sketched a conception of international order based on the rights of humanity. More specifically, he "set forth principles of international right that are binding on all human beings collectively, and only for this reason pertinent especially to those who hold power over states" (Wood, 1998, p. 61). Advocating a federation of states governed by a commitment to respect a "cosmopolitan right" or "universal right of humanity," Kant neither rejected the state nor advocated a world-state; instead, he sought to constrain the military actions of states by appealing to a universal ideal that might noncoercively govern their relations with individuals and one another (Cheah, 1998b; Wood, 1998).

In a well-known essay titled "Patriotism and Cosmopolitanism," the liberal philosopher Martha Nussbaum (Nussbaum et al., 1996) launched a frontal attack against the politics of nationalism, an attack that she associated with Stoic and Kantian philosophy. In the contemporary world, she argued, justice and equality "would be better served by ... the very old ideal of the cosmopolitan, the person whose allegiance is to the worldwide community of human beings" (p. 4). She does acknowledge that "to be a citizen of the world one does not need to give up local identifications," some of which may be "based on ethnic, linguistic, historical, professional, gender, or sexual identities." Rather, she maintains, "we should also work to make all human beings part of our community of dialogue and concern" (p. 9). At its root, however, Nussbaum's position is grounded in a valorization of "human" solidarity, with deeply structured, unequal relations such as race and gender understood as something that one "does not need to give up," as if that were even possible.

Though her call to look beyond the narrow field of vision facilitated by national allegiance is a welcomed corrective, in the end, her appeal too closely resonates with the disembodied universalism earlier embraced by European philosophers and even the world market ideology celebrated by the new managerial class (see Harvey, 2000).

Since much emphasis, however, has been put on Kant as the father of the cosmopolitical spirit, it is worth noting a lesser-known history pertaining to his geographic imagination. In *Perpetual Peace*, Kant declared, "The peoples of the earth have entered in varying degrees into a universal community, and it is developed to the point where a violation of laws in *one* part of the world is felt *everywhere*" (Kant in Harvey, 2000, p. 532). In stark contrast to this universalist proclamation, Harvey (2000) has shown that Kant's *Geography*—a work that has been largely ignored—marginalizes a good part of humankind. He explains, "While most of the text is given over to often bizarre facts of physical geography ... [Kant's] remarks on 'man' within the system of nature are deeply troubling." For example, Kant writes: "Humanity achieves its greatest perfection with the white races. The yellow Indians have somewhat less talent. The negroes are much inferior and some of the peoples of the Americas are well below them." Harvey relays other assertions made by Kant, including "Burmese women wear indecent clothing and take pride in getting pregnant by Europeans, the Hottentots are dirty and you can smell them from far away, [and] the Javanese are thieving, conniving, and servile" (p. 533). Placing Kant's universal ethics against his "geographic" sensibility illuminates the complexities and contradictions of endorsing a cosmopolitan ideology in a world where classed, raced, and gendered fault lines run deep. More to the point, Harvey suggests:

> It boils down to this: either the smelly Hottentots and the lazy Samoyards have to reform themselves to qualify for consideration under the universal ethical code (thereby flattening out all ... differences) or the universal principles operate as an intensely discriminatory code masquerading as the universal good. (p. 535)

The point that oppressive discourses and practices might potentially lie just beneath the cosmopolitan surface must be taken, we believe, very seriously.

Perhaps one way of responding to the problematic presented by this history and the question of whether or not cosmopolitanism can today constitute a more progressive vision is to first acknowledge that the tracing of the origin and history of cosmopolitanism has been rather *un*cosmopolitan. Pollock, Bhabha, Breckenridge, and Chakrabarty (2000) remind us of "how radically we can rewrite the history of cosmopolitanism and how dramatically we can redraw its map once we are prepared to think outside of the box of European intellectual history." They suggest that an essential step toward such a history is to "look at the world across time and space and see how people have thought and acted beyond the local" (p. 586). In other words, there are many cosmopolitanisms, past and present, that might contribute to a reworking from below of present-day hegemonic global relations. "Actually existing cosmopolitanisms," in fact, have been rooted in a spectrum of ideologies from both above and below (Malcomson, 1998). If the historical and contemporary reality of cosmopolitanism is a bricolage of sentiments and practices, then it is essential to clarify the issue of *which* kinds of cosmopolitanism we believe should inform progressive educational work.

On one hand, Vergés (2001) reminds us that universalist discourses, even if rooted in colonialist ideology, can be recast by the colonized in the interest of emancipation. She documents how nineteenth-century Creole intellectuals in the Caribbean French colonies—Martinique, Guadeloupe, and Réunion— reinterpreted the European notion of cosmopolitanism so that "their universal humanism was informed by their opposition to racism and colonial exploita- tion" (p. 169). Referring to this project as *Creole cosmopolitanism*, Vergés explains that:

> A small educated elite of colour emerged, which adopted the vocabulary of French republicanism, creolized it and developed its own claims for rights and justice.... Creoles took seriously the principles of democracy and therefore challenged their violation in the empire.... Travelling across the French empire transformed the Creoles and led them to develop a cosmopolitanism grounded in the understanding of a shared humanity, against racial ideology. (pp. 171–172)

The radical reappropriation of republican principles by Creoles to challenge French colonial power has led Vergés to assert that "the analysis of mimicking, imitating, and borrowing as sources of [political] creativity deserves to be pursued further in Creole societies" (p. 170). She concludes by posing the question: "Can there be a revivification of Creole cosmopolitanism in the context of globalization?" (p. 180). At this juncture, we believe that the ques- tion—and the history on which it is based—requires that subaltern efforts and identities built on universalist discourses and grounded in hegemonic idioms be carefully assessed for their emancipatory potential within particular contexts, rather than automatically written off as evidence of the "co-optation of the oppressed" (e.g., see Gandin & Apple, 2002). Having said this, we still believe that educational work grounded in decontextualized, universal appeals to "care for all of humankind" in an "increasingly interdependent world," as one example, runs many risks—some of which will become clear when we discuss the tradition of global education.

The historical account of Creole cosmopolitanism allows us to consider cosmopolitanism from a colonial perspective that embraces a universalist idiom. Mignolo (2000a, 2000b) also argues that cosmopolitanism is linked to coloniality and subalternity, but he argues for a kind of *critical cosmopolitanism* that issues forth from specific "local histories" that have sought to counter "global designs." He identifies what he believes have been the three dominant global designs of the modern colonial era, including sixteenth-century Christianity and its civilizing mission under the lead of Spanish and Portuguese colonialism; eighteenth- and nineteenth-century imperialism and its secular civilizing mission ushered in by French and English colonialism; and finally, late twentieth-century United States–led transnational colonialism with its mission of neoliberal globalization. In short, global designs are cosmopolitan projects coordinated from above for the purposes of regulation, homogenization, and domination. By contrast, critical cosmopolitan projects are those grounded in particular histories of coloniality and shaped by subaltern epistemologies that confront, from below, global designs.

Central to critical cosmopolitanism is what Mignolo calls "border thinking." Border thinking is "the recognition and transformation of the hegemonic imaginary from the perspective of people in subaltern positions" (2000b, p. 736). To illuminate what is meant by border thinking, Mignolo points out that when the Zapatistas use the word *democracy*, they invest it with a meaning very different from the hegemonic interpretation constructed by the Mexican government—a meaning rooted not in European political philosophy, which centers the individual, but Maya conceptions of community. Yet this is just one illustration, as Mignolo stresses that the contours and contexts of border thinking are diverse. Whereas Creole cosmopolitanism was oppositionally grounded in a universal discourse of shared humanity, critical cosmopolitanism is not a universalizing project. Instead, a network of "subaltern satellites" coexists as part of a multifront effort aimed at "appropriating and transforming Western global designs" (p. 745). We would like to argue that herein lies the transformative potential of critical cosmopolitanism in education. How might curriculum, we ask, support epistemological subalternity? How can schools constitute satellites—connected with others—in the struggle against nationally homogenizing projects and globalization from above?

Posing a related question, Santos (2002a) provocatively asks, "Who needs cosmopolitanism?" He concludes that it is the "socially excluded, victims of the hegemonic conception of cosmopolitanism" who need a sort of "oppositional variety" (p. 460). Rather than calling for universal humanism, Santos advocates a *subaltern cosmopolitanism*, or a cosmopolitanism of the oppressed, which he believes can counter social fascism. As the dominant configuration of relations in the present era, social fascism is "a regime characterized by social relations and life experiences under extremely unequal power relations and exchanges which lead to particularly severe and potentially irreversible forms of exclusion" (p. 456). What are the makings, then, of a subaltern cosmopolitanism capable of confronting this kind of fascism? "Aside from struggles that are originally transnational in nature," Santos includes a "vast set of confrontational ... social struggles that, though local or national in scope, are networked in different ways with parallel struggles elsewhere." Collectively, this network—much like Mignolo's subaltern satellites—constitutes what Santos refers to as "counter-hegemonic globalization from below" (pp. 458–459).

As struggles emerge and develop, whether locally, nationally, or transnationally, the central question is "whether the world is made less and less comfortable for global capitalism by subaltern insurgent practices or whether, on the contrary, global capitalism has managed to co-opt the latter and transform them into means of its own reproduction" (Santos, 2002a, p. 464). Perhaps this criterion, if extended to include not only the economic dimensions of globalization from above but also the political and cultural aspects, could function as a means for assessing the degree to which particular educational strategies actually align with the politics of subaltern cosmopolitanism.

Having discussed the complicated and even yet-to-be-written history of cosmopolitanism, we hope to have clarified what we mean by an education rooted in *subaltern cosmopolitan* multiculturalism. Rather than constructing educational communities around the endorsement of some abstract or universal philosophy of common humanity or benevolent globalism, we believe that schools should instead create a space for border thinking, or epistemological subalternity, and challenge social fascism at whatever level possible. In the same moment, we imagine that classrooms and schools might exist as part of a diverse and interconnected network that seeks to confront unequal relations of power not only nationally, but transnationally. Let us now turn to a discussion of global education and the degree to which it might assist in the project of expanding the horizons of multiculturalism to include a subaltern cosmopolitanism.

Global Education: Toward a *Subaltern* Cosmopolitanism?

We do recognize that the call for schools to look beyond national borders is an ambitious one, even more so with a view toward epistemological subalternity. Since their inception, state education systems have been charged with the responsibility of cultivating "common" values and creating national identity (Apple et al., 2003; Cornbleth & Waugh, 1999; Kaestle, 1983). As such, it must be acknowledged that schools are generally not hospitable sites for the cultivation of counterhegemonic cosmopolitan dispositions—even less so in the post–September 11th environment, which has fueled the most retrogressive kinds of national allegiance.

This becomes especially clear when one looks at neoconservative responses to global education. Writing for the culturally conservative Fordham Foundation, Burack (2003) responds to what he calls the "global education ideology" in the field of social studies education, an ideology that he regrets "is deeply suspicious of America's institutions, values, and role in the world, while uncritically celebrating the institutions and values of most other societies." He contends that global education is "the international equivalent of separatist versions of multiculturalism," meaning that its agenda is to critically recast the position of the United States and the West within the world system, just as multiculturalism attempts to problematize the historic position of European Americans within the United States (p. 41). Burack believes, in fact, that widening the lens to include the study of non-Western societies will lead to a form of "cultural relativism" whereby all cultures are deemed worthy of equal respect—an assertion closely tied to the anxiety that global education will undermine confidence in Western superiority. Proposing a more desirable paradigm of global education, he urges schools to "stress the continuing centrality of the West," then with deep but unrecognized contradiction clarifies: "The goal is not to celebrate the West's glories uncritically. It is to recognize ... that the West is the source of the most important civic ideas and ideals that we want students to understand" (p. 65). Clearly, any kind of education that challenges students to analyze relations of power within either a national or global context is viewed as antithetical to the interests of Western nation-states.

"Transnational progressivism," centered on the notion of global citizenship, Burack (2003) argues, undermines the sovereignty of democratic nation-states and elevates the role that unaccountable international actors should play in governing the world. "Global education advocates want Americans to doubt the ability of their national civil society and its government to deal with global challenges," he writes (p. 58). In the end, transnational solidarity and international civil societies are seen as antidemocratic and unwarranted curtailments on national power, and even understood as decrees for one world government (see also Lamy, 1990).

The reality, however, is that global education in schools does not even remotely reflect such an ideology, a fact that gives Burack (2003) a "reason to hope." Actually, tracing any kind of global education in the United States constitutes a form of not-so-ancient history. Global education is a child of the Cold War era and even more recent trends toward globalization. Curriculum initiatives and educational standards focused on "foreign" language instruction, geography, and world history—particularly world history with a more global emphasis—did not emerge until the 1980s (some much later). Adoption, too, has been uneven (Smith, 2002).

Early proponents of global education in the United States were undoubtedly breaking new ground, but they also argued for global education in quite moderate terms. James Becker, who in 1973 authored *Education for a Global Society*, embraced a kind of universal humanism that resonated with earlier European conceptions of cosmopolitanism. He reminds us that we are "one world" and that although we cannot "afford to ignore the diversity of mankind," global education "should seek to connect rather than divide men; it should make clear their common humanity and emphasize their common fate" (p. 33). He framed his appeal within world system theory, meaning that he believed the world was best understood as a single unit consisting of interdependent parts. Yet the discourse of interdependence hardly brings into view the relations of domination and subordination that exist between nations or the way in which dependencies have been facilitated by colonial relations, powerful states, or international organizations acting on behalf of those states.

A few years later, Robert Hanvey (1976) published his global education manifesto through the Center for War/Peace Studies. Entitled *An Attainable Global Perspective*, its name spoke worlds about its underlying agenda— attainable, implying a "modesty of goals," as Hanvey put it (p. 2). His proposal detailed several aspects of such a global perspective, including consciousness of multiple perspectives, awareness of world issues, cross-cultural awareness, knowledge of the world as a system, and an awareness of potential solutions to global problems. While Hanvey's perspective certainly represented an advance over more narrow conceptions of social education, it did not promote or even necessarily lay groundwork for a perspective comparable to epistemological subalternity, or border thinking. Lacking an explicit ethical imperative and any notion of praxis (Freire, 1993), Hanvey concluded the following regarding global cognition of human problems and their solutions: "I am not proposing that students choose among alternatives—only that they know of them. This in itself is a mildly revolutionary step" (p. 28). It may have indeed been a step, but the origins of global education, and the initiatives set in motion since its inception, have not been conducive to *subaltern* cosmopolitanism. Though Becker and Hanvey at times alluded to asymmetries of power in the world system (e.g., between rich and poor nations), the general thrust of their arguments was on promoting cross-cultural understanding, respect for common humanity (with some knowledge of diversity), and awareness of major world issues and their systemic implications. A transformed world order organized along genuinely democratic lines was not and still is not on the agenda of most global education traditions. If anything, preparing students to compete in the new global economy ranks highest on the present agenda (Reich, 1992).

Tracing the development of global education over several decades, however, does reveal that its meanings have spanned the political map. Graham Pike (2000) reports:

> For some, global education is tantamount to giving a broader geographical perspective to the social studies curriculum so as to equip students to compete more effectively in the marketplace. For others, it represents a fundamental reevaluation of the content, organization, and purpose of schooling in line with a transformative vision of education. (p. 64)

In many ways, these schools of thought and practice represent those that exist within multicultural education, ranging from more conservative approaches to more radically reconstructionist positions. At the same time, Collins,

Czarra, and Smith (1998) provide a broad sketch of global and international studies over the last five decades and note that interdependence or systems thinking has been a dominant frame of reference. Charting conceptions of global education since the Hanvey definition, Kirkwood (2001) has demonstrated that later traditions continue to be relatively congruent with early constructions.

It is important, then, to consider the degree to which alternative global education traditions might enable schools to move toward a *subaltern cosmopolitan* multiculturalism. Merryfield (2001) argues that "it is time for social studies educators to move beyond the global education conceived in the Cold War" (p. 179). Power, ethics, and subalternity lie at the heart of her reconceptualization. For instance, she suggests that students analyze the relationship between empire building and dominant constructions of knowledge. Additionally, she emphasizes that:

> It is critical that students learn from the knowledge and experiences of people who, because of their race, gender, class, culture, national origin, religious or political beliefs, are ignored, stereotyped, or marginalized in mainstream academic knowledge. Unlike the global education of the 1970s, this process brings to the center of the curriculum the voices of people past and present who were silenced because they had little or no power to be heard. (p. 187)

Proposing a global education that "decolonizes the mind," Merryfield provides concrete pedagogic interventions, such as the following: "Students could analyze examples of Europeans' depictions of both white and African women, African women writers own descriptions of their lives and the whites they knew, white American literature about white and African American women, and African American women's writing" (p. 185). This kind of "contrapuntal" reading of history and literature—a pedagogy actually advocated by Said in *Culture and Imperialism*—is an approach that Merryfield believes can transform traditional global education.

The teaching of a "new" world history may also have something to offer to the advancement of a subaltern cosmopolitan multiculturalism. World history has traditionally been "linked to totalizing Western world images and stereotypes." As such:

> The very act of mapping and thinking the world implicated historians from around the world in a nexus of histories of imperial power from which "other" worlds and histories were either excluded entirely— subaltern to the point of nonexistence—or rendered subordinate. (Geyer & Bright, 1995, p. 1036)

Dominant ways of viewing the past have thus necessitated the imagination of an entirely new tradition by scholars from eastern and southern Asia, the

Middle East, Africa, and Latin America, an alternative that seeks to "present the world's pasts ... as a braid of intertwined histories" (p. 1038). This effort has been pursued thus far through two main avenues, the first of which has focused on comparative histories of power and the necessity of positioning the West in a genuinely global context. The second stream has begun to chart histories of mobility, diasporas, and borderlands. Geyer and Bright (1995) argue the immediate significance of this history:

> The recovery of the multiplicity of the world's pasts matters now more than ever ... because, in a global age, the world's pasts are all simultaneously present, colliding, interacting, intermixing—producing a collage of present histories that is surely not the history of a homogeneous global civilization. (p. 1042)

If this is the case—that globalization has engendered a space where diverse but intertwined histories confront one another at every moment—then the study of the new world history constitutes a crucial component of a counterhegemonic global education.

This is especially true because these narratives of the world's pasts reveal that "global integration was ... not a set of procedures devised by the West and superimposed on the rest.... Neither was [it] flatly or consistently rejected." Instead, emergent subaltern histories reveal that dominated groups "engaged Western power in complex patterns of accommodation and resistance" (Geyer & Bright, 1995, p. 1049). If studied in schools, these new world histories from below could provide a context for the rethinking of present conditions from a position of epistemological subalternity. The circulation of these histories in schools will not come easily for reasons already noted. Yet as this tradition —even slowly—begins to rub against the old but still dominant world history, a number of pedagogic possibilities may be set in motion.

The more transformative traditions in global education point toward how a space for cosmopolitan border thinking might be created in classrooms. Notably, there have been efforts to share ways with teachers of bringing together the local and the global in classrooms (see Bigelow & Peterson, 2002; Merryfield, 1996). The potential uses of technology—though accessibility should not be overestimated—may also open the way for a reconstruction of global education in critical directions (McIntyre-Mills, 2000).

Despite the historic mission of mass schooling to engender a national "imagined community" (Anderson, 1991), melding insurgent forms of multiculturalism and transformative traditions of global education may help classrooms and schools to become subaltern satellites linked with diverse efforts beyond schools—all assisting in the project of undermining social fascism within the nation and beyond. Indeed, subaltern cosmopolitan multiculturalism aims to foster a density of affiliations and allegiances, which raises a number of issues that we would like to briefly address.

262 • The Subaltern Speak

A Density of Affiliations: Possibilities and Cautions

Central to subaltern cosmopolitan multiculturalism is a density of affiliations —a complex and layered sense of identification with emancipatory possibility. We contend that curriculum (and schools more generally) should facilitate in students a radical democratic sensibility toward multiple spheres of interest, whether local, national, or global. By failing to support an array of loyalties, or a sort of *triple consciousness*, schools risk contributing to narrow understandings of interest and the inaptitude to grasp the intricate and often exploitive associations that exist between contexts of different scale. Thinking back to the classroom detailed in the opening of this chapter, it is crucial to reflect on one student's vehement call to "stop talking about Puerto Rico" and to proceed toward a history more focused on the United States and its glorious role in the World Wars. That a wider historical view could be so easily dismissed reveals some dimension of the disturbing problematic we are attempting to address.

Yet we recognize that asserting the importance of a density of affiliations is bound to invite any number of criticisms. It might be argued that it is desirable to unconditionally privilege a particular affiliation, such as the local or national; this argument has bolstered both emancipatory and oppressive forms of nationalism. From another standpoint, particular affiliations may be viewed as irrelevant, as argued by those who contend that we are living in an increasingly postnational world that renders local sensibilities obsolete. Alternatively, the point could be raised that affiliations on wider scales lack emotional resonance or historical grounding and are more utopian than politically viable. Beyond this, it is essential to address the degree to which multiple affiliations are rendered problematic by conflicting interests or seeming incompatibility, such as national and transnational allegiances. Allegiances connected to broader domains, it might even be said, are compromised by issues of representation and organization within spheres of association that are weakly developed, such as global civil society. There are powerful arguments and important evidence that must be considered in relation to these positions. We would like here to partly respond to some of these views and concerns.

We begin by acknowledging that there are, indeed, a range of conditions that call for the privileging of particular affiliations. For example, local environmental abuses or racial violence in the neighborhood may require intensive mobilizations within the immediate community, even when broader structures are implicated. At the same time, there are moments when national allegiance should take precedence. Grassroots efforts within various Latin American and Caribbean nations aimed at curtailing the embrace of neoliberal policies by domestic elites or their imposition by international organizations provide examples. Ultimately, there is nothing inherently progressive or retrogressive about centering local or even national affiliations. In our view, it is instead dangerous to assume, without reference to context, the kind of allegiance most conducive to subaltern agency and democratic transformation.

Some nonetheless argue that national affiliations have been and are most central. For instance, Balakrishnan (1996) explains that the nation has constituted the grounds for class action, as international socialism has not historically constituted a basis for mass struggle. According to him, this has been the case because revolutionary agency is uneasily sustained beyond the national frontier and is closely tied to national memory. He writes:

> Imagined nationhood in all its crudity has been the entry ticket for the wretched of the earth into world history. This is because the nation state is the place in which the stakes of this century's great class struggles were defined. The reason why it took place in nation-state frameworks ... was a matter of the scale of effective collective agency.... [And] it is clear that when one speaks of one's dead ancestors one is talking about nation and not international socialism. (p. 212)

Packaging the analysis in these terms implies that memory emanates from local or national pasts alone, and that the energies and forms of coordination needed to sustain political action may only be harnessed in contexts of limited scale. That global affiliations have weak historical roots, minimal emotional purchase, and little political potential, are conclusions potentially drawn from this account. But is this necessarily the case, particularly considering more recent efforts focused on the political, economic, and cultural implications of globalization from above? For example, the World Social Forum (2001) has sought "to strengthen and create new national and international links among organizations and movements of society, that ... will increase the capacity for non-violent social resistance to the process of dehumanization the world is undergoing." There is even evidence that new (though admittedly precarious) forms of labor internationalism are developing as first and third world workers organize against the forces of global capital; a case of international solidarity with Coca-Cola workers in Guatemala provides one illustration, among others (Waterman, 1998). Efforts like these reveal that transnational affiliations can be quite powerful as organizers from across the globe collectively mobilize.

In some quarters, comparatively, global sensibilities are viewed as *more* fundamental than local or national affiliations. According to this line of argument, technologies, diasporic flows, and the decline of the nation-state under conditions of globalization are ushering in a postnational age in which national sentiments and territorially bound politics no longer structure experience in significant ways. For example, Cheah (1998a) demonstrates how particular theories of cultural hybridity and diasporic mobility have assumed the uniquely liberating potential of cosmopolitan identification. In a similar vein, Radhakrishnan (2003) articulates the following critique:

> The poststructuralist appropriation of the diaspora aestheticizes it as an avant-garde lifestyle based on deterritorialization.... The metropolitan

> theory of the diaspora ... has to be demystified before the diasporic condition can be historicized as a condition of pain and double alienation. (p. 323)

Too frequently, cosmopolitan identification is understood as the raison d'être of subaltern resistance and agency, with much less attention paid to the costs of displacement. And while it is undoubtedly true that global affiliations have been prompted by advanced communication technologies, higher levels of international migration, and even the reorganization of the state under conditions of accelerated globalization, it is also the case that "for the majority who remain in peripheral space by choice or necessity," the nation-state remains central "because postnationalism through migration is not an alternative" (Cheah, 1998a, p. 314).

In fact, even global affiliations are often inflected by national loyalties and hierarchies, as demonstrated by Schein (1998) in her analysis of the International Symposium on Hmong People. Within this transnational forum, national affiliations and histories—and even state interventions—influenced the presence of particular groups and the organization of the conference agenda. Considering the overall structure of activities, Schein explains that "the effect was of the 'country representatives,' arrayed for the perusal of the Hmong American audience, offering up their respective country reports in a hierarchy structured by the supremacy of the Hmong American leadership," with one such leader declaring in English at the close of the symposium, "Thank You. God Bless America" (pp. 179–180).

Of course, none of this means that global solidarities are any more problematic, less emancipatory, or difficult to establish than localized affiliations. Clearly, the explosion of transnational social movements from below (Cohen & Rai, 2000) and even the expansion of international education (Rizvi, 2000) reveal the utter importance of global imagination and agency. Again, the problem, we maintain, is asserting the primacy or potential of any given loyalty without respect to political content or context.

A continuum of associations from the local to the global is clearly possible and holds an array of possibilities. There is, understandably, the claim that such an assemblage of allegiances will conflict. We do not deny that conflicts may arise among affiliations of different scale, some of which require careful negotiation, but conflicts of interest and loyalty are not necessarily generated or alleviated by an adjustment of one's loyalties according to scale. Rather, conflict potentially characterizes relations at every level, whether local or global. Perhaps most misguided is the assertion that national and transnational allegiances are mutually exclusive. Quite powerfully, Keck and Sikkink (1998) have documented the relationship of transnational advocacy networks to domestic arenas. Detailing a "boomerang" pattern, they discuss how "domestic NGOs [nongovernmental organizations] bypass their state and directly search out international allies to try to bring pressure on their states from outside" (p. 12). This triangulation of relations reveals the way in which local and global identities, concerns, and campaigns have simultaneously formed— supporting efforts in specific states, contributing to activism across borders, and reconstructing the identities of participants in the process.

Acknowledging the interplay of the national and cosmopolitical does not require denying that transnational mobilizations often evidence unequal relations rooted in differential national power. In the transnational campaign called Education for All, complex alliances were formed between northern and southern nongovernmental organizations in an effort to advocate greater access to free, publicly provided education worldwide, but issues of direct participation and geographic representation within the movement remained a concern (Mundy & Murphy, 2001). In the end, the interconnected nature of each of these spheres of existence must be appreciated, though without romantic notions about particular affiliations either within or beyond borders.

Despite such cautions, these actually existing networks are part of the fabric of subaltern cosmopolitan multiculturalism in which we believe schools represent a crucial strand. Multiple solidarities are possible, but schools must assist in fostering them—albeit in nuanced ways depending on history, context, and the balance of democratic priorities at particular junctures.

Aside from questions of scale remains the issue of the *nature* of affiliation. We have called for a *subaltern* cosmopolitan multiculturalism, but a critical and cautious assessment of subalternities is a necessary part of the process of affiliation. There has been a tendency to romanticize the subaltern as inherently democratic. Recalling one such instance, Spivak (1998) reports an exchange she had while involved in an art show on a migrant community in London:

> When I proposed that we show evidence of the fact that ethnic entrepreneurs were pimping for the transnationals and selling their women and children into sweated labor ... my collaborating artist's response was that he did not want to show sexist exploitation within the community. He wanted to show just white racism. (p. 336)

Such evidence serves to remind us that not all subalternities are rooted in good sense or informed by counterhegemonic consciousness. Within the transnational domain, for instance, a managerial class of Chinese cosmopolitans has established businesses across the globe. While this diasporic regime is partially the result of colonial and postcolonial relations and members of this class remain cultural "others" in Western centers, these executives have built tremendous wealth through a flexible and relatively stateless sense of citizenship, an embrace of economic liberalization, and dependence on patriarchal family relations that foster accumulation (Ong, 1998). At the very least, these illustrations underscore that subaltern and dominant relations may exist simultaneously within communities, and that the identifications fostered by curriculum and schooling must be carefully considered for their democratic and antidemocratic potentiality.

The Girl with a Flag: Conclusion or Beginning?

In the end, each of us is situated in a world of contexts, including national and transnational forces "sometimes acting in concert, sometimes in conflict, articulated at different elite and subaltern levels" (Clifford, 1998, p. 368). We suggest that schools might engender a sensibility of revolutionary character based not on some decontextualized, humanistic affiliation, but on one grounded within local, national, and global contexts where specific negotiations over just arrangements are struggled over. As Robbins (1998) reminds us, "No one actually is or even can be a cosmopolitan in the sense of belonging nowhere.... Nor can anyone be a cosmopolitan in the sense of belonging everywhere" (p. 260). The great irony, then, is that all affiliations assume their significance within concrete sets of relations and particular pasts and presents. Helping students to develop a capacity for thinking and acting in counterhegemonic ways within and across borders is the work that subaltern cosmopolitan multiculturalism can potentially do. But we know this work will not be easy.

Just as we opened this chapter with an illustration of the complexities involved in realizing the vision we have charted, allow us to close with an illustration that once again makes clear the significant challenges. One of us (Paulino) has a daughter who participated in All Nations Day at her high school, which is located in the United States but attended by students from approximately eighty different countries. The day's major event was a flag ceremony during which a procession of students carried the flags of many nations—flags the school later planned to permanently display along a main corridor. According to a group of students with whom we informally spoke—students either from or ancestrally affiliated with Brazil, Iraq, Laos, Peru, the Philippines, Puerto Rico, and the United States—little was done either before, during, or after All Nations Day to ignite a more substantive, long-term, schoolwide conversation about issues of diversity, national identity, global relations, or inequality. Many students, they reported, could not even identify most of the flags, much less speak on the histories and cultures of the nations represented or the position of those nations within the current global regime. While this celebration undoubtedly had cosmopolitan appeal, it demonstrates just how far we still need to travel in order for subaltern cosmopolitan multiculturalism to be realized. It highlights, too, the danger of symbolic gestures that have the potential to make us feel like multicultural world citizens, rather than enabling us to actually think and act in more critically informed ways and to confront oppression at multiple levels. Perhaps this chapter might be read as an invitation to other nations to respond to this proposal, which is not intended to be a universal educational prescription unmediated by debate, translation, or reinvention. Let us begin to talk about how we might ground education in subaltern cosmopolitan multiculturalism, and what that might look like and mean in different contexts.

References

Abowitz, K. K. (2002). Imagining citizenship: Cosmopolitanism or patriotism? [electronic]. *Teachers College Record.* Available: http://www.tcrecord.org/Content.asp?ContentID =11008

Anderson, B. (1991). *Imagined communities.* New York: Verso.

Apple, M. W. (2000). *Official knowledge: Democratic education in a conservative age* (2nd ed.). New York: Routledge.

Apple, M. W., et al. (2003). *The state and the politics of knowledge.* New York: RoutledgeFalmer.

Balakrishnan, G. (1996). The national imagination. In G. Balakrishnan (Ed.), *Mapping the nation* (pp. 198–213). New York: Verso.

Banks, J. A. (1995). Multicultural education: Historical development, dimensions, and practice. In J. A. Banks & C. A. McGee Banks (Eds.), *Handbook of research on multicultural education* (pp. 3–24). New York: Macmillan.

Bauman, Z. (2001). The great war of recognition. *Theory, Culture, and Society, 18* (2–3), 137–150.

Becker, J. (1973). *Education for a global society.* Bloomington, IN: Phi Delta Kappa Educational Foundation.

Bello, W. (2002). Prospects for good global governance: The view from the south [report prepared for the Bundestag, Federal Republic of Germany]. Bangkok, Thailand: Focus on the Global South.

Bigelow, B., & Peterson, B. (Eds.). (2002). *Rethinking globalization: Teaching for justice in an unjust world.* Milwaukee, WI: Rethinking Schools Press.

Brecher, J., Costello, T., & Smith, B. (2000). *Globalization from below.* Cambridge, MA: South End Press.

Burack, J. (2003). The student, the world, and the global education ideology. In J. Leming, L. Ellington, & K. Porter (Eds.), *Where did social studies go wrong?* (pp. 40–69). Washington, DC: Thomas B. Fordham Foundation.

Buras, K. L. (1999). Questioning core assumptions: A critical reading of and response to E. D. Hirsch's *The Schools We Need and Why We Don't Have Them. Harvard Educational Review, 69* (1), 67–93.

Buras, K. L. (2005). Tracing the core knowledge movement: History lessons from above and below. In M. W. Apple & K. L. Buras (Eds.), *The subaltern speak: Curriculum, power, and educational struggles* (see Chapter 1). New York: Routledge.

Burbules, N. C., & Torres, C. A. (Eds.). (2000). *Globalization and education: Critical perspectives.* New York: Routledge.

Cheah, P. (1998a). Given culture: Rethinking cosmopolitical freedom in transnationalism. In P. Cheah & B. Robbins (Eds.), *Cosmopolitics: Thinking and feeling beyond the nation* (pp. 290–328). Minneapolis: University of Minnesota Press.

Cheah, P. (1998b). The cosmopolitical—today. In P. Cheah & B. Robbins (Eds.), *Cosmopolitics: Thinking and feeling beyond the nation* (pp. 20–41). Minneapolis: University of Minnesota Press.

Clifford, J. (1998). Mixed feelings. In P. Cheah & B. Robbins (Eds.), *Cosmopolitics: Thinking and feeling beyond the nation* (pp. 362–370). Minneapolis: University of Minnesota Press.

Cohen, R., & Rai, S. (2000). Global social movements: Towards a cosmopolitan politics. In R. Cohen & S. Rai (Eds.), *Global social movements* (pp. 3–17). London: Athlone Press.

Collins, H. T., Czarra, F., & Smith A. F. (1998). Guidelines for global and international studies education: Challenges, cultures, and connections. *Social Education, 62* (5), 311–317.

Cornbleth, C., & Waugh, D. (1999). *The great speckled bird: Multicultural politics and education policymaking.* Mahwah, NJ: Lawrence Erlbaum Associates.

Dahl, R. A. (1998). *On democracy.* New Haven, CT: Yale University Press.

Diaz, C. F., Massialas, B. G., & Xanthopoulos, J. A. (1999). *Global perspectives for educators.* Needham Heights, MA: Allyn & Bacon.

Dimitriadis, G., & McCarthy, C. (2001). *Reading and teaching the postcolonial: From Baldwin to Basquiat and beyond.* New York: Teachers College Press.

Farahmandpur, R. (2004). Essay review: A Marxist critique of Michael Apple's neo-Marxist approach to educational reform [electronic]. *Journal for Critical Education Policy Studies, 2* (1). Available: http://www.jceps.com

Fraser, N. (1997). *Justice interruptus.* New York: Routledge.

Freire, P. (1993). *Pedagogy of the oppressed*. New York: Continuum.

Gandin, L. A., & Apple, M. W. (2002). Challenging neo-liberalism, building democracy: Creating the Citizen School in Porto Alegre, Brazil. *Journal of Education Policy, 17* (2), 259–279.

Geyer, M, & Bright, C. (1995). World history in a global age. *American Historical Review, 100* (4), 1034–1060.

Ghai, Y. (2000). Universalism and relativism: Human rights as a framework for negotiating interethnic claims. *Cardozo Law Review, 21*, 1095–1140.

Giroux, H. A. (1995a). Insurgent multiculturalism and the promise of pedagogy. In D. T. Goldberg (Ed.), *Multiculturalism: A critical reader* (pp. 325– 343). Oxford, UK: Blackwell.

Giroux, H. A. (1995b). National identity and the politics of multiculturalism. *College Literature, 22* (2), 42–57.

Gonzalez, J. (1998). "Puerto Rico had never seen anything like it": The meaning of the general strike. *The Progressive, 62* (9), 24–27.

Grant, C. A., & Sleeter, C. E. (2003). *Turning on learning: Five approaches for multicultural teaching plans for race, class, gender, and disability* (3rd ed.). New York: John Wiley & Sons.

Hanvey, R. G. (1976). *An attainable global perspective*. New York: Center for War/Peace Studies.

Harvey, D. (2000). Cosmopolitanism and the banality of geographical evils. *Public Culture, 12* (2), 529–564.

Hirsch, E. D., Jr. (1992). Toward a centrist curriculum: Two kinds of multiculturalism in elementary school. Charlottesville, VA: Core Knowledge Foundation.

Huntington, S. A. (1997). *Clash of civilizations and the remaking of world order*. New York: Touchstone.

Kaestle, C. F. (1983). *Pillars of the republic: Common schools and American society, 1780–1860*. New York: Hill & Wang.

Keck, M., & Sikkink, K. (1998). *Activists beyond borders*. Ithaca, NY: Cornell University Press.

Kirkwood, T. F. (2001). Our global age requires global education: Clarifying definitional ambiguities. *Social Studies, 92* (1), 10–15.

Kymlicka, W. (1995). *Multicultural citizenship: A liberal theory of minority rights*. Oxford, UK: Clarendon Press.

Lamy, S. L. (1990). Global education: A conflict of images. In K. A. Tye (Ed.), *Global education: From thought to action* (pp. 49–63). Alexandria, VA: Association for Supervision and Curriculum Development.

Malcomson, S. L. (1998). The varieties of cosmopolitan experience. In P. Cheah & B. Robbins (Eds.), *Cosmopolitics: Thinking and feeling beyond the nation* (pp. 233–245). Minneapolis: University of Minnesota Press.

McIntyre-Mills, J. J. (2000). *Global citizenship and social movements: Creating transcultural webs of meaning for the new millennium*. London: Harwood Academic Publishers.

McLaren, P., & Farahmandpur, R. (2001). Class, cultism, and multiculturalism: A notebook on forging a revolutionary politics. *Multicultural Education, 8* (3), 2–14.

Merryfield, M. M. (Ed.). (1996). *Making connections between multicultural and global education: Teacher educators and teacher education programs*. Washington, DC: American Association of Colleges for Teacher Education.

Merryfield, M. M. (2001). Moving the center of global education: From imperial world views that divide the world to double consciousness, contrapuntal pedagogy, hybridity, and cross-cultural competence. In W. B. Stanley (Ed.), Critical issues in social studies research for the 21st century (pp. 179–207). Greenwich, CT: Information Age Publishing.

Mignolo, W. D. (2000a). *Local histories/global designs: Coloniality, subaltern knowledge, and border thinking*. Princeton, NJ: Princeton University Press.

Mignolo, W. D. (2000b). The many faces of cosmo-polis: Border thinking and critical cosmopolitanism. *Public Culture, 12* (3), 721–748.

Mundy, K., & Murphy, L. (2001). Transnational advocacy, global civil society? Emerging evidence from the field of education. *Comparative Education Review, 45* (1), 85–126.

Nussbaum, M. C., et al. (1996). *For love of country: Debating the limits of patriotism*. Boston, MA: Beacon Press.

O'Byrne, D. J. (2001). On the construction of political identity: Negotiation and strategies beyond the nation-state. In P. Kennedy & C. J. Danks (Eds.), *Globalization and national identities: Crisis or opportunity?* (pp. 139–157). New York: Palgrave.

Ong, A. (1998). Flexible citizenship among Chinese cosmopolitans. In P. Cheah & B. Robbins (Eds.), *Cosmopolitics: Thinking and feeling beyond the nation* (pp. 134–162). Minneapolis: University of Minnesota Press.

Pieterse, J. N. (2004). *Globalization and culture: Global mélange.* New York: Rowman & Littlefield Publishers.

Pike, G. (2000). Global education and national identity: In pursuit of meaning. *Theory into Practice, 39* (2), 64–73.

Pollock, S., Bhabha, H. K., Breckenridge, C. A., & Chakrabarty, D. (2000). Cosmopolitanisms. *Public Culture, 12* (3), 577–589.

Radhakrishnan, R. (2003). Postcoloniality and the boundaries of identity. In L. M. Alcoff & E. Mendieta (Eds.), *Identities: Race, class, gender, and nationality* (pp. 312–329). Malden, MD: Blackwell Publishing.

Reich, R. B. (1992). *The work of nations: Preparing ourselves for 21st-century capitalism.* New York: Vintage Books.

Rizvi, F. (2000). International education and the production of global imagination. In N. C. Burbules & C. A. Torres (Eds.), *Globalization and education: Critical perspectives* (pp. 205–225). New York: Routledge.

Robbins, B. (1998) Comparative cosmopolitanisms. In P. Cheah & B. Robbins (Eds.), *Cosmopolitics: Thinking and feeling beyond the nation* (pp. 246–264). Minneapolis: University of Minnesota Press.

Said, E. W. (2000). *Reflections on exile and other essays.* Cambridge, MA: Harvard University Press.

Santiago, R. (Ed.). (1995). *Boricuas: Influential Puerto Rican writings.* New York: Ballantine Books.

Santos, Boaventura de Sousa. (2001). Nuestra America: Reinventing a subaltern paradigm of recognition and redistribution. *Theory, Culture, and Society, 18* (2–3), 185–217.

Santos, Boaventura de Sousa. (2002a). Can law be emancipatory? In Boaventura de Sousa Santos, *Toward a new common sense: Law, science and politics in the paradigmatic transition.* London: Butterworths.

Santos, Boaventura de Sousa. (2002b). Toward a multicultural conception of human rights. *Beyond Law, 9* (25), 9–32.

Schlesinger, A. M., Jr. (1992). *The disuniting of America: Reflections on a multicultural society.* New York: W. W. Norton & Company.

Shein, L. (1998). Importing Miao brethren to Hmong America: A not-so-stateless transnationalism. In P. Cheah & B. Robbins (Eds.), *Cosmopolitics: Thinking and feeling beyond the nation* (pp. 163–191). Minneapolis: University of Minnesota Press.

Smith, A. F. (2002). How global is the curriculum? *Educational Leadership, 60* (2), 38–41.

Spivak, G. C. (1998). Cultural talks in the hot peace: Revisiting the "global village." In P. Cheah & B. Robbins (Eds.), *Cosmopolitics: Thinking and feeling beyond the nation* (pp. 329–348). Minneapolis: University of Minnesota Press.

Stiglitz, J. E. (2002). *Globalization and its discontents.* New York: W.W. Norton & Company.

Sunshine, C. A., & Menkart, D. (Eds.). (1999). *Caribbean connections: Classroom resources for secondary schools.* Washington, DC: Ecumenical Program on Central America and the Caribbean.

Tomlinson, J. (1999). *Globalization and culture.* Chicago, IL: University of Chicago Press.

Torres, C. A. (1998). *Democracy, education, and multiculturalism: Dilemmas of citizenship in a global world.* New York: Rowman & Littlefield.

Tye, B. B., & Tye, K. A. (1992). *Global education: A study of school change.* Albany: State University of New York Press.

Ukpokodu, N. (1999). Multiculturalism vs. globalism. *Social Education, 63* (5), 298–300.

Verdery, K. (1996). Whither "nation"and "nationalism"? In G. Balakrishnan (Ed.), *Mapping the nation* (pp. 226–234). New York: Verso.

Vergès, F. (2001). Vertigo and emancipation, creole cosmopolitanism and cultural politics. *Theory, Culture, and Society, 18* (2–3), 169–183.

Waterman, P. (1998). *Globalization, social movements and the new internationalisms.* Washington, DC: Mansell.

WLIW. (1999). The Puerto Ricans: Our American story [video]. New York: Author.

Wood, A. W. (1998). Kant's project for perpetual peace. In P. Cheah & B. Robbins (Eds.), *Cosmopolitics: Thinking and feeling beyond the nation* (pp. 59–76). Minneapolis: University of Minnesota Press.

World Social Forum. (2001). World social forum charter of principles. Available: http://www.forumsocialmundial.org.br/eng/qcartas.asp.?id_menu=4&cd_language=2

11
Speaking Back to Official Knowledge

MICHAEL W. APPLE AND KRISTEN L. BURAS

This concluding chapter will not be of the usual kind. We do not wish to draw all the conclusions that one can from these chapters. In fact, we believe that doing so could foreclose the kinds of debate that are important for the development of generative and effective actions on the complicated relations of domination and subordination in our societies. Because of this, we choose instead to raise a series of issues and questions that we hope will lead to more reflective and successful actions that challenge these relations.

In doing this, we also want to suggest that those in critical education studies need to have less romantic visions of the issues surrounding the politics of subalternity so that more effective tactical and strategic understandings and interventions are possible. We say this because we believe that all too much of what counts as "radical" theory in education is overly rhetorical (Apple, 2006), and is therefore less able than it might be in interrupting neoliberal and neoconservative forces today. Of course, this must be done in a way that continues the long tradition of generating and opening spaces where subaltern voices are made public—and heard.

In what follows, we raise a number of important questions and suggest some of the implications raised by the arguments and issues that have played such an important role in this book.

I: How, and in what ways, has the right captured the discourse of subalternity, and in support of what purposes?

In one of the early chapters of this book, Michael Apple reveals how religious fundamentalists and evangelicals have attempted to assume the identity of a subaltern community. Following the lead of those involved in the African American struggle for civil rights, for example, conservative, middle-class, white women within the home schooling movement view themselves as among the "new oppressed." They are simply defending an assemblage of religious beliefs and cultural forms that have been unrecognized or eschewed by traditional public schools. Positioned within overlapping relations of subordination and domination, these mothers have turned the domestic sphere into a realm of activism in which children are taught, ironically, about the righteousness of particular forms of marginalization (e.g., homosexuals who are "living in sin") and are trained to go out into the world and defend these commitments. Likewise, Kristen Buras has shown how E. D. Hirsch—representing a particular faction within a broader neoconservative bloc—has partly embraced and redefined subaltern demands for recognition and redistribution through a discourse described as rightist multiculturalism. Weaving an educational vision that appeals to the concerns of both dominant and subaltern groups, integrating an array of differently situated communities into the movement, and even writing a "*new* old history" for Core Knowledge schools that conditionally incorporates the subaltern, the power of strategic compromise and appropriation is clear.

Yet the discourse of subalternity is still situated within a set of peculiar, tense alliances, as demonstrated in both the Core Knowledge movement and the efforts around vouchers in Milwaukee. As Thomas Pedroni reminds us, subalternity is not always so easily sutured into hegemonic discourses, but rather there are fractures within such alliances. Because of this, those of us deeply involved in struggles in education and in the larger sociocultural arena need to ask whether the adoption of subaltern discourses and courting of subaltern communities within both of these reform movements dilutes the power of the right or stretches it. What are the effects of this? What does this mean for our efforts to build counterhegemonic alliances to counter the right?

II: What might be gained by taking a less romantic view of subalternity and examining the contradictions of subaltern voices? Alternatively, what are the dangers of problematizing the subaltern?

Kevin Kumashiro opens his chapter by sharing some of the resistance he has faced in his attempts to look at both racially and sexually oppressed communities in less romantic ways, and to reveal the contradictions within those communities. He criticizes what he describes as the "willful partiality" of many who work in anti-oppressive education. What is too often overlooked in these important traditions, which have undeniably contributed to the democratic project, is the multiplicity of positions occupied by each of us. Think here, for example, of the struggle documented by Glenabah Martinez over the building of a monument to honor the conquistador Juan de Oñate. Each faction in the dispute—Indigenous peoples and *Nuevos Mexicanos*—has traditionally been subordinate to dominant groups. Yet without less romantic and more complicated understandings of the mixing and mingling of dominance and subalternity within each of our identities and histories, we do not have the theoretical tools to grasp the nexus of power and disempowerment embedded in this conflict. What does it mean when a traditionally marginalized group demands the recognition of its history through a monument that some in the community believe honors Hispanic culture, while many disregard that this history entailed the subordination of yet another subaltern group—Native Americans whose lives and land were taken under Spanish conquest?

To return yet again to the women involved in home schooling, those subordinated along gender lines have nonetheless found a way to bolster their power within the domestic sphere by teaching children, ironically, about the "righteousness" of marginalizing particular "others," such as gays and lesbians (or even those who are not "sufficiently Christian"). This is, after all, the kind of content endorsed in the Bible curriculum used by so many. In the case of Core Knowledge, moreover, not all marginalized communities see the need to recontextualize Core from below. They see it as something of a blessing, one that should be embraced. At one low-income, African American school in Atlanta, for example, the Core Knowledge curriculum stands in sharp contrast to the curricula in similarly populated schools that stress African and African American themes. Core students, the principal touts, are instead "listening to Mozart and Beethoven, speaking French and reading classics like 'Robinson Crusoe'" (Donsky, 2005). The embrace of dominant and even retrogressive forms by women or communities of color does not correspond with the way subalterns are *supposed* to believe and act. But this is exactly our point.

Existing theories of cultural recognition, especially within education, have been largely premised on the assumption that a particular brand of consciousness is, by and large, always associated with subalternity—one that rejects dominant culture, resists assimilation, or refuses to perpetuate existing relations of unequal power. While it is the case that very real histories have contributed to the development of particular tendencies and sensibilities within oppressed communities, these are not always uniform or progressive, and they are mediated by multiple identifications based on class, race, gender, sexuality, language, "ability," and national origin. We would like to argue, then, that it is crucial to account for the contradictions of subalternity and even the internalization of the consciousness of the "oppressor." If we do not understand this, we may actually contribute to pushing oppressed people into the arms of dominant groups, by being seen as arrogant and as not listening to the complicated voices coming from below that may not be saying what we expect or want to hear.

Our failure to do so has only fueled the attacks of many cultural conservatives who criticize multiculturalism for its "relativistic" stance on culture —meaning that such a tradition unconditionally elevates the oppressed while demonizing the oppressor. Perhaps the cause of emancipatory educational efforts around diversity, we suggest, would be better served by a more nuanced exploration of kinds of diversity and the specific criteria that might be used to distinguish which cultural forms deserve recognition and which do not (e.g., see Fraser, 1997; Fraser & Honneth, 2003). This is a *very* knotty issue. But the real world and a politics that tries to deal with it in progressive ways can't be built by simply wishing it away.

We very much understand that there is a danger in problematizing the subaltern. Oppressed groups are already vulnerable, and are already too frequently seen as backward, responsible for their own subordinate status, and even guilty of "reverse discrimination." If not done carefully, this kind of work could rebound on progressive theorists and activists, weaken collective bonds within and across subaltern communities, and leave oppressed communities only more vulnerable to claims that we are *all* oppressed and oppressor in one way or another. Recognizing that these are very real dangers means that we must also recognize the kinds of challenges that will need to be addressed in future theoretical work, carefully considered within grassroots efforts, and worked out on the ground in classrooms as critical educators address students situated along multiple axes of power.

III: Under what conditions do subaltern groups "become right?" Under what conditions do they instead tactically occupy a "third space," one in which they support educational reforms and movements under the primary direction of conservative forces, but do so for reasons that sit only uncomfortably alongside the purposes and interests of dominant groups?

Following Apple and Oliver (2003), even with his and our strong support for the impressive reforms being built in Porto Alegre, Luís Armando Gandin reminds us that even those with relatively progressive political commitments can be pushed to the right. In the context of the Citizen School project in Porto Alegre, Brazil, he warns that the tendency within the Municipal Secretariat of Education (SMED) to frame particular teachers as conservative—specifically those who express concerns about or appear resistant to the kinds of changes represented by the project—may only foster greater resistance in these teachers. Moreover, he stresses, the good sense in their resistance will fail to shape the direction of the project if they are viewed only as counterrevolutionaries getting in the way of progress.

At the same time, Pedroni has demonstrated that not all subaltern groups "become right" in their support of conservative educational reforms. In the Milwaukee alliance around vouchers, he has revealed how African American parents rarely offered intact neoliberal discourses as explanations for their participation in the voucher program. These kinds of conditional alliances have instead enabled traditionally oppressed groups to act within the spaces provided by conservative educational reforms. This does not mean that such conditional alliances should always be applauded; but it does mean that we should not infantilize oppressed groups by seeing them as necessarily duped when they do so.

It is important to recall, for instance, that the Core Knowledge curriculum was recontextualized by a variety of educational actors—something that helped the movement to grow, but also required the disciplining of less conservative forces within it. Thinking again of the contest over the statue of Oñate and the efforts around vouchers, both Martinez and Pedroni reveal how the often privileged and conservative subject position of *tax payer* was assumed by subaltern groups—in the first case by Indigenous peoples to justify their contestation of the use of public monies for building the statue, and in the second case by African American parent Sonia Israel who indicated that the public schools acted like they "were giving you something" when her "taxes help pay for pubic education." Again, we need to think carefully about those factors that push people to the right and those conditions under which they assume what may *appear* to be rightist positions, but for purposes that, upon closer examination, at least partly run counter to rightist efforts. What does this mean for how progressive alliances might be built? But just as importantly, can this recognition of the tactical uses of rightist positions and resources by subaltern groups lead us to simply uncritically *accept* this support, to not argue against it, or to assume that there isn't vigorous debate about such tactics within oppressed communities themselves? This would be a real mistake as well.

IV: Is the left being honest enough about the power of conservative moderniza-tion? Are we thinking tactically enough? In a related vein, what might be learned from the right's success? What lessons should the left reject if "democratic means" are to be used to achieve "democratic ends?"

As Kumashiro pointed out in his analysis of politics in the post–9/11 era, "there is great profit in the business of fear." The cultivation of fear has undoubtedly been a powerful weapon in struggles over common sense, and the forces of conservative modernization have used this weapon skillfully. Detraction, too, has served dominant groups well. Being told to look *here*, at the so-called cultural illiteracy of poor families, when we should be looking *there*, at the politics of marginalization within the canon of dominant knowledge, has also been a strategy effectively utilized by the right (and as Kumashiro points out, sometimes by the left as well).

Compromise has likewise been a strategy for the maintenance of hege-mony, as was recognized by Antonio Gramsci, who we discussed in the open-ing chapter of this book. School district officials "allowed" Indigenous students to wear Native attire during the graduation ceremony, but only if covered by the cap and gown. Taiwanese ethnic groups are accommodated in their demands for indigenization education that is rooted in Taiwan as long as it is mindful of the mainland. Subaltern groups will be incorporated into Core Knowledge history texts, but only under particular conditions. Compromise and conditionality have served the interests of the right in powerful ways. We

276 • The Subaltern Speak

believe that it is necessary for progressive educators and activists to begin to think carefully both about the strategies being employed and about what we might learn from this. One thing is certain, however; we must not simply copy rightist tactics. To do so would be to give up some of our most important and lasting core principles.

The right has also found ways, through particular appeals and the disarticulation and rearticulation of particular subaltern concerns, to build hybrid alliances (Apple, 2006). Might the left learn something from the right in this regard? This issue must be approached cautiously. While it is true that particular alliances among disparate groups may have progressive possibilities—as is the case in a coalition between groups left and right against the commercialization of children by Channel One—there are also significant dangers in entering into these alliances and/or adopting the strategies used by conservative forces. Appealing to the everyday sensibilities of dispossessed groups in an effort to redefine them in ways that further relations of subordination and domination is hardly desirable. Neither is the (mis)appropriating of subaltern voices, as evidenced by Hirsch's speech about James Farmer's support for Core Knowledge when, in fact, Farmer's support was far less definitive. What might be learned (actually returned to, since many progressive movements inside and outside of education do have a powerful history of doing this; see Anyon, 2005 for more on this) by the left, however, is to seek out those concerns that resonate with oppressed communities, and to use these as starting points for building more progressive alternatives. This must be done with deep respect for the perspectives and arguments being advanced by subaltern groups—and especially with due recognition of the elements of good sense even in those positions with which we may initially disagree.

But there is more. As we have argued elsewhere, exposing subaltern communities to counterevidence regarding the claims and promises of the right may also be a key strategy for activists (Buras & Apple, 2005). An overly romantic vision that teaching doesn't have to go on, that there aren't things that need to be told to the dispossessed by deeply committed organic intellectuals, is exactly that—romantic. There are, in fact, lessons to be learned from both above and below, which brings us to the next question.

V: What are the characteristics of successful counterhegemonic struggles?

The above question about the right's success should lead us to ask questions about the successes of counterhegemonic struggles, a number of which have been documented by contributors to this book. In his chapter, Apple underlined the importance of identity work within conservative educational movements, but he also acknowledged that identity politics are a crucial part of all social and educational movements, including counterhegemonic ones.

Even before such struggles are waged in collective and organized ways, the process of identity formation is often underway, as Boal's Theater of the Oppressed aptly recognizes. Thus, while the opposition of Indigenous students to cultural domination (as documented by Martinez) never assumed the form of mass resistance, the unwillingness of a Native student to believe that Odysseus could "set the values for a civilization," and Indigenous pride and knowledge of culture fostered by Native American studies, are essential components of the kind of subjectivity on which broader mobilizations depend.

Speaking theoretically, as mentioned above and as stressed by Gandin, counterhegemonic struggles take seriously the work of rearticulating dominant subject positions and discourses for counterhegemonic purposes. In clearer terms, this is actually what occurred in the Citizen School project when activists redefined neoliberal tenets such as autonomy and decentralization to suit their own purposes—that is, not to discipline the public sphere, but to democratize it. As Chen points out, oppositional movements recognize that the state is *always* in formation, which opens the space to mediate its relationship to and between subaltern groups, education, and other social arenas. While Gandin speaks of working in the "gaps" and Chen speaks of finding the "gray areas," both mean to reference the idea of reorienting dominant frameworks and building new forms of common sense under the conditions daily faced by less powerful groups. Perhaps this is also what Aronowitz means when he refers to a Swedish ethnographer who insisted that we must "dig where we stand"—in that case, progressive academics within their own universities.

In an equally powerful way, Delgado Bernal reminds us in her analysis of the East Los Angeles Blowouts that successful mobilizations embrace a multidimensional concept of grassroots activism and leadership. By recognizing multiple ways of participating or "leading," counterhegemonic struggles can be strengthened. While official spokespeople are essential, she reminds us that networking and organizing to build a broad base of support and developing consciousness, "subtly and outright" (whether leaving radical newspapers in bathrooms for students to read or standing atop a car to give a spontaneous speech to a crowd), all are important and utterly essential contributions to the success of oppositional efforts in education and beyond. This broad base of support, in fact, was essential to the success of oppositional movements in Taiwan, where educational efforts were bolstered by efforts to win seats in the legislature as well as to command media time.

The broad, collective character of these movements cannot be overstated. As Gandin has shown, the Workers' Party and the Citizen School project did not aim to govern from above, but to democratize governance and decision making—something that must be taken very seriously if disparate subaltern groups are to be organically and democratically integrated into collective educational struggles. Conservatives surely recognize this, as evidenced by Hirsch's populist appeal to teachers and his insistence (although clearly only partly true) that Core Knowledge "has been from the start a bottom-up not a top-down movement." Of course, the right is not the only set of groups who can use others to support its long-term goals. Indeed, considering the Core Knowledge Foundation's use of subaltern segments for its own legitimacy purposes, the less powerful might also use the powerful in counterhegemonic ways, as when those organizing the blowouts worked to obtain the support of Bobby Kennedy for their cause. Here, too, we have a long history of creatively doing this, and this history needs to be returned to and thought about as part of a long-term set of strategies in education and social action.

VI: Are there subaltern voices and forms of agency whose transformative potential has gone unrecognized? Who are the subaltern among the subaltern?

We would like to suggest that we must begin here by looking at how subaltern voice and agency have often been understood in highly gendered ways. It is white women who are doing much of the hidden and rather intense work of home schooling. It is African American women who are often making educational decisions around vouchers in Milwaukee. And although all of the L.A. 13 arrested for their involvement in the blowouts were men, women—as shown through Delgado Bernal's oral histories—played a crucial role in mobilizing and sustaining mass resistance. Yet much of this goes unrecognized. This brings us back in particular ways to Spivak's concerns about whether or not the subaltern can speak and be heard. The challenge, we think, is to begin recognizing that there are subaltern among the subaltern—voices and forms of action that reside within the margins of the margins. We need to interrogate the existence of these margins and make visible the essential knowledge and contributions of such groups. Rather than expecting particular groups to convert, pass, or cover, we need to see how the refusal of particular identities and voices to be pushed into the background, or assimilated, actually constitutes a powerful critique of relations of dominance.

At the same time, we need to think about how conditional visibility and invisibility have also been used by particular groups in counterhegemonic ways, as was described by one Chicana activist who indicated how gendered positionality itself was used to mobilize greater support for the blowouts. Her traditionally feminine, "goody two shoes" demeanor helped win the support of school administrators and an older and more conservative generation of Chicano/as within the community. We might think here, too, of religious conservative women whose domesticity is nonetheless understood as a form of social housekeeping, meaning that the education of children has the potential to transform the public sphere in ways that align the civil society and the state with their religious vision. But can such religious sentiment and a traditional concern for one's children be employed in progressive as well as retrogressive ways? The progressively inclined evangelical, Jim Wallis (2005), for instance, claims that this can be and is the case.

The above questions are also centrally tied to relations between center and periphery. In the *favelas* of Brazil, poor communities, rather than being viewed as culturally deficient, have sought to validate popular knowledge through the Citizen School project, and by suggesting generative themes around which the curriculum might develop. Alongside these efforts, however, have been discourses by the SMED about the need to challenge common sense, again instantiating the struggle to be heard, what counts as speaking, and so forth. Though caught in a double bind between regular classes and Native American studies, Indigenous students valued community-based projects as a means for maintaining identity and becoming educated, although clearly the presence of these voices in the "normal" classroom could (and sometimes did) challenge hegemonic curricula. When we think, too, about the Core Knowledge movement, we need to ask ourselves: Whose voices and knowledge rest outside the Core? And can a concern with a core itself turn into a set of articulate challenges of who has decided and should decide what counts as something "common" among us? The very question of what a core should be can serve as an entry point toward decentered unities that might be able to unite us around the idea of a common culture as not a thing, but an ever-evolving process of deliberation and a political/educative arena for further debate (Williams, 1989).

VII: What are the limits and possibilities of the subaltern resisting, rearticulating, and reinventing conservative modernization, particularly in terms of curriculum and educational reform?

Let us recall the way in which Core Knowledge has sometimes been reinterpreted at the classroom level in ways that trouble the official educational vision of neoconservatives. Students learned about Thomas Jefferson, but they learned different lessons: president as enslaver versus president as hero. This kind of curricular deviance has, in part, generated efforts to discipline diversity within the movement and to bring its supporters into closer alignment with dominant conceptions of cultural literacy. Native American students clearly accommodated particular pressures to enhance their transcripts and futures by taking "normal" classes. But as one student indicated when asked *when* he would be an educated Native person, he responded: "When I speak Navajo." In a similar vein, Chicano/as in East Los Angeles pressed for bilingual education, while activists in Taiwan rejected the notion that native languages represented only local dialects or illiteracy, while standard Mandarin represented a "common language." Likewise, Gandin reveals the power of groups from below to support democratic schools by redefining the language of neoliberalism. Kumashiro, too, challenges us to think about how particular anti-oppressive educational reforms might also be reconstructed in ways that challenge dominant forms rather than expecting the assimilation of the oppressed—which clearly is not automatic, as the above examples reveal.

If we recollect the Mexican American Youth Leadership Conference discussed by Chicana activists, we will remember that its official purpose was to assimilate students into Anglo ways and culture. But students reported their experiences at the camp as pivotal moments during which a more radical consciousness as Chicanas was fostered and then channeled into various activist causes once back at school. We need to take seriously the idea that conservative modernization has a correlate, as suggested by Pedroni, in progressive modernization. What would this look like? What are the spaces within dominant educational practices where this can *and does* go on (see, e.g., Apple & Beane, 1995; Gutstein & Peterson, 2005)? These spaces for making and remaking curriculum and for engaging in critically oriented educational reforms need to be thoughtfully assessed, not simply something dealt with rhetorically by waving the theoretical flag of critical pedagogy. We need to be specific, not only sloganizers.

VIII: How can progressive scholars use their skills of analysis and commit themselves to subaltern struggles when their work is being increasingly proletarianized, commodified, privatized, and the economic and ideological crisis is so severe?

"We are entering a new phase of subalternity," warns Aronwitz in his chapter. Intellectual labor is being increasingly commodified (see also Apple, 1995). Corporate, military, and state forces have undermined academic freedom and open inquiry by making knowledge serve private industry, by relying on business partnerships, and by allowing funding sources to dictate what constitutes useful knowledge. This situation harkens back to the struggles of Native students to define the utility of different forms of knowledge within existing sets of economic relations and the need for a future career. In certain parallel ways, progressive scholars in the academy obviously must struggle against the forces of capital in defending the utility of particular forms of knowledge as well as the importance of publicity of knowledge. Yet doing so may likewise undermine the future of their career in academia, if tenure is denied for nonacademic reasons or because their work is not neutral enough or challenges the interests of funding sources. A new managerial class, argues Aronowitz, has overtaken the administration of the university and has begun defining agendas in teaching and research. Under such conditions, we ask, can radicals in the academy engage in subaltern struggles as precisely those kinds of epistemological and political/cultural commitments are themselves rendered peripheral? Bringing us back to the question of what supports successful counterhegemonic struggles, Aronowitz challenges us to find the "concrete instances" by which more "abstract ideals" are violated, and to use these as a means for instigating activism. This challenge should be carefully considered, we think, since this book has made clear that the voices of the subaltern are strengthened and magnified when articulated in collective ways.

IX: *Is the development of a* triple consciousness *that incorporates local, national, and global concerns and affiliations and centers epistemological subalternity within the sphere of education desirable or even possible? To what degree might globalization from above be undermined by cross-border educational efforts from below? What are the limits and possibilities of* subaltern cosmopolitan multiculturalism *within and outside of the United States?*

One of the points raised by Aronowitz is that the solidarity of progressives in the academy with those in other domains can only serve to strengthen subaltern movements all over. Within our own institutions of higher education, he suggests, is one of the places where the transnational movement against global capital might begin. This point resonates with the vision of subaltern cosmopolitan multiculturalism developed by Buras and Motter. We need to be thoughtful about the potential of such local histories to interrupt global designs (Mignolo, 2000). Likewise, the Citizen School project would appear to be just the kind of subaltern educational "satellite" that Buras and Motter suggest could be potentially connected with other counterhegemonic sites. Gandin indicates, in fact, that the project has unfolded in a spirit resonant with insurgent multiculturalism. Beyond this, within the project, subaltern knowledge at the local level (e.g., through thematic complexes) is made to rub against both Brazilian and world history, although from a critical rather than traditional perspective. The Citizen School would appear to have the potential to foster the kind of *triple consciousness*, or multiple affiliations, that are central to subaltern cosmopolitan multiculturalism.

Likewise, the struggles of activists in Taiwan reveal the importance of making critical connections between the local, national, and global. Oppositional movements there seemed to closely align with the "nationalism of the oppressed" described by Buras and Motter, and sought to give root to local ethnic cultures and to construct a broader Taiwan national identity against the colonial Chinese state. Importantly, struggles over constructions of geography and sovereignty only further underscore the significance of border thinking—in more ways than one. In a related way, Apple's discussion of technology and its retraditionalizing effects within the home schooling movement should also cause us to think about the place of technology, and the context of its use, within potentially detraditionalizing projects directed toward subaltern cosmopolitan multiculturalism.

X: In light of debates over the construction of the historical subaltern subject—the debates in which Spivak has been so central—what might be said about the importance of identity work and struggles over the construction of history for forming the contemporary dominant/subaltern subject? To what degree does the subaltern subject speak within particular histories, speak back to official histories, and participate in the very making of history?

Chen reminds us that the struggle over the narrativization of the February 28 Massacre was central to a sense of collective identity. Yet despite the countermemories sought and validated by activists, the official narrative failed to mention utterly important details, such as who was responsible. Likewise, the collection of Chicana feminist oral histories by Delgado Bernal, and the tensions between narratives of the past in U.S. history classes and Native American studies, reveal that our sense of the past has much to do with our struggles in the present. Within Core Knowledge history texts, Buras has illustrated how a *new* old history has been strategically constructed, one that exceeds the limits of additive histories through the embrace of more sophisticated forms of historical recognition and incorporation. Those narratives, however, often actually *disunite* America's history by either masking the relations of power that have shaped the intertwined histories of subaltern and elite groups in the past, or by centering the narrative around cooperative rather than conflicted relations.

Yet consciousness of relations of subordination and domination is the first step in moving toward the critical sensibility needed to build counterhegemonic movements in education and elsewhere. It was Gramsci who said that part of the project of building a new common sense was coming to see how sediments of the past are embedded within present-day conceptions of the world and teasing apart the progressive from the retrogressive elements. Must the past be remade or reenvisioned before the future can be remade by subaltern groups? Of course, asking the question this way makes the process of transformation too linear, but the point remains. Remaking and reenvisioning a past provides crucial countermemories that can play significant roles in the project of building a "thick" democracy.

The School Bus Returns

In the introductory chapter to this book, we said that we were going to put the subaltern on the school bus and take a ride through urban schools, home schools, the academy, and various educational reforms and movements. All the while, we wanted to center on Spivak's important question, "Can the subaltern speak?" We hope that we have made clear that the answer is not a simple "Yes" or "No." Within unequal relations of power and disparate educational struggles, there are a range of limits and possibilities. Our work, then, is to assess those spaces carefully and unromantically and to be as tactical, strategic, and democratic as possible in reconstructing those spaces in more progressive directions. Part of what we are suggesting, too, is a retheorization of the politics of recognition along lines that take seriously the complexities and contradictions of dominance and subalternity both right and left.

The challenge for all of us is to think within and across borders about the implications of the arguments made throughout this book for the theories and practices involved in the critical and democratic reconstruction of curriculum, schooling, and the theater of education in the broadest sense. As we have said, this will require returning to Boal's insights that speaking occurs in many ways, at many levels, and in many voices.

One of the things we have sought to do in this volume is to urge progressives to be more strategic, to understand that neither overly romantic visions nor overly rhetorical approaches are sufficient. In doing so, we realize that this may make it harder for us to find easy solutions. However, if reality is ideologically complicated, simply repeating the Gramscian mantra "Pessimism of the intellect, optimism of the will" doesn't change much. This is one of the reasons we have also focused not only on complexity, but on lasting and successful struggles that have made a real difference.

We do not want to be misunderstood. While we have integrated some elements of what have come to be called postmodern and poststructural concerns into this book, we strongly believe that all of this occurs in real and determinate material contexts. Neither economies nor class relations are simply "texts." They exist as massive structuring relations and we ignore them at our risk. However, we are not in a church, so we should not be worried about heresy. Critical political, cultural, and educational projects may require new resources. The justification for their use should not be whether or not they are true to some vision of past glory or of *the* correct political position, but whether they help us envision, continue, and build powerful forms of intervention into the relations of dominance and subordination that so clearly characterize our society.

As you read this last page and close this book, it may be a good idea, ironically, to return to the first page—that is, the cover. We said that Gramsci attended to a host of cultural forms as part of his educational project. We want to leave you with that image and the complexities that it suggests about subaltern voices.

References

Anyon, J. (2005). *Radical possibilities*. New York: Routledge.

Apple, M. W. (1995). *Education and power* (2nd ed.). New York: Routledge.

Apple, M. W. (2006). *Educating the "right" way: Markets, standards, god, and inequality* (2nd ed.). New York: Routledge.

Apple, M. W., & Beane, J. A. (1995). *Democratic schools*. Alexandria, VA: Association for Supervision and Curriculum Development.

Apple, M. W., & Oliver, A. (2003). Becoming right. In Michael W. Apple, et al., *The state and the politics of knowledge*. New York: RoutledgeFalmer.

Buras, K. L., & Apple, M. W. (2005). School choice, neoliberal promises, and unpromising evidence. *Educational Policy, 19* (3), 550–564.

Donsky, P. (2005, February 27). Capitol View Elementary looks past poverty, employs classics to enrich students' world. *Atlanta Journal Constitution.*

Fraser, N. (1997). *Justice interruptus.* New York: Routledge.

Fraser, N. & Honneth, A. (2003). *Redistribution or recognition? A political–philosophical exchange.* New York: Verso.

Gutstein, E., & Peterson, B. (2005). *Rethinking mathematics: Teaching social justice by the numbers.* Milwaukee, WI: Rethinking Schools.

Mignolo, W. D. (2000). *Local histories/global designs: Coloniality, subaltern knowledge, and border thinking.* Princeton, NJ: Princeton University Press.

Wallis, J. (2005). *God's politics.* New York: HarperCollins.

Williams, R. (1989). *Resources of hope.* New York: Verso.

About the Contributors

Michael W. Apple is the John Bascom Professor of Curriculum and Instruction and Educational Policy Studies at the University of Wisconsin-Madison. Among his recent books are *Educating the "Right" Way: Markets, Standards, God, and Inequality, The State and the Politics of Knowledge,* and the 25th Anniversary third edition of his classic *Ideology and Curriculum.*

Stanley Aronowitz is Distinguished Professor of Sociology at the Graduate Center, City University of New York. Long involved in the labor movement and in education, he is founder of the Center for Worker Education at the City College of New York. He is the author of over eighteen books, including *The Knowledge Factory.*

Dolores Delgado Bernal is Associate Professor at the University of Utah in the Department of Education, Culture, and Society and the Ethnic Studies Program, Salt Lake City, Utah. Her research draws on critical race theory and U.S. third world feminist theories to examine the educational experiences of students of color. She has authored numerous articles, some of which have appeared in *Harvard Educational Review* and *Urban Education.*

Kristen L. Buras is a doctoral candidate and Wisconsin-Spencer Fellow at the University of Wisconsin-Madison. She is interested in the cultural politics of curriculum and reform. Her research on the Core Knowledge Movement has been published in *Harvard Educational Review.* She has also written on issues of culture, citizenship, and conservative educational reform in journals such as *Education Review* and *Educational Policy.*

Jyh-Jia Chen is Assistant Professor in the Institute of Education at Chiao Tung University, Hsinchu, Taiwan. Her research has focused on state formation and educational reform movements, and she has written on the politics of textbooks in journals such as *Pedagogy, Culture, and Society.*

Luís Armando Gandin is Professor of Education at the Federal University of Rio Grande do Sul, Porto Alegre, Brazil. He has a master's degree in sociology and a Ph.D. in education from the University of Wisconsin-Madison. He is the editor of the journal *Currículo sem Fronteiras* and has published four books.

Kevin K. Kumashiro, Ph.D., is the director of the Center for Anti-Oppressive Education, in Washington, D.C., and is also a senior program specialist in human and civil rights for the National Education Association in the United

States. He is the author of several books on anti-oppressive education, including *Against Common Sense: Teaching and Learning Toward Social Justice.*

Glenabah Martinez (Taos/Diné) is Assistant Professor in the Department of Language, Literacy, and Sociocultural Studies at the University of New Mexico, in Albuquerque, New Mexico. Her research interests include curriculum and instruction in high school settings and the educational experiences of Indigenous youth. Her forthcoming book is *Native Pride: The Politics of Curriculum and Instruction in an Urban, Public High School.* She formerly taught high school social studies.

Paulino Motter has a background in critical policy studies and currently works in the Ministry of Education in Brasília, Brazil.

Thomas C. Pedroni is Assistant Professor of global education studies and social studies methods at Oakland University, Rochester, Michigan. His recent research, published in *Teachers College Record* and *Urban Review,* has centered on issues of identity formation and subaltern agency among urban low-income, predominantly African American and Latino parents within otherwise conservative coalitions for publicly financed vouchers.

Index

Made in the USA
Columbia, SC
15 January 2018